Home and Work

HOME

and WORK

Negotiating Boundaries through Everyday Life

Christena E. Nippert-Eng

THE UNIVERSITY OF CHICAGO PRESS *Chicago & London*

Christena E. Nippert-Eng is assistant professor of sociology in the Department of Social Sciences, Illinois Institute of Technology.

The University of Chicago Press, Chicago 60637
The University of Chicago Press, Ltd., London

Printed in the United States of America
05 04 03 02 01 00 99 98 97 96 1 2 3 4 5

ISBN: 0-226-58145-4 (cloth)
0-226-58146-2 (paper)

Portions of this book are contained in "The Home/Work Nexus: Boundary Work in Everyday Life," the author's unpublished doctoral dissertation, State University of New York at Stony Brook, 1995.

Library of Congress Cataloging-in-Publication Data

Nippert-Eng, Christena E.
Home and work : negotiating boundaries through everyday life/Christena E. Nippert-Eng.
p. cm.
Includes bibliographical references and index.
1. Organizational sociology. 2. Work and family. 3. Corporate culture. 4. Social psychology.
HM131.N498 1996
306.3′6′0973—dc20 95-39967
CIP

♾ The paper used in this publication meets the minimum requirements of the American National Standard for Information Sciences—Permanence of Paper for Printed Library Materials, ANSI Z39.48-1984.

to Gretchen, my joy

CONTENTS

Prologue xi

Acknowledgments xvi

Introduction

NEGOTIATING HOME AND WORK:
FROM INTEGRATION TO SEGMENTATION 1

Boundary Work: Sculpting Home and Work 7
Home and Work as Experiential Realms 18
Summary 28
The Lab 30

Chapter One

TERRITORIES OF THE SELF:
RECOGNIZING THE HOME-WORK BOUNDARY 34

Calendars 43
Keys 48
Clothes and Appearance 50
"Identity Kits": Wallets and Purses 57
Eating and Drinking 60
Money 63
People and Their Representations 67
Talk 76
Reading 83
Breaks 91
Conclusion 98

Chapter Two

COGNITIVE ENGINEERING:
BRIDGING TIME, SPACE, AND SELF 105

The Cognitive Structure of Transitions 106
The Behavioral Support of Mental Movement 110

Bridges between Home and Work 117
Transitional Acts as Rituals 145
Conclusion 148

Chapter Three

STRUCTURAL CONSTRAINTS AND PERSONAL DISCRETION: WORK STAKES ITS CLAIM 152

The "Bureaucratic," the "Greedy," and the "Discretionary" Workplace 154
Privacy: Time, Mailboxes, Telephone, and Work Space 162
Boundary Reference Groups 171
The Physical Environment 189
Work Accessibility 191

Chapter Four

BE IT EVER SO HUMBLE, THERE ARE ALSO SURVEYORS AT HOME 194

From Explicit Permission to Tacit Omission: Spouses and Our Realms' Reach 194
The Sacredness of Children and the Primacy of Parenting: Kids and the Polluting and Purifying of Realms 202
House and Home: The Possibilities and Probabilities of Space 221
Conclusion 226

Chapter Five

JIMMY, ELEANOR, AND THE LOGIC OF BOUNDARY WORK 229

Jimmy's Homecoming 231
Eleanor's Escher 246
Art Appreciation 267
Older Dogs and Newer Tricks 273

Conclusion

Beyond Home and Work: Boundary Theory 277

Appendix

Interview Questionnaire for *Home and Work* 293

References 307

Index 313

PROLOGUE

Consider your keys; calendars; purse and/or wallet contents; commuting, drinking, and reading habits; your lunchtime and vacation plans; the photographs in your living room and work space; and the people with whom you socialize. These items, along with numerous others that I address in this book, have one thing in common. They are dimensions through which each of us draws the line between home and work. Often practical yet eminently symbolic, publicly visible yet intimately revealing, these are the kinds of things with which each of us places a mental, physical, and behavioral boundary between these two realms.

Boundaries, all boundaries, are socially constructed; they are artificial and arbitrary (Zerubavel 1991). Over the natural nonorder of things, we impose boundaries on everything, including our daily activities and the places and people with whom we pursue them. These boundaries may be purely mental, as in the conceptual lines drawn around categories. But, more often, boundaries also reflect and result in physical forms that reinforce and make visible their more important, mental foundations.

The process of classification results from our boundary-imposing propensities. Cultural groups constantly negotiate the grounds of distinction, seeking consensus on the places and ways in which boundaries reflect what we see and shape what we think. As a result, we produce and find ourselves constrained by systems of classification. These systems are comprised of interrelated categories in which each category encompasses a more or less distinct conceptual territory, like the categories of "home" and "work." Classification systems are of special interest to social scientists, therefore, for they reflect and reproduce what is meaningful to a people.

More specifically, by shaping the very ways we think about and act toward each other and things (Foucault [1966] 1973), classificatory boundaries are the most essential element of culture. These are the girders supporting all interpretation, all experience. By internalizing certain combinations of specific conceptual borders (such as those demarcating what is "home" and "work"), we perpetuate a distinct, cultured way of thinking (Durkheim [1912] 1965) the definitive aspect of social group membership (Mannheim [1936] 1985).

Socialization is nothing less than the lifelong process of learning, adopting, rejecting, and challenging classificatory boundaries and systems, given the behavioral and political implications of assigning artifacts, actions, people, and thoughts to one category or another. Aristotle's discussion of who belongs to the "Polis," for instance, is not simply an ivory tower exercise in the definition of a category.[1] People who belong to the Polis possess rights to life, happiness, and economic protection that do not apply to outsiders. Nonmembers may be killed with no hesitation; they aren't really "people" at all. We still contribute to a history full of widespread violence against certain ethnic, religious, political, and sexually oriented groups (not to mention other species), showing how this logic and some of our most reprehensible forms of "boundary work" persist.

What is a family? Who is your parent? Who is an adult? Who is black? A Palestinian? A Bosnian? Rwandan? Who is human? Who is alive? What is public? What is perverse? What is masculine or feminine? Who is intelligent?

The greatest debates and ethical dilemmas of our time are about drawing boundaries. This is because placing lines here or there has definite implications for how we treat each other and the world around us. Depending on which category she or he belongs to, someone will or will not receive medical insurance coverage; will or will not be taken from the caretakers they've known all their life and placed with a stranger having similar DNA; will or will not be subjected to hard prison terms, the military draft, or parental notification for medical procedures; will or will not be formally or informally entitled to live, vote, work, buy a house, and/or go to school in a certain place; will or will not be slaughtered, resuscitated, and so forth.

Home and Work: Negotiating Boundaries through Everyday Life is a project that emerged from my interest in the interplay between cultural, conceptual boundaries and their personal, practical enactments. I am fascinated by the process in which boundaries emerge, transform, and even disappear altogether, the process through which boundaries become more or less meaningful, more or less real. This process is certainly interesting at the level of society or a cultural group, but I am especially interested in it at the personal level.

Cultural boundaries must be created, maintained, or cast aside by

1. See Ernest Barker, ed. and trans., *The Politics of Aristotle* (1946; New York: Oxford University Press, 1973), xlvii–lii, 92–116.

real people. Each of us actively decides boundaries' salience and propriety through our actions, noticed and unnoticed. It is at the level of the individual that new ways of looking at things and new ways of making them real begins, of defining old distinctions/boundaries as less important and making new ones more so. This happens largely according to very pragmatic criteria: how well these distinctions and ways of looking at the world actually mesh with what we and others experienced before and what we see, feel, and aspire to now. Through the aggregation of these personal boundary negotiations, culture is preserved and changed as conceptual frameworks are shored up, bent, or restructured to accommodate more private realities and visions.

How do we place, maintain, and change personal mental boundaries and conceptual territories in light of cultural ones? What physical and behavioral forms do we give these mental points of distinction and their subsequent negotiations? Why do we place these boundaries in particular places? How is their placement affected when interpersonal views of boundaries and territories conflict? In short, how do cultural directives, social constraints, and individuals' different ways of conceiving and enacting categorical boundaries come together?

The answers to these questions have to do with two related processes. First, ever-changing social contexts constrain individual visions and enactments of cultural boundaries. Each of us is immediately caught up in numerous social dynamics, politics, power relations, commitments, and conflicts. These unquestionably affect our on-going boundary negotiations, whatever the boundary at hand. Second, these questions are also concerned with what I now call "boundary work." This is the never-ending, hands-on, largely visible process through which boundaries are negotiated, placed, maintained, and transformed by individuals over time.

In this book, I attempt to answer these questions and illustrate these processes by looking at the boundary between home and work. This is a boundary that is, perhaps, not as flashy, not so media-hyped as those I mentioned before. Indeed, debate about my chosen boundary is often tacit, compared to others, and played out in highly symbolic ways. It also takes place constantly, unlike some boundary debates, right under our noses in every home, workplace, and institution. It sometimes recedes into the background and sometimes takes forms that mask the real issue of contention. But the instant the household and/

or workplace order is challenged—whether that order is based on normally assumed or contentious categorical boundaries—it may rage to the forefront of our consciousness.

The careful consideration of one concrete case, one boundary's characteristics and implications, seemed to be the best way for me to clarify and enlarge the body of thought about all boundaries and classificatory acts. I have given my attention to the home-work boundary rather than some other border for several reasons. First, it is important to address questions about extremely pervasive, social phenomenon like conceptual boundaries and their negotiation from an extremely pervasive angle. The home-work boundary is certainly a pervasive, and, as I will show, quite a problematic issue for most members of our society.

The home-work boundary also lets me bring together many of my long-standing interests in sociology. My imagination has long been captured by the study of work and occupations. But I am also fascinated by the sociology of culture, knowledge, organizations, science, leisure, gender, time and space, social psychology, and the newly emerging field known as "cognitive sociology" (Zerubavel 1996).

I am further drawn to the sociology of everyday life. I like work about things that are meaningful to most people, not just members of Academe. But—what is even more important—everyday actions and choices are some of the best places to show off the power of sociology; the perspective makes these things anything but mundane for an interested observer. Indeed, I like sociology so real I can taste it. I certainly want to see it happening around me.[2] I also like my theory so thoroughly embedded in practice that when I'm reading or listening to a professional presentation, I forget to distinguish between them. That's how the discipline produces good theory and still offers our audiences new and interesting takes on the ways people really think and act.

Throughout this book, then, I take my sensitivity to and fascination with what people do everyday and give it a new twist. I not only want to find out more about wage work and its varied roles in people's lives, but about broader principles of social organization and interaction, how we use space and time to support these principles and how we balance the remarkable tension between what is personal and social. And always, my interest is focused on what work and all its practical constraints and symbolic manifestations mean to the people doing it. This

2. As in what Patricia and Peter Adler (1991) call "backyard sociology."

means paying acute attention to the social and physical environment in which work gets done, including the cultural, domestic, and leisure environments that surround and permeate it.

Accordingly, for this project on boundaries, I turn to the multi-dimensional, highly variable border between two of the most important mental and experiential categories of Modern social life: "home" and "work."

ACKNOWLEDGMENTS

This project would not have been possible without dozens of people at "the Lab," where I conducted extensive interviews for this book. I regret that I cannot list them by name, but I hope this book has repaid them in some way for their uniformly good will, valuable time, and insightful conversations.

There are a few people whose identities I do not have to hide, however. I have been assisted, supported, nurtured, and otherwise helped by many individuals over the course of this project. Before I even began this work, the thoughts of John Alt, Judith Best, Karen Cerulo, Stephen Cole, Eugene Ericksen, John Gagnon, Sherri Grasmuck, David Halle, Kyriakos Kontopoulos, Magali Sarfatti Larson, Leo Rigsby, and Patricia Roos were especially important to me. I eagerly took whatever I could from their lectures and private conversations and put it to my own use. This project partly results from their generous attention.

Later, throughout the various stages of this project, the following people provided encouragement, conversations, and written comments, and/or tolerated my analyses and queries about their boundary work: David Adler, Lynn Adler, Laurie Anderson, Jorge Arditi, David Beam, Jim Botts, Karen Cerulo, Ivan Chase, Libby Chute, Ken Dauber, Kevin Delaney, Katje Dugan, Paul DeForest, Rick Eckstein, Carolyn Ellis, Cynthia Fuchs Epstein, Ken Evans-Lutterodt, Michael Flaherty, Greg Franklin, Tom Gorman, Carolyn Hasman Gorman, William Grimshaw, Chris Guryan, Jeff Heyer, Lorrie Krebs, Bruno LaFontaine, Geraldine Lamble, Cheryl Laz, Helena Lopata, Patrick McGuire, Bill O'Hern, Gail O'Hern, Scott Peters, Pat Powers, Ian Robinson, Ann Rotchford, Nancy Sacks, Stefan Schubler, Rolf Schuster, Ullica Segerstrale, Joyce Seltzer, Allen Shelton, Detlef Smilgies, Shivaji Sondhi, Zhen Quan Tan, Rueyling Tzeng, Vered Vinitzky-Seroussi, Karen Hurd Waldeck, and Barbara Wille.

The Department of Sociology at the State University of New York at Stony Brook supported me through much of my tenure there. In addition to providing me with graduate assistantships, invitations to talk about my work, and a truly stimulating atmosphere, it gave me a small grant to help with the administrative costs of this research. Norman Goodman, Mark Granovetter, and Richard Williams were quite supportive. The Center for Academic Advising at Stony Brook supported me for another year, and I am thankful for their conversations and encouragement, as well.

Some of the material in this book was included in two papers I wrote that received Graduate Student Paper Competition Awards from the American Sociological Association (ASA). "'Mommy, Mommy,' or 'Excuse Me, Ma'am,': Gender and Interruptions at Home and Work," received the ASA Culture Section Award for 1992. "From Home to Work and Back Again: Commuting and the Transformation of Self" received the ASA Social Psychology Section Award for 1993. I could not have attended the meetings either year without the financial support of these sections, nor would I have benefited from the delightful encouragement of the section members I met there, especially Gary Fine, Elizabeth Long, Jane Sell, and Peggy Thoits. I am also grateful for the comments of numerous people (especially Stanford Lyman) who attended ASA and Society for the Study of Symbolic Interaction paper sessions in which I presented various bits of this work from 1988 through 1993.

At all stages of this project, there were people who provided me with the most consistent, insightful guidance I could want. My thesis committee, with whose aid I produced the first draft of this book, was a panel of exemplary proportions. Few graduate students have been as fortunate as I. Robert Zussman, Paul Attewell, and Naomi Gerstel provided support, camaraderie, insights and often extraordinarily helpful comments from near and afar. I benefited equally from their diversity of viewpoints and uniformly good will.

I have been the beneficiary of Barry Schwartz's smart, generous attention for several years. He has had a distinct impact on my work and my professional goals, encouraging me more than he probably knows. Later, he provided an extended, extremely thought-provoking and crucial review of the entire manuscript, a lovely gift and a model of professional criticism. He continues to amaze me with his ability to target strengths and weaknesses, suggestions of how to turn the latter into the former, and willingness to use these talents on my behalf.

Much to my delight, Ira Cohen presented me with yet another insightful, detailed, and extremely useful review of the entire manuscript. Ira's enthusiasm and sharp eye were essential for my final revisions. His wonderful sense of humor and willingness to hold the hands of people he hasn't even met are astonishing and also a model for the profession.

Too many years ago, at my first ASA meeting, Doug Mitchell took the time out from a long day and even longer queue of people standing in front of him to talk to me about a very different image of this project. He never forgot my name or face. He gave me encouragement, substantive guidance and much, much later, a contract. He has left his indelible fingerprint on me twice: once through his sure shaping of some of the best my discipline has to offer, once through his much more personal attention. I hope this book gives you back a little something for your effort, Doug, with the promise of more cookies and tea to come! Thanks also to Matt Howard, Kathryn Krug, Andrea Federle-Busci, and David Blair.

Finally, and most important, there cannot be a better mentor than Eviatar Zerubavel, nor a member of our discipline with a better, more sociological imagination (or integration-tolerant family!) Without his excitement, encouragement, energy, and exceptional scholarship, I would have followed a very different path. Permission to do unusual work is a rare commodity in graduate school. When I could not give it to myself, he did, and he carried me along until I could, too. Eviatar came to Stony Brook at the perfect time with a perfect combination of invitation, feedback, and sensitivity, and this book is the result. Thank you. For everything.

I might say almost the same about my husband, Peter. Thank you for everything, too. I've loved you through it all, I couldn't have written this without you (really), and I'm so glad we finally have something to show for all the insanity! Thanks for your continuing encouragement, insights, incredible tolerance for half-crazed women, your paycheck, last minute take-out meals, hours of computer, clerical, and CAD support (the figures look great), and, most especially, for our daughter, to whom I dedicate this work.

I sometimes thought you would have your Ph.D. before I got mine, Gretchen, but I simply couldn't have done this without you. You make me laugh, you make me work, you make me look in new ways at the things I take for granted, and in many ways you've given me more insight about my subject matter than any other person. Thank you.

And many, many thanks to all the rest of our family, whose conversations, baby-sitting, meals, and financial and moral support have made this project possible, especially: Rotena and Victor Nippert, Terry and Jack Eng, Edith and John DuBois, Teresia and August Hoegel, Phyllis and Victor Nippert, Ann and Conny Erbes, Susan and Peter Hoegel, Ann Wells, Steve Nippert, Gretta and Chip Nippert, Trina and Dave Plummer, Julia and John Nippert, and Terry Ann and Bob Izzo. Naturally, whatever shortcomings and mistakes exist here I shall call my own, but the credit for whatever is good must be shared with all of you, too.

introduction

Negotiating Home and Work: From Integration to Segmentation

"What I want to know is why you didn't ask me anything about sex," John asked. All ears, I stopped putting away my notes and asked what he meant. "You're interested in how my personal life and work life intermingle. All I'm saying is I've had my share of sex in the lab over the years. And I used to keep love letters in my desk drawer, too. Of course, that was before I was married. But years ago . . . I've done it in a couple of places. I would think you'd find that interesting. Why didn't you ask me about that?"

Why, indeed. Well, I thought on my way home, perhaps that's a starting point for another book. Sex in the workplace: the ultimate in Modern boundary blurring—between self and others, home and work, private and public.

Mostly, though, the words and image of Ed came to mind as I drove along rehashing my last three hours with John. No wonder. For someone interested in the process of placing boundaries around home and work, these two men are logical counterpoints. Their characters are quite similar, and each provides a vivid example of what this process entails. But they also show how very differently this kind of boundary work might be done.

A machinist, Ed is just as colorful as John, who is an experimental scientist. They have much in common. I could listen for hours to both men, entertaining me with their vivid narratives, delivered with a wonderful sense of timing, humor, and intrigue. They share healthy egos, sincere, often teary-eyed devotion to loved ones, and an obvious passion for life. In addition, they both work at the same scientific research facility, which I call "The Lab."

But that's about where the similarities end. Where John intermingles the time and space of home and work along so many dimensions, one of which I hadn't even included in my interview schedule, Ed draws it clearly and indelibly, countering John point for point. Until recently, for instance, John was married to his scientific collaborator. So, not only did he freely do and discuss his work with his wife, but he shared much of what others might consider his "private" life with his "coworker." Ed's wife, on the other hand, has never been to his workplace and knows little about the actual tasks of machining. He dislikes talking about work with her, seeing no reason to expose her to much of what goes on there or the "boring" details of his work. When he gets home, he wants to forget about work, not drag it into the living room behind him. Ed also steadfastly refuses to divulge personal information to his coworkers. He firmly believes that the less other workers know about his life outside the Lab, the less they can use that information against him. Family photographs taped to his tool box are his only advertisements about home.

Over the years John frequently could be found in his laboratory any day of the week, any time of the night or day. At other times he could be found working at home, reading work materials, puzzling out a problem, planning strategies and discussing his work with his wife, or visiting colleagues. And the work day and space were just as riddled with quick, random phone calls or in-person conversations with his wife about domestic issues and plans. Ed, however, clocks in and out of work at the precise times mandated by his contract and vehemently insists on his right to evenings and weekends with his family. He "never" thinks about work while at home and literally never socializes with colleagues, much less invites them to his house. His wife calls him only occasionally at work, mostly during contractual breaks in the day, what Ed calls "my," rather than "the Lab's" time.

The primary reason John works is because he loves the work and the notoriety it offers. The money is more of a fringe benefit than the driving rationale behind his effort. In many ways John's fusion of self with work is best represented by the copies of journal articles he proudly hands out, his name (and his ex-wife's) prominently displayed on each. Ed, on the other hand, works only because he needs the money to support the family he loves. In spite of his dislike of machining, he stays with it because he can make more money at this than at anything else. In his workplace the very system of handing out, negotiating, and collecting assigned jobs seems designed to inhibit Ed's identification with his work. For Ed, there is no personal glory at work. On some days only love for his family and repeated glances at their photos keeps him at the milling machine.

Much of Ed's and John's lives prepared them for their very different juxtapositions of home and work. Extensive training in college and graduate school and postdoctoral fellowships encouraged John to expect he would work and live within the same circle of people. The experimental scientist subculture taught him early on that times and spaces were interchangeable, that, essentially, one could work in bed and bed people at work. Private offices, secluded laboratories, little immediate supervision or accountability, a task mix requiring a lot of "thinking" (a highly mobile activity), sexually mixed work groups, and hours spent pulling the experimental night shift encourage John's more flexible ideas about the purposes of time and space. This is precisely what allows him to tell anecdotes about sex in the lab with no more compunction than we might expect to hear about the journal articles he writes there or his experiments with *molecular* kinetics.

In the traditions and spaces of his occupation, Ed also has fertile ground for his ideas about the intermingling of home and work, time and space. However, even if the opportunity presented itself for Ed to have sex in his workplace, which it never would, chances are that Ed would not actually do so. Long the backbone of organized labor in this country, machinists' history is predicated on the idea that a worker's interests and those of her or his boss are separate and in direct conflict. One manifestation of this is the clear distinction between employers' and employees' time and space, between public and private turf. Working in great, huge rooms where privacy is almost impossible, Ed and his coworkers are closely supervised and their work is carefully scrutinized, taking place at specific, virtually nonnegotiable times of the day and week. From the time they begin their apprenticeships, machinists' folklore, contractual disputes, equipment requirements, and sexually homogeneous environments continually reinforce the idea that time and space is dedicated to work *or* home, public *or* private pursuits. The lesson is that, ultimately, these cannot be the same. Because of its learned, exclusive mental association with one realm and not the other, then, the more we are like Ed, the more even the thought of sex in the workplace is outrageous.

So, how does a sociologist talk about the meaning of "home," of "work," and of the ways they are related, given that people like John and Ed must be simultaneously, conceptually accommodated? To date I know of no comprehensive attempt to theoretically or empirically account for the marvelous variations of life experience embodied by these terms. Social scientists generally have written about "home" and "work" as if we all know what these terms mean, as if the territories they encompass and the ways they are related are the same for everyone. If we acknowledge variations, we do so only about one side of the commute at a time, most often one variation at a time. But "home" and "work" are inextricably, conceptually defined with and by each other. Exploring one without exploring the other cannot get to the heart of what it's really like to experience either, independently or jointly, for one person or many.

As a result, we have no image or language to describe the undeniably rich variations on these themes composed by real people living real lives.[1] We have no conceptual framework that allows for ambiguity and

1. Actually, a huge array of works provides evidence for the often fuzzy distinctions we make between home and work. However, none of them try to simultaneously account for all the variations in these realms or to show the consistency in the numerous dimensions across which wage workers develop their home-work boundaries, as I do. In fact, the following excellent works support the existence of variations from the classic (and largely mythical) image of a suburban commuter whose work and home do not mix. See Rosabeth Moss Kanter's excellent review essay *Work and Family in the United States: A Critical Review and Agenda for Research and Policy* (1977b) and her discussion of corporate wives in *Men and Women of the Corporation* (1977a). See also, Martha Fowlkes's essay "The Myth of Merit and Male Professional Careers" (1987); Arlie Hochschild's article "The Ambassador's Wife" (1969); and Hochschild's *The Managed Heart: Commercialization of Human Feeling* (1983), which is striking in its implications for the degree to which work can subsume the individual and private life through the exploitation of emotion and self. Graeme Salaman's *Community and Occupation: An Exploration of Work/Leisure Relationships* (1974) shows similar kinds of blurring between work and home seen in William Whyte's classic, *The Organization Man* ([1956] 1957). This kind of blurring is also seen in C. Wright Mills's "craftsmen" in *White Collar* (1956). Mills also addresses variations in the meaning of work, much as Robert Dubin does in "Industrial Workers' Worlds: A Study of the 'Central Life Interests' of Industrial Workers" (1956). These variations are also seen in Studs Terkel's classic and delightful essay collection *Working* (1972). In *Engineering Culture* (Philadelphia: Temple University Press, 1991), Gideon Kunda briefly mentions the need for corporate members to "place boundaries around their work," although he does not elaborate on this process, while Robert Zussman's *Mechanics of the Middle Class* (1985) also addresses the boundaries between engineers' wage work and private lives, as does David Halle in *America's Working Man* (1984). An extremely interesting

order, sameness and difference across the categories of "home" and "work" or across the people who create them. By default, we have written with a "univocality" (Levine 1988) that does a disservice to our disciplines as well as to our incredible ability to simultaneously impose and accommodate multiple social orders.

I have found it useful to see the myriad ways we conceptualize and juxtapose "home" and "work" as a continuum (Nippert-Eng 1991). These possibilities range from "integration" to "segmentation." Within the ideal-typical position of "home" and "work" as fully *"integrated,"* no distinction exists between what belongs to "home" or "work" and when and where they are engaged. "Home" and "work" are one and the same, one giant category of social existence, for no conceptual boundary separates its contents or meanings. Within this integrated paradigm, all the components we usually associate with these different realms are intertwined and understood with the same mental framework. People, motives for involvement, thoughts, tasks, and the intellectual and emotional approaches used to engage in them—even objects—are experienced in the same way, no matter where we are or what the task at hand. That is, the extreme integrator possesses a single, all-purpose mentality, one way of being, one amorphous self. She or he thinks and acts the same way with anyone, boss, coworker, spouse, or child, no matter where she or he is found, no matter what social role obligations are at hand. Moreover, any traditional realm contents may legitimately take place, appear, and/or demand attention in any location. Whether designated by outsiders as "home" or "workplace," for the extreme integrator, all space and time is multipurpose.

At the other end of the "integration-segmentation continuum," however, these aspects of social existence are conceived of and experienced as completely separate, *"segmented"* worlds. Here, the mental

account of what happened in a workplace where the time and space of the home-work boundary was intentionally blurred yet eventually demarcated in the strongest of capitalist traditions appears in Kathleen Weston and Lisa Rofel's "Sexuality, Class, and Conflict in a Lesbian Workplace" (1987). Perri Klass's novel *Other Women's Children* (1990) is a wonderful look at a woman physician's difficulty trying to separate her private and public lives and ways of thinking and acting. Homeworkers also provide great food for thought regarding this phenomenon. Betty Beach's *Integrating Work and Family Life* (1989) and Kathleen Christensen's article "Women, Families and Home-Based Employment" (1987) provide great insight on the potential difficulties of setting the home-work boundary.

boundary between realms is clear and impregnable, resolutely preserving the distinctive characteristics of each sphere. There is no classificatory ambiguity for the extreme segmentor: everything belongs to "home" *or* "work," two mutually exclusive categories. With no conceptual overlap between realms and their contents, there is no physical or temporal overlap between them, either. Moreover, two distinct, realm-specific mentalities guide the extreme segmentor, so that she or he operates according to two very different interpretive and behavioral frameworks. As a result, and unlike the constant, asituational self of the extreme integrator, the extreme segmentor of home and work alternates between two different "selves" or ways of being, depending on her or his location and the realm-specific demands at hand.

The ways real people conceive of and relate "home" and "work" fall somewhere in-between these two ideal-typical approaches. As we negotiate our own home and work realms, the vast majority of us, including John and Ed, do not approach "home" and "work" as a single, all-encompassing and amorphous category of experience. Nor are these entirely mutually exclusive realms. Rather, along numerous dimensions, we combine segmenting and integrating visions and practices to create personal realm configurations. We do this within the structural constraints of either realm. The result is that at a given time and repeatedly subject to change, we are *relatively* more or less integrating/segmenting in how we experience home and work, but we fall short of either ideal type.

The full range of integrating/segmenting views and relationships between home and work is interesting to me because it implies that these categories, their contents and their boundary, must be negotiated. These negotiations must be done within a number of constraints, using a number of "tools." That is, one's personal position along the integration-segmentation continuum is highly dependent on three elements. The first is internalized, cultural images of "home" and "work." The second is unique permutations of social-structural constraints that emanate from both realms. The third is the personal practices through which we enact and elaborate images of these categories and situational constraints.

Practices—like surrounding ourselves with different or similar objects or people at home and work, or developing commuting routines that help us transform between home and work ways of being—play an important, mediating role between sociocognitive constructs and social-structural constraints. On the one hand, we continually learn what the concepts "home" and "work" mean, fine-tuning the cultural images we begin to internalize as children. On the other hand, we find ourselves continually pressed to meet the expectations of those around us and the material constraints that delimit the ways our home and work may meet. In large part, each of us makes sense of these mental and structural constraints on what "home" and "work" mean through personal, boundary-producing practices.

In other words, through everyday choices and practices, we each continually work toward some level of integration/segmentation, enacting, reinforcing, and modifying our ideas of what is "work" and "home" and how they should relate. This process, through which we concretize the mental territories of "home" and "work" into physical ones and learn to transcend as well as preserve these realms, is what I call the "boundary work" of home and work. It is uniquely social, despite its personal appearance. Each of us engages in it according to specific sociocognitive and social-structural constraints and draws from a common repertoire of cultural activities, symbols, and organizing strategies to do it.

Boundary Work: Sculpting Home and Work

In general "boundary work" consists of the strategies, principles, and practices we use to create, maintain, and modify cultural categories. In this book, I focus on a specific case of boundary work: the process through which we organize potentially realm-specific matters, people, objects, and aspects of self into "home" and "work," maintaining and changing these conceptualizations as needed and/or desired. Through boundary work, we impose our views of "home," "work," and their relationship on a fairly malleable world of possibilities.[2]

Boundary work is first and foremost a mental activity, but it must be enacted and enhanced through a largely visible collection of essential, practical activities. It is this physical side of boundary work (e.g., wearing different or similar clothes at home and work; using "personal"

2. For a different, yet not inconsistent use of the term "boundary-work," see Thomas F. Gieryn, "Boundary Work and the Demarcation of Science from Non-Science: Strains and Interests in Professional Ideologies of Scientists," *American Sociological Review* 48 (1983), December: 781–95. Gieryn explores the ways scientists attempt through rhetoric to distinguish between what they do and what nonscientists do.

money for "work" expenses, or not; listing work and home engagements on the same or different calendars; having coworkers over for dinner, or not; bringing children to the workplace, or not; putting a family photo on one's desk or colleagues' pictures on the fireplace mantel, or not; changing clothes upon arriving home each day, or not; consuming differently drugged drinks in the morning and evening, or not) that helps us tangibly reinforce and even challenge cognitive and situational distinctions between "home" and "work."

Accordingly, boundary work is the key process that reflects and helps determine how much we integrate/segment home and work. It is what ultimately allows each of us to repeatedly define and refine the essence of and relationship between our home and work realms—what is unique to each place and what is shared between them. It is the process that lets us create, challenge, defend and change categories of social existence within the mental and structural constraints of that existence.

There are two kinds of boundary work. The first focuses on boundary placement. The second focuses on boundary transcendence. Both are essential to place and maintain boundaries. The former more visibly draws the line between realms and the latter helps keep it in place by allowing us to jump back and forth over it. The activities associated with both forms may be continually adjusted to accommodate different conceptualizations of these realms.

Both forms of boundary work are affected by and reflected in three components: (1) the degree to which the people of either realm overlap, (2) the degree to which the objects (ranging from task-specific "tools," in the most general sense of the word, to decorations) and ambiance of surroundings are similar/different; and (3) the degree to which we think, act, and present ourselves in either realm in similar/different ways.

Throughout this text, I freely switch from discussing one of these aspects of integration/segmentation to another. This strategy reflects one of my most important points—that is, that there are multiple, equally important fronts along which the home-work boundary must be simultaneously negotiated. However, the degree of integration/segmentation we enact along each of these components can vary independently of the others. Of course, what we do along one of these fronts is often heavily influenced in the same integrating or segmenting direction by the same factors that guide our actions along other fronts. Nevertheless, any one of us might be highly segmenting in how we manage the people of both realms, extremely integrating via the inanimate objects of both realms, and more in the middle ranges in how we manage our appearance, talk styles, and eating habits. One's position along the continuum at a certain time is a composite, a summation of how one manages each of these broad components and their multiple dimensions.

For example, Irene is a scientist who engages in wage labor work at home at almost any time of the day or night. She has similar reading materials, computers, telephones, artwork, writing supplies, lights, and furniture in her workplace and home offices. She regularly brings her children into institutional workspace, entertains mostly colleagues at home, and is married to her collaborator. Like John, the scientist described at the beginning of this chapter, these strategies place Irene toward the integration pole of the continuum.

Yet Irene also maintains numerous pockets of privacy, reflecting more selective distinctions between "home" and "work." These distinctions are encouraged simply because she possesses a separate workplace and residence. In addition, she does certain work and leisure and domestic activities only at home, while others occur only at the workplace. Only her spouse is privy to certain thoughts and behavior. Only family attends certain social functions. Certain workmates are engaged only outside the home. These more segmenting distinctions offset her more integrating influences and practices and keep Irene from approaching the integration pole more closely.

Sal is a machinist who also has a policy about mixing "home" and "work," but his efforts (like Ed's, the machinist who appeared earlier) are designed to keep them separate. He never brings coworkers or wage labor tasks home, and he strictly adheres to a 7:30 to 4:30 workday, Monday through Friday. There are no common objects between his home and his workplace except himself, his lunch box, his underwear, and his jeans. (He wears different shoes and shirts in both places, even keeping his home and work shirts in separate drawers at home.)

Yet Sal makes and receives personal phone calls at work. He occasionally shares bits of more impersonal information between coworkers and family and attends colleagues' retirement parties and the funerals of their relatives. He brings the family to an annual workplace picnic and has a family portrait hanging at his workspace. So, while Sal is far more segmenting than John or Irene, he too falls short of an extreme type, some practices off-setting the segmenting effects of others.

Integrating through these three components presents three possibilities in terms of the direction of integration. First, we may create an overall effect in which "work" is heavily infused with elements conventionally associated with "home." Or we may heavily infuse "home" with the traditional elements of "work." Or, of course, we may obtain a fairly even balance in our integrating efforts, interweaving both realms with ways of being, people, activities, and artifacts commonly associated with another realm.

The amount of discretion we have for personal boundary work is a most important constraint on the direction and forms of our integration. For reasons I discuss later, the discretion to infuse work with home-related elements is often much less than the discretion to infuse or absorb home with work. Nonetheless, theoretically, and for some people even practically, the integrating of realms may be a fairly well-balanced endeavor, or one in which *either* side of the commute claims more turf from the other.

Wherever we currently fall along the continuum, however, we use different practices in many different ways to create, preserve and change the experiential categories of "home" and "work." The process is like sculpting. In its classical, artistic sense, sculpting is an activity in which boundaries are physically imposed on matter, creating new forms and evoking new interpretations of raw material in the process. If an artist is working with stone, for instance, she carves out negative and positive spaces, defining each from and with the other, to form a new, critically interrelated whole. Hence, the sculptor's activity is a kind of "boundary work," in which matter is envisioned, divided up, and related to itself with virtually endless possibilities. This boundary work transforms relatively undifferentiated material into artificial, socially embedded "works of art."

Delineating and relating the concepts "home" and "work" is similarly a mental and physical sculpting process, and it too can result in endless different experiences. Consider a raw chunk of stone that represents all the items potentially divided into "home" and "work": people, objects, activities, even ways of thinking and being. Like the marble worker whose creations emerge from undifferentiated lumps, each of us must mentally carve out our own categories and relationships of "home" and "work" from an otherwise amorphous social existence. The process is embedded in the systems of cultural concepts and demands we are born into, as well as those we consciously choose or are forced to embrace later on. These ideas are reflected and modified through the tangible, physical side of boundary work, like the presence or absence of phone calls from home while at work, talking about work with one's family, using a briefcase or computer modem to bring personal reading materials and children's fund-raising forms to work or wage work to home, or carrying bag lunches from home to work.

In the extremely segmented approach to home and work, material is purposefully transformed into two distinct categories, "home" and "work" (i.e., negative and positive space), each inversely defining the other. The fully integrated "home-work" category lacks further internal boundaries, though, remaining an undifferentiated lump. It is enacted through people, objects, activities, and a self that are utterly interchangeable across time and space. It pointedly resists subdividing matter into "negative" and "positive" space.

At some point, however, the sculptor's job turns from the placement of boundaries to their maintenance. He must stop chiseling, stop imposing new variations on the boundary between negative and positive space. At first, he does this sequentially, perhaps repeatedly returning and adjusting what he's done in some places, while leaving others alone. Eventually, though, he must do whatever is necessary in order to uphold all of what he's done, allowing the boundaries to exist as a particular, final arrangement of negative and positive space. To maintain this boundary, he might sell the sculpture, so he's not tempted to keep tapping away forever. He might make sure that another chunk of stone will be ready to go, diverting his energy from the old to the new. He may (re)train himself to simply accept the ways these particular negative and positive spaces join at each juncture. Whatever it takes, this, too, is part of the work the sculptor must do in order for the work to exist.

In the same way, home-work negotiators must turn to different forms of boundary work whenever we are, or must be, satisfied with the boundary we've imposed. Whenever we finish with the work of *placing* the boundary, we must turn to the work of *transcending* it. Rather than continuing to chisel away, we work on making transitions between realms, in order to preserve both "home" and "work" as they currently exist.

However, because of the multidimensionality and dynamic status of the home-work boundary, just as we manage to negotiate a good boundary along one dimension, another boundary point is liable to require our attention. Indeed, at any given time, we may find ourselves dividing our attention between placing and re-placing the home-work boundary at some junctures, and focusing more on simply accommodating it at others. And each time we adjust the line along any specific dimension, we produce a new work of art, despite any similarity to what preceded it.

Of course, any sculptor faces certain constraints, so that often unseen influences limit how she approaches, fashions, and leaves each stone. Creating a work of art is not simply a matter of exercising personal choice or "free will." Many constraints take the form of social expectations about what is culturally meaningful to both artist and audience and what sculpting is all about: what should the process be like and what kind of an outcome should we expect. The thoughts of the sculptor's teachers and commissioners will be especially important to her regarding cultural, conceptual issues of what "works of art" look like and how they are made. Other constraints are much more tangible, like the shape and physical characteristics of the stone, the tools the artist has to shape it, the dimensions of her studio, and how much and how soon she's relying on the income a work might generate.

Because of these constraints, some choices are already made for the artist before he even begins his work, especially choices about what the stone will *not* become. These choices are largely made at the unconscious level, reflecting the fact that boundary work occurs here, according to internalized principles, as well as at a more conscious level. The sculptor embraces some options yet does not even consider others. (This may be, as Steven Lukes [1974] argues, the most insidious form of social control.) Social, cognitive constraints thus manifest in personal experience, imagination, and others' expectations. This makes boundary work both visible and invisible, conscious and unconscious.

Accordingly, while there is plenty of room for personal innovation in sculpting, the most basic rules that guide the sculptor's hand are predetermined and virtually impossible to ignore. These rules may be so fundamental that they are taken for granted; only the most systematic exploration uncovers them. Like a good cook, experimental scientist, or home-work negotiator, a sculptor takes her mental constraints and the physical resources at hand and produces a wonderfully synergistic result. And, as is the case with these other people, the end product causes the sculptor to reflect back on the concepts, understandings, techniques, and material situations that originally guided her hand. Through her practical sculpting activity and the artifact it produces, new light is shed on the way she sees these things, the importance they have for her work, and the way she might negotiate them next time.

Likewise, sociocognitive and social-structural constraints abound for us as we practically negotiate the meaning of "home," "work," and their "proper" relationship. First of all, individual thinking is nothing less than the embodiment of group thinking. This is the common thread of the works of Emile Durkheim ([1912] 1965), Max Weber ([1904] 1976), Karl Marx (McLellan 1977), Alfred Schutz (1973), Schutz and Thomas Luckmann (1973), Peter Berger and Luckmann (1968), Michel Foucault ([1966] 1973), Karl Mannheim ([1936] 1985; 1982; 1972), Ludwig Fleck ([1935] 1981), and Thomas Kuhn ([1962] 1970) for instance. All students of philosophy and the sociology of knowledge and science, they note the primacy of the social group for personal thought. "Worldviews," "thoughtstyles," "paradigms," "class consciousness," etcetera, shape any individual's conceptual framework.

Hence, one person's conceptualization of "home" and "work" and their proper relationship is predicated on cultural understandings of these terms. But, as Durkheim ([1912] 1965) reminds us, while cultural constructs precede and inform personal ones, personal ones are never the mere embodiments of social ones. Raymond Williams ([1976] 1985) explicitly argues that the perpetuation of a multiplicity of meanings for cultural concepts is a result of variations in personal experience. A concept must be commensurate with a person's experience for her or him to cognitively embrace it, in whole or in part. This mutually constraining effect results in cultural categories like "home" and "work" that inform and are informed by personal experience.

In addition to more mental, conceptual social constraints, more readily apparent social factors influence what each of us can understand home and work to be, as well as what we can shape them to look like. For instance, just as a sculptor's teacher encourages him to chisel in a certain way, so do spouses' and children's demands influence the way we divide our time between wage and domestic work. If an artistic school of thought leads the sculptor to envision a piece in a certain way, so too do a work group's expectations guide the home-work negotiator. For instance, formal and informal workplace rules about making "personal" phone calls, taking "personal" breaks, and using "work" equipment, materials, and money for "personal" reasons undoubtedly shape the way we distinguish between home and work. The size of a studio limits the dimensions of a sculptor's work of art, just as workplace danger may prohibit the otherwise integrating presence of children or spouses. An artist may not have enough money to buy better tools or study with a more eminent teacher, which would allow him to change his understanding of sculpture. Similarly, the single mother living on her wages and possessing few marketable skills may not have the chance to move beyond her present boss's boundary expectations, whatever they are. Even cultural norms about things like the ideal relationship between parents and children and the forms of day care that should be available shape possible juxtapositions of home and work.

The process of socialization regarding what "home" and "work" mean starts with models presented during childhood. As we grow, our own employment and education experiences provide confirmation or alternatives to these ideas. Soon, spouses', employers', and coworkers' expectations—even children's demands—are crucial in shaping our decisions of what can and will belong to each sphere, or even if there will be two spheres. These classificatory negotiations largely result from expectations about how and why one does certain kinds of wage and domestic work, and the kinds of family, work group, and daily lives we and significant others desire and require of ourselves.

As a result of these factors, for instance, the occupations of university professor, diplomat, family business owner, cleric, and medical doctor and those in cottage industries push members toward the integration end of the spectrum. So do the home-related constraints of people married to coworkers or highly wage work–supportive spouses. Part-time cashiers, insurance claim processors, construction laborers, and "job shop" machinists, however, are examples of occupations that tend to make us segment home and work more. So do the constraints of new parents, those who do most of the daily domestic work, and those whose spouses steadfastly insist that we draw the home-work line at the front doorstep.

Sociologically, the home-work boundary varies for any given person largely according to expectations associated with the following: occupation, work organization, work group, and hierarchical position held within these, gender, family structure, spouse's wage work, one's parenting role, and domestic labor role. Each of these social statuses encapsulates historical, cultural norms about the meaning of home and work, the kinds of activities and ways of being each entails, and the ways each "kind" of person should experience these realms. These normative guidelines are part of what we internalize during our lifelong socialization in making classificatory distinctions.

Furthermore, any individual negotiates these statuses within specific physical environments. The selves, roles and activities institutionally and personally associated with certain statuses are carried out within the real world. A laboratory feels very different from a living room, while a powerful administrator's office may be quite similar to it. Thus, physical, ambient conditions also constrain the way we experience either realm and the extent to which we perceive differences between them.

Change in these statuses, the activities associated with them or the environments in which they are carried out is thus likely to bring about change in the way someone categorizes and experiences "home" and "work." This is because these changes frequently invoke new, modified understandings of what home and work mean. They may also change the available ways in which we may carry out these understandings.

When a sculptor's constraints change, for instance, the kind of piece produced also is likely to change. If she gets better chisels and polishing techniques, she can use these to create a new, different kind of piece. If her old tools are thrown out, she will be forced to. If she has discovered something new about herself or society through a significant life experience, she may have a new theme for the next work. An exercise or assignment from the artist with whom she studies can present new problems to be solved and new constraints on possible solutions. She may shed the inhibitions on her old gifts of imagination and approach her next piece with a tradition-shattering, innovative "eye" she had not previously possessed. There are even more mundane changes that may affect the kind of piece she will produce next. She may have only enough money to purchase certain kinds of stone. She may have only a seven-foot ceiling in a ten- by twelve-foot room for her studio. She may develop arthritis and become incapable of making certain strokes with the strength and dexterity they require.

Chances are, maintaining the status quo would result in the sculptor's next work being quite similar to a previous creation. Change in any of these things, however, quite a probable event, virtually assures change in the next work of art. In this way, the sculptor displays a range of continuity and discontinuity between her sculptures. Certain constraints carry over to manifest again in new works of art, while others are replaced with new considerations and new responses to them.

In the same way, each of us responds to changing constraints on the ways we see and experience home and work. If a sculptor's arthritis causes him to abandon certain forms of stone working, so may the onset of a parent's or child's terminal or chronic illness cause us to become more segmentist in the interweaving of our home and work. Or, bosses and family permitting, our own illness may promote a more flexible approach to the time and space of both realms, as we try to work and recuperate simultaneously. The adoption of workplace policies like flextime and flex-place can offer far more integrating possibilities. The sudden institution of bureaucratic workplace policies, however, encourages a more segmentist approach to home and work, demanding that we remove "personal" items and activities from workspace and time. A promotion to management may mean expectations of greater investment of self in work. It may require and promote more thinking about work while at home, more extra-workplace socializing with coworkers and more business travel. A new job in a work group with fairly segmentist expectations, though, can lead us to become more segmenting, as people repeatedly refuse invitations to chat about domestic matters or socialize "on the outside." On the other hand, a likable coworker's enthusiasm can just as easily rope us into playing on a departmental softball or bowling team, extending our relationships with coworkers into the physical and social space and time outside the workplace proper. Likewise, marriage to a spouse who positively throws herself into furthering our career by networking, entertaining, and typing on our behalf may greatly increase a previous level of integration.

Over time, certain realm and boundary expectations and ambient conditions generally hold constant. But new expectations and physical arrangements demand or allow us to change home and work arrangements beyond our previous conceptualizations. We abandon or adopt specific segmenting and integrating practices along numerous dimensions as needed and desired. At the same time, these new practices react back on the social influences that give rise to them, causing us to modify both our visions of "home" and "work" and the temporal and spatial territories they previously encompassed.

Sometimes the change in our home-work configurations will be quite radical. Other times it will be more of a fine-tuning of present configurations. It depends on the changes we experience and how severely these test and constrain the previous conceptual framework and practical ways of distinguishing between home and work.

Of course, while boundary work is firmly and consistently embedded in the social structure, it also allows for discretion in personal responses to these constraints. For example, if it is not required in our job descriptions, we must still decide if we will have nothing to do with our colleagues outside the workplace and workday. Will we socialize with them in a neutral, social place like a softball field or a restaurant? Will we invite them into our homes? How often and for what kinds of occasions? And if we make a decision about these things today, what will we do tomorrow, if a new, quite likable colleague joins the department or our marriage hits a low point?

Boundary work thus gives us room for personal innovation as well as the accommodation of cultural and sociostructural expectations. It allows us to constantly modify our understandings and experiences of home and work, providing an important link between self and society, what is personal and cultural. In this respect, the home-work negotiator is no different from the artistic sculptor, whose work links him and his unique propensity for creation with the rest of the art community.

Thus, each person may move in any direction along the continuum, reflecting the new ways she or he is asked by others and herself or himself to perceive and enact "home" and "work." Integration and segmentation are not personality types. They are typifications of the ways we classify and juxtapose items, acts, thoughts, and aspects of self to accommodate social and personal expectations.

For a given person, however, there may well be differing levels of social-psychological comfort with certain positions on the continuum. Yet that comfort is more a function of two situational factors. First, how closely are we allowed by others to enact our socialized views about the "proper" relationship between home and work? Second, how well can we muster the resources that allow us to adjust when we're forced to abandon old views and adopt new ones?

For instance, Didi grew up as an important presence in her parents' prestigious family business. In its purest form, the presence of family and business were inseparable in this social unit, whether its members were at home or the office. Now a wife and mother of two, Didi still helps run the company. Her husband, however, shares no such integrated background. Despite a highly lucrative, professional career and long hours at work, he is far more segmentist in his views, as are his colleagues. He is quickly annoyed if even the smallest amount of paperwork from Didi's job lays on the living room coffee table. Alan firmly believes that when she's at home, Didi should do only "home" things. Of course, throughout Didi's childhood, "home" things included "work" things and vice versa. The definition of "home" things was an early and continuous point of contention for this couple.

Didi now finds she is more segmentist too, a result of the births of her two children within one year, her acceptance of most of the family's domestic and child-related work, and the desire to dedicate their small amount of shared time to family activities. She still "sneaks in" a little "wage work" in the evenings, however, after the kids are in bed. Through evening thoughts, paperwork, and phone calls, Didi retains some of her old ideas about home, work, and their relationship. At the same time, she's adopted some new practices to handle the changes in her personal situation and in what "home" and "work" mean to her and those around her.

Home and Work as Experiential Realms

In our society, for historical reasons, segmentist approaches to home and work generally are assumed and understood far more often than integrating ones. We take Alan's perspective for granted more than Didi's. In fact, the "myth of separate spheres" permeates our culture (Kanter 1977b). With the exception of a few elite and/or unusual occupations and lifestyles (e.g., rural doctors, clerics, politicians, soldiers, commercial fisherwomen and -men, farmers, migrant workers, and hoboes) we rarely expect that home and work will be intimately, inextricably linked for members of our society.

The normative expectations of a segmented home and work experience have resulted from the separation of the values, activities, social functions, and people of home and work into separate spatio-temporal locations. Throughout the nineteenth and twentieth centuries in the United States, "work" and "home" became increasingly distinct, mentally and physically. At this time, these realms also acquired a conceptually inverse, inseparable, semiotic link with each other. Old themes of public and private, men and women, production and consumption became respectively concretized into the new places and times of "work" and "home."[3] As some of society's most fundamental structures changed, so did the classification systems that reproduced them.[4]

3. The following works have been most helpful in drawing the connections between today's constructions of home and work and those of the last two centuries: Jean Bethke Elshtain, *Public Man, Private Woman: Women in Social and Political Thought* (1981) (see especially Part I); Mary P. Ryan, *The Cradle of the Middle Class: The Family in Oneida County, NY, 1790–1865* (1981); Nancy F. Cott, *The Bonds of Womanhood: "Women's Sphere" in New England, 1780–1835* (1977); Alice Kessler-Harris, *Out to Work: A History of Wage-Earning Women in the United States* (1982); Lynn Weiner, *From Working Girl to Working Mother* (1985); Ruth Schwarz Cowen, *More Work for Mother: The Ironies of Household Technology from the Open Hearth to the Microwave* (1983); Christopher Lasch, *Haven in a Heartless World: The Family Besieged* (1977); Richard Sennett, *The Fall of Public Man: The Social Psychology of Capitalism* (1977); and Nancy Folbre and Heidi Hartmann, "The Rhetoric of Self-Interest: Selfishness, Altruism, and Gender in Economic Theory" (1988).

4. This is the central point underlying Emile Durkheim's and Marcel Mauss's *Primitive Classification* ([1903] 1963).

It was during this time that "work" became the public realm of wage labor. It was increasingly conceptualized as the masculine, political, artificial (i.e., instrumental, rational, and socially valued) world of economic production. It took place away from the homestead during a "shift," a specific part of the twenty-four-hour day. "Home," on the other hand, became identified as the private territory where one resided and found activity symbolizing a woman's love for her family. It gradually became thought of as the feminine realm, a nonpolitical, natural (i.e., affiliative, irrational, emotional, biologically necessary) world focused on social and biological reproduction, economic consumption, and, in terms of leisure, physical, and mental restoration for the wage-laborer.

An asymmetrical value judgment also became part of the home-work bifurcation during this time. Wage work was a source of social power and its activity was relatively highly esteemed. For many, it also became one of the last places that a person would choose to be, except for the money it provided. Home became a refuge from that public world of work, where the nurturing, expressive ambiance created by mother and wife served as a retreat for all (except women, perhaps). The "Cult of True Womanhood" and the myth of the "Self-Made Man" epitomize the patterns outlined here.

A number of these themes are highlighted in the ways we think of the terms "work" and "home" today. First, "work" is both a place and an activity, a function of its present association with a dedicated work-place and time. We "go to" work "in order to" work. Further, to describe something as "work" often implies a tedious and even distasteful activity, requiring a great deal of effort, self-discipline, and sometimes skill. So much so, that those who enjoy their wage labor will make comments to the effect, "This is too much fun to be work" or "I'd pay *them* to let me to do this!"

Moreover, in spite of the consciousness-raising efforts of feminists, "work" is generally equated with "wage work." It referentially excludes domestic, nonpaid labor, and must be preceded by the qualifier "volunteer" when done outside the home for no wage. The implication is that wage work is a fundamentally different kind of activity from these other things, even if the tasks done are the same. The further implication is that wage work, fundamentally men's territory, is necessary, is central to the economy, and requires effort and skill. The historical myth is that domestic and volunteer work, as women's work, is not and does not. We further resist equating domestic labor with (wage) "work" because this demeans its symbolic value as a "labor of love" (i.e., of "home") (DeVault 1987). Women especially see domestic work as a gift to loved ones (Hochschild [1989] 1990) and an extension of purer motives and relationships than we assume in wage labor.

Because we think of "home" and "work" as gendered territories, we also have a propensity to think of "work" as fundamentally *"men's"* wage work. The sexually segregated activities women do for wages are less recognized as "real" work (Halle 1984) and are valued and rewarded less, accordingly (Reskin and Roos 1990). Of course, seeing home and work as gendered territories means that while men's activities are the standard for "real" wage work, women's activities are the standard for "real" parenting and homemaking.

In our culture, we tend to actively contrast "work" with "play" or "leisure," using the former to buy the latter. We seek escape and individuality through our leisure, rarely expecting to do so through our work. We see "work" even more broadly as a means to an end. It's what we do to obtain necessary and desirable commodities to maintain our "home" along several dimensions: as a coherent family unit, as a residence, as a place of leisure, and as a refuge from "work." It's a "bonus" if our work is pleasurable; its ultimate purpose is to provide money for the expected pursuit of pleasure elsewhere.

Furthermore, we see "work" as a public activity requiring a public presentation of a carefully constructed self. Appearance, speech, emotions, and the portrayal of intellect must be attended to in specific, situationally defined ways "at work." As a private realm, however, "home" ideally is the place where we can "be ourselves," "put up our feet," "let down our hair," relax among those who see us, "warts and all" but aren't supposed to hold it against us. In fact, one of the foremost attractions of wage labor for some wage earners interviewed for this book and unemployed previously is that it makes them "get dressed in the morning." This counteracts the self-described sloppy, sluggish patterns they fell into while at home all the time. When they have their "work selves" to contrast with "home selves," however, they look forward to opportunities for both sets of attitudes and presentations of self.

Because of assumptions about work's "public" nature, we further assume great involvement by the State in observing and regulating the activities, physical conditions, and wage and interpersonal exchanges of "work." At the same time, we expect correspondingly little involvement of the State in our homes, for "home" is *ours,* private. Tax assessors may not come inside our homes for the same reasons we have resisted the national census since its inception: what exists and goes on inside our homes is nobody else's business.

For this reason, we have strict limitations on police intervention and their rights to search within the home. This includes historically placing a low priority on police involvement in cases of domestic violence. Only when one or more family members repeatedly denies others the most rudimentary elements of a "decent" home life (such as being free of extreme physical abuse inflicted over a substantial period of time) can police and social workers interfere. Indeed, our private homes are the places we are most likely to selectively show our most abusive, inhuman sides, as well as our most affectionate and tender ones.

We have extensive laws about trespassing, in some states including the right to kill someone who enters one's home uninvited. We may drive, fish, or shoot guns on our properties without a license and (in most states) engage in any sex acts in our homes with consenting adults. We fully expect these activities to be regulated at the workplace, however. Likewise, we can be legally reprimanded or prosecuted for sexist or racist or agist comments and actions at work, yet this remains an unimaginable scenario within our homes.

Thus, "home" and "work" became ideologically distinct in the last two centuries, each imbued with expectations that counter the other's. The segmentist experience of home and work and their relationship is predicated on this conceptually contrasting imagery. Individual realities aside, we culturally contrast "home" and "work," point for ideological point: "home" is "not work" and "work" is "not home," each defined inversely by the other within a conceptually closed system. Invoking one of these concepts immediately invokes the other, by way of contrast.

Semiotics, which includes the study of syntactics and semantics, allows us to focus on just such a way of uncovering the meaning of symbols (de Saussure [1919] 1959; Zerubavel 1987). In this case, the concepts "home" and "work" symbolize contrasting ideas or meanings, for specific historical, cultural reasons. Regardless of which is the "marked" or "unmarked" point of inquiry (Waugh 1982), both meanings are signified simultaneously. The study or conceptualization of either one must therefore be viewed in light of the other.[5]

5. For a general discussion of semiotics, see Ferdinand de Saussure, *A General Course in Linguistics* ([1919] 1959). In addition, the semiotic relationship between two structurally related, contrasting symbols and the meanings they represent is discussed fully and accessibly in Eviatar Zerubavel's "The Language of Time: Toward a Semiotics of Temporality" (1987). It is here that the notion of the "semiotic quadrangle"

In the case of these semiotically linked concepts, if work is perceived as an artificial, masculine realm, then home is the natural, feminine realm. If work is seen as the center for productivity, home is the locus of consumption. If we expect work to be a place where we do things primarily in exchange for wages, home is the site of voluntary activity, done simply because it is "right" and perhaps because it makes us feel good to do so. If work is expected to be a string of temporary jobs and Tonnies's gesellschaft-like, specific, limited relationships and goals, home is the center of gemeinschaft-like relations, all-encompassing and unlimited over the life course.[6] Home is where we seek the predictable continuity of families' presence and their long (and rather unforgiving) memories of who we are. It is the place we expect to most thoroughly embed ourselves, past, present, and future. If we now expect work to be a public world of rational relationships and interactions, home is the world where we carry out the private search for intimacy. Home is a place of refuge, perhaps, but mostly because we expect to explore and create selves there with a range of emotions and activities and relationships totally unexpected and inappropriate to the workplace. Of the two places, home is where we expect to get the support and resources necessary to grow into autonomous, loving, and productive citizens. Thus, if work is a place we temporarily occupy each day as another interchangeable cog in the institutional machinery, home is a place we seek to possess. With a freedom alien to the workplace, we shape, decorate and fill our homes with people, pets, and objects that reflect and reinforce our individuality and sense of belonging. If work is supposed to be the means to an end, home is the supposed end for which we are working.

In short, we have moved away from the "craftsman" model of work in which work, home, and leisure are merely different facets of a single crystalline existence. Instead, our culture has largely adopted a "utilitarian" model of work (Mills 1956). In this view, we separate the complementary functions of work, leisure, and family into two distinct institutions, two entirely different matrices of order and meaning, each

is introduced, where the syntactic relationships between (a) contrasting symbols and (b) contrasting meanings is related to the semantic relationships between the associated symbol and meaning of each side of the pair. On the nature of marked and unmarked symbols that are semiotically linked, see Linda R. Waugh, "Marked and Unmarked: A Choice between Unequals in Semiotic Structure" (1982).

6. Ferdinand Tonnies, *Gemeinschaft and Gesellschaft* ([1887]; New Brunswick, N.J.: Transaction Books, 1988).

associated with a particular time and place. As distinct locations where we are fairly reliably found at certain times, the terms "home" and "work" now encapsulate and symbolize for us all the other things we associate with the places so named.

This includes a certain set of expectations about what goes on where, who should be involved and how we and others should negotiate all of it. We categorize aspects of our selves, the people with whom we associate, the activities we do, and the objects around us into two different geographical places, keeping them fairly distinct. Some elements are located "at home" and others "at work."

We also split up our time, dedicating different blocks of it to "home" and "work." A segmentist culture produces the workday and the holiday, the work week and the weekend, and the work year and the vacation, differentiating between them as much as the house and the workplace. Under the segmented model, work is relegated primarily to the workplace and workday; home is relegated to the house, the evening and the weekend.[7] A more integrating approach to home and work would leave all times and all places more multipurpose. (Of course, this creates far less experiential variety across time and space, as well as within the self among those who integrate more.)

Suburban living, for instance, is predicated on this historical, segmentist model of home and work, time and space.[8] It is no coincidence that a temporal and physical separation of home and work coincided with the cultural separation of the themes and people just mentioned.

7. A rather intimidating number of Marxist reflections on work and the workplace assume the current bifurcation of work and family/leisure interests as a direct result of capitalists' exploitation of alienated workers. Several works in particular may be helpful in summarizing various themes of the segmentation of the concerns, activities and people of work from those of home: John Alt's "Beyond Class: The Decline of Labor and Leisure" (1976); Richard Edwards's *Contested Terrain: The Transformation of the Workplace in the Twentieth Century* (1979); Andre Gorz's *Farewell to the Working Class* ([1980] 1982); and Christopher Lasch's *Haven in a Heartless World: The Family Besieged* (1977).

8. A number of sources on the development of the suburbs and the suburban way of life help elaborate the structural dichotomy between home and work. See especially Kenneth Jackson's *Crabgrass Frontier* (1985); Barry Schwartz, ed., *The Changing Face of the Suburbs* (1976), especially the essay by Scott Donaldson, presenting themes of suburban life in John Cheever's work. (309–22), and Schwartz's conclusion (325–40); *The First Suburbs* by Henry C. Binford (1985), especially the introduction (1–13), chap. 5 on commutation (125–49), and chap. 6 on Suburban Society (154–86), and Robert C. Wood's *Suburbia: Its People and Their Politics* (1958).

The key organizational tools that reflect and reinforce any conceptual boundaries are space and time (Zerubavel 1991).

Not only did the suburbs emerge for this reason, but in designing and marketing their product, suburban developers relied heavily on the logic that led to it. According to them, the city was suitable only for the workday and -week, while the suburb was for the evening and weekend. The city was the center of serious work, coworkers, and adult matters; the suburb was the place for leisure, family, and especially children. The city was filthy and unhealthy; the suburb was clean and dedicated to robust, "All-American" lifestyles earmarked by lots of fresh air activities. The city was for those who had not earned the right to leave it; the suburbs were for those who had and who could then insulate themselves from those who had not, while securing advantages for their children that would further ensure their upward (outward) mobility. In short, the development of the suburbs was a response to structural and conceptual changes, but it also enhanced and made more distinct the separation of home and work that stimulated the movement.

The historical bias toward the segmentation of home and work makes it difficult to conceive of them in any other way. Like all dichotomies (Epstein 1988), segmentist language/imagery, here additionally concretized into space and time, constrains us from seeing home and work as anything else. Variations across the continuum exist, but our historical bias is manifested in seeing these categories as more or less distinct, not more or less the same. Helena Lopata (1993) argues that this conceptual inversion presents a real challenge to academics, one which must be met if better understandings of women's experiences, in particular, are to emerge.

Rooted in history, then, present cultural norms and personal understandings of home and work lead us to "frame" (Goffman 1974; Bateson [1955] 1972) or experience our physical surroundings, the time of day, and what goes on at home and work in specific ways. Even if we do similar things with similar kinds of people at home and work (think of a mother who is also a day-care provider), these may be experienced as quite different activities. The physical places in which they are done and the realm-specific motivations, goals, and constraints on behavior in either realm change the experience of these activities.

Of course, individual realities rarely meet historical, normative expectations of what home and work are about. Our actual situations may encourage realm-specific framings to diverge in any number of directions. For some people, home and work are not nearly as distinguishable as the segmentist model leads us to expect. We may have highly integrating conceptual frameworks and lifestyles. If work is "greedy" (Coser 1974), for instance, demanding long-term commitment, goals, accountability, and the embedding of self there, it may absorb home altogether. This leaves little distinction between the public and private lives, times, and places that other, currently more segmenting people possess.

Furthermore, even if these realms are quite distinct qualitatively and geographically, they may not possess the phenomenological norms presumed by our historical, cultural model. *Work* may be the place we can really "be ourselves." *It* may be the locus of power, autonomy, freedom, and relatively unaccountable consumption. Home may be associated with temporary and utilitarian relationships, short-term goals, limited commitment, and distasteful "work." Or, perhaps, neither realm may provide the kind of supportive environment and relationships in which we can empower and embed our selves.

This is why individual meanings of home and work and their relationship do not begin and end with those of the segmentist, Modern model just described. Rather, these historical expectations combine with personal realities as we create our unique images and juxtapositions of these categories. We use these cultural expectations to interpret personal situations, and vice-versa. But the power of culture over individual experience encourages us to give special weight to the images of the segmentist model; these are seen as the norm. Any actual, individual deviations from this model are seen as exactly that: deviations from the normative, culturally expected view of what home and work mean and how they are related. We would have no need for a "Take Our Daughters to Work Day," for instance, nor would it be such a special event, if the activity and the conceptual framework it could stand for was more common throughout the rest of the year.

"Home" and "work" are not merely places, then, but "experiential realms." They are combinations of conceptual, social-structural and spatio-temporal categories, guided by a historically-given model. We see "home" and "work" as distinct locations in space and time, but, even more importantly, as places dedicated to largely separate sets of tasks, people, relationships, things, and specific ways of thinking about and responding to them. Home and work are experiential, not merely physical realms, because there is a fundamental, cognitive distinction between their designated agendas and rules for interaction in our society. This greatly influences the "frames" that guide our actions in each realm and the boundary work we do to distinguish between them.

The use of distinct framings to interpret what happens at home and work is actually key to the degree of segmentation/integration we experience. Extreme integrators understand everything of "home-work" within a single frame, while extreme segmentors use two entirely different, if not antithetical, framings to experience "home" and "work." (To use the terminology of Schutz and Luckmann (1973), there is a single "finite province of meaning" for the former, two "provinces" for the latter.) Given that real people fall between these two extremes, we all use two different frames of mind to engage in work and home. *How* different these are is what places us in a particular spot on the continuum.

Frames become activated in the form of "mentalities," ways of thinking and being when we're mentally and/or physically "in" either place.[9] It's the invocation of a particular mentality that imbues otherwise subjectively meaningless places, things, times of day, tasks at hand, and role relations with their experiential significance. If we think in pretty much the same way, feel like pretty much the same person, and go about our activities and interactions in much the same frame of mind, paying attention to the same kinds of things and having similar expecta-

9. My concept of a "mentality" is informed by a number of works and concepts in philosophy and the sociology of knowledge and science. See Karl Mannheim's *Ideology and Utopia* ([1936] 1985) for the concept of a "weltanschauung" (worldview), as well as chap. 2 in *Essays on the Sociology of Knowledge* (Mannheim 1972). Peter Berger and Thomas Luckmann's *The Social Construction of Reality* (1968) is a good source for a general understanding of the perspective used here, as well as Alfred Schutz's "On Multiple Realities" (1973, 207–59) and Alfred Schutz and Thomas Luckmann's *The Structures of the Life World* (1973). Ludwig Fleck's provoking concept and use of a "thoughtstyle" is presented in *Genesis and Development of a Scientific Fact* ([1935] 1981). Thomas Kuhn's similar but slightly more elusive concept of a "paradigm" is elaborated in *The Structure of Scientific Revolutions* ([1962] 1970). Somewhat more accessible work on the substance of mentalities and experiential realms is presented in Erving Goffman's *Frame Analysis* (1974), although an important distinction between my view and Goffman's is that, like Fleck, I do not believe there is the possibility of social creatures observing an "untransformed reality"; observation entails interpretation. In *Smut* (1983) Murray Davis also provides a highly accessible and interesting treatment of this material in his "everyday" and "erotic" realities.

tions of those around us no matter where we are, we have a more continuous, more integrated experience of home and work. If, on the other hand, we find ourselves feeling like two different people, acting out two different personae, approaching our activities with different perspectives, and interpreting what others do differently at home and work, we have a more segmented experience of these realms.

This is at least partly because the more similar we see home and work, the more integrating are the practices we innovate and adopt. Our boundary work emerges to confirm and strengthen whatever the degree of similarity/difference between our framings of home and work. Despite what others might think, the less similarity or overlap we see in what we do, why we do it, and who we are when we do it, the more segmenting the practices we create and adopt will be. We use whatever discretion we have in either realm to enact personal views of home, work, and their relationship through noninstitutionalized, personal activities and routines.

The varying distinctiveness of our home and work selves contributes greatly to the problematic nature of our boundary work. The more we integrate, the easier it is to turn from one way of being to another, to make the transition from one experiential world to another. This is because home and work and the selves associated with them are closer approximations of each other. For this reason, the more we integrate, the more the problematic part of our boundary work tends to focus on boundary placement. The more we segment home and work, however, the greater is the transformation we must make between each world and the realm-specific mentalities associated with them. The more we segment, then, the more our attention focuses on transcendent boundary work.

It is because of segmentist influences, then, that we must learn how to visibly, behaviorally induce the mental transformations required by physical movement between realms. The ways we use our journeys between home and work, clothing, drinking, eating, hellos, good-byes, and other ritualized activities are important forms of boundary work for this reason. They help us transcend home-work boundaries, even as we place them. And the more we segment, the more heavily we must rely on these activities to help us through the day.

This is just one more way that tangible, visible behavior helps us physically negotiate and delineate what is mentally distinct. Through the ways we manage our selves, objects, people, thoughts, and tasks, we not only concretize mental boundaries but our mental journeys over them. This is how we turn classificatory boundaries into existential ones and existentially move between mental ones.

Summary

"Home" and "work" are conceptual categories, differentially imposed by mentally and physically drawing boundaries around activities, self, people, and things. Daily boundary work helps us sculpt these concepts into experiential realms and, in the process, maintain the boundaries we impose. The boundaries we draw reflect and reinforce our perceptions of what does and does not belong together, what might go together (and under what circumstances), and what is the relationship between all of them. Boundary work thus helps us create and constantly modify the mental frameworks used to experience social life. Indeed, without boundary work, any conceptual distinctions between "home" and "work," and any experiential framework based on them, become moot.

Of course, for the boundary work of "home" and "work," the social constraints on our products and the tools used to create them are different from those of the artistic sculptor. Like the sculptor's product, though, we use these tools to create a work of art that has a distinct, consistent logic to it. And, like the sculptor, we use physical boundary work to reflect and enhance the mental, conceptual boundary work on which "home" and "work," our daily works of art, are based.

Chapter one of this book focuses on visible yet highly symbolic ways of separating the objects, people, activities, and thoughts of our daily lives into "home" and "work." These aspects of the boundary work of "home" and "work" cover a range of practices and inanimate and animate objects, from calendars and keys, clothing and purses, address books and photographs, lunches and vacations to reading material, money, and people. Throughout this discussion, I especially focus on how time and space are shared and divided in the process of sculpting realms as we attempt to delineate and juxtapose these "territories of the self."

In chapter two, I turn my attention to transformational activities: commutes and phone calls, hellos and good-byes, changing clothes, and eating and drinking. Here, I focus on frequently ritualized, transitional boundary work. I argue that transitions between realms may be easier or more difficult for us depending on how segmenting/integrating we are at a given time and our greater or lesser awareness of the home-work boundary.

In many ways, the dimensions of our boundary work presented in these first two chapters are the equivalent of a sculptor's tools. And inasmuch as conceptual images of home and work fall along a continuum, I show how each tangible boundary dimension appears in more integrating and segmenting forms. This range of options makes it clear that our works of art are the result of the numerous choices that we make and that are imposed on us at every juncture of the home-work boundary.

Having established what I mean by "boundary work" in the first two chapters, I next turn to the social constraints from home and work that encourage us to put boundaries in certain places and ways. In chapters three and four, I put more structural and cultural meat on the symbolic, social-psychological arguments of the first two chapters. Like the constraints shaping the sculptor's product, those presented here range from the more unconscious and insidious to the extremely obvious. The options employers, coworkers, and families give us, for instance, reflect a combination of situational factors and cultural assumptions embedded within them. Each of these greatly influences the extent to which we segment or integrate along the dimensions discussed in chapters one and two. So do the ambient, physical characteristics of realm environments and the geographical distances between them. Chapter three offers some thoughts on constraints emanating from the workplace and chapter four focuses on those from home.

In chapter five, I bring together my observations about the logic of boundary work with two case studies. Through extensive interview quotations, I offer biographical sketches of people I met during the fieldwork for this study: "Jimmy" and "Eleanor." Representing two points well apart on the integration-segmentation continuum, Jimmy and Eleanor illustrate the variety and consistency of personal boundary work. With Jimmy, a married, thirty-year-old machinist and father of three, I focus on the issue of transitions. Eleanor, a married, forty-five-year-old personnel manager and mother of one, shows how combinations of realms cause some of us to pay more attention to boundary placement work. The chapter ends with some thoughts on the appropriateness of various positions along the integration-segmentation continuum.

In my conclusion, "Beyond Home and Work: Boundary Theory," I take the issue of classificatory boundaries to their most abstract level. Here, I enumerate what I have found to be the most important structural aspects of any categorical boundaries, reflecting on the behavioral and scholarly implications of their variations. This is where I also offer a few more comments on the study of classification, the questions of classification that this study allows me to explore in detail, and how this kind of inquiry is subsumed within the emerging field of cognitive sociology.

The Lab

My observations in this book are informed by seventy-two, two- to six-hour interviews with employees at "the Laboratory," or "the Lab," a research laboratory in the Northeast United States. (A copy of the interview schedule I developed is included as an appendix to this text.) I also incorporate observations made on-site while conducting the interviews. Six pretest interviews and dozens of less formal discussions with family, acquaintances, and other members of the Laboratory supplement the formal interviews. Altogether, these are the conversations that helped generate and illustrate the thoughts that appear here.

There were several reasons that I selected the Lab for my field work. First, I am fascinated by scientists' work. The ways scientists approach their work and the ways they are trained and interact with one another are amazing. The organizations dedicated to scientific research are interesting to me too. It is quite a trick to support scientists' disparate goals, cowboy-like work attitudes, and intolerance for bureaucracy and still maintain a collegial, well-focused enterprise. I had no doubt that the Lab and its members would keep my interest sharply peaked during and after my fieldwork.

Second, after some preliminary investigation, I decided I wanted a place where I could enrich my theoretical work and less systematic observations by talking to people in a variety of occupations. I expected boundary work to be greatly influenced by occupational membership. I wanted to talk to family members too, people who had others making demands of them and relying on them at home, as I anticipated this would play an important role in personal boundary work. I also wanted a place where neither women nor men held token employment status, for I expected that gendered divisions of labor at work and home would affect boundary expectations and practices. And I wanted a place where I could find considerate, helpful people. I needed a sympathetic administrative staff that might grant me access to the employees, as well as individuals who might be willing to discuss the details of their everyday lives with a stranger, whose only source of legitimacy was being a Ph.D. student.

The Lab offered the perfect resolution of all these constraints. Its mission is the furthering of scientific knowledge within the natural science disciplines. It conscientiously fosters employer-employee relations through numerous in-house programs and policies. This predisposed all levels of its staff to my interests and needs. The Laboratory payroll includes many occupational groups, so I had a great deal of choice in the groups on whom I could focus my efforts. Several scientific departments employed enough Ph.D. women scientists so that I could get a sense of any gender differences in what home and work mean and how they relate, while holding work demands relatively constant. The Lab also has a reputation of employing mature, family-oriented people. In fact, a number of people I met belong to several generations of family members employed at the Lab. Many met their future spouses at the Lab. I could talk to people who only lived with another adult, single parents, those in two-parent households with small children, with older children, and still others with "empty nests." I was granted work time to meet with all my conversants and given all the assistance I needed with logistics and introductions. Very few of the people I approached refused to meet with me, whether out of politeness, curiosity, a need to talk, the desire to get away from work for a little while, or even sympathy for someone trying to do a dissertation.

In short, the Lab was an ideal research environment for this project, and I quickly found myself beginning interviews there. I conducted the interviews between January of 1991 and January of 1992, with most of them taking place between June and December of 1991. Over and over again, I met and talked with smart people who graciously accommodated me in every possible way.

Of the formal interviews, twenty-six were with Personnel employees, across the division hierarchy. Twenty of these were with women, holding a variety of jobs in the recruiting, hiring, and firing of employees and providing employment-related services and benefits. Six interviews were with men in this division, five of whom were supervisors across all levels of management. Twenty of the interviews were with male machinists, specializing in light- and heavy-tool and instrument making, representing all levels of the division hierarchy. Twenty-six interviews were with Ph.D. scientists from two disciplines, evenly split between women and men. These scientists work in decentralized, academic-like departments, pursuing personal research agendas and collaborating as desired. They also represent a number of levels in division and work group hierarchies.

Participants were selected from those living with at least one significant other, stratified along a variety of life-course/family configurations. Where I had some choice about whom to interview, I often followed the advice of administrators and assistants who knew of my interests, some having been interviewed already. My aim throughout the interview process was to obtain rich, insightful interviews rather than strictly "representative" ones. Of the eighty-one individuals I approached, nine elected not to participate in the interview. Five of these were high-ranking, male Ph.D. scientists in the "Unhappy" department described in chapter three; the rest were unsystematically distributed by sex across departments and seniority levels.

Throughout the following discussion, I have protected the confidence of the people with whom I spoke in several ways. First, I have used pseudonyms in place of real names. I also use multiple pseudonyms for the same person whenever possible to limit the possibilities of identifying her or him. Further, I have regularly changed demographic, workplace, and familial information about individuals and within their stories wherever it does not affect the point under discussion. Finally, I have intentionally preserved the anonymity of the Lab, not only as part of the conditions under which I was invited to learn from this organization but to better protect the identities of my conversants.

One implication of this decision is that I have chosen to withhold certain descriptive information about the Lab that may well have appeared in other studies by other people. Those who study organizations or conduct classic ethnographic studies will be the quickest (perhaps the only) readers to notice this. I was forced to omit this information because organizations like this are dramatically unique. Anyone in scientific circles, especially, could easily identify the Lab if I gave too much information about its organizational profile. Quantitative information reveals organizational identities especially well. This is why information like the number of departments, specific nature of those departments, number of employees at the Lab or within each department, as well as information on its institutional affiliations will not appear here.

Nevertheless, this decision poses few analytical problems, for this is not a study of the Lab. It is not a study of Lab employees. This is a book about a process, "boundary work," what might influence it and what might come out of it. The Lab was a convenient place where I could talk to a bunch of people about these things. I use the Lab and the individual workers there only to help illustrate the process with which I am concerned, its range of possibilities, and the ways extrapersonal factors constrain it at the personal level.

In fact, my focus on the process of boundary work lets me use the information gleaned from these interviews in a fairly untraditional way. I am generally unhappy with the way interview material is used in scholarly books. Rarely do conversants' insights appear as more than two or three decontextualized lines punctuating the author's text. This is the convention, of course, and, along with publishers' and editors' preferences for short quotes (since they save space and keep printing costs down), tradition goes a long way in perpetuating a genre. Nonetheless, these bits of dialogue often do little to shed light on the author's point better than the author does, or to provide enough "data" for the reader to independently judge a point's validity. The pages of the text become punctuated with brief bursts of self-legitimating ammunition. Moreover, while these (sometimes mistakenly) raise the author's pedestal of comprehension ever higher, they do so at the expense of the speakers, presenting the latter and their thoughts in a fragmented, unenlightened state.

I have at least temporarily settled the issue of how to use my interview material in the following way. Throughout most of this book, I do not present much in the way of quotes from my conversants. I summarize their stories, aggregate their various habits, and present these in my own voice, as illustrations of whatever point I am trying to make. It is not necessary or efficient to do otherwise.

However, in chapter five, readers will probably find some of the lengthiest quotations they've ever seen in a scholarly book. Here, I let Jimmy and Eleanor do much of their own talking, trying only to direct readers toward the various points they made during our conversations. This is as good a way as any, and better than most, to carry out my agenda for this chapter, namely, to provide a more experiential, "real life" summary of the previous chapters while raising a few new points too. In this way, I intend to stay true to my prejudices about how conversants and quotes should be treated, especially when they say important things better than I can.

one

Territories of the Self: Recognizing the Home-Work Boundary

In a segmenting society, interaction tends to occur within single-purpose, institutional environments. The self becomes separated, parceled out so that certain aspects of identity are emphasized in one realm, others in its opposite. The ways we spatially and temporally divide up objects, people, and activities reflect and promote the mental boundaries we place around these certain ways of being, of thinking, and of acting.

To the extent that anyone makes distinctions between home and work, we each experience and exhibit realm-specific notions of who we are. Through boundary work, we create a more or less continuous sense of who we are in each realm. We separate and assign certain aspects of self to distinct places and times, allowing and encouraging others to appear anywhere, anytime. In this light, boundary work is the process of creating and maintaining more or less distinct "territories of the self."

The idea of a *territory* of the self implies that a self does not end with a mentality. Rather, we portray and reinforce that self, that way of thinking, through our bodies and our physical, tangible surroundings. As a particular sense of self extends outward, manifesting in visible artifacts and behavior, it can be located in space and time. We embed it in and associate it with a particular environment and its contents, including the people and objects appearing there.

Once this association is made, any realm-specific person, activity, or item is capable of evoking its associated, realm-specific self, inducing us to think and act in a particular way. Moreover, any opposite, or "cross-realm" item can threaten one's immersion in a particular version of self. Seeing one's child or spouse, for instance, can instantly shatter some people's immersion in a distinct work self.

The more or less problematic conflict that may exist between home and work ways of being helps account for a range of visible behavior. Consider, for instance, when an employee quickly, furtively pulls loved ones out of workplace hallways and into his office, turns his back on coworkers to engage in murmured telephone conversations with a family member, or stops a living-room conversation with coworkers when his spouse walks in. When someone receives publicly audible phone calls at work from a spouse who laughingly refuses to hang up until the worker says "I love you," or when she receives an even more distressing call from children fighting at home, we get some sense of the discomfort that sometimes happens when ways of being meet.

In general, certain items are more evocative of selves than others. Physical appearances, certain artifacts and activities, and the people surrounding us are particularly important reflections of who we are. As such, they are extremely effective at inducing certain ways of being. The ways we manage these (largely a result of work mates' and family members' demands) helps us resist and promote the separation and cohesion of self across the home-work boundary. Through the visible presence of a variety of living and inanimate "props," we enhance and attenuate the mental distinctions between realms and selves.

Emile Durkheim ([1912] 1965), Arnold Van Gennep (1960), Murray Davis (1983), and Mihalyi Csikszentmihalyi and Eugene Rochberg-Halton (1981) have been remarkably sensitive to the evocative power of objects and people, in general. Durkheim addresses the issue through his innovative work on the creation, maintenance, and invocation of sacred and profane mentalities and realms. Van Gennep is also extraordinarily sensitive to the use of space and time to keep status-related objects and people physically distinct in order to keep distinct the ways of being that they evoke. Davis pursues this process through his work on containing "everyday" and "erotic" realities and their contents. Csikszentmihalyi and Rochberg-Halton also note how the objects around us promote specific senses of who we are and how we think, making an explicit connection between objects and identity:

> Men and women make order in their selves (i.e. "retrieve their identity" [Arendt, 1958, p.137]) by first creating and then interacting with the material world. The nature of that transaction will determine, to a great ex-

> tent, the kind of person that emerges. Thus the things that surround us are inseparable from who we are. The material objects we use are not just tools we can pick up and discard at our convenience; they constitute the framework of experience that gives order to our otherwise shapeless selves. (1981, 16)

Realm-specific contents not only promote a realm-specific sense of self, but they insulate us from our other-realm selves. Thus, realm-specific contents encourage a more segmenting approach to home and work, supporting two distinct senses of self. Correspondingly, the more we share objects between realms, the more we create an all-purpose "framework of experience." Interfacing with this more continuous backdrop supports a more continuous sense of self across time and space. The extreme segmentor, for instance, keeps different aspects of self in their appropriate places by keeping associated realm contents to their mutually exclusive locations. The extreme integrator freely exchanges the contents of each physical location, however, so that the same aspects of self are evoked and propped up whether she or he is at home or the workplace.

In this way, a comparison of realm contents and the ways they are managed directly reflects the extent to which aspects of self are situated at or shared between home and work. In fact, change the kinds of objects in our realms, change the way they are divided up and shared, and it's possible to induce change in the very ways we see ourselves at home and work. Over time this is one of the ways we may be encouraged to change positions along the integration-segmentation continuum.

That is, by including other-realm artifacts and memorabilia within our workspaces and homes, we invite ourselves and others to cross any spatio-temporal lines that might serve as prefabricated realm boundaries. This is a personally integrating strategy, because it encourages us to mentally fuse at least certain aspects of otherwise realm-specific selves. For instance, vacation photographs and souvenirs on office walls remind us of certain times or sequences of events that are personally meaningful and enjoyable. But they also evoke a certain sense of self. They remind us of who we were when we took that vacation, who we are now, and, probably, who we hope to be and what we want to do in the future, on our next cruise, hike, tour, ski trip, etcetera. This effect is compounded because we are reminded of who was with us at the time, evoking images of our selves in relation to others—that is, the ways we think and act in that company.

Surrounding ourselves with cross-realm, identity-evoking items promotes an internal resolution of potentially opposing selves. It's a way to help erase the artificial, social rift between home and work encouraged by a segmenting society. One of the reasons this works, though, is because this is not only an *inwardly*-directed strategy, but also an *outwardly*-oriented one. By displaying these items, we solicit the integrating support of others. These items not only say something to us about who we are but they say something to anyone else who views them. Publicly displayed, these items become conversation pieces, enticing people to ask us about them and the realm in which they originated.

At work, for instance, Stan is a scientist who has model airplanes he built hanging from his office ceiling. Sam is a machinist with pictures of his pets and children on the back of his tool box. Tony, another scientist, has signs for music concerts featuring his family on his office door. His colleague Jason has politically radical, witty posters hanging on his office walls. Over in Personnel, Glenn has numerous pictures of her child facing her desk and the doorway. At home, François displays a hallway photograph of himself with his Nobel Prize–winning mentor. Jesús, Kim, and Jay have pictures in their dens and hallways of work projects for which their labor was instrumental. James's wife keeps a copy of all the books and articles he's written on the mantel in the living room. Dan keeps structurally flawed, machined parts that convey the nature of what he does at his basement workbench, retrieving them for company. Lisa has a china cabinet in her dining room, filled with figurines and glasses from years of coworkers' Christmas gifts. Some of us wear items like workplace-awarded watches, jackets, and clothing patches and hang plaques received for outstanding service in our homes. Displayed for others to see and providing a focus for "cross-realm talk," these cross-realm items invite otherwise realm-specific associates in a powerful but unspoken way to blur the conventional spatio-temporal lines of home and work.

Naturally, the constraints of space at home and work affect the extent to which we're able to display any artifacts. Yet in spite of what we have to work with, we still manage to impress ourselves upon our surroundings in ways ranging from the seemingly small and trifling to more impressive, undeniable forms. Eleanor, for instance, has a huge office compared to Heather, both spaces reflecting their relative workplace status. However, Eleanor's office collection of artwork, photographs, and souvenirs brought from home is no more effective at promoting integration than is Heather's. Heather's collection is merely a scaled-down version, where one item does the boundary work of Eleanor's three. Such is the case with many women at the Lab who share "gang" offices and have a minimum of private workspace.[1]

Likewise, Lab machinists have no offices, but they display remarkable ingenuity in achieving integration through objects. Machinists typically own the tool boxes and tools they use at the Lab, which allows them to do whatever they like with these implements. Many machinists choose to make special symbolic statements by attaching tall boards of pegboard, cork board, or Plexiglas to the backs of their tool boxes. This is where they proudly display photographs of their wives, children, pets, and even cars, boats, and homes. After seeing something like this, it becomes quite clear that Lab machinists who do not display souvenirs of home do so by choice, not because the nature of their workspace prevents it.

Decisions about what times and places are appropriate for specific activities, people and objects are based on cultural and personal assumptions about the meaning of certain times and spaces. "Public" time is that during which we are normally accessible and accountable to others. During "private" time, however, we are relatively inaccessible and unaccountable to others. Both concepts form the ends of a continuum in the classification and experience of temporal location (Zerubavel 1985). The same may be said of "public" and "private" space. "Social territories" include both these spatial and temporal components, so that certain times and places are seen as more public, others as more private.

The historical segmentation of work and home results in people generally associating work with more public temporal and spatial areas, while "home" is associated with more private territory.[2] As a result, our

1. Among the members of the Lab Personnel Division and the Ph.D. (or older, equivalently credentialled) scientists in the two research departments I studied, 50 percent of the women in these three departments shared offices, while 0 percent, 13 percent, and 29.8 percent, of the men shared offices, respectively.

2. At the personal level, a variety of factors can cause us to push the experience of time and space toward the public or private ends of the spectrum. For instance, consider the introduction of an office mate into a previously private office or a child into a previously two-adult home. Either can transform previously "private" times and spaces into much more "public" versions. When this happens, previously private territories can be constricted into much smaller islands. These are scattered preciously throughout the day, week, or year, or routinely appear at a predictable time in the daily, weekly, or yearly cycle. Only when the office mate or child leaves, for however long, can time and space reapproximate its previously private character.

culture encourages us to do more of our wage work, relatively public activity, in relatively public times and space. We reserve more of our home-related thoughts, activities, people, and objects for more private space and time.

As we move along the home-work continuum, however, we differ in the variability of the public/private-ness of time and space, both within and between realms. That is, the more we integrate, the more our space and time is malleable, accommodating home *and* work, private *and* public agendas. The more we segment, the more time and space is dedicated to work *or* home, public *or* private concerns. This pattern exists across realms, comparing one spatio-temporal location with the other, and even within the domicile and workplace.

Moreover, the more we segment, the more we reify the temporal and spatial boundary between residence and workplace. That is, we tend to treat as "given" the respective, arbitrary, artificial associations of wage work and domestic concerns with workplace and residence. However, the more we integrate, the more we make traditionally private territories public and traditionally public ones, private. This spatio-temporal blurring is a crucial part of integrating boundary work.

For example, the bedroom and the late/early hours of the day can easily become more public to accommodate wage work. The more we integrate, the more likely we are to have a bedside telephone that connects us with work mates, who predictably call at unpredictable times for assistance and advice. We're more likely to read work-related articles and talk to spouses in bed about our work. We'll fall asleep at night thinking about work and wake up and lay there in the morning making plans for the workday. We may toss and turn and lose sleep altogether while thinking about work. In fact, the more we integrate, the more we may find ourselves waking up in bed having discovered or even solved a "work"-related problem while we slept. Even dreaming may be an integrating activity, then, as problems, fundamental anxieties, and reconceptualizations of work and self are settled or brought to the fore of consciousness.

Likewise, the more we integrate, the more our public workspace and the customary hours of the workday facilitate traditionally more "private" time and space. Recall John, who not only thinks about and does scientific work in bed, but laughingly tells of sexual exploits in a variety of workspaces, from his private office to shared laboratories, during the day and night. He stores love letters in his office desk, just as others store scientific publications on their bedside night tables. Indeed, John discussed his work and domestic matters anywhere with his scientist wife, whether in bed or their offices.

More typically, however, Laboratory workers "privatize" workplace time and space through private and sometimes even intimate conversations over workplace telephones during the workday. There are occasional visits from family and close friends, too. Of course, office conversations with coworkers during the day may be far from strictly business. And if occupational and work-group norms allow, "normal" work time and/or workspace are used by some Lab members for activities like jogging, swimming, calisthenics, and cycling.[3] It is also commonplace for Lab members to occasionally engage in activities like leisure reading, music appreciation, poetry composition, and personal letter writing during "work time" in "work space."

The more we segment, though, the more we enhance the mental home-work boundary by insisting on the clear demarcation of public and private territories. This can take the form of legally binding contracts and informal sanctions that recognize and enforce the difference between these times and places and assumptions about what is appropriate for each. One of the biggest points of contention for organized labor at the Lab, for instance, is what time and space "belongs" to whom: what social territory is the employer entitled to, and what remains for the employee?

This theme underlies numerous territorial disputes over time in all kinds of work organizations. Common points of contention include: the hours just following the normal workday or work week (i.e., whether an employer can make weekday or weekend overtime mandatory), the duration of the workday and breaks in the workday (before and after which employees may be required to punch a time clock to show precise compliance with employer requirements), the time required to change into and out of appropriate or mandatory work clothing and clean up at the end of the day, or even the time necessary to cash a paycheck in an occupation traditionally paid in cash.[4] In addition, the

3. Of course, anyone may see these and other activities as "work"-related. The extra energy and visually pleasing body that results from exercise are often important for occupational success. Thus, "work," not "leisure" or "personal," reasons may explaining why some of us engage in these actions, especially during "work" time.

4. Machinists with whom I spoke are given 30 minutes' paid time off to cash their paychecks each time they are disbursed. They are contractually entitled to leave their workbenches ten minutes early each day to clean up and change their clothes so

time one spends on the phone for "personal" phone calls is a frequent source of contention for blue- and white-collar workers, as is the classification of "sick" days, "personal" days, "vacation" days, and holidays.[5]

Machining, for instance, is an occupation riddled with a history of employer-employee antagonism in this country, and machinists and management have constant disputes over the above issues. In union shops, grievances and reprimands are typically focused on the presumption that time and space is dedicated to *either* work *or* private interests. These segmentist assumptions of time and space are seen in the following story. Here, Harold frames a run-in with management according to the classification of the time in which the incident occurred.

> We're sitting in the lunchroom. *On my break.* All right? Somebody's reading an article in the newspaper and says hey, look at this. At Boeing, in Seattle, they feel that they pay the custodians and the nonskilled too much money and the toolmakers too little money. So, what they're gonna do with all new hires, they're reducing the amount that they pay for their nonskilled and they're gonna raise the toolmaker rate. I said boy, I wish I worked for Boeing. Now, the supervisor heard me say that. He called me in after break. Lu[cky]—I'm glad there were witnesses there. He started to holler at me. "You'll get everybody upset and you have no right to tell, you, you wanta go to Boeing, you—" . . . I brought him up on charges of violating my First Amendment freedom of speech rights. . . .
>
> **I find it an interesting twist to the story that you said this was while you were on break.**

they may leave the building at the exact, official quitting time. Even if they transform themselves quickly and are ready to leave "early," they must still stay inside the doorway until the precise quitting time.

5. One year at a local university, for instance, staff members were informed unexpectedly that they should take their vacation over the Christmas intersession, for the university would turn off the lights and electricity at that time in order to save utility costs. Quite rightly, employees insisted that if they had other vacation plans and were willing to show up to work on those days, the university had no right to expect them to take vacation then. According to staff members, the university responded that it wasn't demanding anything, merely informing employees there would be no lights and no heat if they chose not to take vacation then. Sociology Department employees showed up in snow suits, working by flashlight to preserve the right to vacation when they chose. As a result of workers' outrage, employees who do not wish to vacation at this time are now routinely reassigned to temporary workspace in one of the few buildings that remain heated and lighted over the intersession.

> Yeah, well, that's why I said it violated—Oh yeah, they tried to make it sound like "During working time, you can't say—" I said wait a minute! This isn't during working time.
>
> **First of all, can they even say that you can't**—No.—**say that during working time?** No. Well that's, that's the Union's contention. What I said, I can say any time.

The clarity and mutual exclusivity to the different categories of time in this story is amazing. No less so is the extent to which real decisions about people's autonomy, careers, and litigation depend on them. Even the supervisor implicitly defined the situation as "private" time, for he waited until *after* the break to reprimand Harold. In fact, one might argue that the supervisor's quandary is really rooted in an inability to separate and classify the space Harold occupies in the same way that he separates and classifies Harold's time. Most important, though, despite Harold's threatened legal action on First Amendment principles, Harold primarily grounds his innocence in the private-public time principles that frame so much of the union member's existence.

The varying uni- and multipurpose use of space and time associated with segmentation/integration reflects a range of uni- and multipurpose selves. Harold's coworkers and bosses largely share the assumption that machinists' home-related interests and ways of being have nothing in common with the ways they must think and act in the workplace. Hence, time and space are carefully managed and monitored by both parties to insulate each way of being from the other.

The most logical way to manage multiple personae is to locate each of them within a particular time and place. If we must think and act differently among our family members than our colleagues, then it's easiest to relegate our interaction with them to different times and places. If we find that looking at certain objects makes us think in a certain way, then it's easiest to keep those objects only in the places where it's okay to think that way. The more we segment, then, the more we create dedicated, single-purpose spaces and times in which to embed and protect our dedicated, single-purpose selves. And the more we integrate, the less we need protective territorial borders for our more all-purpose selves. Our space and time are made more all-purpose, accordingly.

Any and every time we see someone distinguishing between the space and time of home and work, of each related self, *there* is the home-work boundary. Accordingly, boundary work takes many forms.

Numerous artifacts constitute the tools we use to do it and offer evidence of how it's done. Calendars, keys, clothes, what we eat and drink, money, people and their representations, talk, reading materials and habits, and daily and yearly work breaks all show us busily placing mental and physical boundaries around "home" and "work."

Calendars

The number and type of calendars someone uses is one of the most telling indicators of where she or he falls along the integration-segmentation continuum. Because our spatial and temporal maps reflect our social ones (Zerubavel 1985a), calendars reflect our classification of activities and people into more single- or all-purpose worlds. Moreover, by visually concretizing a particular mental configuration of home and work, the calendars themselves help reinforce that configuration whenever we look at them. Accordingly, calendar maintenance shows how we help maintain a given relationship between the contents of home and work, including the selves we locate there.

There are two more integrating strategies of maintaining calendars. Like Keith, a common choice for those who integrate realms more is to carry a small pocket calendar virtually everywhere all the time. This lists "home"-related as well as "work"-related events. Keith's calendar includes everything from get-togethers with family and friends, shopping expeditions, and birthdays to appointments with work assistants and colleagues, conference abstract deadlines, purchase and shipping information for work equipment, leisure and wage work travel information, and expenses to be vouchered through his department head. An alternative, integrating calendar strategy is to list the same information on multiple calendars, including those anchored to office desks, kitchen or study walls, etcetera. By providing the same access to the same information no matter where we go, this multiple-calendar strategy has the same integrating effect of a pocket calendar.

The more we segment, however, the more we use calendars that are realm-specific both in their locations *and* their contents. These dedicated calendars rarely include references to other-realm activities. Because the times and places for the people, tasks, and things of each realm tend to be mutually exclusive, family and leisure commitments appear on home calendars; work events appear on others. Viola, for example, uses a hanging calendar in her kitchen at home, and the communal, wall calendar in her gang office at work. There is no overlap between their contents. The kitchen calendar typically lists doctors' appointments, children's special events and bus information, and family and church engagements. At work, her calendar lists only special training sessions and planned vacation days, information that concerns everyone there.

Occasionally, these more segmenting, discrete calendars include other-realm events that trespass on the time normally reserved for a given realm. Overnight business travel is listed on home calendars, for instance, as it usurps what is normally "home time." Likewise, daytime family events like lunch with a spouse, a child's concert, or a repair or delivery appointment requiring someone at home are listed on dedicated work calendars. These references to domestic concerns at work are unusual, though, appearing only because they transgress the normal, segmentist temporal boundary between realms.

Certainly, an element of practicality helps promote more integrating and segmenting approaches to calendars. The more we segment, the more blocks of time are mapped out and dedicated to one particular realm or another. The more we integrate, the less time is cordoned off and reserved for realm-specific concerns. It remains more malleable and accommodating of multiple purposes, a *tabula rasa* for whatever we wish. For this reason, the more we integrate, the more we need to have all aspects of our schedules available simultaneously. We must be aware of all commitments no matter where we are, whether these originate in domestic or workplace spheres. The more we segment, the less we need to know what's going on with our family schedules while we're at work, or vice-versa.

As with all boundary work, dedicated, segmenting calendars and all-purpose, integrating ones help us manage the mental as well as the practical realm. Like suddenly seeing other realm-specific artifacts or people, a glance at an item on a calendar triggers a certain mentality, much as Durkheim's ([1912] 1965) religious totems evoke associated ways of being. A visual reminder of an up-coming event tends to invoke at least certain aspects of the concerns, attitudes and expectations associated with that event. If the mentalities invoked by domestic and work events are so different, so incommensurate for someone, she or he needs to minimize the risk of triggering an inappropriate mentality at an inappropriate time. Relegating realm-specific events to appropriate calendars, seen only during certain blocks of time in certain places, helps achieve this.

Joan's configuration of calendars is quite effective at managing this evocative effect. She has two work calendars. On her small desk-top, flip-to-the-next-day calendar, she haphazardly scrawls all her daily appointments, deadlines, and reminders with an assortment of writing implements. A big wall calendar hangs prominently across from her desk, however. In large, spacious, carefully printed block letters, this calendar lists three types of events, all in the same bold marker ink: her vacation days, her departmental softball games, and weekend visits from her family.

Joan says she needs to be reminded of these things while at work so she can plan around them. The wall calendar reminds her to bring sportswear for the right day, meet visitors at the right time, and prepare colleagues for her absence. Yet these easily could be listed on her desk calendar. Rather, the events listed on Joan's large wall calendar are three of the most cherished parts of her life. This is what entitles them to careful notation on a separate, easily seen, monthly wall calendar.

Joan simply has to look up to be reminded that, at a certain time, she'll be doing something she really enjoys, something more personally exciting perhaps than the task at hand. The type of calendar and kind of lettering she uses, its placement in her direct line of sight if she lifts her head all reflect Joan's anticipation, her "looking forward" to these events. This is in direct contrast to the haphazardly scribbled items jammed onto each page of her desk calendar. The management of these items reflects and reinforces the relatively downcast mental posture she has toward them.

Joan's system also reflects the logical principle of using daily calendars to schedule our less desirable events but monthly ones for those to which we look forward. A calendar showing a single day at a time structurally inhibits anticipation of its monthly contents. It forces one to think in daily terms. Contrast this with children's Advent calendars, for example. These show an entire month's worth of days at a glance, each day's window hiding a delightful illustration or piece of candy. This design cleverly reinforces the wonderful sense of anticipation that precedes Christmas, just like Joan's monthly wall calendar reinforces her selective sense of anticipation.

Each of Joan's calendars is functionally equivalent in that it stimulates and props up the adoption of a certain mind-set. But because these mentalities are so different, Joan keeps them visually segregated into different, and amazingly appropriate, fields of view. This allows her to stay as immersed in her work mind-set as needed, occasionally treating herself to brief mental excursions into what may be a freer, happier, home-related frame of mind.

Of course, other variations on integrating and segmenting calendar systems exist. Joe is self-employed in addition to his full-time machining job. During the evenings, he freelances as a drafter, using his home computer and more traditional techniques to produce technical drawings. Joe uses three calendars, one for each of his work "lives" and one for his family time. He keeps a small calendar in his tool box on-site, which lists his overtime, personal vacation days, and holidays. A larger wall calendar over his office desk at home shows deadlines and projected progress and jobs for his freelance work. Joe also shares with his wife a calendar hanging by the phone in the kitchen. This lists mostly weekend social engagements with family and old high school chums, as well as dates to remember about household services and the like. As all three of his "lives" are kept temporally and spatially distinct from the others, Joe logically relies on different calendars to keep track of them. Thus, his three calendars reflect his cognitive classification of commitments into three distinct categories and help maintain the desired relationship between all of them.

In another segmenting variation, Alice clearly and happily segments her home and work lives most of the time, but carries a pocket calendar in addition to her work and home calendars. This pocket calendar is used for one reason only. Before she began working at the Lab, Alice was friends with a woman who recently became employed on-site. Now, every couple of weeks, one of them makes an on-site call to the other during the day. At this time, they set a date to meet on the weekend with their families. Each time, Alice writes this date in her pocket calendar. She transfers it to her kitchen calendar when she gets home.

Alice's pocket calendar helps preserve her otherwise distinct borders around these realms. Alice's friend does not "belong" to her work realm, despite her employment at the Lab; she "belongs" to Alice's home realm. The pocket calendar is Alice's way of transferring the stuff of "home" to its proper place, that is, her kitchen calendar, after it appeared out of place; that is, at work during work time. In this way, realms remain intact.

Marie's calendrical choices are fascinating, for they reflect her process of moving from a relatively segmenting home-work configuration to a more integrating one. During her recovery from an illness, Marie received permission to come to her workplace office twenty hours per week, working at home the rest of the time. At this point, she found it difficult to manage her new time configuration in past ways. The old distinctions between "work space" and "domestic space," "work time" and "home time" were gone, muddled by numerous doctors' appointments, the discretion to rest when she needed it and to tend to family and wage work when and where she could.

At a practical level, Marie knew it didn't make sense to keep separate home and work calendars anymore, for she might need information about all of her commitments, anywhere, anytime. Yet her hard-won understanding of what "home" and "work" meant prevented her from switching to one, all-purpose calendar. Marie had a thirty-year career built on more segmenting understandings of home and work and did her boundary work accordingly. As a result, she continued to draw mental lines around her activities in spite of these new arrangements. Practically, a single calendar was called for, but Marie resisted this solution; it just didn't feel right.

Marie finally came across a bound, folder-sized calendar that had two identical, vertical schedule forms on each side of the same page. It immediately struck her as the perfect solution to her problem. She now dedicates one column to "home" and the other to "work," keeping each schedule separate, but alongside the other. Practically, this gives her a better sense of how each schedule needs to accommodate the other. Symbolically, however, it also reflects Marie's new mental relationship between her home and work realms. With the spatial configuration of the two vertical schedule forms, she enjoys the integration-reinforcing option of seeing domestic and work events simultaneously. Or, by focusing only on a single side of each page, she reinforces a more segmenting view of these realms. Her calendar allows her to vacillate between seeing time in the old way, as dedicated, single-purpose, segmentist blocks, or in newer, more integrating terms, as amorphous, multipurpose, smaller units, each of which is available for anything.

As all these cases show, segmenting calendar strategies not only reflect, but reinforce a more segmenting configuration of home and work. They do this in part by controlling the triggering of incommensurate mentalities that might be associated with specific events. More integrating versions of calendars also reinforce mental, categorical boundaries around home and work. However, these calendars downplay any border that exists between realms, promoting the mental intermingling and accommodation of realm contents.

Keys

Like their calendars, the ways people manage their keys reflect and reinforce their mental and experiential levels of segmentation/integration between home and work. And, like calendars, keys reflect combinations of symbolic and practical reasons that lead us to manage them in certain ways. The result is that the more we integrate, the more we display a marked preference for carrying our home and work keys on the same ring, jumbled together in a clump of metal. The more we segment, however, the more likely we are to separate our keys onto distinct rings, at least one dedicated to home and one to work.

In the case of keys, the association of a particular item with a particular realm is a bit more obvious than some calendrical contents, for keys are blatantly location-specific. They provide access to specific physical structures. Yet keys are also highly symbolic. With the turn of a key, we can unlock certain aspects of self and ways of thinking. We can expose ourselves to rooms filled with animate and inanimate objects that, like reminders on calendars, trigger mentalities, thoughts, and behavior. Remembered pasts and imagined futures are unlocked with our keys. (This is precisely what allowed Freud [(1917) 1966] to argue that the "slip" of trying to unlock a door with the wrong key betrays a wish to be somewhere else, where that key would have worked.) Accordingly, and practicality notwithstanding, we keep keys more together or apart in accordance with the mental distance between the worlds and ways of being they signify.

Naturally, as with calendar systems, there are enlightening variations on integrating and segmenting key-managing strategies. For instance, Dave provides a great example of how daily practices may be driven by the desire to maintain a certain cognitive order in spite of their practical implications. Dave is a scientist terrifically attuned to the practical world and the inefficiencies of most people's daily routines and ergonomic environments. However, his key-handling system creates a glaring hole in his own self-described quest for the convenient and the efficient.

On several occasions, Dave has duct-taped the holes in his pants pockets rather than give up the forty-odd keys he carries with him. He repeatedly bumps his knee on his keys as they swing in the car ignition. His key ring is so full, there is barely enough space to isolate and hold any given key. Though he enjoys trying to shave off seconds from daily tasks, he more than loses these small bits of gained time fumbling through his keys in front of doors.

Just after he defended his doctoral research proposal and moved permanently out of the classroom and into the lab, Dave transferred his home and work keys onto separate rings, connected by a spring clip. It is no coincidence that this reorganizing, more segmenting strategy came about at this time. It reflected Dave's overall frame of mind in which he thought he would shed the holistic, integrated life of the graduate student for saner, more well-defined boundaries as a wage-working experimentalist.

In the four years since, the only times Dave has actually used the spring clip feature to separate his keys were to temporarily loan out one side or the other, take a leisure trip to Europe, and once while he moved house. Through long weekend vacations to relatives up and down the East Coast, conferences all over the country, trips to stores and many other mundane and special occasions, Dave takes both his work and home keys with him. In other words, in spite of a rather clever attempt to manage his "key problem" using segmentist principles, his integrative approach still holds.

If anything, the life of a wage-working experimentalist encourages a more thoroughly integrated lifestyle than Dave had before. So his keys stay together even now that he can separate them easily. In fact, Dave's implicitly redefined his "key problem" as a "pocket problem" and finds sturdier pants with bigger pockets a more appropriate solution.

The metaphorical power of this real-life story is beautiful. A more segmenting solution to Dave's problem is to separate all his home and work realm contents into two more manageable key rings, two organizing categories kept in correspondingly distinct physical locations. His consistently integrating demands and approach leave them lumped in one category, however. Dave expands the boundary of his more singular home/work category to include more contents, rather than subdivide it into two smaller, separate realms. The more we integrate, the bigger we make the "pocket," rather than parcel out its contents into different locations.

Like Dave's, Patty's boundary work with keys also shows how concrete, visible actions reflect mental classification systems. Patty is a singular case in that she carries all her keys on one ring, despite her otherwise highly segmenting existence. To be precise, she uses a triple-folding packet for her keys. When unsnapped, it displays a line of about a dozen separate clips along the top of the packet's center, each for a different key. Despite the integrating possibilities here, Patty does not intermingle her keys. She "draws" clear boundaries around them by separating the clips into three segments: her home keys are clustered to the left, her work keys to the right, and both groups are separated by a cluster of empty clips in-between. She physically helps prevent the mental intermingling of realms in this tremendously subtle way, despite the more integrating opportunities her single key holder offers.

Nobody really "needs" their home keys while they're at work, or vice-versa. What keys show us is something more fundamental about the way people mentally juxtapose categories of home and work. Very simply, the more we integrate, the less it bothers us to cluster home and work keys together. In our minds, home and work are not separated enough to result in consciously separating them onto different key rings. Home and work are more of a "package deal" in the integration approach, and key rings reflect this. Because realms are not so clearly associated with specific places, the keys associated with the places are not so distinctive, either. The more we segment, however, realms are quite different, so that we actually separate our keys into mutually exclusive clusters, usually found on separate rings.

The parallel between the boundary work of home-work negotiators and artistic sculptors may be a bit clearer now. The artistic sculptor decides the specific ways each kind of space—negative and positive—will complement the other along each cubic inch of his creation. So, too, do we place the home-work boundary through extensive, detailed decisions at each possible meeting point between realms. Choices to place our calendars somewhere and to use each for certain things are countered by choices of where *not* to put our calendars and what kinds of activities each will *not* include. Likewise, the boundary work of home and work does not end with the decision of whether or not to carry home and work keys and how many to take. It extends through the more detailed and far more interesting choices we make about which keys we allow to touch and which ones we insist on separating into particular clumps. Choices about physical appearance in each realm also reflect detailed decisions about the way our worlds relate.

Clothes and Appearance

Given their close connection with the selves they signify, the clothes we wear and other alterations we make in appearance are some of the most self-evocative of realm contents. Nothing reflects the varying identities we assume more than our clothes (Davis 1992; Stone 1962).

Wearing a particular costume is probably the single best way to induce ourselves to mentally assume a role.

A number of factors contribute to clothing's essential linkage with self and its provocative power. Social images associated with the costume combine with the sensual feel and look of the clothing to evoke or "trigger" a certain mentality. In part, this is because clothing is a most immediate mental prop: it is unremitting in reminding us of itself. Against our skin and combined with the rest of our appearance, clothing provides a more or less constant background source of self-awareness.

Consider, for example, the different experiential feel evoked when a woman wears each of the following: an exercise bra, leotard, leggings, and sneakers; an old pair of jeans, favorite baggy sweater, and slippers; a studded, spangled, beaded black cocktail dress, black stockings, and high heels; a wedding gown with crinolines, white, wedding-bells textured stockings, garter, and white silk heels; or a two-piece business suit, silk blouse, clear stockings, and flat pumps. Unquestionably, each different costume (including the face and hairstyle accompanying it) encourages a different awareness of one's self. It reflects and reinforces the "person" we wish to be at that time.

The more we segment home and work, the more likely we are to feel as if we are "two different people" when we're at home and work. So, the more we segment, the more we rely on wearing different clothes to help us adopt and maintain each realm-specific persona. Switching from one "uniform" to another—most often casual jeans, shorts, and sweat clothes at home and "dress-up" or protective, sturdy clothes at work—is a highly significant, segmenting form of boundary work. The more we integrate, though, the more we tend to wear all-purpose clothing for home *and* work, regardless of whether that clothing conforms more to any norms of "dressing-up" or "dressing-down."

In fact, clothing provides a wonderful example of how policies and practices in our work and home realms encourage us to become more integrating or segmenting. Certainly, there are cultural customs about what clothes should be worn where. These, along with employers, colleagues, and families, encourage us to demarcate territories of self by formally or informally requiring us to wear certain things within each realm.

For instance, the military has long required both on-and off-duty soldiers to wear uniforms while on base. Always being in uniform enhances the sense of home-work integration already promoted by on-base housing and frequent family relocations, albeit heavily weighted on the side of wage work absorbing the home. As part of their "uniform," "Women Marines" are even required to wear certain kinds of make-up in certain ways, receiving instruction and supplies for this in mandatory classes (C. Williams 1989).

Police, however, like nurses and doctors, are required to wear their "uniforms" only when they're on duty. (This may constitute any number of costumes, given undercover work.) This encourages police officers to distinguish between private and public senses of self.

(Of course, there are numerous other factors that actively counter that distinction. Some district members are required to wear a gun at all times when in public. This costume "accessory" acts as an ever-present reminder of one's work self, lessening the distinction between this and any "home" sense of self. It functions in the same way as the requirement of special unit members to wear beepers twenty-four hours a day, keep squad cars in their driveways in-between shifts, and/or search dogs at their homes: it makes it impossible for police officers to keep their work selves out of their homes and "private" lives.)

Other workplace groups may expect different kinds of "uniforms." They may require us to wear ties and/or jackets, suits, dresses and dress shoes, replete with nonballistic accessories and make-up. Although the colors, textures, and styles of these uniforms may change daily, they are the functional equivalent of other work groups' name-embroidered coveralls and shirts, "Dress Whites," ministerial robes, or basketball shirts, shorts and sneakers.

At home, different expectations may lead to wearing certain kinds of "uniforms." Infants are notorious for unexpectedly spitting up or leaking onto our clothes. So, when we have an infant in the house, wash and wear costumes, not "good" clothes, are in order. Babies increase our need to clean the areas around them, too, which also calls for "smudgeable," casual clothes. Even chasing after and playing with them requires durable, practical clothing that preserves modesty, protects knees and elbows, and can be worn out. Pets also encourage us to wear only certain clothes at home, as they leave their hair on our furniture and slobber and jump all over us. And if we regularly engage in certain activities within the house, like cooking, cleaning, plumbing, painting, or crafts and hobbies, these too can call for different kinds of clothes than those worn to work.

Through our clothes, practical workplace and home constraints like these translate into even more powerful, symbolic influences on the home-work boundary. The practical demands of realm participation may well translate into fabric-based signs that symbolize and even evoke that participation. People with babies, for instance, are certainly encouraged to segment home and work if there is a baby at home and not at work. The work, noises, and objects involved with tending to a baby, the attention and "continuous coverage" (LaRossa and LaRossa 1981; Zerubavel 1979) she or he demands from parents are obvious points of realm distinction. However, infants' segmenting influence is extended even beyond this, through the clothes-wearing patterns they encourage. This is because simple acts, like changing our clothes, experientially enhance whatever other mental and practical points of distinction already exist between realms.

At some level, it really doesn't matter why we wear different or similar clothes in either realm, or what exactly it is that we wear in either place or time. What matters is whether or not we change clothes depending on the realm locations we're going to occupy. If one's "work" clothes are silk dresses and wool blend slacks, there are many practical reasons for not wearing them at home. With the expense of dry cleaning, the probability of getting them dirty quicker by wearing them at home means we'll wear them only as long as we "have" to. Of course, the discomfort and constricted movement that may come from wearing them and their accouterments also are incentives to wear something else at home. For others, though, there are just as practical reasons for not wearing "good" clothes to work. There may be a high probability of getting them dirty, contaminated, torn or burned, as is the case for experimental scientists and machinists.

There are other, just as practical but maybe longer-term reasons for wearing certain clothes only in one realm. For example, there is no formal "dress code" for scientists in Leigh's work group. However, despite her love of bright colors and comfortable, lightweight skirts, she will not wear them at work. She feels it reinforces her fellow scientists' views of her as a woman rather than a "scientist." She believes her colleagues are incapable of seeing her as both and already emphasize her sex at the expense of her scientific-ness. The more they associate her with traditional femininity, the more negative she feels are the consequences for her career. As a result, she wears drab, functional slacks, shirts, and sweaters at work and changes into the far more feminine clothes she would prefer to wear in both places when she gets home.[6]

Of course, our presentation of self often extends beyond the articles and accessories we wear to things we directly do to our bodies. We shave or apply make-up to our faces and color to our nails; we style hair, clean our teeth, and/or give ourselves purchased smells. Again, there may be numerous practical reasons that we do these things or not in certain ways. There are occupational reasons, for instance, that chemists don't polish their nails, that actors do or do not shave each day, and that dancers grow and wear their hair in certain ways. What matters is not why but how differently we do these things for each realm. To the extent that there is a difference, these choices reflect and reinforce differences in the ways we think and act between realms. The fact that so many men skip shaving on weekends or vacations, or that so many women wear make-up only outside the home, reflects and enhances a certain level of segmentation between realms. No systematic distinction in how we look at home and work reflects and enhances a more integrating experience of realms.

From a mentality-maintenance perspective, wearing certain kinds of clothes in one or both realms can be quite practical, too. Consider the discomfort of wearing "dress" clothes, for instance. If it is difficult to maintain one's work mentality, for instance, constrictive clothing and shoes may act as ever-present, subtle reminders, propping up a certain "work" sense of self, of thinking and acting. They help prevent us from falling into more informal and private selves.

Where work groups wish to *enhance* a more informal, casual approach to work, "dressing-up" is as actively stigmatized as "dressing down" is elsewhere; it too can create a normatively inappropriate awareness of self. The prohibition against dress clothes in some compa-

6. Many professional women share Leigh's view, according to Fred Davis (1992). Candace West (1984) provides an explanation of the dynamics underlying this belief in her work on patient-doctor interactions. Women physicians, argues West, do not share the "master status" (Hughes 1945) of being male, which is normally associated with their profession. As a result, they must work harder than men to prove their legitimacy as doctors, because patients (and possibly other physicians) see them as women first. In Davis's work, this translates into dilemmas about clothing choice for women who hold or aspire to more powerful statuses in male-dominated settings. As a solution to this problem, women professionals often assume workday clothing styles and colors that are more traditionally male. This is an attempt to downplay their gender association in favor of their occupational status.

nies certainly attracts those who wish to integrate home and work more. But it also signifies a company that wants its employees to so thoroughly identify with their work that they see work as an integral part of their selves. Given the symbolic, integrating influence of wearing the same clothes at home and work, informal wear at the office promotes just such a fusion of work and home selves. This can be a remarkably effective policy that speaks volumes about a fundamentally trusting relationship between management, employees, and the role each is to have in the other's life.

Where this fusion of selves is undesirable, especially given the malleability of time and space that often goes with it, the effects of realm-specific clothing also can be used effectively. "Workaholics" are extreme but asymmetrical integrators whose public personae are constantly poised to absorb their families' space and time. For them, wearing casual, comfortable clothes at home can help stave off slipping into a more public, work frame of mind. Changing clothes upon arriving home can be an important signal to themselves and the rest of the family that they're trying to place some limits on their work. "Dress codes" in the workplace capitalize on this same dynamic, of course, but encourage employees to place limits on their home ways of being.

For women in our country, purses are part of costumed appearances. These too may be realm-specific or not, both in their presence and in the type we use for either or both realms. The gendered nature of purses at least partly contributes to their cross-realm or realm-specific nature.

Because of cultural norms in this country, a purse symbolizes feminine identity. Choosing to carry a purse is an obvious sign of gender awareness in little girls, as is the choice not to carry a purse for little boys. This taken-for-granted equation of purses with femininity was brought glaringly to the forefront by Wesley, a married, heterosexual Lab scientist. He carries a beautifully tooled, leather, purse-sized shoulder bag that normally contains his wallet and a few other items. He and another male scientist bought and adopted the habit of carrying these while postdoctoral fellows in Europe, where it is quite common for men to carry purses. Laughing, Wesley explains that he and his friend jokingly refer to these as their "fag bags," reflecting the feminine gender association with purses in this country. A person who enjoys testing and rankling others, he seems to carry this at least in part because of its startling effect on those who are not as sure about his gender as is he.

The purse-carrying habits of women scientists and Personnel staff also reflect the gender association of purses. While women Personnel workers I met uniformly carry purses, roughly half the women scientists do not. As Leigh intimated in her choice of less-feminine dress, the pursuit of high-powered, scientific occupations leads some people to conclude that the obvious display of femininity in the lab is detrimental to one's career. A purse is one such obvious display. Scientists also regularly use other vessels like briefcases, tote bags, and backpacks to carry work and home artifacts back and forth between realms. Both of these factors may result in women scientists finding it less desirable, consciously or otherwise, to carry a purse.

Nonetheless, most of the same scientists who do not bring a purse to work regularly take one with them on outings, to the theater, the store, or wherever. Perhaps this is because they do not carry their backpacks, tote bags, and briefcases on these occasions, but need something in which they can put a few things. Whatever the reasons, though, the realm-specificity of their purse-carrying behavior reflects and reinforces the realm-specificity of the gender their purses symbolize. Even purse-carrying behavior, then, shows how costumes and appearances can intimate and evoke the segmentation of home and work. Through their purses, some Lab scientists segment realms according to the relevance of gender, promoting their association with femininity in one realm, and down-playing it in another.

The segmentation of home and work according to the relevance of gender is further reflected in the appearance-related items found in Laboratory women's purses. Women Personnel workers have far larger "presentation repair kits" than scientists at the Lab. Personnel workers have assortments of combs and brushes, hair clips and bows, nail files, glues and polish, make-up for every part of the face, and assorted breath and body perfumes in their purses. Whatever kind of vessel scientists carry, though, they tend to contain only a single brush or comb, virtually no make-up (perhaps a single lipstick for special occasions) and no perfume or nail polish.

The women scientists who carried purses also had less fashionable, less "feminine" purses than their Personnel counterparts, much like their shoes. This is consistent with the general tendency of scientists of either sex to spend less time than women and men Personnel staff on workplace appearance, avoiding the expensive, coordinated clothing, cosmetics, hair schemes, and dressing rituals of the latter. Personnel workers tend to have multiple purses, swapping items from one to the other as outfits and practicality demand. Scientists, however, are more likely to have one, all-purpose and neutrally-colored purse, used constantly, for any occasion, if at all. This is consistent with their all-purpose clothing and the minimal attention given to clothes and clothes-changing throughout the day.

Of course, there are exceptions to this general pattern, made obvious precisely by their unusualness. Martha is a scientist who is extremely feminine in her dress and appearance: lean, shapely, and well-groomed, she often appears in body-hugging skirts and dresses, well-styled and highlighted hair. She carries a full-fledged assortment of cosmetics and hair-care items in her fashionable purse. Martha expresses her "real" self (R. Turner 1976) through dance in addition to her science, displaying similar prowess in and attraction to both disciplines. She takes five dance classes a week and carries numerous dance mementos in her purse, from lesson receipts to recital programs. Martha also holds a lower-level scientific title than any of her similarly-credentialed male departmental colleagues. It is interesting to consider whether the obvious display of her femininity across the home-work boundary, her lack of segmentation in this respect, is in any way responsible for the relatively lower scientific position she holds.

"Identity Kits": Wallets and Purses

But purses do not only symbolize gender identity. Along with wallets and myriad equivalents like tote bags, backpacks, briefcases, and sports bags that go everywhere with us, these are more fundamentally "identity kits" (Nippert-Eng 1992a). Simmel (1955) argued that the modern notion of self is found in the intersection of a unique web of social affiliations. The evidence of those affiliations is most systematically brought together in our wallets, purses, and their substitutes. Whether their contents reflect our institutional (R. Turner 1976) or interstitial identities, wallets and purses serve as private locations for personally meaningful artifacts.

We carry wallets and purses with us everywhere, reflecting the expectation that we may never know when we might need much of what is in them—practically or emotionally. Through the artifacts in purses and wallets, we can see whether or not someone's home-based and work-based selves are contained to one place and time or carried beyond the domicile or workplace. In this way, an inventory of identity kits helps uncover current levels of integration/segmentation.

However, an asymmetrical bias exists in our culture's version of home and work segmentation. This is manifested in the expectation that we will keep work and work selves confined to the workplace more than we will keep our home selves to the house. In varying degrees, we expect to infuse our work lives with some of who we are at home, but we do not necessarily expect to do the reverse. In our segmentist culture, paychecks and workday stress are seen as the main points where work penetrates our homes (Zussman 1987; Kanter 1977b).

In a collection of autobiographical essays by sociologists (Berger 1990), this bias is reflected in John Gagnon's observations.

> Naming the ways in which the events of an individual's life have influenced his or her works is necessarily a trickster's task. It requires a decision that, first, there is some work separate from the events of life and, second, that the order of effect is from life to work. How much more interesting it might be if one asked how writing a certain article affected the way the author reared children or loved friends. (213)

This may be a more interesting question precisely because it's less likely to be asked, given not only our segmentist culture but our bias about the direction of what little realm penetration we expect.

This bias is clearly present in the contents of Lab members' purses and wallets. While almost all Lab employees carry home-related items in their identity kits, the presence of work-related ones cannot be assumed so easily. Of course, even the most segmenting of Lab employees carry a few practical, access-related work items in their wallets and purses. These are usually limited to a health insurance card, an employee identification badge, and sometimes workplace keys. Machinists may sometimes carry cards that verify training and the right to use certain equipment, although many of them leave these in their tool boxes, rather than carry them off-site. Few Lab members carry anything beyond these kind of immediate, location-specific items, however. Even the presence of one's own business cards is so exceptional that it shows a relatively greater degree of integration. If nothing else, carrying business cards shows that we (even our employers, if they ,provide the cards) believe our work and work selves might, perhaps should, be evoked outside the time and space of the workday. Otherwise, along with everything else, these cards could be kept in or around one's workspace; they need not be carried around.

The work-related items carried by Lab members vary from the obvious and practical to the extremely symbolic. For example, business cards and slips of paper with names and phone numbers of professional contacts may appear here. Phone, cash, and credit cards for professional use are sometimes present. So too are car rental, hotel discount, frequent flyer, and airline club membership cards. Professional association and union membership cards and pocket calendars appear here too.

Scientists' and academics' kits include things like lists of equations and chemical formulas. They have computer specifications and software "help" phone numbers, as well as state tax-free purchasing numbers. Their identity kits also include publishers' and colleagues' phone numbers and addresses. And they carry notes about references to look up during the next trip to the library or bookstore.

The practical, obvious purposes of these items do not negate their symbolic, integrating value. However, the symbolic value of kit items is especially visible when wallet and purse contents are expired or otherwise "useless" for daily activities. An old employee badge from a former institution, an expired driver's license from another country where our work took us, a four-leaf clover picked by a visiting collaborator as she walked around our home, and a necklace from a colleague in Italy all signify work selves. So do the cards Jane carries, certifying her as a member of a number of human resource organizations and a graduate of a series of seminars. She readily acknowledges that there is absolutely no practical value or use for these cards, and she has never even shown them to anyone else. Yet each year, she replaces expired cards with their updated versions, keeping them next to the frayed, irreplaceable ones.

We may keep these items purely for ourselves, for their internally integrating, evocative, and sometimes comforting power. Or we may keep them handy as props, to substantiate stories told to others. Of course, the more we integrate, the more likely we are to talk about home and work outside their dedicated spaces. For people who integrate more *and* like to carry around story-telling artifacts, this means there'll be more work-related items to serve that purpose.

For instance, Hal is a scientist who carries an American Civil Liberties Union (ACLU) membership card in his wallet, years out of date, because he still likes to think of himself as the rebellious, political type of his student days. When he encounters conservative acquaintances, he enjoys teasing them by showing this card. Similarly, Troy is a machinist and ex-sailor. He carries a kind of membership card, signed by his battleship captain and proving he'd been to "Davy Jones' Locker," meaning he'd crossed the equator while serving in the navy. Whenever he thinks strangers are boasting about duty they haven't seen, he produces his card and challenges them to do the same. Both of these men see these aspects of their work selves as fundamental to who they are, anywhere, any time. All kinds of work-related items, then, from the practical to the impractical, help create a sense of continuity among our identities. They support more integrated, consistent identities across the past, present, and future, as well as across the time and space of home and work.

Eating and Drinking

As countless nutrition, diet, and psychological experts can attest, in this culture, eating and drinking are activities closely connected to our self images. These activities reflect a way of thinking not only about food but about who we are and who we wish to be. It is no wonder, then, that we distinguish between home and work and their associated ways of being through the things we eat and drink. This is complemented by differences in patterns of consumption: the times, places, amounts, and ways we eat and drink in either place. The more we integrate, the more similar are the foodstuffs and patterns of consumption at home and work. A more segmenting approach, however, reinforces differences in our home and work selves as we eat and drink different things in different ways at home and work.

For instance, Stan is a scientist whose life completely revolves around his work. He spends at least fourteen hours of the day, seven days a week thinking about and doing his work and being with colleagues, whether at home or the workplace. Stan drinks coffee throughout the entire week, wherever he is, from the time he gets up until two or three hours before bed. Sabrina, however, is a Personnel worker who makes clear distinctions between her work and home selves. She maintains distinct, more balanced places and times for both throughout the day, week, and year. She also drinks tea at home, but coffee at work. Meals at home are always accompanied or followed by tea. But Monday through Friday, from the moment she enters her office in the morning until mid-afternoon, coffee is Sabrina's choice of drink.

What Stan and Sabrina suggest is that, like the rest of our boundary work, eating and drinking choices follow the designation of space and time into more single- or multipurpose locations, more single- or multiple-purpose selves. This is reflected in consumption within as well as between each realm. Institutional constraints and personal preferences mean that drinking and eating at the Lab tend to become highly routine endeavors. For instance, Bruno has coffee at exactly 9:45 each morning, because that's when his shop takes its collective break. He repeats this at exactly noon and again at 3:00 P.M. for the same reason. Janet eats lunch at exactly noon each day, coordinating with others so that her work group can maintain phone coverage.

Yet even where our work groups do not demand scheduled breaks, we may fall into patterns of workplace eating and drinking. Free to get coffee or take lunch when we wish, we nevertheless schedule ourselves into routines. (I will expand the argument later that this routine/habit-making behavior appears so frequently because it is so functional. With daily lives so full of decisions to be made and commitments to be kept, routines are wonderful ways to limit the mental costs of what we must think about and do. They let us take care of things with a minimal amount of attention and chaos.) And certainly, our work groups have nothing to say about our choices of *what* we eat and drink at any given time. Nonetheless, we tend to fall into routines about this, too.

For instance, Tammy breaks between 9:30 and 9:45 each workday morning to pour a cup of tea from her thermos and eat a special cheese Danish she buys from the same place and time each day on the way to work. Likewise, Sam chooses to walk to the cafeteria each morning at about 10:00 for coffee and a corn muffin. Roseanne has a cup of chicken bouillon and a rice cake each workday afternoon at 3:00. Maggie has a Diet Coke at 2:30 P.M. each workday, and, Monday through Friday; David raids the vending machines for a candy bar at about 3:30 P.M. None of these people take these "breaks" or eat these items at home on the weekends. They are hard-pressed to identify any routines during their weekends, much less point out those focused on eating and drinking certain foods at a certain time. Rather, these highly patterned eating choices and habits have become appropriate only for the workplace, playing a critical role in propping up the workplace/day mentalities for each worker.

Eating habits at home may similarly support a certain sense of self, albeit a different one than that of the workplace. Indeed, if numerous advertising campaigns are to be believed, most of us gain our additional pounds through postwork, evening and weekend binges. In this respect, the consumption of food clearly reflects the preponderance of a segmentist life style.

Terry, for instance, found the most effective way for her to lose weight was to acknowledge the hopelessness of watching what she ate on weekends. Accordingly, she used routine and busy-ness during workdays to satisfy herself with carefully controlled meals at carefully controlled times. She then ate whatever she liked on weekends, just as she normally did. This wonderfully sociological diet capitalized on the segmentist patterns she already made in the time, space, and ways of being associated with each realm.

In fact, just as the lack of distinct work and home space may make it difficult for homeworkers to concentrate on their wage labor (Christensen 1987), they may also face more problems with overeating than their commuting counterparts. Homeworkers lack most wage workers' public, workplace constraints on constant snacking and drinking. Just as participation in the public realm frequently constrains us to dress, talk, and sit differently than when we're at home, it exudes a similar effect on our eating.

Certainly, our culture encourages us, especially women, to be more conscious of the amounts of food we consume and the frequency with which we eat in more public settings, as well as the kinds of manners we display in the process. We learn at an early age that we need not be so self-conscious in the privacy of our homes. Accordingly, it may take unusually higher amounts of will power for homeworkers and homemakers to compensate for the free-wheeling patterns of eating associated with the house. Homeworkers not only lack distinctions between realm-specific utensils and containers and the places in which they use them, but they also lack distinct, realm-specific constraints on the extent and frequency of their eating.

Of course, the reverse pattern may hold true, and eating may be relatively uncontrolled and unconstrained at work. Gus works in a food manufacturing plant. The temptation to eat was bad enough when he was on the line, taking preset, clocked breaks. Now, as a manager, he has constant access to a lunch room filled with hundreds of pounds of the products they produce. He and his colleagues can help themselves to what they like, any time, even having items cooked to order. Gus can rely on his wife to make well-balanced, lean, and portion-controlled meals at home. On Monday morning, though, his appetite combines with a workplace emphasis on food and the relatively less temporal accountability associated with his status to leave him pounds overweight from his current workday eating.

The semiotic contrasting of foodstuffs has received a serious treatment from Claude Levi-Strauss (see especially 1978, 478–90). Following his insights, we see that it doesn't really matter what foodstuffs we substitute at home for our choices at work. The important point is whether or not we distinguish between them. Perhaps it'll be as simple a distinction as having something cooked for lunch at home on weekends, but a yogurt, sandwich, salad, or otherwise cold, bag lunch at work. Or vice versa, as is the case for Gunter. A scientist living on his own, he eats a cooked, cafeteria meal for lunch each workday (continuing the German tradition of a hot midday meal) and keeps only cold cuts, bread, and cereal at home for his meals there.

Perhaps even more important, though, is the issue of whether we semiotically change our routines of eating in either place, at either time. Eleanor's family has a tradition of sprawling with the *New York Times,* bagels, lox, and cream cheese each Sunday. They don't shower or change into daytime, casual clothes until almost noon, as an extension of their Sunday morning indulgence. On weekday mornings, though, Eleanor breakfasts lightly and efficiently on toast and tea, immediately dressing for work.

It doesn't really matter how Eleanor distinguishes in her breakfasts throughout the week, only that she does. It doesn't matter if we have regular, elaborate and/or nutritious evening meals during the week, but not the weekend, or vice versa. The important point is that patterns of how and what we eat complement dozens of other visible actions to help enact and create more continuous or discontinuous senses of who we are between realms.

Money

Perhaps even more than eating habits, money is perceived as a direct extension of one's self in our culture.[7] The distinction between one per-

7. This general connection was made remarkably clear during my initial interviews with machinists. However, my experience also suggests that the connection between self and money may vary according to certain social categories, like occupation. For instance, when I asked to see what was in their wallets, a number of machinists balked. I had said that I was interested in what these contents could tell me about who they are. It was only after I explained that I was interested in the other items they carried in their wallets, not the amount of cash they had, that these men agreed to the exercise.

At the time, I was a perpetually "broke" graduate student whose occupational aspirations and view of self were not linked heavily to my earnings potential. It took me a while to become sensitive to the source of my conversants' reluctance. Once I realized there was patterned resistance here and what words overcame this resistance, it frankly astonished me that these men considered the amount of cash they carried to be a more private matter than, for instance, notes from and photographs

son's money and another's is acute and ingrained from an early age in many ways. We use our money for our own purposes. The variability across time and space of "one's own purposes," though, betrays assumptions of more multi- or single-purpose selves across the home-work boundary. As we segment more, our distinctions between the financial accounts of home and work grow greater. The more we integrate, our selves transcend location more, so that our money does too. Money becomes more multipurpose, as do the bills we pay with it.

Hence, there are several logical possibilities for keeping "our" money to and for "our selves." Segmentist personal and/or institutional rules about money, for instance, forbid "polluting" a personal bank or credit card account with work-realm transactions. In addition, it may be literally impossible to reimburse an employee for work-related expenses paid out of her or his "own pocket." The very concept of someone using personal funds for work expenses is unthinkable in some places, and such policies keep it that way.

Sometimes we ourselves refuse to use our own money for work-related purchases, whether or not we would be reimbursed. To do so might set a dangerous precedent in keeping the line between one's home and work firmly drawn. Lab machinists, for instance, frequently suggested that if they were asked to pay work expenses with personal money it would be a most invasive and abhorrent demand.

Keeping our money to ourselves may also translate into workplace prohibitions against polluting one's work accounts with personal, domestic transactions. The outrage against Oliver North in the Iran-Contra hearings almost immediately focused on the use of government, work-

---

of loved ones. Likewise, I only noted, but did not initially appreciate the emphasis I repeatedly heard on some machinists' possession of "gold" credit cards and stock brokers' business cards. When I heard it for about the fourth time, I suddenly realized the extent of my own obliviousness to the important link between money and self for these men.

My personal attitudes were more consistent with the scientists' I interviewed. When I asked if we could take a tour through their wallets and purses, scientists would often silently, instantly pull them out and begin counting out their cash, sometimes asking if I wanted to know about pocket change too. They did so whether they had very little or a lot of cash, and never once emphasized the "color"/extent of their credit lines. Nor did they emphasize the fact that they often carried stock brokers' cards. I had to tell scientists too that I was not interested in the amount of cash they had but only so they would stop counting it and get to what *I* thought was the really interesting stuff. This suggests that there may be some occupational variation in the extent to which members of our culture identify with money.

place money for personal use. United States prosecutors and the media zeroed in on the purchase of his daughter's dance school tights with government travelers' checks and the installation of North's home security system, billed to the government. North's office practices of borrowing travelers' checks from the safe and replacing them the next day, and of using the checks as reimbursement for out-of-pocket, petty cash expenditures were breaches of segmentist accounting procedures. Surely, the international and domestic power struggle in which North was involved was far more important than these realm-blurring financial practices, but it was almost given secondary consideration by the press and Congress. (It could be, of course, that segmentist accounting violations are simply the most obvious and easiest violations with which to prosecute and remove federal employees.) This suggests just how strictly drawn the lines of money may be in our culture's view of home and work and what remarkable priority we place on this aspect of boundary work.

On the other hand, keeping one's money to one's self may mean the flat-out expectation of freely intermingling "personal" money with "work" expenses and accounts. In these situations, the expectation that one's "personal" interests are totally intermingled with one's "work" interests translates into a highly integrating monetary policy. Cross-realm expenses and expenditures are the norm in this more integrating approach, as are the accounting procedures to accommodate them.

Of course, here I am talking about more intentional integrating monetary practices. There is at least one scenario in which accounts become quite interchangeable, although this was not the original plan. I know of several individuals who were self-employed with incorporated businesses and who subsequently had to declare corporate *and* personal bankruptcy. As with so many self-employed people I've met, their "personal" interests *were* their "business" interests. Accordingly, when the business encountered financial difficulties, personal accounts also were depleted in an attempt to save the business. Unfortunately, this integrating gamble did not pay off.

The more typical situation I have in mind applies to academics and scientists, whose institutions commonly expect these workers to purchase work-related items with their own money first, then get reimbursed. These include airline tickets and per diem expenses like food and housing for conferences and experimental runs out of town. Likewise, the costs of photocopying, postage, and computer supplies may be legitimate workplace expenses, even if purchased and used outside the workplace. These, like telephone calls made from home, even the cost of electricity to run wage labor machinery, lights, heat, and air conditioning at home, may well be reimbursable expenses. But all must be paid for "out of pocket" first. These professionals not only expect to use personal checks and credit cards to pay for work items but regularly declare unreimbursed work expenses on their personal tax returns.

Furthermore, any and all of these professionals' expenses may appear on domestic bills and personal bank and credit card account statements. These documents are treated as legitimate workplace receipts, and rarely questioned for authenticity or motive. In fact, scientists carry a plethora of seemingly personal phone, photocopying, photograph developing and credit card bills with them, which include receipts for restaurant meals, motels and supplies and tools. These appear in part because frequently, domestic bills include workplace receipts that their carriers submit for reimbursement.

Scientists also carry domestic bills with them because they freely use work space and workday time to take care of these kinds of things, just as normally domestic space and time are used to take care of workplace administrative tasks. In general, the interchangeability of "personal" and "workplace" monies simply reflects the interchangeability of the places and times where purchased items and services are used. It is expected, for instance, that Lab scientists will keep equipment purchased with work money at home and use it freely. By the same token, they regularly usurp things like household furniture, extension cords, machinery, computer manuals, and household members' labor and insights for workplace endeavors.

Renee shows just how much someone may have to patrol the home-work boundary where money is concerned. An account manager, she works in the market research industry. To a large extent, management assumes that Renee's personal credit card is at their beck and call; reimbursing her is their preferred way to handle corporate expenses.

When she has to travel to other cities to meet with clients or hold press conferences, Renee's bank account is the first one depleted. When her boss wanted a Christmas tree put up in the lobby to create a better atmosphere for clients and employees, Renee's credit card was commandeered. She is the one who purchases meals, drinks, and gifts for clients and coworkers, then patiently waits for a check dispersal.

Renee knows this is an important part of the job. She also knows firsthand of several people who have had to avert aspirations for promotion because of this demand. They simply do not have the personal funds to front for clients, nor can they wait for weeks to recoup spent money.

Ordinarily, Renee doesn't mind this. These are, after all, the "rules of the game"; if she wants to play, she has to follow them. Yet at one point, Renee found herself forced to assert the boundary between home and work at this most crucial point of distinction, via her credit card.

Renee and her boss were to attend a conference in another city. Room reservations were hard to come by and had to be guaranteed with a credit card. Her boss, in another city, told his secretary to use Renee's credit card to secure their rooms. However, Renee was in the middle of purchasing her first home and under close scrutiny for a mortgage approval. Having been careful to avoid all credit card activity for months, she was not about to let any new charges appear on her statement now. When forced to choose, Renee's credit card literally was going to be used (or not) for her home, not her work. (She was lucky. Following a lengthy, heated discussion with her out-of-town boss, she finally got him to put the charges on his card instead of hers.)

Max Weber argues that Modernity and the disintegration of the household as the economic unit hinged on the separation of household and business monies, even more than their physical separation ([1918] 1978, 2:379.) Kevin Delaney (1992) argues that corporate bankruptcy today is constrained by this historical separation of family and business accounts and the distinct forms of sanctions that emerged for financial improprieties in either realm. It is logical, then, that segmentist approaches to money are the most common in our Modern society.

But in keeping with Weber, we may also consider the inverse implication of his argument and current, more integrating approaches to money. When certain occupations, work groups, and workplaces treat personal and business monies as closely intertwined, if not interchangeable, they show what are essentially the pre-Modern roots of these groups and organizations. These roots have been preserved through centuries-long battles over highly integrative professional status, power, and lifestyles (Abbott 1988; Larson [1977] 1979) and/or centuries-old models of conducting "family businesses."

People and Their Representations

Who we are is largely a synergistic result of the responses we get from people around us and the ways we interpret those responses (Mead

1934). For this reason, other people and the objects that represent them are some of the most self-evocative of our surroundings. Seeing or hearing other people calls forth aspects of our selves more instantaneously and more thoroughly than anything else. Creating and maintaining territories of self therefore requires particularly acute attention to managing others' presence. We need to do this not only by managing their appearances "in person," but through the telephone and other electronic media like fax machines and computers, through correspondence and notes containing information about others, and via photographs, gifts, and souvenirs of time spent with them. Our management of people through all these avenues helps ensure only those aspects of self that we and others deem appropriate are activated and supported at a given time and place.

This is one of the reasons why, given a certain amount of personal discretion, the extreme segmentor has a distinct lack of home-related others and objects in the workplace or of work-related people and artifacts at home. It is also one of the reasons why there may be no difference in the people and objects of the extreme integrator's home or workplace. Like choices of how to manage calendars and keys, the ways we decorate, fill and use our homes and workspaces show us protecting and bolstering more or less distinct mentalities. While there certainly are practical reasons to surround ourselves or not with these kinds of things, these do not negate the more subtle, symbolic reasons we may have for doing so.

Address and Phone Books

One focus of boundary work aimed at managing representations of people is address and phone books. People's addresses are separated or intermingled across realms in the same way that their bodies are, promoting a certain mental juxtaposition of the actual people through their written representations. The more we segment home and work, the more we segregate traditionally "home"-related addresses and phone numbers from "work"-related ones. The more we integrate realms, the more we keep information on the people of home and work together.

The more we segment, for instance, the more we store information about how to reach family and friends at home and information about work acquaintances in the workplace. Information on home-related individuals typically appears at home in a dedicated address book, on a piece of paper hung by the telephone, on a published phone book cover, or maybe in a file stored in a home computer. Listings of coworkers and professional contacts are kept at work, though, in a tool box, taped on a wall, and/or compiled in an institutional "speed-dial" telephone, phone book, computer, or Rolodex.

The physical separation of this information into realm-specific, mutually-exclusive lists reflects one of the principles guiding the use of calendars. The more we segment, the less overlap there is in the times and places reserved for certain people. This is a practical reason why the more we segment, the more our collections of addresses and phone numbers are organized by and stored within the realm of affiliation, usually in alphabetical lists.

This segmentist strategy is so pervasive that it is sometimes difficult to imagine alternatives. Nonetheless, Keith, a scientist of international renown and an exceptional home-work integrator, has quite a different way of handling this information. He keeps all his significant phone numbers together, compressed-printed from his computer in a long accordion list that unfolds from his pocket calendar. This all-purpose phone list goes everywhere with him, from home to laboratory, from the United States to Europe and Asia.

Even more interesting, though, Keith sections off his list not by realm and alphabetical order, but by the telephone country code of each person. Even the few individuals who can be designated as truly belonging uniquely to one realm, like his in-laws and parents, are lumped in with everyone else. They appear under their appropriate phone prefix, in a seemingly random, rather than alphabetical ordering.

Of course, Keith's integrating address-management strategy is remarkably consistent with integrating calendar strategies. It is no wonder he keeps this accordion-pleated phone list inside his pocket calendar. The more we integrate, the more we keep everyone's names and numbers in a single vessel, be it a calendar, an address book, Rolodex, or electronic notebook. And the more we integrate, the more we carry this vessel with us everywhere, or have duplicate lists available in multiple places, for we are as likely to need a coworker's phone number at home as a friend's at work. Indeed, like others who integrate more, Keith typically finds it impossible to catalog people as coworkers *or* friends, for they are almost certainly both. This task is made even more difficult for some people at the Lab, who are married to coworkers, are coworkers' off-spring, or perhaps gave birth to their collaborators.

Variations on these mutually exclusive and inclusive address sets abound. For instance, I once received two Christmas cards from a friend: a personally selected and hand-signed one from her and her husband, and an institutional, prestamped one from her company. I not only appeared in Kathy's address book at home, but in her Rolodex at work. We not only went to college together and were best friends, but I was also a consultant for her company. I was not the only person who appeared in both address locations, however, for Kathy keeps a selection of family and friends' numbers in her workplace Rolodex. Nonetheless, I was the only person who received dual cards. Why? Because I appeared in the large Rolodex section designated for work contacts, not the small one reserved for family and friends.

As we move across the home-work continuum, what changes is the number of addresses shared across realms. The more we segment, the smaller are the chunks of home addresses kept at work and work addresses kept at home. But no matter how many numbers and addresses we share across realms, many of us, like my friend, rely on spatial partitioning to keep cross-realm numbers distinct from those that seem to belong more properly to the realm of occupation. Home numbers are kept in the workplace in a separate Rolodex section, computer file, file folder, or drawer. Work numbers appear on a separate page in our home address books, on a separate sheet of paper by the phone, or next to a different phone in another room. Only the most integrating of people, like Keith, will spatially intermingle information for the people of both realms on single, all-purpose lists. The subtle use of space, reflecting more detailed boundary decisions, is made clear even in this form of boundary work.

Photographs and Gifts

Cross-realm representations of people are mentally more dangerous to us as we increasingly distinguish between who we are with the people they represent and who we are where these people are absent. The more we segment, the more we relegate gifts, memorabilia, and facsimiles of people to the realm of their subjects' origin. The more we integrate, though, the more likely it is that any of these representations will appear in workplace or home spaces.

In the workplace, photographs are the most common, sometimes the only artifacts people use to achieve a greater degree of integration between home and work.[8] It is the highly symbolic nature of photographs

8. It struck me early in my fieldwork that European-born scientists at the Lab are less likely to display family photos than their U.S. counterparts. When questioned about this, each European agreed that workplace family photos are much rarer in

that empowers them with the ability to bring us closer to people—and aspects of our selves—just by looking at them. These artifacts are incredibly evocative, triggering emotions quickly and effectively (Csikszentmihalyi and Rochberg-Halton 1981, 66–69.) Although photographs of vacation places, projects, cars, boats, workplaces, and homes appear at the Lab, the most common workspace photographs are those of significant others.

One reason for their proliferation is that, despite their evocative power, photographs allow us to integrate others in a highly controlled way. On the one hand, we may not want to totally deny cross-realm-specific others and the self associated with them. On the other hand, their presence in person or even on the phone might be too much of an integrating influence for us (and/or our families and employers) to handle. Photos acknowledge those on the other side of our commutes without risking the mental self-consciousness and incapacitation (and possibly disapproval) that the actual subjects might bring about.

Boundary work with photographs begins with the initial decision of whether or not to bring the likenesses of cross-realm-specific people to home or work. Subsequent choices must be made about whether or not to display these photos, and the size, framing, action/scene, and placement of any we finally do display. Along with the directions they face (i.e., toward us, toward others, or both), these decisions confirm and promote the extent of other-realm-specific people's presence in a given place. The more photographs of realm-specific others we display and the more these are displayed toward visitors, the greater is their integrating impact.

Through her humorous manipulation of photographs across all these dimensions, Rachel shows the often taken-for-granted status of these more segmenting and integrating photograph decisions. Rachel surrounds herself with personal mementos in her office. At the moment, however, she is miffed at her boyfriend and wants everyone to know it.

Rachel has "allowed" one of her boyfriend's photos, normally thumb-tacked directly in front of her, to fall down behind her desk. She retrieves it from there to show people, then promptly drops it down again. She carefully arranged the extremely large leaves of a corner plant to cover up another photo he had given her as a gift. And a

their home countries. Several remain puzzled by the preponderance of this practice in the United States. Their observations suggest that this may be a uniquely American form of display/integration.

thumbtack is placed squarely through his likeness in another picture facing her on her bulletin board. With a twinkle in her eye, she says she *might* rearrange things again when he's done sufficient penance.

The open, visible display of home-related significant others (including pets) on office desks, locker doors, and tool boxes is quite common at the Lab. Like the other objects surrounding Lab workers, these items promote a certain degree of continuity across time and space within ourselves. The thoughts they provoke are an internal source of continuity. The comments they promote from the people around us are external sources. It is relatively unusual to see pictures of work colleagues at Lab members' homes, however. Again, this reflects the asymmetrical, segmentist bias among Lab members, who expect to bring more of their home selves to the time and space of the workplace than their work selves into their homes.

Most Laboratory members keep any work-related photographs they might have *at* work, either displayed or, more often, stored in drawers. Work photos kept at home also usually are put away or appear in dedicated work areas within the house: at a workbench, or in an office or den. The display of photographs of colleagues and projects on the mantel or bookcase amongst those of family and friends is a very rare occurrence. When this happens, it indicates and reinforces a very high degree of integration indeed.

If the photographs we display are also gifts from significant others, their ability to remind us of another realm is strengthened. The ways we store and display any gifts from people associated with a particular realm reflects and reinforces a certain degree of segmentation/integration, just like photographs. Marcel Mauss argues in *The Gift* (1967) that presents symbolize the people who give them to us. The ways we manage them are additional ways of keeping the people they represent to a given place and time, or allowing them to transcend the thresholds of homes and workplaces.

Here, again, we see that the more we integrate, the more we bring gifts from one realm into the other. The more we segment, though, the more gifts are kept in their realm of origin. However, here too we see the asymmetrical bias of Lab members bringing more reminders of who they are at home into the workplace than the reverse.

Of course, many gifts given to Lab members by family and friends are specifically for their workspaces, like paper weights, calendars, briefcases, pen and pencil sets and holders, tools, coffee mugs, and photographs. There are also nonspecific, decorative gifts that Lab members bring in from home that remind them of the gift givers. This includes everything from plants to figurines, from paintings to radios.

Gifts from work mates tend to stay at work, though. Photographs of and by colleagues, coffee mugs from salespeople and conferences, Christmas grab-bag items, souvenirs from work trips abroad, and thank-you tokens sent from international colleagues typically stay in Lab members' offices and toolboxes. Even jackets embroidered with the Lab's name are commonly worn only to and from work on work days. Perhaps the only gifts from work mates not typically kept at work are those specifically designated for home, like engagement, wedding, retirement and baby shower gifts, and cash bonuses, including things like gift certificates for dinner and tickets to sports events and theatrical productions. Given their "personal" nature, it is logical that these are often presented to Lab employees in nonwork spaces, during nonwork times, ranging from lunch rooms during lunch time to off-site restaurants on the weekend.

People

If managing the things that represent people helps define territories of the self, the presence or absence of the actual living, breathing people has an even greater impact. The most self-evocative of all, people's cross-realm absence/presence is one of the most important dimensions of boundary work. People induce and support an intense kind of "self-consciousness" in us, and different associates bring different aspects of self to the surface. These are the self-aspects that experience has taught us are appropriate for interaction with given people. The more we integrate, the more most aspects of self are "appropriate" no matter where we are, no matter who we're with. Essentially, we're only slight variations on the same theme, whether with coworkers or family, at the institutional workplace or at home. As we segment more, ways of thinking and behaving among colleagues, in the workplace, can be quite incommensurate with ways of thinking and behaving with family and friends at home.

As a result, the more we integrate, the more mentally free we are to mix associates emanating from one realm with those from the other. We experience less mental and behavioral conflict when simultaneously amongst work and home associates: we are not very "self-conscious" in these situations. Accordingly, colleagues frequently are found in our homes and family members frequently are found in institutional workplaces, in person and otherwise (assuming this is permitted by the residents of either realm.)

The more we segment, though, the more we keep people within the spatio-temporal boundaries of their realm of origin. Mixing the people of both realms causes varying degrees of discomfort and indecision (i.e., self-consciousness), for the different clusters of people call for different, often conflicting aspects of self. The extreme segmentor cannot even handle photographs of realm-specific others in the opposing realm. She or he may have an almost paralytic experience when the living beings of home and work meet. Each group of associates expects her or him to behave as usual, yet these two modes of being cannot be accommodated. In these situations, it becomes quite difficult for the family member/employee to say or do anything that would meet both groups' expectations. So, she or he says and does very little at all or ignores one realm-specific party entirely while being extremely "self-conscious."

This is why the more we segment, the less likely we are to introduce coworkers and family members even if they meet by chance in a store or movie theater. This is also why we might avoid bringing family members to office parties or inviting coworkers to house parties. It is more comfortable to engage colleagues at work only and family at home only.

Those who integrate a bit more than this may allow a qualified meeting of selves and realms. Occasional socializing with work mates occurs, but it is kept to neutral, public spaces, sometimes including family members. Sports facilities and fields, or restaurants, bars, casinos, parks and museums all support a less worklike mentality. They allow an employee to present an expanded view of her- or himself to colleagues, but one that does not extend all the way into the distinctive self-territories of each others' homes. Some Lab workers have met outside the workday and -place for years to pursue mutual dining and recreational interests but have never visited each others' homes.

The Lab has dozens of active recreational clubs comprised of employees and their families. These associations cover all sorts of athletic pursuits, such as softball, volleyball, swimming, tennis, bowling and weight-lifting, as well as instrumental and vocal music-making, archery, rifle shooting, photography, astronomy, amateur radio, public speaking, cooking, power plane flying, painting, dancing, and martial arts. Each of these clubs meets with different periodicities for narrowly defined purposes, in public spaces.

These activities are so popular at least in part because they allow otherwise segmenting employees to explore and present a fuller range of self with coworkers, but within carefully controlled, relatively nonthreatening situations. If clubs met at people's houses, they might not be nearly so attractive. This is not just because of the geographic centrality of meetings held on workplace grounds. Rather, it's because colleagues who come to our homes force us to immediately accommodate the full range of selves evoked by their presence, on the one hand, and the physical setting and occupants of our homes, on the other. The more we segment, the more this evokes fairly oppositional selves, which are normally enacted only sequentially over the course of the day and week. So, containing extra-work activities to a neutral, public place, helps minimize the self-consciousness that might occur if the events were held in the home or workplace proper.

Family members, neighbors or high school chums who appear at work during the workday may bring on the same dilemma. The more we segment, then, the more we engage these associates only outside the workplace. On the rare occasions family must come to the workplace, we ask them to drop us off at the door, wait outside in the car to pick us up, or stay secreted in an office or lobby corner. This reduces the chances of colleagues noticing their "contaminating" presence, possibly even making the connection between them and us, and demanding a self-conscious introduction and conversation.

The more we segment, the more phone calls between realms are kept to a minimum for this same reason. We'll routinely schedule these for break times or entirely forbid them, except in case of emergency. We not only have difficulty switching between selves in the instantaneous fashion demanded by cross-realm phone calls, but we are extremely uncomfortable carrying on a meaningful conversation with family in our workspaces, sometimes in front of work mates. Increased integration, however, not only permits *more* cross-realm phone calls but more *random* calls, as we are less troubled by the unpredictable switch from one self to another.

Levels of segmentation/integration are apparent when we consider the relative visibility of any of these self-evocative realm contents. If children periodically appear in a dedicated workplace, it is certainly more integrating than if they do not. In Personnel, for instance, workers bring in their children each year for the half-day of work on Christmas Eve. But if the children appear regularly and randomly throughout the year, are openly paraded about, introduced to colleagues, brought to meetings, and freely visit colleagues, this is more integrating still.

For instance, CMP Publications in Manhasset, New York (its real name and location), is a corporation with the first on-site, private day-care center on Long Island. Here, employees commonly take their young children to the cafeteria for lunch, causing much head-turning among visitors. Children's ready visibility every day amongst silk-dressed, suited grown-ups creates quite a different effect within the organization than if they were restricted to their classrooms.

Likewise, Glenn has several pictures of her son facing her on her desk. However, she also has an entire table covered with dozens of his brass-framed photos. This table sits across the office, perpendicular to her desk and facing the door, clearly visible to coworkers and the myriad clients she interviews each week. The additional volume and position of these photos induces an even greater degree of integration than that of most people's office photos of children. Marian creates a similar effect by hanging sketches and paintings of dogs throughout the length of her shared office, each representing her own cherished pets, past and present.

Whether we ensure other-realm people's varying absence or presence, we convey clear messages about what kind of involvement we want from them in a given realm. Never inviting coworkers to our homes makes just as active a statement about the role we want them to have there as when we invite them over. Never inviting family or friends to join us at work gives the same message about how much we expect them to be involved in our activities there. And when employers, spouses, and even children refuse to allow other-realm people to join us while they're present, they help ensure that our personal boundaries are spatially and temporally drawn around the workday and place. At best, the alternative is to meet realm-specific people on neutral turf. This extends the boundaries around home and work selves a bit, maybe or maybe not as far as we'd like.

Talk

The extent of the boundary work we do around realm-specific selves is clearest when we suddenly find ourselves engaging previously realm-specific associates on both ends of our commutes. Coworkers who decide to share living quarters quickly find out the extent to which each other previously separated her or his home and work selves. So do family members who take jobs working with or near each other.

Kim, for instance, found his father's "lives" separated in a way not unlike the clothing that so many people use to frame their work and home selves. The first time Kim ever heard his father swear was when Kim took a summer job at his father's workplace. He quickly found out that his father's style of talk was not only chock full of expletives at work but that these were often hurled in red-faced, yelling fits at his subordinates. The all-male, blue collar, industrial environment promoted a side of his dad that Kim never fathomed. It also earned his father a workplace reputation Kim wouldn't have believed without seeing.

Whether it's a liberal use of profanity, scientific jargon, or gender-insensitive comments, we can only imagine how many people would be surprised to hear how their loved ones talk at work, given the ways they express their selves at home. Or, for that matter, how surprised our colleagues would be to hear how we talk in our homes. In fact, the degree to which realm-specific others would be surprised to hear how we talk in our other realm is an excellent measure of just how much we segment/integrate—just how different is each of our realm-specific selves.

The differences in how we talk in different places *within* realm locations further shows spatio-temporal distinctions around selves. Do we talk differently during lunch than the rest of the workday? In our boss's office than our own? On the weekend than the week, in our homes? On our living room couches than in our beds?

Boundaries around styles of talk may be the most accurate in showing just where the essence of home and work, of evermore intensely private and public selves lies for us. They show just how much spatio-temporal territory surrounds the unique selves we associate with home and work. The more we segment, the more obviously our styles of talk are traded at home and work doorways, at "work" time and "personal" time. The more we integrate, though, the less we break into distinctive styles of talk at these socially prefabricated points. Rather, unique forms of talk are associated with far more retracted borders. Territories of talk styles may include only those times and spaces surrounding specific, realm-defining tasks (frequently the most mentally demanding of activities), such as having a heart-to-heart talk with a child, making love to a spouse, or fighting with a sibling at home.

Accordingly, we could imagine a map depicting where and when we engage in distinct styles of talk. It would show just how much we rely on our houses and the traditional workplace and -day to mark the most distinctive, exclusive "core" of our home and work selves. The more we segment, the more exactly talk-style territories match the culturally embedded, segmentist map of dedicated spatial and temporal locations. The more we integrate, the less we vary our talk styles at these exact points.

The place we trade styles of talk at least partly depends on the extent to which we discuss one realm while physically located in the other. The more we engage in cross-realm conversations, the more likely we are to cross-fertilize realms with the distinct styles of talk cultivated in our homes and workplaces. We talk sweetly or bitterly about family at work and use occupational and organizational jargon in conversations with family or guests at home.

Of course, this means that simply by talking about one realm while in the other, talk styles lose their realm-specificity. Refusing to engage in cross-realm conversations therefore helps preserve realm-specific talk styles. So, like the people who might stimulate them, the ways we manage cross-realm conversations also reflect and affect our views of the home-work boundary.

For instance, where people produce written materials as part of their wage labor, the line between home and work is blurred when family and friends type, read, and/or offer feedback on these writings. The more such feedback resembles the give-and-take of a discussion, the greater the integration level it discloses and promotes. For a discussion to occur, family members must be fairly well versed in the details of an employee's work: the subject matter, audience, and appropriate style of writing. The more we talk about and show our work at home, the more our families can engage in discussions about it, however useful, painful or annoying we find their comments. The more we segment, the less we can engage in such debates with our families, for we exchange little information about the goings-on of either realm in its opposing world. Family members have little background to guide their feedback.

Details about cross-realm talk are quite important for disclosing just where we fall along the continuum: what kinds of things are talked about, and when and where does the talk occur? The more we segment, the more we keep cross-realm talk to a minimum, engaging in it at fewer, fairly predictable times. The more we integrate, though, the more frequently and randomly we discuss myriad aspects of each world while physically located away from it.

The more Lab members segment, the more commonly talk about work at home is limited to the following kinds of topics: paychecks and benefits, brief news bulletins about someone whom a spouse has met or heard of, and/or some extraordinary event, perhaps a social infraction made by one's colleagues or management. Little is shared about the work itself. Families typically know more about what the traffic was like on the way home than what their loved ones actually did at work that day.

There is a dearth of information flowing in the opposite direction, as well. Work mates in segmentist settings like the Lab's machine shops rarely know much more than superficial, demographic information about coworkers' home lives. Classic, quick exchanges are typical on how the wife/husband and kids are or how the vacation went. Other shared information is limited primarily to leisure pursuits, household repair, and family members' material upkeep. Car restoration, boat maintenance, cooking, clothes shopping, interior decorating, and plumbing, electrical work, painting, roofing, etcetera are common topics of conversations. These topics focus on coworkers' commonalties as homeowners and managers, more "public" topics. Although these home-related issues are more private than workplace activities, they are public enough to constitute safe conversational ground for those who more conventionally draw the line between home and work, private and public.

These exchanges are "publicized" further through their typically brief and/or instructional framings and the places in which they occur. First, the more we segment, the more likely it is that conversations focus on referrals to knowledgeable experts, places, or resources. These are not emotional, intimate discussions about why people do these things and the meanings these activities and objects evoke, but more distanced, "safer" talk. It is as if conversants were merely substituting for a good phone book or consumer service agency.

Moreover, the more we segment, the more we tend to engage in these less personal discussions outside proper, dedicated workspaces. One or both parties tend to hold these discussions while standing in a hallway, lobby, walk-through area, or office doorway. Conversations about home may be habitually reserved for lunchrooms, bathrooms, and space altogether outside office buildings. In other words, the more we segment, the more cross-realm talk is limited to the times and spaces that are neither strictly "home" nor "work": interstitial, or "liminal" (Van Gennep 1960) spaces and times.

Consider, for example, one of the very few occasions that segmentist workplaces actually dedicate to integrating talk: holiday office parties.

To promote more personable, seasonal, integrating exchanges, the office Christmas party typically occurs in more liminal space and time. This may be the only time of the year when coworkers reliably talk to each other about families and personal plans. And, as one colleague laughingly told me, it is in just this kind of setting where he and a coworker were tersely reminded by department mates *and* family not to "talk shop." As he pointed out, this may be a difficult rule for people used to doing nothing *but* talking shop with their coworkers.

At home, too, there are more segmenting and more integrating ways to talk about work. Brief and infrequent exchanges that take place either just after arriving home at the end of the day and/or at the beginning of dinner reflect and reinforce a more segmenting approach. These transitional periods, marked by physical movement into the house, or from one room and activity to another, also provide liminal time and space. Here, more segmenting family members might bring up other-realm concerns before fully embracing home again.

On the other hand, the more we integrate, the more we talk about both realms in all kinds of places. Work is not only read, but discussed in bed late at night and in the morning. It is freely interchanged with family happenings as an important focus of dinner conversations. Frequent phone conversations with people met through work often contain exchanges about family, as phone conversations with family include exchanges about work and colleagues. We make cross-realm comments about work while watching television in living rooms, during car rides, and while sunbathing on family vacations. The more we integrate, the more difficult it is to pinpoint any specific place or time in which we see the subject matter of work "off limits."

Murray Davis's (1983) comments of appreciation to his wife in the forward to *Smut* illustrate this point beautifully. In this book, Davis describes in minute detail the "slide" into "erotic reality" and the instant flinging back into "everyday reality" after sexual satiation. A systematic comparison of these different realities and their accomplishment occupies a good portion of the work. The foreword states,

> Finally, I would like to thank my wife, Catherine Schmidt, for sharing her numerous insights into my topic, and especially for her amused forbearance whenever I made notes on unseemly matters at untimely times. (xii)

As a synthesizer of "work" and "home," Davis is extraordinary for one or both of two reasons: because of the extent to which he integrates through subject matter, activities, people, space, and time and/or because of the extent to which he publicly admits doing so!

Cross-realm talk in the reverse direction, however, usually does not occur as freely. Davis notwithstanding, even people who integrate more tend to talk less about home and home-based interests while at work than vice versa. This happens for at least two reasons.

First, whether we currently segment or integrate realms more, segmentist employers and cultural norms indoctrinate us with the belief that we should "work" while we're at the workplace or, at the very least, allow others to do so. There is no equivalent, inverse, cultural norm about home; this is precisely the place we expect to talk about what we want, whenever we want, relatively speaking. This suppresses cross-realm talk at work, compared to home, and makes us engage in such talk at carefully chosen times within the workplace. In this way, we generally show greater sensitivity to situations at work and (more powerful) work mates' agendas than to situations at home and (less powerful) spouses' and children's agendas.

Second, in our society, certain areas of social experience (i.e., "private" matters) are typically associated with home, as the "private" realm. These are comprised of particular subjects, activities, feelings, and goals shared within specific, well-defined social circles. For instance, our culture generally believes in the relative privacy of the emotional, sexual, and religious aspects of one's life. These concerns are typically associated with "home" rather than "work" and are routinely discussed and enacted there with only certain people.

For instance, when asked, "Have you ever been uncomfortable because a coworker started to tell you about (their) personal life? What happened? Why did you feel this way?" no one in this study described a particular subject as "off limits" in the workplace. Virtually everyone said they would listen to a coworker about whatever she or he wanted to talk about. It is not the subject matter of a conversation, per se, but the appropriateness of them listening to it that makes Lab employees uncomfortable. Discomfort occurs when the listener does not feel emotionally close enough to the talker to hear what they are saying. The desperateness or simply the lack of social sense of a talker who inappropriately seeks them as an audience is what makes listeners uncomfortable. This suggests that when people draw the home-work boundary in conversations, social circles—the networks associated with territories—are more important than the topic, per se.

Nonetheless, certain topics are generally viewed by Lab members as inappropriate for the workplace. Sexual preferences and exploits and the emotional, intimate details of relationships, negative or positive, were mentioned most often. Thus, while it might not make them tremendously uncomfortable to hear about these things from someone else, few people in this study said they would initiate conversations about such "private" matters with coworkers. Davis's work, for instance, is so remarkable (and, within the discipline and university, politically "loaded") precisely because so few of us are likely to discuss such revealing subject matter so publicly with coworkers.

The more we integrate, the larger is the range of other-realm matters we discuss at work; it is probably just not as large as the range of work matters we might discuss at home. Given institutional demands for secrecy, the more we integrate, the more family members know about the nitty-gritty details of our work. Family members may be intimately involved in this work, actually doing parts of it, as well as offering advice about what was or should be done.[9] The therapeutic and counseling services of spouses and even older children may make them extremely well-informed of workplace trials and tribulations. In the same way, the more we integrate, the more colleagues ask and are told a great deal about children's, spouse's, and our own exploits. They may offer solicited and unsolicited advice about "personal" problems and help out with domestic projects like house renovations, car repairs, and entertaining. This is largely because they are not only coworkers, but also "personal friends."

And, of course, the more we integrate, the less discriminating we are in the times and places we talk about "domestic" matters when at work. We may be more sensitive to the timing of our cross-realm conversations here than at home, but there is no self- and/or other-imposed, "blanket" principle telling us, like more segmenting colleagues, not to discuss domestic matters unless it's "break time" or we're in the lunchroom. The more we integrate, the more we'll tell coworkers about family member's exploits in each others' offices, during committee meetings and "business" phone calls, at "working lunches," in official memos, even in documents published and read by strangers.

In addition to Davis's *Smut* (1983), for instance, consider the beginnings of Eviatar Zerubavel's *Seven-Day Circle* (1985b) and *The Fine Line*

9. For some especially insightful work on the role of wives in accomplishing "their husbands'" work, see Fowlkes (1987), Hochschild (1969), and Kanter (1977a, 104–26).

(1991), Douglas Harper's *Working Knowledge* (1987), Carolyn Ellis's *Final Negotiations* (1994), Mary Catherine Bateson's *Composing a Life* (1989), Arlie Hochschild's introduction to *The Second Shift* (1990), and the prologue and overview of Patricia and Peter Adler's *Backboards and Blackboards* (1991). This arbitrary collection of published academic works explicitly weave personal and family histories throughout the authors' more purely "intellectual" observations. These works fall closer to the integration end of the integration-segmentation continuum represented in academics' works. The subjects of inquiry, methodologies, kinds of data and forms of writing portray varying but fairly high levels of integration between the authors' homes and work, their "personal" and "public" lives.

Reading

Reading practices further uncover a great deal about how segmenting/integrating we see home and work. These too point to the importance of social customs about time and space in identifying and doing boundary work. Four kinds of details are relevant about reading: what is read, where and when it is read, where it is received, and where it is stored.

Extreme integrators read conventionally "work-related" or "home-related" materials anywhere, anytime. They are just as likely to have work-related journals sent to their homes as to their offices; these materials are just as likely to be found on their living room coffee tables and bedroom night stands as their office desks. On behalf of themselves and their families, they lend novels, recipes, "how to" books, and leisure material to work colleagues as well as their journals, tools, and equipment. They borrow the same from coworkers.

Extreme segmentors read "work-related" material at work only, during "work time" (i.e., not during official breaks or in nonwork spaces). They also receive and store these things only at their designated workplaces. Likewise, "home-related" materials are read only at home or temporarily kept among private belongings at work, to be read during official breaks, during relatively "private" time. They pick up these items during home-related shopping trips or from home-related friends, or have them mailed to their houses. They do not read these things at their actual workspaces, whether during "private" or "public" time. Rather, the more we segment, the more we remove ourselves from work areas to read "personal" items, perhaps going to another corner of the office, a lounge, lunchroom, bathroom, or car. Workspace cannot accommodate what is so clearly a nonwork activity, promoting a nonwork mentality and presentation of self.

Naturally, variations on these themes exist. For instance, Bob's actions and attitudes are consistently guided by a segmenting approach to home and work. Through the reading of "personal" material in the workplace, he shows how he partitions his day spatially and temporally.

After leaving home in the morning, Bob buys a cup of coffee and the newspaper on the way to work. He usually arrives "early" and indulges in both. At exactly 8:30 A.M., the official start to his department's workday, he moves the newspaper from his desk to the top of the radiator alongside the adjacent wall. Other than lunch, there are no official breaks in Bob's work day. Accordingly, it is only at lunch time that he brings the paper back onto the top of his desk.

However, some days things are slow at work. Bob can't quite get into a distasteful task at hand. He's already gone to the bathroom, said good morning, and cracked a joke to everyone down the hall. The paper calls to him. Bob swivels his chair toward the radiator, hunches over the paper, and steals a few more paragraphs. He does not fully open up the tabloid, but leaves it resting on the radiator, using only one hand to partially peel back a few pages. Everything about him conveys the message to others, but most importantly, to himself, that this is a "side involvement" (Goffman 1963a), literally and sociologically.

Upon Bob's demonstration of this technique, I was reminded of elementary school children sneaking glances at comic books hidden in desks or someone cheating on an exam. There is at least one major difference here. There is no teacher present. Indeed, there is no supervisor nor even a colleague present, for Bob has his own office with a thick, solid wood door to ensure his privacy.

What Bob does have is a conscience, a product of a plethora of assumptions grounded in segmentist principles about work and family and leisure. Bob's actions reflect beliefs that before 8:30 A.M. and during lunch, it's quite all right to openly read the newspaper at one's desk. In-between, however, is "work time." The sports pages are not permissible then, "taboo," so "sneaking" or "cheating" is the only alternative.

Segmenting reading practices abound. Many Lab machinists and Personnel workers, for instance, bring personal reading material to and from work each day or leave it in their lockers overnight. Although they have the more integrating option to leave personal items at their workspaces, they do not take it very often. Moreover, these people generally have very little mail sent to the workplace, certainly not things like magazines they have personally paid for or household bills. Union, health insurance, and Laboratory correspondence are the only kinds of mail they receive at work.

Those leaning toward the integration pole, however, like many Lab scientists, keep all kinds of "personal" reading materials at work and receive numerous mail items here. These include magazines and journals they have personally purchased, "household" and "work"-related bills and materials. (The latter are also received at their homes. In fact, as far as bills are concerned, personal credit card and telephone statements may be completely riddled with "home"- and "work"-related expenses. This eliminates even the usual classification logic that determines to which address these are mailed.)

Magazine and journal mailing patterns are particularly enlightening in terms of where we draw the line between home and work. Anyone can transport magazines and journals between realm locations. Subscriptions, however, present a forced choice about where we think it's most appropriate to receive our magazines. For this reason, subscriptions uncover people's fundamental assumptions about what topics and literary treatments belong where, a manifestation of their (and others') views about home and work. An extreme integrator, for instance, would be just as likely to receive *Playgirl* or *Penthouse* at work, as the *Journal of the American Chemical Society* or the *American Journal of Sociology* at home. (This is precisely what might happen for a homeworker, of course, who receives, uses, and stores a range of "personal" and "professional" material at home. In fact, the image of a private mailbox with all these items resting against each other suggests the enormous range of boundary work homeworkers face in managing their selves, time, and space each day without the advantage of two places in which to do it.)

In large part, the place subscriptions are mailed to reflects boundary assumptions about what each of us is willing to spend "our" money on. The more we segment, the less likely we are to spend "our" money on something "work"-related. If a subscription is so important for work, we'll expect the boss to use her or his budget to pay for it. We'll reserve "our" money for things associated with home, with our "private" interests. The more we integrate, however, the less distinction we make about what reading material we'll spend "our" money on. This is because neither occupational or domestic interests, the money dedicated to them, or the places associated with them, are so distinct.

Nevertheless, a typical pattern for Lab members who integrate home and work more but still fall short of the extreme is to have more serious, specialized trade subscriptions sent to the office. Subscriptions concerned with more general "work" interests are frequently sent home, however. Here, they are kept alongside more conventionally "home"-related subscriptions.

For instance, Elliot is a chemist who gets *Science* and *Science News* sent to his office but has *Popular Science, National Geographic* and *Windsurfing* sent to his home. Margie is a biochemist who gets and keeps *Science* and *Nature* at her office. Her scientist husband, Mark, similarly receives and keeps his copies of *Physics Today* and the journal for the *Optical Society of America* at work. They both read the more general periodicals *Scientific American* and *National Geographic* at home, however, where they also receive *Consumer Reports.* Mark also occasionally brings home some of the laser and computer trade magazines he gets at the office. At home, he gives these a leisurely, "I wonder what kinds of 'toys' are available now" reading, reflecting the overlap between his "personal" and "occupational" technology interests.

The more we integrate, then, the less obvious is the classification of a subscription or any other reading material. Similar interests and ways of thinking exist no matter where we are found. As a result, the more we integrate, the less reading something at home or work indicates why or how it's being read, that is, for "home" or "work" purposes. While Murray Davis was writing *Smut,* for instance, who could possibly guess why he might have been reading "steamy" materials in his university office *or* in his home?

Lab members who integrate more sometimes choose to have work-related journals and magazines sent home simply because they prefer to read there. Reading may be the only part of their work easily done away from the office, workshop or lab, so it's reserved for home. Moreover, home is sometimes the only place these people are free from the interruptions and hectic schedules of the workplace. By reading there, it's possible to concentrate on the material at hand.

The more we integrate, then, the more we sound like Eleanor, a powerful Lab administrator. She thoroughly intertwines "personal" with "professional" reasons for reading the *New York Times.* She is fascinated by international and domestic politics and relishes reading this paper. But she also must solve numerous problems for a community of international scientists every day and faces new constraints in doing her job whenever there are changes in the business world and the federal government's domestic agenda. So although she is personally interested in the *Times* and would read it just for leisure, she also does this for her work. And she does it at home each morning before going to work, because once she enters her office building, she has no time to herself.

In other words, while Eleanor enjoys reading the paper as much as Bob, there is an important difference in how they classify their activity. For Bob, a relative segmentor compared to Eleanor, reading the paper is "not work" and should take place during "not work" time. Eleanor, however, currently much further toward the integration pole, sees her newspaper reading as essential to her work. So much so, that she unselfconsciously stays home an hour later than her staff to read the paper in peace. It gives her necessary background information in which to embed her similar interests and activities at work *and* home. (Of course, this difference in how Bob and Eleanor see the newspaper certainly is influenced by the very different jobs they do within Personnel. Occupation and organizational position are extremely important influences on boundary work, as will become clear later in this book.)

Bob's and Eleanor's newspaper habits converge in one respect: where they store their papers. Eleanor simply leaves her paper at home in the morning. Bob brings his newspaper to work with him then takes it back home at the end of the day. Both store their papers at home, then, despite the fact that Bob's paper is strictly classified as "personal" material, while Eleanor's paper is inextricably "work"-related, too.

Perhaps the place we intend to store items is the main consideration guiding decisions on where to receive mail and other reading material. The more we segment home and work, the more we store categories of artifacts in one physical space *or* the other, depending on the activity with which an artifact is associated. Consider items like newspapers, paperwork, schedules, children's fund-raising items, spouse's walkathon sponsor sheets, or professional articles and memoranda. Occasionally, we may bring these realm-specific items into the opposing realm. However, if these items are to be saved, the more we segment, the more we return them again to a "proper" storage space in the realm of origin.

The more we integrate, the more frequently we bring all sorts of things back and forth between realms, as seen in a comparison of Lab members' wallets, purses, briefcases, tote bags, and backpacks. More important, though, the more we integrate, the less we care about where we leave these transcendent things: a tabletop at home is just as good as one at work. Because the mental distinctions between realms are not so diametrically opposing, artifacts representing these realms can be stored in either place. Seeing these things in either place then helps reinforce an integrating view and experience of realms. Only when a particular item is used at one place but not the other—that is, when segmentist principles apply—do those who integrate more care about the realm in which belongings are stored. Practicality or convenience thus guides an object's final resting place for all of us. But the number of mental options for that resting place are different as we move from one end of the integration-segmentation continuum to the other.

There are further variations on storage themes. Some ways of managing cross-realm artifacts are even more integrating than others. In general, the more items appear outside a well-defined and isolated place within a realm location, the greater the degree of integration their presence indicates and promotes. That is, the greater the visibility of realm-specific items across realms, the greater the degree of integration they reflect and encourage.

For instance, it is obviously more integrating to do wage labor at home than not to do so. Yet a more segmenting strategy to working at home is to have a designated study, in which all wage work items are carefully contained and all work activity is done. A greater degree of integration is seen when artifacts are used and haphazardly strewn throughout one's house. Their appearance in the bathroom, bedroom, dining room, living and television rooms, and mixed in with all kinds of household items on counters, tables, and benches is a sure sign of an even greater integrator in residence. Similarly, consider the containment of a personal computer for wage work to one's home office or bedroom with its own phone number/line for a modem. Placing the computer in the dining room, kitchen, or living room and using the single house phone number to run the modem is a spatially more integrating approach to "working" at home.

United States tax laws, for instance, are clearly based on segmenting assumptions about home and work. The guidelines for declaring a "home office" on one's income tax are quite stringent, allowing one to declare as a home office only that floor space exclusively dedicated to wage work. As numerous auditors and newspaper articles inform us in April, the mere declaration of a "home office" is grounds for the IRS to immediately "flag" a tax return. In an environment of segmentist accounting procedures, the IRS is apparently quite suspicious of more integrating uses of space and equipment.[10]

A parallel, temporal dimension uncovers the same continuum of integrating and segmenting possibilities. For instance, a temporally more segmenting approach is to engage in one's wage work at home only after children have gone to bed or during a set block of time on Saturday or Sunday afternoon. A more integrating approach is to do one's work at home while the children are still up and running around, while fixing dinner or giving baths, or while sitting with others who are watching television. In the former, more segmenting approach, "work" is cordoned off from domestic life much more than in the latter approach. Intermixed with other events, the relatively more integrating practice consists of thoughts about work that freely flow in and around domestic life. Specific wage tasks are tended to within the rhythm of the household. In this way, the temporal intrusion of "work" elements into "home" time may complement its increased visibility within "home" space.

Similarly, those who bring home-related items to work surely have more integrating relationships between home and work than those who do not. A more segmenting strategy, however, is to keep all these "personal" items in one desk or file cabinet drawer, perhaps within one's private office. A more integrating strategy increases their visibility by carefully displaying these things on a desk corner or section of a

10. Similarly, while exploring insurance coverage for my computer at home, I found my broker was incapable of understanding that I use it for employment and a range of more and less obviously "personal" reasons. He had no difficulty with the idea that a car can be used for leisure, household errands, and wage work. I began by explaining that my husband and I used our computer to run experiments and analyze and write up research. At that point, he insisted that either our university had to cover its replacement costs, or we would have to incorporate to cover it ourselves. I tried to explain that not only had we, not the university, purchased the computer, but that I also wrote letters to family and friends and shopping lists and the like on it, as well as exams and classroom materials. In addition, my husband, a pilot, practices on "Flight Simulator" and occasionally plays games on it. It took a forty-minute phone call from my broker to another, with me answering a battery of questions from both of them to find out how much it would cost to cover my computer. (They finally clung to the idea that I was "a teacher," which seemed to somehow disperse the fog.) It seems that the assumptions of segmenting home and work are so strong, that unless one has legally adopted a self-employed classification, it may be very difficult for some institutions and their representatives to comprehend and accommodate the all-purpose functioning of tools and space other than cars.

wall. But an even more integrating strategy is to mix personal things throughout the piles on one's desk and table tops and intersperse them with the official memorabilia and institutional art work covering all the office walls. Likewise, consider people who freely read "personal" material, do handicrafts like knitting or crocheting, or write "personal" letters throughout the "workday." This approach is temporally more integrating than doing these things only before the official start of the workday or afterwards, perhaps while waiting for a ride or forestalling the return home to an empty or unhappy household.

This is why, as a signifier and supporting practice of segmentation/integration, it is extremely relevant to know not only what materials people read, but where and when they read them: in one location only or in both? Are "work" materials read in a home study, only, or also in the living room, bathroom, or bed? Are they read during weekday evenings and/or the weekend? Are they read while providing "secondary" attention (LaRossa and LaRossa 1981, 49–56) to someone or something else in the domestic realm? Are "home" or "personal" materials read in a workplace office, at one's desk during "work time," official breaks in the day, or both? Or are they reserved for only certain places, like lounges, outdoor benches, or one's car? Boundary work does not begin and end with the decision to read realm-specific materials across realms or not, but continues through these more subtle kinds of questions. By answering these, we establish even more segmenting/integrating experiences of home and work.

This is apparent when we consider other typical, potentially realm-specific items: paper, pens, forms, floppy disks, computers, stock room supplies, and machined parts or domestic items repaired at work. Promotional items like T-shirts, mugs, refrigerator magnets, knickknacks, and jackets and clothing patches also cross-fertilize realms. The home-work boundary is further established by the travels of items like handicrafts and edible goods and children's and spouse's fund-raising items, commonly brought into the workplace to show and share with colleagues.

With these items, as with reading materials, the principle of increased visibility indicating and promoting increased integration applies. Integration is higher if family members actually wear the T-shirts rather than store them on a closet shelf; if stationery lies on the kitchen counter rather than in a desk drawer; if brochures appear on coffee tables not tucked away in-between books in the den; and if mugs and magnets are used every day not collecting dust in basement boxes. The same is true when children's fund-raising or concert posters are displayed on one's office door, locker, or tool box rather than kept in a desk or mail tray, and when food from home invitingly rests on a desk, table, or cart rather than hidden away in a drawer or lunch box.

Breaks

Whether for coffee, lunch or vacation, any formal break in the workday or work year provides an opportunity to demarcate public and private time. In fact, it actually encourages us to do so. However, just because an organizational break policy entitles or even encourages a worker to make this distinction does not mean she or he must. The choices individuals make on how to spend their breaks tell a great deal about if and where they draw the line between their "work" and "personal" lives.

Historically, segmentist assumptions underlie the very idea of "taking a break" in today's workplace. Marx describes the temporal dynamics of the segmentist contract, which hinges on the exchange of labor for a specific amount of time and money. The time encompassed by the workday is sold by the laborer to the employer and transformed into more "public" time for the duration. The workday thus becomes time during which we are officially accountable to the people we work for. During "breaks," however, we temporarily repossess that time. When we "take a break" (i.e., take our time back from an employer), time becomes personal or "private" (Zerubavel 1985a) again for a short, predetermined period of relative unaccountability.

C. Wright Mills describes a historical alternative to this segmentist view of a work "break" (1956, 215–38). The "craftsman" neither distinguishes between the realms of private and public interests nor the time in which they are pursued in the way of the Modern, segmenting wage worker. The integrative life of the "craftsman" thus manifests in a more integrative view of work "breaks," where neither this pocket of time nor that which surrounds it are so distinct. Rather than seeing breaks as a qualitatively, diametrically opposite kind of time, the "craftsman" sees a work break only as a temporary reprieve from a specific task. The craftsperson seeks a refreshing, relaxing opportunity away from the work at hand in order to return to it with renewed vigor and insight and do it right, which might even be achieved by turning to another work task for a while.

The more we segment, the more we embrace the historical, segmentist, Marxist-like view of "breaks." We see these as explicit, often formally-defined instances of private time. The more we integrate, though, the more we see a break as the "craftsman" does, as momentary relief from a task at which we're no longer working efficiently, but this may well be accomplished by tending to another work task.

I want to be quite clear that I do not mean to equate more "segmented" home-work juxtapositions with Marx's alienated workers and meaningless work, however. A handful of currently relative segmentors from the Lab are anything *but* alienated. They enjoy their wage work and worlds, are proud of what they do, and clearly maintain a great deal of control over it. There is, however, a time and a place for everything. Work and home are cordoned off from each other for reasons of variety and simplicity. The segmenting form of breaks is undoubtedly exhibited by classically alienated workers (like some Lab machinists) for the reasons Marx enumerated. However, it is also seen in workers who are simply taking a break away from work and toward home for reasons of dual-realm task management.

So, the more we integrate, the more we take breaks from a specific task or group of tasks, but not an entire realm. We may turn our attention to matters originating at work *or* home for a temporary reprieve, freely intermingling work and home concerns throughout breaks, whether of the daily or yearly variety. We do not distinguish between "our" time and "company" time so much, so we do not capitalize on opportunities to enhance this distinction with the same fervor as our more segmenting counterparts.

Daily Breaks

Accordingly, the more we segment, the more daily breaks in the workday are used for relatively personal pursuits. These are the times we are more likely to bring forth children's fund-raising items and personal reading material, or make personal phone calls. This is also when we feel we can most legitimately give personal opinions about the world (like Harold, the machinist who'd "like to work for Boeing") or tend to creature needs. We eat or drink, go to the bathroom, stretch our legs, and repair presentations of self most unselfconsciously during workday breaks.

The more we integrate, though, the less likely we are to do these things solely during predetermined, exclusive breaks in the workday. We'll do them during "work time," just as we'll work through even formally designated breaks in the workday. Unlike our more segmenting counterparts, we tend not to remove ourselves from work spaces, drop or put away all "work" material, and/or leave phones unanswered during "breaks." Nor do we avoid conversations about work during breaks, whether or not these are spent with work mates. The more we integrate, the less fully we remove ourselves from work during breaks, in the same way that we do not completely remove ourselves from home-related selves and concerns during the rest of the workday.

A close look at the ways Lab members spend workday lunches shows these differences in integrating and segmenting break strategies. Typically, the more we integrate, the more likely we are to blur the distinction between what we do during lunch and the rest of the workday. Such Lab members generally follow one of two integrating patterns for this break on any given day.

First, they may eat with colleagues at some collective spot, whether it's someone's workspace or a dedicated cafeteria or lunchroom. During this time, they freely discuss work and personal topics, covering a wide range of work tasks, schedules and issues, leisure interests, and family activities and concerns. Second, more integrating workers also eat at their desks, alone, continuing to work in one respect or another. Sometimes they do less difficult work-related reading, catching up on newsletters, browsing through a journal, possibly targeting something for a more serious reading later. At other times, especially when deadlines are imminent, they simply continue working on whatever the task is at hand, risking coffee and mayonnaise stains on the paperwork.

The more Lab members segment, however, the more likely they are to leave workspaces for lunch, whether they plan to eat by themselves or with others, or attend to some domestic errand or leisure pursuit. Like other breaks, this time can put an amazing amount of mental distance between these people and their work selves. Maggie drives herself to a serene, unoccupied athletic field, sits in her car and eats a bag lunch in solitary bliss each day. She keeps a good novel handy and a blanket in the car for her cherished daily "fix" of private time. Rebecca and Al are each the primary parents of their respective families. They use their lunch times for running to the grocery store and taking care of all kinds of errands, grabbing a bite to eat somewhere off-site. Regina likes to roller skate or walk during lunch, but also meets extradepartmental friends for the occasion, driving off-site for something to eat.

Segmentation also means avoiding discussions of work when we meet others for lunch. The whole point of these meetings is to talk about nonwork matters. We share stories about families, vacations, leisure interests, and personal triumphs and tribulations, sometimes told during shopping expeditions for personal items. We like to talk about work "at work" not "at lunch." Like other breaks, lunch time is fundamentally defined as private time. This is why lunch time is the period when fund-raising solicitations on behalf of children and spouses are most likely to occur at the Lab, when special foods brought from home are likely to be shared, and when currently more segmenting colleagues tend to be in their most personable moods.

Many Lab members also choose this time to call family members or to meet them at home or some other place for lunch. This may be one of the few times some work groups allow their employees to make "personal" calls. However, even those who enjoy the discretion to phone at any time frequently choose lunch time to do so. It gives them a break from work and work mates, distancing them from workplace surroundings and identities.

So does a quick trip home for lunch. Chuck is a machinist who only has thirty clocked minutes for his lunch break. Nevertheless, he drives home to eat with his wife and youngest child each day, losing half that time to the round trip. Similarly, Catherine and her husband are scientists working in different departments. They have no children, however, and each drives their own car to and from work. While they have all sorts of options about what to do for lunch, their typical pattern is to call each other at some point in the morning and arrange to drive home together for their midday break. For these three, the return home (like others' phone calls to there) reactivates senses of identity based there. This may counter a less desirable sense of who we are at the workplace, or simply provide a little more variety in the senses of self experienced during the day.

While those who eat at the workplace cannot accomplish the same experience of those who eat lunch at home, bag lunches can bring home a little closer. The presence of a bag lunch is often attributed only to financial considerations or time constraints in obtaining food. Nonetheless, these are subtle souvenirs of home. They are often packed by a significant other, containing leftovers of the latest family meal or an item prepared especially for the preferences of a loved one. One group of men has even succeeded in getting their wives to good-naturedly compete with each other through the cookies they send each day. Some Lab members' lunches also contain little visitations, with a note of some sort saying "I love you" or "Don't forget the dry cleaning."

The meaning and intimacy of bag lunches for adults undoubtedly has its roots in elementary school days, where children carry lunch boxes and bags packed by nurturing parents, almost exclusively mothers. As I moved into junior high school, for instance, it was almost a "rite of passage" (Van Gennep 1960) that children stop carrying such obvious tokens of a mother's love and childhood status and buy an institutional, "grown-up" version of lunch. This was a way for children to actively distance themselves from home and their identities there. The same principle guided my peers' choices to abandon childhood identity–betraying cartoon lunch boxes at this time, opting for the adult "brown bag" whenever we were forced to carry lunch from home.

A current television commercial focuses precisely on the symbolic significance of bag lunches. A young boy's mother has gone on a business trip, leaving his father in charge. Surrounded by his buddies, the child opens his lunch box in the school cafeteria to find nothing there. As his face and his friends are quick to point out, this is just about the penultimate test of whether his father really loves him and can take good care of him. As the devastation and ridicule climaxes, business-suited Dad rushes up to the table, apologizes for forgetting his child's lunch and hands him a bag from McDonald's. As the child breaks into smiles, his friends fall silent with astonishment and envy. Of course, there are numerous lessons McDonald's wants us to internalize from this. The most important point for my purposes, however, is how this commercial relies on the symbolic value of lunches brought from home. The identities, relationships, and values a bag lunch represents is something learned from a very young age in our culture.

For this purely symbolic reason, a number of people prefer bringing a home-made lunch to work if given the choice, especially if it's made for them by a loving spouse. The lunch helps invoke home-related thoughts and identity. It pushes the experience of lunch away from a purely public, purely utilitarian event toward a more treasured, "private" experience. This is also why some people may prefer *not* to bring a lunch when they have the choice, but to buy a prepared meal in a cafeteria or restaurant. If we feel the need to keep lunch public, staying focused on work and relationships with colleagues, we may avoid the sense of intimacy and ties to home that a bag lunch evokes.

Regardless of all the practical reasons that people do and do not bring bag lunches to work, their symbolic value helps explain why we make the lunch choices we do and why we eat them where we do. From this perspective, only those of us with relatively high degrees of integration *can* eat a bag lunch from home and do wage work at the same time. Even if an extreme segmentor wanted to work through lunch, it would be quite difficult to do so over such an obvious parcel of home.

Vacations

The more we segment, the more yearly breaks from work reflect the work-distancing, home-embracing patterns of daily breaks. The more we integrate, however, the more likely it is that vacations include both home- and work-realm activities and people. As with daily breaks, both of these forms of boundary work reinforce the degree of integration/segmentation that leads to them initially.

For instance, Sam, Tommy, and Angelo are machinists who stay as far away from machining and the Lab as possible during their vacations—physically and mentally. Sam is a member of a van club, an association of people who take great pride in the unique attributes and decorating of their vans. He, his wife, and children plan vacations around the club's trips whenever possible, caravanning their way across the States. When this is not possible, they take off on their own camping sprees, returning just in time for Sam to return to work. Now that his children are grown, Tommy and his wife also take off by themselves during his vacations from work. In their motor home, they head to the southern states, seeking warmth, beaches, and quiet campgrounds for their reprieve. Angelo packs his family and pets into the car and heads back to the rural town where they previously resided. They visit with family and old friends during his work vacations, doing "old-fashioned, family things."

Cruises, plane trips to scuba dive in the Bahamas or hike in the European Alps, and bus trips to Atlantic City for gambling, eating, and shows are simply more expensive, flashier kinds of segmentist vacations from work. The whole point of these breaks is to put work and the rhythm of everyday life it encourages as far behind as possible. And it's not even necessary to leave home to do this. Those who spend their vacations renovating their houses and/or simply "doing nothing" may achieve the same affect.

Penelope, for instance, puts an interesting twist on this home-based mode of segmentist vacations. She has a large family and cannot afford to go away for her vacations. Instead, she escapes from wage work *and* domestic chores by declaring a one-week moratorium on *any* of her services during her annual vacation. She shops the day before vacation begins and not again until it's over. Laundry, cleaning and cooking are completely forsaken for this one week out of the year. Instead, Penelope reads trashy novels all day and night, interrupting herself only to go to a movie or out to dinner with her husband. Her vacation from work is simultaneously combined with a vacation from home, despite remaining in her house.

These practices are quite different from more integrating options. Charlotte, for instance, is a Lab scientist married to a scientist. Just after finishing graduate school, Ralph and she embarked on a classic, if spectacular, example of a more integrating "vacation." In the preceding year, Ralph received numerous invitations to give presentations throughout Europe and the Soviet Union. Charlotte and Ralph decided to devote several weeks touring through numerous countries, sightseeing their way from one of his talks to another. Schlepping diapers across Siberia for their nursing infant and toilet paper for their five-year-old, the family lectured and toured their way across this giant land mass. They ate dinner with dozens of hosting scientists' families as well as in restaurants and train cars on their own.

It is quite common for Lab scientists to combine "pleasure with pleasure" when it comes to "vacations." In fact, their "vacations" are often quite close to what more segmenting types would call "business trips." Yet, for scientists, this is often as close as they come to a "vacation" in the customary sense of the word. First, while they do not leave their work behind, they do abandon the rhythm of normal, everyday life for the duration of these breaks. Second, scientists' families may come along on these trips. They also frequently extend a stay in a particular place beyond the minimal time required to give a talk or attend a conference, devoting a few days afterward to see the local sights. For all these reasons, these scientists do not see such trips as strictly "work"-related, even if they are not "vacations" in the most segmenting sense of the word.

Recall John and his ex-wife, for instance, scientific collaborators and spouses. They regularly combined the invitation to present a paper or attend a conference with a couple of extra days wherever they went. In fact, if they weren't interested in exploring the leisure offerings of a certain part of the world, they frequently declined the invitation to discuss their work there.

Dinah, another scientist, keeps her travel to a minimum since it is so disruptive to her family's routine and so difficult for her to manage them "on the road." Because her husband will not mind their young children while she's gone, though, they all go to her one annual, traveling event: her professional association's yearly conference. This also is the family's vacation. Dinah attends talks while her family makes trips to local attractions and the hotel pool. She takes all meals with the family, in-between. (In the past, this time has included the task of nursing the babies.) In the evening, instead of socializing with other conference attendees, Dinah stays in the hotel room with her family, keeping her husband company even after the children are asleep. Dinah's integrating version of a "vacation" clearly includes "work" as well as "home."

Changing views and choices of vacations are good indicators of how we view and juxtapose home and work. For years, Giuseppe made a practice of using his annual vacation time to visit his and his wife's extended family in Sicily. Before Giuseppe joined the ranks of Lab management, this trip provided a distinct break in what he did during the rest of the year. Giuseppe rarely even thought about work while in Sicily. All that changed once he became a machine shop manager, though. Now, trips to Sicily include much pleading from his wife to stop thinking and talking about work and indulge in a more proper vacation like he used to.

Giuseppe's promotion to a managerial role has allowed his involvement with work to blossom. It permeates so much of his self, now, that he neither distinguishes much between his thoughts and ways of being at home and work anymore, nor makes this vacation such a clean break. Now, he thinks constantly about how things are going at the Lab, even when he's in Sicily. When he packs for vacation, he makes sure he has a list of home phone numbers for other managers and a fax number to transmit schematics if he needs/wants to. Just as he now covers his workspace with pictures of his beloved grandson and gifts from the rest of his family, so does his work infiltrate even the previously exclusively home-oriented time and space of their vacation.

Conclusion

Everyone actively and passively makes numerous decisions about whether and how they bring "work" into "home" and "home" into "work." These decisions repeatedly push us toward either end of the integration/segmentation continuum, reflecting, reinforcing, and challenging the boundaries we place around each realm. The management of objects and activities over space and time is an extremely important part of the boundary work between home and work. Institutional and personal (often unconscious) policies about the display of cross-realm artifacts and people help us separate and locate aspects of our selves. We share some of these contents and ways of being across time and space, but distinguish between others.

Accordingly, at least part of what we see in the sculpting of home and work is the creation of territories of the self. The more we segment, the more we use different spatio-temporal places to support different ways of being. This counteracts the more continuous sense of self we might otherwise experience as part of a more integrating home-work configuration. The ways we manage calendars, keys, clothes and appearances, eating and drinking, money and people, etcetera reveal and support the ever-emergent, mental and physical configurations of "home" and "work" as self territories.

Mary Douglas ([1966] 1985; 1975) provides a fruitful framework for understanding the interplay between objects and activities and the cognitive order they signify. Douglas argues that the purity of a given cultural category is threatened by nonmember elements. Cultural membership tells individuals what does and does not belong to any category, and just how threatened members should feel by people or things that threaten to pollute the contentious category. Through various activities, we actively segregate the extraneous matter, what we might think of as figurative, mental "dirt."

Literally, for example, "dirt" is acceptable if it's outside the home, but not inside—that is, it "pollutes" the inside of our homes. By keeping it where it belongs, the essences of the "outside" and the "inside" of one's house (i.e., two different cultural categories) are preserved. In this way, the action of sweeping one's floors becomes a physical, visible attempt to maintain a mental, categorical purity and order.

The more we segment home and work, the more we show evidence of analogous, antipollution activity. We use a pocket calendar for transferring dates to their proper, realm-specific calendars and keep home keys on a separate chain from those of work. We keep family phone numbers and addresses in a separate section of a workplace Rolodex. At home, we keep work reading materials in our briefcases or in the den, while at work we keep personal reading materials in our purse or off to the side, on a radiator. We do not invite colleagues home for dinner, nor do we decorate our workspaces with personally meaningful gifts and photographs. Nor do we wear the same clothes at work and at home, or use the same credit card to purchase items or services for both realms. Actions like these help maintain the integrity of both categories. They preserve the orderliness of one's mental framework, which defines home and work as distinct, separated realms.

What is "orderly," of course, varies tremendously according to classificatory frameworks. The less we see "home" and "work" as mutually exclusive mental, social, and physical worlds, the less "disorder" we see in the intermingling of domestic and wage-labor artifacts and reminders. Listing all activities on one calendar or carrying all keys in one lump can preserve just as "orderly" a state of being as more segmenting choices.

Through trial and error, spousal threats, children's demands, extended family's expectations, and the pleasing and disappointing of one's self, colleagues, and bosses, we each learn where to draw the lines around "home" and "work" and who we are when we're in a certain place. Cultural membership, represented across all these categories, directs us to more restricted or expanded notions of these realms. However problematic the process of demarking them, though, the more we integrate, the more "home" and "work" are defined by smaller cores of truly distinctive places, principles, people, thoughts, and feelings. That is, the more we integrate, the smaller the mutually exclusive territories of "home" and "work" become. As a result, fewer things are seen as

"dirt," as pollution threats to the essence of each realm. More concepts, aspects of self, artifacts, and people are shared between spatio-temporal locations for they do not challenge what we see as the essential differences between "home" and "work." Conversely, the more we segment, the larger the mutually exclusive territory of each realm becomes. Overlap between realms becomes more and more inappropriate and undesirable. As a result, each category is more threatened along more points by the potentially polluting effects of the other.

When the mental (and subsequently social, spatial, and temporal) territory exclusively dedicated to each category is larger, its perimeter requires more defensive patrolling. The extreme integrator doesn't think twice about going to a colleague's house for dinner, but the extreme segmentor must. The extreme integrator feels no compulsion to change clothes when arriving home from work each day, but the extreme segmentor does. The extreme integrator assumes and enjoys phone calls about work at home. The extreme segmentor resents them to the point of outrage, perhaps demanding "overtime" for the call's duration. And the extreme integrator couldn't care less about what keys or appointments are jumbled together; the extreme segmentor keeps them carefully apart.

Douglas suggests, then, that "dirt" is a relative thing. This has at least two implications. First, across cultural groups, some people will see "dirt" long before others do. This reflects the different classificatory frameworks and rules that distinguish cultural groups. Second, because of this, some people will be quicker to clean up than others, putting dirt in its "proper" place and combating the polluting effects of its presence.

As I see it, the relative perception of dirt and any other categorical "pollution" is a function of the retraction or expansion of categorical boundaries. What is pollution to one person are perfectly legitimate realm contents for another. Household divisions of labor notwithstanding, people who feel the compulsion to "clean" quicker than others exhibit a particular conception of "the house," with all its ramifications for purity, order, and maintenance work. This conception is simply a more narrowly defined view of what constitutes "the house" than that held by their more integrating, less meticulous counterparts. The latter possess a less mutually exclusive concept of "the house," one that is not fundamentally challenged by dried mud on their carpets or spider webs on the inside of window frames. Whether this conception of the "house" is narrower or broader, though, cleaning fanatics as well as their more slovenly counterparts possess distinct, conceptual frameworks that guide their actions.[11]

11. To elaborate, time spent cleaning the house is not simply a function of personality. Different cultures give us different ideas of what should be inside and outside of the house, and where precisely any item or creature should be found. In addition, of course, gender socialization encourages different members of our culture to focus on different categorical borders and to take the responsibility for maintaining them. For example, women generally are more directed by our culture to patrol for and eliminate interior "dirt" and "disorder" while men are directed more toward exterior varieties. So, gender socialization greatly influences the subsequent, related boundary work that we do, that is, the places and things that we tidy up, the tools we use to do so, and the frequency with which we do it.

My discussion of "cleaning" and categorical expansion or contraction does not refer to the differences between people who have and have not internalized the responsibility for household cleaning. Rather, I am referring to variations in categorical borders/contents that are found among those who accept similar levels of responsibility for domestic (dis)order. Among those individuals, the line between what belongs inside and outside of the house—and the boundary work it necessitates—is more easily seen as a function of influences such as cultural, subcultural, and familial ideas of where this categorical border belongs.

Likewise, all home-work negotiators impose classificatory order on their existences. However, as we move along the integration-segmentation continuum, that order includes different amounts of mutually exclusive mental territory. The more we segment, the more "dirt" we see, and the more effort we dedicate to the never-ending process of "cleaning up." We show our larger mutually exclusive realm territories by separating out a larger amount of artifacts, activities, and associates into their "proper" realms. There is a distinct time and a distinct place for everything, as people, objects, thoughts, actions and behaviors are assigned to *either* the "home" *or* "work" territories. As we integrate more, possessing smaller mutually exclusive home and work territories, we display less of these visible, segmenting strategies. Compared to our more segmenting counterparts, we are ready for most of these artifacts and endeavors, any time, any place, paying very little attention to their classification and containment.

Across the continuum, the purity of time and space reflects the degree of mental, categorical purity guiding its allocation. As we distinguish between and merge categories of objects, our actions not only enact, but help reinforce and reproduce the cognitive relationships between home and work that lead to these decisions. In this way, strategies for managing numerous items visibly concretize a range of mental home and work configurations. At the same time, our practices substantiate and challenge more segmenting and integrating views of our selves.

Our boundary work is not limited to the creation of home and work realms and selves. We also must develop skills that allow us to move between realms while still preserving them. Transcendent boundary work focuses on getting us over the home-work boundary, rather than placing it. Often, we develop routines to help us do this, comprised of conscious and unconscious decisions about how to manage potentially realm-specific elements and selves. The extent to which we create and rely on them, however, changes as we move along the integration-segmentation continuum.

The more we segment, the more we must become something of a chameleon, able to transform ourselves from one distinct way of being to another, given a certain sociocognitive backdrop. In fact, at the extremely segmenting end of the continuum, we must become adept at moving between two totally different worlds. We need to learn how to turn mental "light switches" "off" for the realm we physically leave and "on" for the one we occupy next. (In fact, in the best of the energy-conservation tradition, extreme segmentors operate most efficiently when these two "switches" are never on at the same time.)

At the extreme integrating end of the continuum, however, cognitive movement between worlds is unnecessary, for everyday life exists in only one world. Here, the "lights" are always on (or off altogether!), for all activity takes place within one "room" only, controlled with one light switch only. The extreme integrator merely looks from one corner of the room to the other, turning her or his attention from one facet to another of her or his crystalline existence. Place and time of day are evermore irrelevant as we integrate more, so the need to develop transitional routines lessens considerably too.

In real life, since each of us falls short of these polar extremes, there are always two mental switches that signify home and work realms. Moreover, these are more like dining room dimmer switches, analog counterpoints to the discrete, digital components created by extremists. While the lights in one mental realm may be significantly lower than those of the other, neither is ever off altogether. Each set of lights, each mentality, simply waits, hovering in the background until we turn it back up.

The extent to which associates, artifacts, and activities originating in one realm are found in the other is a good indication of how brightly we leave on the mental lights of another realm. The more someone approaches the segmentation pole, the more these switches are inversely coupled, approximating the energy conservation approach of extremists. She or he *sequentially* turns her or his attention to home or work while minimizing the need to repeatedly switch between realms. As a result, this person severely limits the cross-realm transport and presence of all kinds of realm-specific items. This allows her or him to keep one set of "lights" very low indeed, while fully illuminating the realm of mental and physical occupation.

The more someone approaches the integration pole, the more independently her or his mental switches work. Either set of lights may be increased or decreased at any time and both tend to remain on at a higher level than those of the relative segmentor. This is why the more we integrate, the more there is such an obvious cross-fertilization of realms through a variety of elements. These items, activities, and people indicate and prop up a greater simultaneous awareness of and immersion in both realms: they support a more amorphous, all-purpose self.

In this way, the problematic nature of transitions between realms becomes a bit clearer. This is the work we must do to rotate or push these dimmer switches in either direction. Of course, this aspect of boundary work varies tremendously according to what position these switches are left in and how independently they operate. Accordingly, the sociocognitive structure of mental transitions and the practical ways we achieve them are another important aspect of the boundary work of home and work.

two

Cognitive Engineering: Bridging Time, Space, and Self

As we construct the boundary between home and work, so must we negotiate whatever rift emerges between our realm-specific ways of being. The more we segment, the more distinct, perhaps even contradictory, are our realm-specific senses of self. Within this framework, it's easy to see how segmentist influences create a daily, problematic situation for wage earners. Somehow, as part of our boundary work, each of us except the most extreme integrator must repeatedly affect a mental and behavioral transformation as we turn from home to work and back again.[1]

It is this transitional work to which I now turn my attention. Why do we have to do this work? What forms does it take and how do the incumbent tasks vary along the integration-segmentation continuum? An analysis of commutes shapes much of my discussion, with special attention to hellos and good-byes; the consumption of food and drugged drinks; clothes and appearance-changing routines, including patterns of wristwatch wearing; our choices of routes and listening hab-

1. The relationship between Robert J. Lifton's (1993) "protean man" and Kenneth Gergen's "multiphrenic" personality and the need for chameleon-like transformations in a segmentist society merits some reflection. These personality types certainly facilitate integrative boundary work. But they may be even more essential and more precisely suited to segmenting boundary work, given the tremendous transformative skill demanded of us when we face more segmenting situations. It is not integrating infrastructures but segmenting ones that are more precisely responsible for producing, reinforcing, and honing the protean man and the multiphrenic personality.

its to and from work, and the function of sleeping on mass transit. I conclude by looking at interrealm phone calls as the transitional counterpoint to commutes, while arguing for the ritualistic function of all these transcendental activities.

The historical influence of segmentation generally makes us think of the movement between home and work as *physical* movement, a transition from one place and time to another. We tend to overlook our far more definitive *mental* movement between realms, which we simply assume accompanies our physical travels. Just because we physically leave one location and arrive at another, however, does not mean we always complete our mental journey between them.

The mental journey is what home and work transitions are all about. Physical journeys and visible behaviors simply facilitate the cognitive side of the process. Despite their visibility, driving to work, putting on and shedding coats, locking and unlocking doors, reading mail, and the numerous other minutiae that constitute personal transitional behavior are not the essence of transitions. Rather, they are the tangible grease that help our mental gears shift between the ways of thinking and being associated with either place.

The deceptively physical nature of the home-work transition becomes even more transparent if we consider people who wage work at their residences. Here, the mental nature of transitions from domestic to wage labor is more obvious. However, for homeworkers, too, transitions are extremely difficult to obtain by relying on purely mental gymnastics. They also use space and time and physical acts to substantiate mental boundary crossing. People who work at home may get up from the breakfast table and walk into a home office or workshop to do their wage work. This extremely short "commute" substantiates gear shifting, just like neighbors' car rides. Even the routine of those who merely clear the dishes before spreading out their work on the kitchen table helps them turn from one mentality to the other.

The Cognitive Structure of Transitions

If the lights in a room have been merely dimmed rather than shut off altogether, it takes less work and time to fully illuminate them again. The same kind of work is needed when lights are off or dimmed, but the latter requires less energy than the former to fully light the room again. The amount of work needed for more integrating or more segmenting individuals to make the transition between home and work varies similarly. They do the same kinds of work to make these transitions but do more or less of it and rely on it more or less heavily. On average, the mental starting and end points of these daily transitions differ for people falling more toward one pole or the other. Accordingly, the difficulty of accomplishing cognitive dis- and relocations differs too.

The more we integrate, the less mutually exclusive are our realms and senses of self. We do not engage in one only at the expense of another; both may remain more toward the foreground of consciousness. As a result, the more we integrate, the less severe are transitions between realms. Transitions are noticeably problematic for us only if we're fully immersed in the smaller, truly distinctive core of elements that distinguishes realms and realm-specific selves.

The more we segment, however, the more each realm includes primarily mutually exclusive, truly distinctive elements. The mentalities and physical objects of each realm have little in common with the other. As a result, moving from mental locations within one realm to those of another usually requires greater effort from us, in order to cover greater mental distance.

In other words, the problematic nature of transitions between home and work varies depending on how different are these realms. The integration of home and work encourages the cross-fertilization of each realm and emphasizes similarities in who we are in either place. The segmentation of realms rigorously enhances the boundary between realms to maintain the purity of each unique, contrasting world and sense of self. The importance and difficulty of daily transitions varies, therefore, according to the amounts and kinds of territory our home-work boundaries delimit.

Eviatar Zerubavel argues that the classificatory boundary demands a quantum, cognitive leap between categories. For him, the most rigid boundary creates categories that are mutually exclusive and well-defined. These are transcended only by a mental leap over the chasm that separates one class from another. The existence of a more malleable, permeable boundary leads to less rigid, more flexible, and sometimes ambiguous classification (Zerubavel 1991). As I see it, this latter type of boundary calls for more of a mental "stroll" from one category to another as the juxtaposed territories merge.

Differences in home-work transitions are more easily understood with Zerubavel's spatial metaphor. As home-work negotiators approach the segmentation end of the continuum, they must successfully "leap" between more intensely different mentalities and worlds each time they go to work, come home, or get a cross-realm phone call. Extreme cases must negotiate a mental and practical "abyss" much like that which separates Durkheim's sacred and profane worlds (1965, 357). Those toward the integration end, however, need not exert so much energy to cross the home-work boundary. They travel an ever smaller, less strenuous distance to immerse themselves in a useful frame of mind or task.

Georg Simmel's reflections on "the bridge" provide another useful image of this mental travel. Simmel argues that bridges allow us to transcend the limits of one territory or another. In the process, bridges enhance the distinctive characteristics of the territories they join (Simmel 1985). It is for these two reasons that I see home-work transitions as *mental* bridges. They allow us to transcend realm boundaries, including different senses of self, while also drawing our attention to what is unique to each territory. They facilitate our alternating movement between mental territories while preserving the integrity of each realm and sense of self.

There are crucial, structural differences in bridges that help shape the experience of crossing them. Bridges come in all shapes and sizes. They may be long or short. Some are sturdy and enclosed, creating a secure feeling for the traveler. Others are open to the air, noticeably shaking with the wind and traffic that passes over them. These allow us to see the scope of our natural surroundings, even what's underneath us, increasing a sense of precariousness.

The kinds of bridges we build largely depend on the nature of the lands they connect, the space over which they hang, and the creative use of available resources. The sociocognitive "land" differs radically from one side of extreme segmentors' commutes to the other. A wide mental and, subsequently, behavioral chasm separates their home and work territories. For these reasons, the extreme segmentor of home and work possesses something like the Verrazano Narrows Bridge between New York and Staten Island, or the Golden Gate Bridge in San Francisco. These bridges are long, covering deep, wide bodies of water and connecting lands experientially distinct from each other as well as the water. The bridges between extreme segmentors' home and work territories are just as great as these, although they are feats of *cognitive* not civil engineering.[2]

2. For a different use of the term "cognitive engineering," see Cohen and Taylor 1978, 15–16.

The tenuousness and importance of crossing monstrous bridges is usually quite clear to passengers. This is why the Golden Gate and Verrazano bridges make some travelers extremely nervous. It is quite far from one body of land to another and difficult to get to either territory if something goes wrong in-between. Falling off such a bridge would be almost certainly catastrophic. The need to concentrate, the tenuous position of the steering wheel, and/or one's location in space are eminently clear while crossing these structures.

Similarly, the more we segment, the more conscious we are of transitional home-work movement and its absolute necessity for participation in either realm. The more we segment, the more preoccupation with other-realm thoughts in an other-realm frame of mind is a formidable barrier to effectively participating in either realm. If we fail to complete our "bridge" crossings, we may feel stranded in a kind of mental "Never Land." Still partially immersed in the mentality of one realm, we cannot fully adopt that of our destination. We find ourselves physically at home or work but not mentally, unable to cope with our assigned tasks or the activity surrounding us. Failure to complete transitions may leave us disappointed in ourselves as well as subject to the chastisement of others for not participating in a realm as expected.

At least partly because of the overall difficulty of mental trips between home and work, the more we segment, the more we limit the number of crossings we make. For instance, we limit the number of cross-realm phone calls we make or receive. We stay late at the office rather than try to do work at home after dinner. We do not invite coworkers into our homes. And we resist hosting home-related visitors in the workplace, especially in the middle of the day. All of these strategies reduce the number of times we must mentally travel between home and work, given the amount of energy that must be expended doing so.

The more we integrate, however, the smaller mental bridges need to be. The more diffused borders of our home and work territories and identities effectively bring these shorelines closer. In addition, the more we integrate, the more the "lay of the land" for each realm is similar. Accordingly, the more we integrate, the more our bridges may go relatively unnoticed. Rather than the Golden Gate or the Verrazano Narrows bridges, most of the time we need traverse only the mental equivalent of short foot bridges crossing narrow, shallow streams.

As we increase the degree of home-work integration, then, we can get away with paying less and less attention to most bridge crossings and still make them successfully. First, crossing these bridges is not such a tremendous undertaking. Second, should a distracted traveler fall off a bridge like this, she or he may risk nothing more than mild embarrassment at her or his wet clothes. Similarly, the more we integrate, the less mentally paralyzing it is if we fail to complete a transition. Each frame of mind, each "self" is close enough to the other that if we get stuck in-between, we can still function fairly effectively in either realm, at least temporarily. Our failed transitions may be "discovered" at some point, but this may leave us only a bit frustrated, perhaps embarrassed at being caught slightly out of mental sorts.

With more probable success in crossing our mental bridges and less dire consequences if we fail, the more we integrate, the more readily we embark on these journeys. We'll make these transitions more frequently and randomly, relying less on routine, ritual and predictability to help us along. We'll bring work home for the evenings and weekends. We stop off at the office or lab while running domestic errands. We'll frequently make cross-realm phone calls. We'll invite family and friends to visit with us "any time" in the workplace and expect a steady presence of coworkers in our homes. More consistent in who we are in both places, we more freely intermingle and switch between the people, tasks, thoughts, and expectations associated with either/both realm(s).

The Behavioral Support of Mental Movement

We generally use space and time to enact more elusive, mental distinctions between things (Zerubavel 1991; Van Gennep 1960; Durkheim [1912] 1965; Bourdieu 1973; Tuan 1982). Transitional home-work behavior is a direct result of this spatio-temporal enactment of mental categories. Since conceptualizations of home and work are manifested in spatio-temporal, physical territories, it commonly takes physical behavior over time and space to induce or substantiate mental movement between realms. Behavioral "tricks" and physical movement help us substantiate the more fragile mental transitions underlying them. Such visible behaviors concretize mental movement. They activate and reinforce mental gear-shifting and the conceptual borders surrounding each realm.

Whether travel is mental or physical, getting from one place to another is a problematic task. Just as drivers must learn how to shift without grinding the gears and bucking or stalling the car, so must home-work negotiators develop smooth transition skills. Eventually, like more experienced drivers who have learned the idiosyncrasies of their cars, experienced home-work negotiators may not even notice when or how they shift their mental gears. Only when the structural demands for mental shifting change might they realize and refine their previous habits.

In general, transitions into mentalities that are harder to obtain and maintain require greater concentration from the mental traveler. To accomplish these transitions, we rely heavily on specific, visible, and sometimes sequential activities. For instance, Murray Davis (1983, 45–85) describes the utter concentration needed throughout a sequence of activities for sexual partners to shed "everyday reality" and immerse themselves in "erotic reality." Erotic reality is a difficult and tenuous mentality, carefully guarded and reserved for only certain times and places. As a result, Davis argues, a sequence of evermore erotic mental states helps us "slide" into erotic reality.

So tenuous is the adoption of this fragile mentality that it may be shattered at any point. Partners must work hard to force everyday reality (and its associated self) well into the background, doing whatever mental and physical tricks are necessary to alter their consciousness. Conversely, because of our training to think and experience life from the view of everyday reality, it is not nearly so difficult to re-adopt this frame of mind after sexual activity. Davis describes the adoption of this relatively easier mentality upon satiation with Heidegger's term, "Geworfenheit," an "instantaneous falling down into the world that is there."

Davis's work suggests we must work harder to adopt *any* mentality that is more difficult. Moreover, this harder work may take the form of visible, tangible, even sequential activity that builds upon itself. Howard Becker (1986, 2–3) also brings this principle to mind when he writes of graduate students' personal rituals preceding the formidable and distasteful task of writing. Some of these are quite lengthy and elaborate. I would wager, however, that none of these students need such crutches in order to *stop* writing. They can quickly return to a less taxing frame of mind. For many of us, the instantaneous "I'm outa' here" jump from the desk chair or workbench at the end of the day visibly contrasts with the painstaking, routinized, and pedantic way we get into the work day. As Lab workers show, it is more common to rely on a greater variety of more elaborate transitional activities in the morning, taking us from sleep to a proper work mentality, than when we move from work to home mind-sets at the end of the day.[3]

The following list, for instance, includes some of the most common elements of Laboratory members' weekday morning activities. Naturally, we each pick and choose from a variety of activities as we construct our own morning routines. Yet it is surprising how common it is to do things like these as we "gear up" for work. The mornings find us showering; getting dressed and "made-up"; making beds; tending to curtains and windows and straightening up a bit; taking care of pets; preparing children for their days; acquiring and drinking coffee or its substitutes; eating; making lunch; acquiring and reading the daily newspaper; planning and partially preparing evening meals; engaging in farewell rituals at home; thinking and listening to favorite radio programs during the trip to work; greeting people at work, and chatting with favored coworkers; tending to the physical plant at work, for example, unlocking doors, turning on lights, booting up computers, and warming up office machinery; organizing desks; collecting materials needed for the day; and establishing meetings and schedules of activity with coworkers. All of these actions are preparation, what we do before

3. Of course, while the transition from sleep to work may be considered the most difficult for some of us (see, for example, Schwartz 1970), it can obviously work the other way for some people. For instance, it struck me early in my daughter's life that motherhood gave me distinct transitional problems waking up and being productive in the middle of the night and in the morning, as a result of getting up repeatedly in the night. My daughter's problems, however, were focused on *going* to sleep. She required no apparent transition time getting up but more than made up for it at bedtime.

It is quite common for infants to have difficulty with bedtime transitions. As a result, the folklore of parenthood abounds with stories of parents like myself running through entire liturgies of goodnight rituals: story-telling, lullaby-singing, mobile-playing, and kissing and wishing sweet dreams to everything in sight. Eventually, thank goodness, children get old enough to accept the whole concept of going to sleep, developing their own ritualized routines to help their transitions. At the same time, parents develop their own morning routines to take them from bleary-eyed states to more useful, work frames of mind. Certainly, the increased number of things we have to do each day with a baby in the house contributes to this. However, the increased need to behaviorally induce and prop up the transformation from sleep-deprived parent to productive employee or domestic manager can lead us to do these things in highly routinized ways in the early morning. In this way, we "buy time" in which we can gear up for the day and mentality ahead of us.

"getting down to work." They help us along as we try to push ourselves away from home and toward our work mentalities.

People tend to be much briefer in what they routinely do at the end of the day. They quickly scrub up or turn off computer and light switches, grab coats, and shut office doors as they head out of the building. They'll throw a "g'night-see-ya-tomorrow" to anyone they pass on the way but rarely engage in the easy conversations of the morning. Different radio shows or blessed silence may accompany them on the way home. And once there, shorter, simpler routines than in the morning take over: closing the garage; taking care of pets; changing into comfortable clothes; browsing through the mail; having a refreshing drink; watching the news or stock market reports on television; and tending to dinner. All of these may be accompanied by the predictable and unpredictable needs of children, as some of the tasks that help us mentally put work behind and home in front of us.

One of the purposes of routine or habit is to reduce repetitious decision-making and limit the number of things to which we must attend while trying to accomplish specific goals. In fact, if one's goal is to gear up into a certain mentality, routines are essential. They buy us time in which we can gather our wits. This is why the creation of morning routines is such an important part of the transition to work. The routine acts as a "warm up" for the nonroutine; the mindless prepares us for the mindful. And the sequence of activity not only allows a mental transformation to take place, it actually encourages it. It pulls us along, taking us toward the given mentality that we have come to associate with the routine tasks at hand. Simply by doing acts associated with a given mentality or mental transition, we can induce ourselves to adopt that mentality or transition.

June, for instance, is unique among Lab employees in that she vacuums her kitchen floor every morning just before going to work. She has several pets and a white floor and feels this activity is necessary to maintain her house. The fact that she vacuums while others take food out of the freezer for supper, pack a diaper bag for day care, or start a load of laundry does not matter. What matters is that June does some particular task every day just before leaving the house. In this case, June's activity not only keeps her house in order but her home and work selves. Vacuuming the floor has become a transitional activity, helping her put one realm behind her while signaling the need and providing the opportunity to begin embracing next.

Routines at the end of the day serve the same purpose. However, because the home mentality is so much easier to obtain for many people, an exact, elaborate collection or sequence of events is not as crucial for this mental transition. The transition to an easier mentality can hinge on one single, highly significant act. Melissa pinpoints one such activity upon arriving at home each day: the instant she walks in the door, she drops her coat and takes off her bra, through the sleeves of her blouse. Mary kicks off her dress shoes into the corner by the couch. In an extremely efficacious way, both shed what's left of their work mind-sets along with these most telling symbols of their public selves.

Our asymmetrical needs to tend to transitions into work are especially apparent on Friday afternoons and Monday mornings, given the segmentation of the work week from the leisure-oriented weekend.[4] The work self and mentality can be so difficult to obtain and maintain that people may adopt weekend, anticipatory leisure modes early on Friday afternoons, hours before "quitting time." We may struggle to keep this from happening any earlier.

This contrasts visibly with the slower adoption of appropriate work frames of mind on Monday morning. Redistancing one's self from the weekend mentality can be so difficult that some Lab members refuse to schedule any activities for Sunday afternoons and evenings. They use this as quiet, transitional time to put the weekend, home, and leisure mentality behind and prepare again for Monday's workplace demands. Thus, the ease of adopting the home mentality and the difficulty of adopting its work counterpart contributes to lower work productivity on Friday afternoons and Monday mornings than during the rest of the week.[5] As a way of compensating for these weekly, transitional difficulties, though, we may reserve organizational tasks and activities that require the least concentration for this time.

4. On this phenomenon, see Eviatar Zerubavel's *Seven Day Circle* (1985b), where the creation of a five-day work week alternating with a two-day, leisure weekend is discussed at length.

5. See especially Zerubavel 1985b, 86–120, which includes his discussion of the anticipation of the weekend and dread of Monday mornings. The author also notes slower productivity on Fridays. However, he attributes this to fatigue (90–91) rather than the difficulty we have maintaining the work mentality and the ease of falling into the home frame of mind on this transitional day. His observations on the feeling of Sunday afternoons and Monday mornings are more consistent with my analysis, however. Zerubavel also attributes their experiential flavor to transitional difficulties

The need to work harder at the transition from home to work is also seen in experiential differences between morning and evening commuting train trips and those on Mondays as opposed to Fridays. The kinds of activities in which we engage, the kinds of foods and drinks we consume, the general presentation of self (in terms of body tension, composure, completeness, and correctness of dress, make-up and hair style), the level of interaction between riders and, correspondingly, the noise level, all vary greatly according to at least two compounding factors. These are the time of the trip, according to a daily and a weekly cycle, and the direction of the commute, that is, whether one is going to work or home.

The morning commute is far more sedate than the evening commute. In general, morning passengers are more introspective, keeping quietly to themselves. For some, this is because they're still waking up and/or dosing. Along with others quietly contemplating the day ahead of them and the home behind them, they breakfast and drink strong coffee out of styrofoam cups with tear-away lids. Still others are obviously concentrating on tasks connected to work and the preparation for work. These especially include newspaper and report reading, report writing and note taking. A few read novels and magazines, do crossword puzzles or handicrafts. Others engage in murmured conversations, frequently punctuated by long, contemplative silences. Regardless of the activity in which they're engaged, though, morning commuters attend to it with a singular, silent, independent focus missing on the way home.

Evening commutes are almost raucous in comparison. Strangers and acquaintances talk more, joke much more, and make a great deal more noise. Passengers concentrate less, picking up and putting down reading material and conversations as though looking for interruptions. This is not only due to postwork fatigue and the level of distractions, but to the underlying message of those distractions: now we're heading to the less serious, more relaxing realm. People have literally "let loose" in appearance; ties are stuffed in pockets, hair is disarrayed, shoes are kicked off and lying under seats. Many enjoy ice cream, salty snacks, and sodas, beer, and wine coolers. Just in the type of drug present in commuters' drinks—caffeine or alcohol—we can tell which direction they're heading.

---

in moving from a weekend leisure mode into a work week, productive mode of thought (90, 110, 111).

The same pattern exists between trips at the beginning of the work week, compared to those at the end. Morning trips on Mondays are even more quiet and focused than those on Fridays. And evening trips on Fridays are even more relaxed, noisy, and dispersed than on Mondays. Alcohol and food consumption appears to increase on Fridays, as well, as relieved passengers celebrate the impending, two-day hiatus from the difficulties of adopting and maintaining their work selves.

Culturally, we tend to think of work as the more serious, more difficult frame of mind in our day or week. Yet, as anyone who has had trying times at home can point out, the home mentality can be just as foreboding and challenging, depending on how things are going there. Although Edith's devastating and nasty divorce from her husband of forty years is final, she spends more and more time in her workplace. She dreads the thought of going home at night and does a variety of activities to brace herself before resigning to the inevitable need to go home. She fixes a stiff drink the moment she arrives to help her handle being in such a big, empty house full of memories and to go to sleep more quickly. She also sets about doing chores right away to fill her time before going to bed. She gets herself out the door as soon as possible after waking up, barely staying there long enough for the coffee to brew.

Kevin, too, found himself taking every bit of work possible to his office while initiating his divorce, staying away from home as long as possible. At the end of the workday, he'd organize his research notes, pay bills, plan the evening meal and shopping list, and think about his legal and social plans of action. Then he'd pick up his daughter from day care, go to the store and, after settling her in at home, immediately launch into cooking dinner and straightening up the house. From the time he set aside his research at work, he was mentally bracing himself for his wife's return from work and the ways he found himself thinking and acting in her presence.

Whichever realm provides the most challenge for mental immersion, the transition that precedes its occupation requires more concentration and more elaborate preparation. Its accomplishment is more likely to be interrupted, for its tenuousness leaves us more open to distractions and less able to recover from them. As a result, there tends to be an imbalance in the weightiness, crucialness, and tenuousness of our morning and evening routines. Of course, the extent and direction of this imbalance changes over time. When everything is easier at home, we may concentrate on the more difficult transition to our work selves.

When the reverse is true, we may pay more attention to coaxing ourselves into the home mentality. And whatever differences there might be in our morning and evening transitions, the more we integrate, the easier are our transitions in any direction.

Bridges between Home and Work

For my present purposes, I think of "bridges" as objects and activities that facilitate, even encourage, mental transitions between home and work, between one way of being and another. Briefcases, computers, fax machines, telephones and bag lunches are more obvious "bridging" items. There are others, too: commutes; other daily periods of time formally and informally set aside for mental adjustment between realms; customary morning and evening drinks, often laced with drugs, and the foods consumed with them; and ritual activities and routines performed prior to leaving one realm and just before full immersion in the other. Either alone or in endless permutations, these common bridging elements provide a framework for innovative and purposeful transition behavior. A detailed discussion of commuting, a bridging activity that incorporates many others, provides a rich background for exploring each of these elements more thoroughly.

Commuting

A segmentist daily schedule structurally creates the transitional character of certain times of the day and of the spaces where we spend that time. Allowing for individual preferences and needs, these include the times prior to mentally leaving a realm of occupation, those following the occupation of a different realm, and the time it takes to move from one to another. These times are usually signified by physical movement, that is, the journey to and from work.[6]

This need not be the case. A schedule may substitute for physical travel as the impetus for mental transitions. For instance, a scheduled break or appointment in the workday may call for a change in mentalities. Likewise, people who at least partly work for a wage at home do not have a traditional, physical trip to stimulate their transitions. Yet a

6. I am aware that, when pushed, people share little consensus about what constitutes a "commute." I have dealt extensively with the normative issues underlying the use of this term elsewhere (Nippert-Eng 1988). Here, I simply use it as a shorthand term for the more accurate "journey between home and work."

schedule or even a sequence of events can easily provide the framework for their mental dis- and relocations.

For instance, I find it very difficult to write before my husband and daughter leave the house each day. In the past, their departure time varied over the span of about an hour. Accordingly, I took my transitional home-work cue not from the clock, but from their final trip down the hall to the bathroom and the process of putting on coats. I walked them to the car, kissed everyone, and waved good-bye. Once they were out of sight and I turned away from the street and toward the house, I was ready to "go to work." In other words, my family's departure guided my own, noncommuting (but nonetheless behaviorally enhanced) transition from "home" to "work."

A transition can be seriously interrupted and prolonged if something happens after a transition has already begun. This can certainly frustrate or at least distract the mental traveler. Once we've begun our transitions, we are no longer prepared to deal in the usual way with the contents of the realm we've already begun to leave. And the more we segment realms, the more problematic this grinding, mental shift into "reverse" can be.

Consider, for instance, the homeworking parent who sends his child out the door to school and then turns to his work. He may be rather unprepared for the child's presence when she reappears fifteen minutes later, having missed the bus. Or, consider what happens if we leave the house for work only to discover we've forgotten a book, lunch, sports gear, or something. Our frustration at going back is not simply due to "lost" time and finding a place to turn the car around. It's also because this destroys the flow of our transition. We don't want to physically go back to the place we've already mentally left. This is one reason why, even if we remember an item at the end of the street, we may choose to do without it, rather than return and undo the flow of our transition. We might get so used to the unique feel of our transitions and to bracketing them within certain times and places, we sometimes find ourselves defensive about anything—including forgotten items and other highway or train commuters—that seriously interferes with them.

Similarly, many of us run errands on the way home from work. Despite pressures to get home by a certain time and the exhaustion of the workday, we may still insist on doing these errands before, rather than after dinner. We do this at least in part for the same reason that we leave forgotten-then-remembered things at home in the morning. Once we've completed the transition from our public, work personae into our home selves, going back out again into the public world, in however anonymous a form, is a lot of work. It takes effort to settle into the home mentality, however blissful it is and however easier it is than adapting a work mentality. Not wanting to do this work again, to make two extra transitions that night, adds to fatigue and fossil fuel conservation as disincentives to going back out again on errands.

A Liminal Experience

Relative to home and work, the journey between them is a spatially, temporally, and socially "interstructural" location. For this reason, it offers the perfect opportunity for mental transitions between realms. As the journey physically dislocates and relocates us, it simultaneously encourages us to mentally detach from and reattach to the realms and selves on either side.

Because of its interstructural location, commuting is best understood as an everyday instance of Arnold Van Gennep's (1960) concept of "liminality." Liminality is a transitional status Van Gennep originally proposed for status changes over the life course. It refers to a transformational period in which people leave one social status and enter another. This transitional experience consists of three phases: a shedding of the original status; a transitional, preparatory period prior to embracing the new status; and, finally, the full adoption of a new social position. In Van Gennep's terms, the "rites of passage" that signify these three phases are preliminal (separation), liminal (transition), and postliminal (incorporation,) respectively.

Liminal periods between various statuses in our own society include adolescence, which mediates the movement from childhood to adulthood. The transition from being single to married is commonly known as "being engaged." The transition from full employment to retirement often includes a period of semiretirement. Rites of passage like birthday, engagement, and retirement parties; graduation ceremonies; and weddings, as well as more informal rituals, mark the beginnings and ends of each of these life course transitions and statuses.

Van Gennep and anthropologist Victor Turner (1967; 1974) argue that liminal periods are interstructural in nature because the status positions on either side of them are fully recognized as part of the structural fabric of society. The liminal period itself, however, occurs outside of the official social structure. It may become so extensive that it acquires a quasi-structural position of its own, but liminality is fundamentally defined by its transitional, "sandwiched" position relative to the official statuses on either side. Liminal beings are "betwixt and between," marginal beings falling in the interstices of society.

Nonetheless, Turner reminds us that while liminality is a status, it is not a "state." It is a process of becoming, a transformation of the liminal being from what she or he was to what she or he is going to be. The liminal person is engaged in actively shedding one status or role and acquiring its replacement. Movement between statuses is facilitated because the liminal period is a sort of "neutral zone," where neither the time nor the place in which it occurs are committed to a particular structural activity or social circle.

The concept of liminality has not yet been applied to a *daily* sequence of status dis- and relocation. Yet it is quite a useful way to view the commute as a daily process of separating from one realm and version of self and incorporating into another. Van Gennep's work on liminality concerns ceremonial patterns that "accompany a passage from one situation to another or from one cosmic or social world to another" (1960, 10). Surely, this movement is the most definitive characteristic of commuting, where the realms of home and work are two separated social worlds. These realms demand what are often acutely different, if not antithetical, rules for thinking and acting. As a result, moving between them requires us to existentially switch between more or less differentiated aspects of our selves. The commute, as an interstructural, astructural experience, greatly facilitates this transitional task.

Although we rarely acknowledge its positive, transitional benefits, the commuting experience can be a mentally powerful one, due to its liminal nature. Mary Douglas ([1966] 1985) argues that liminal statuses empower us because they free us from the more conventional patterns of thought and behavior demanded by the social structure. If we manage to physically and mentally survive liminal periods, she argues, we obtain unique, socially valued insights and analytical skills.

Our journeys between home and work offer such empowering, transformational experiences every day. Free from the structurally embedded ways of thinking and acting associated with either realm, commuting gives a unique opportunity to adjust between these worlds, to transform ourselves. In the meantime, we have the chance to see aspects of our realm-specific selves from a more distanced perspective and to take those insights with us when we leave the car, train or bus.

Cognitive growth and adjustment may constitute the primary, perhaps single advantage of those who have long journeys between home and work. Many people feel physically and emotionally drained from extended commutes, feeling they must stop commuting before commuting stops them! Yet this free-thinking period provides crucial time to daydream, envisioning future events and solving problems in ways often not possible at home or work, given our interruptability there.

Long-distance commuters with years of experience understand this benefit to their travels. Other than keeping the rules of driving or train riding somewhere in the backs of their minds, they are free to think about what they wish. This at least partly accounts for some people's continued choices to spend two to five hours a day on a train or in a car, just moving between realm locations. As part of their thoughts and activities, a significant commute gives family members/employees enough time to make a complete mental transition between home and work realms.

Like other liminal beings, but relative to home and work, commuters rely heavily on the relative privacy and freedom of the commute to achieve their transformations, an activity well-suited to any "waiting period" (Schwartz 1975). In fact, exempt from most of the mental and social constraints associated with either of these realms, commuting offers us a cherished opportunity for Zerubavel's (1979) relatively inaccessible "private time." Essentially, commuters get a "time out" from the demands of both realms, leaving them free to mentally vacillate between and outside of home and work.

The assumption of private time clearly underlies the behavior of mass transit commuters. Novices must quickly learn not to unduly disturb other passengers and how to defend their own privacy from the socially obtuse. Many of Goffman's (1963a; 1971) observations about public behavior can be seen here. Goffman's norms of civil inattention (1963a) and the irrelevance (1971, 17–28) of others are particularly visible.

At least one obvious exception seems to prove this rule. Occasionally, small enclaves of friendly commuters emerge, what I call "commuter clubs." They converse; eat and drink; play card, computer, and (magnetic) board games; and save seats for each other every day. These clubs develop only when people mutually agree to ignore the general rule of privacy that prevails. Their existence further depends on two of the most crucial structural characteristics of commuting. First, the cyclical nature of commuting provides reliable opportunities for repeated contact among passengers. Second, the insulating nature of the commute protects members from the social demands of work and home that might otherwise compete for their attention. Both of these conditions allow for close, long-term friendships to develop among passengers, provided they initially break the prevailing norms of (non)interaction.

Commuters' "out of time" and "out of place" status further suggests that the commute is a "free area." Stanley Cohen and Laurie Taylor (1978, 94–95) suggest that free areas are pockets of space and time in which people are permitted to develop and define their essential identities, usually via the use of fantasy. Society "flags" specific times and kinds of activities as free areas, often structuring these escape periods into the day, week, or year. In a segmenting society, coffee breaks, weekends, and vacations are examples of free areas, but commuting also serves this function. During these times, relatively unconstrained by having to tend to "paramount reality," to use the words of Berger and Luckmann (1968), we are free to escape the social structure in which we otherwise would be embedded.

It is precisely this freedom from structure, from either of our daily social worlds, that leads so many commuters to become spatially and temporally "lost" at times. Unanchored by demands for participation, dislocated, as it were, we may even find the need to assign ourselves some "spatio-temporal benchmarks"[7] during the commute.

The freedom and privacy of commuting contributes greatly to the suppression of carpooling among employees. The segmentation and multiplicity of roles that characterize modern life create more, ever greater fronts of accountability and accessibility. One of the ways people counter this is by creating and maintaining relatively inaccessible pockets of privacy throughout the day. For some of us, journeys to and from work are the only places we can retreat into privacy. Locked in our cars, commutes offer a working woman or man the legitimate equivalent of a teenager's bedroom, often complete with stereo system and favorite music. For this reason alone, many of us resist sharing the ride. If given the option, I suspect many commuters would refuse to carry cellular phones on the train or in their cars for the same reason. (Or, at least, they would not give out the phone number.) As Joanne, a professor, explained, her train ride is the only time she can't be interrupted by the

7. In *Timetables* (Indianapolis: Bobbs-Merrill, 1963), Julius Roth proposes the idea of a temporal benchmark in his study of tuberculosis patients. As the patients quickly learn, these are institutional events that signify progress along the road to recovery. Interestingly, Roth notes that when the institution fails to provide these (for patients who are not progressing, actually) the patients will invent them in order to locate themselves.

phone or by someone knocking on her door. As a result, she reserves her most serious thinking for the train and purchased a lap-top computer for this venue, despite desk-top models waiting for her use at home and work.

The journey between home and work is usually repeated twice a day, five times a week, sometimes for years or decades. Over the life course, the commuter is constantly entering, experiencing, and leaving this particular type of liminality, giving it a "relative autonomy" of its own, like other liminal periods. Moreover, it is not uncommon for commuters to spend one-quarter or more of their working day traveling between realm locations. As such, the proportion of time spent in this status alone contributes to commuting's importance as a transitional activity. Like liminal beings whose marginality varies over the life course, the commuter also enjoys a "sufficiently elaborated" period of marginality. However, this is spread out in effective, daily allotments over the span of her or his working life.

In short, during the journey between home and work, commuters exist in an interstructural, transitional, transformational, liminal status. A perfect bridging opportunity for the traveler, the commute connects the realm-specific mentalities and ways of being associated with either side of the trip by providing a neutral, transitional time and space between them. In this way, the journey to and from work preserves territories of the self by facilitating their transcendence. As a transitional activity that takes up a significant amount of our time and energy, it is a crucial location for boundary work.

Transformational Activities

As a result of segmentist influences and their mental and physical movement between realms, commuters engage in classically transitional activities. Most often, these activities change according to the direction of the trip, that is, our destination and the self associated with it. Arriving and departing activities and the realm-specific nature of drinks, food, and appearances play a particularly important and visible role in self-transformations.

Hellos and Good-byes Commuting is not the only kind of travel that signifies transitions in status and self. Van Gennep (1960) observed that life course status passages are often identified by a territorial passage, such as moving one's residence. Today, for instance, the college student moves from her childhood home to the dorm, the newlywed moves from his place of "single" residence to the couple's new home, and the recent retiree moves to Florida. Commuters' territorial passage signifies and substantiates movement between statuses and the ways of thinking and being associated with them, just as residential moves accompany life course changes.

Van Gennep also describes rites of passage used to demarcate the separation and reincorporation of travelers as members of a social group (1960, 26–30). In some cultures, people lose their status as members of the community while traveling outside the group's physical territory. They become nonmembers for their travels' duration and must reclaim their membership when they return. In these cases, preliminal, liminal, and postliminal rites separate travelers from their structural positions within the group, send them off to the liminal (travel) experience, then reintegrate them into their previously held statuses when they return.

The more we segment home and work, the more we approach Van Gennep's model of virtually losing group membership while traveling away from one realm and occupying another. Most of us leave our houses in the morning and go off to the worlds of work and school.[8] Practically speaking, we more or less become nonmembers or, at least, nonparticipants in the household for the duration of the school- and workday. That is, the more we segment, the more we sequentially alternate between social statuses, withdrawing more fully from one world in order to occupy the other. The more we integrate, though, the more we maintain a presence in and contact with the other realm. We maintain more of both our home and work selves simultaneously, although we probably rely on one more fully at any given time. It's as if we "keep our seat warm" or our "foot in the door" at the other realm, rather than leave it altogether.

In other words, when we physically exit from our homes in the morning or our workplace in the evening, the length and extent of our mental absence is variable. In the morning, for instance, our mental absence from home may last until we do some domestic task at work,

8. The relatively marginal status of some members of society is rooted/reflected in the fact that they do *not* "leave the house" each morning. This includes young children, the chronically ill or impaired, and the unemployed, whose marginal status is increasingly attributed to homemakers but increasingly rejected for retirees. Of course, the status of both these last groups is changing largely because of the numbers of people in each category. Institutionalized people share an enhanced form of this stigma in addition to their other sources of negative sanctions (Goffman 1963b).

have lunch with a family member, or phone her or him to "touch base." Or it may last until we reappear at the end of the day, with no contact between realms for the duration.

The more we segment, vacating home selves while at work, the more we rely on social convention and others' good will in order to resume these selves and statuses when we return. The same holds true at work. Here, we reappear after a night's or weekend's absence to be greeted by coworkers, who welcome us back to the positions we more or less forfeited during our absence. At the end of the day, they bid us farewell again, with the tacit promise to "save our places" until we return the next morning. The more we integrate, though, the more we maintain our own places in both realms; nobody has to "save" them for us for we don't fully leave them.

In this way, the ritualized, morning activity of breakfasting, handing someone a bag lunch, kissing her or him good-bye, and waving from the front step or another car functions for everyone like send-off parties for family members suddenly called to war. These parties tell servicewomen and -men that it's time to think less like members of a household and more like soldiers who have a job to do. They tell the families and friends left behind that temporarily (they hope), they must start thinking and acting without relying on the presence or assistance of the people who are leaving.

The difficult work of reorientation doesn't end with someone's departure, though. As when the soldier returns to a welcome-home party, daily homecoming rituals help the whole family readjust to forms of thinking and acting that incorporate members who were absent. For the soldier, the welcome home marks the time others expect her or him to leave the combat mentality behind and try to resume a non-, even prewartime, everyday sense of self. For the wage earner, "Hi, Honey, I'm home" routines also signal the time to put one mentality behind and resume another—for everyone.

The same process happens at the workplace, of course, where increased segmentation means decreased contact with the people, thoughts, and tasks of work between "quitting" and "starting" time. However much we ignore it overnight, in the morning we are expected to pick up work right where we left off the previous day. Ritualized greetings and chats with one's colleagues and briefings with assistants help us accomplish this task. And the more we segment, the more pronounced and crucial these activities become for everyone's self-transformations. Morning greetings to one's colleagues may not be mere procrastination, then, but essential, re-orienting, refocusing actions.

In other words, the more we segment, the more we actually, totally "go home" or "go to work," since our mental and social presences strongly correlate with our physical ones. When we physically leave either realm, we not only leave certain tasks behind, but who we are when we're there. Hellos and good-byes are more appropriate and necessary to get us through the day, then, for not only are we greeting or bidding farewell to the people around us but to the "self" about to be distanced or embraced.

The more we integrate, though, the less we actually "leave" either realm and the aspects of self associated with it. Our presence is more or less obvious, more or less emphasized, but never entirely missing. Though we may physically change locations, we never really mentally, socially leave either realm, either in our own minds or, very often, in our colleagues'. We stay accessible and accountable to both realms no matter where our bodies are, freely drawing on a more constant, all-purpose sense of self as needed. We talk on the phone instead of in person, work on a computer at home instead of the office, or think about a child's problem while tending to "work" tasks in the workplace.

We take brief breaks from each realm, but we do not take full-blown, eight-hour "vacations" from them and the selves located there. We just don't "go home" at the end of the day, nor do we "go to work" in the morning, not in the sense of more segmenting people. And it's absurd to say hello to someone when they've made no entrance, or good-bye when no exit is forthcoming. As a result, the more we integrate home and work, the more we downplay hellos and good-byes, for these mental rites of passage have less separational, transformational significance.

Another phenomenon related to greetings and farewells also aids workplace arrivals and departures and shows the link between physical, mental, and social mobility. Workplace organizations sometimes display signs for employees arriving at or leaving work grounds. At one quiet, wooded access road to the Lab, a sign facing in-coming traffic says: "Think. On-The-Job Safety Begins Here." At another, more popular entrance, in-coming traffic signs remind people of on-site events that day, so that they might better plan their schedules. Signs for out-going traffic say "Take Safety Home With You," "Wipers On? Lights On, Too," and "Buckle Up—It's The Law." These last directives reorient those still too absorbed in their work, mentally turning them toward the outside world. These signs tacitly acknowledge the self-transformations that accompany our physical journeys between social worlds.

In-between the hellos and good-byes that bracket commutes, numerous activities continue to reflect and encourage self-transformations. During the journey to work, choices of foods and drinks and appearance-changing efforts tell something about who we are at the moment, as well as who we wish to become.

Drugs, Drinks, and Food Two aspects of foods and drinks compound each other to make these useful tools for mental transitions and ever-present artifacts during our commutes. First, the inherent, chemical characteristics of some foods and drinks physiologically help induce transitions in certain directions. Second, these same and other foods may be socially and/or personally associated with distinct realms. When we consume them, frequently in ritualized ways, we help trigger or complete mental transitions not merely because of their physiological effects but because of their even more overwhelming, symbolic characteristics. In this way, what we consume prior to, and just after, our arrival at each realm helps us embrace the mentality we must assume there.

A frustrated and insightful Jack, for instance, describes recurrent transition problems leaving work behind him each day. Absorbed and fascinated with his scientific work, Jack is unable to put it behind him by the time he reaches home and greets his two-year-old daughter. He adores her, yet still has not adjusted to the segmenting effect of her demands, having spent his years prior to her arrival thoroughly interweaving home and work as he wished. He has quite a bit of difficulty winding down from the hectic pace and problems of his workday and settling into what he thinks is a proper, supportive, attention-giving role toward his daughter. Jack says he currently helps himself get into the right frame of mind when he arrives at home by drinking a couple of beers. He's not happy with this for physical reasons, but it seems to help his mental transformation a lot.

The ritual of an alcoholic drink after work is a common custom. We stop off at a bar on the way home, have a drink on the train or when we arrive at home. Cheri was in elementary school when she learned to mix a martini, for her IBM engineer father required one each day when he came home. Recall Edith too, now single and returning home each day to an empty house that once held six children, a husband and a variety of guests. The first thing she does when she gets home is fix herself a glass of scotch.

Alcohol is a choice transitional drink from work to home largely because of its relaxing effects. It helps us "unwind" from a tense or intense, hectic, public work mentality into one more appropriate for home. From this perspective, the more someone segments, the more logical it is that she or he turns to alcohol to achieve these transitions. The more we integrate, the less we need to turn to alcohol, though. We do not need to alter our pace and orientation so much, for the home mentality is so much closer to the work state of mind. There is less of a structural need to rely on this or any other particular bridge.

Keeping in mind that situational, structural factors encourage us to segment/integrate more, we can imagine how *combinations* of work and family situations might contribute to a greater consumption of postworkday alcohol. Incommensurate situations that demand incommensurate mentalities/selves demand more transitional "tricks." Alcohol consumption is part of this tactical repertoire, as reflected in the many "Attitude Adjustment Hour" specials held in bars at the end of each workday and week. The more radical the transformation a certain home-work configuration demands, the more a home-work negotiator might rely on alcohol to make the transition—or avoid it altogether.

When we mentally move in the opposite direction, however, from home to work mentalities, caffeine is the common choice of drug. It might be impossible to count the number of people who have a transitional reliance on this drug or the number of disposable cups we use for our transitional drinking. Caffeine and alcohol have important and virtually opposite effects on the human body. This substantially contributes to their mutually exclusive, semiotically linked associations with each realm. As a stimulant, caffeine affects the nervous system to artificially enhance the transformation from a sleepy to a wide-awake state. In moderation, it sharpens our ability to concentrate and attend to sensory information. Alcohol, however, is a depressant, working to reduce inhibitions and slow down interpretations of and responses to most sensory information. In excess, coffee makes us jumpy and nervous; alcohol makes us dull and sleepy.

Physiologically, drinking a cup of coffee may well sharpen us for what lies ahead, helping us to work harder and think more clearly. But it does so partly because the *act* of drinking it signifies to us, in a purely symbolic fashion, that we *are* hard-working, both in character and action.

In our society, one of the symbolic contexts for coffee drinking is the preparation for serious, concentrated endeavor. In this context, we associate the image of someone drinking coffee with people who are fighting natural states of mind to engage in the utmost artificial activity: important, hard work. When we see others sitting in cars, at desks, or standing at workbenches and drinking coffee, we realize how socially, not merely physically, significant is this act. This is why children try to drink it, testing their status and proving their seriousness and importance with it, despite its initially bitter, unappealing taste.

In a purely reflexive, ritualistic way, then, coffee drinking promotes transitions into "work" frames of mind, as we "become" what our drink symbolizes. In this day and age, coffee may be the metaphorical equivalent to a Nuer tribal member's ever-present spear, as described by Evans-Pritchard in Csikszentmihalyi and Rochberg-Halton (1981, 233). Drinking coffee may well convey the superior power, strength, speed, and stamina of today's "warrior," just as the Nuer's spear does. In fact, argue Csikszentmihalyi and Rochberg-Halton, the Nuer's spear spurs on its carrier, its very feel causing him to strive for the power and character it symbolizes but he may lack. A cup of coffee may be very similar, indeed.

When we drink our coffee at regular, predictable times, this activity can promote our mental transitions in yet another way, as part of a sequence of routine, ritualized actions. Some people routinely stop at a deli for a cup of coffee on the way to work. Others walk down the hall to get some after hanging up their coats each morning, leisurely drinking it while perusing their desks or the newspaper, reading mail, or chatting with a coworker. As a prop, coffee-drinking forms an important part of our daily, background routine.

Of course, drinking coffee often requires that it be made first—ritualized, transformational behavior in its own right unaffected by whether the maker actually drinks it or not. Regina describes her coffee-making activities in the office kitchen as "warm-ups" for her day's activity. After turning on her light, depositing her coat and bag in her own office, and booting up her computer, she heads down the hall to tend to the morning pots of coffee. In the process, she thinks about her schedule, greets each of her colleagues, and chats with them about their homes and plans for the day. Ten or fifteen minutes later, she heads back down the hall to her own office, hot mug of coffee in hand, and "gets to work."

Most of the time, then, we can tell which direction commuters are heading just by the drugs in their drinks. Alcohol, associated with a leisure, home self, helps people transition out of work and into home at the end of the day. Coffee drinking begins in the morning and lasts throughout the early afternoon, though, as it is generally more difficult to adopt and maintain the workday mentality.

Yet, where "home" is as much or more "work" than wage work, it may call for caffeine, too. Alma, for instance, shows what can happen when going home is more difficult than facing who and where we are at work. Alma is a single mother who lives only fifteen minutes away from her workplace. She finds this a totally inadequate period of time in which to brace herself for her five demanding children. Frequently, she forestalls her arrival at home by going to a girlfriend's house for a half-hour visit and a cup of coffee. The fact that she's drinking caffeine is a telling sign of the kind of transition she must make.

At work, Alma says she can really be herself: soft-spoken, well-dressed, helpful, witty, and stimulating. At home, she finds herself reduced to a loud-mouthed nag, an emotional victim of her and her children's knee-jerk reactions to everyday events and their shared abandonment by Alma's missing husband. This is compounded by Alma's physical exhaustion and the frustrating self-image produced by relentless domestic chores each evening.

It is no coincidence that Alma frequently helps herself into a home mentality by (1) artificially lengthening her trip home at the end of the day, and (2) drinking coffee not alcohol. It is also not surprising that Alma uses no tricks to forestall her arrival at work in the morning. She leaves her house as early as possible, "escaping" from domestic responsibilities and her children's demands. She arrives at work well before it is required, settling in at her desk without anything to drink until much later in the day.

Naturally, coffee is not the only beverage people use to fulfill its transitional function. Anything can do the trick, but custom results in the common substitutes of tea and hot chocolate. With or without caffeine, these drinks all have one thing in common: they're *warm*. Hence, the prototypical characteristic of transitional morning drinks may not be their caffeine content but their heat. On the other hand, whether one drinks alcohol, soda, juice, or any other heading-home substitute, custom frequently finds us relying on *cold* drinks at this time.[9] Literally, then, our morning drinks "warm us up" to the wage work at hand, while our evening drinks "cool us down" for the return home. In the

9. I am grateful to Eviatar Zerubavel for pointing out this contrasting dimension of morning and evening drinks.

best of Levi-Strauss's (1978) "culinary anthropology" tradition, this dimension adds to the oppositional drug contents of pre- and postwork-day drinks. By using the symbolic and physiological aspects of drinks, including drug content and temperature, we help ourselves place and maintain our home-work boundaries, even as we cross them.

"Snacks" are *the* transitional food, by definition. They take care of us in-between dedicated meal times and places. The transition between realms is frequently accompanied by snacking. Children, for instance, often have a snack when they get home from school, when they must readjust to their home lives and agendas.

At the beginning of the day, many people treat "breakfast" as a snack, rather than a meal in its own right. They grab a quick, frequently sugar- and carbohydrate-loaded snack, whose sole purpose is to tide them over until lunch, their first "real meal" of the day. A Danish, bagel, muffin, doughnut, Pop-Tart, or roll can be quickly consumed in the car, on the train, or in the office or lunchroom. Typical foods for the transition into work, these can form a crucial link in the routine sequence of symbols and activities that mentally takes us there. When we eat them, like when we drink coffee, we concretize and enact the mental direction of our commute.

On the way home, other snack foods serve the same mentality-triggering purpose. In Penn Station, New York, or Thirtieth Street Station in Philadelphia, for instance, hundreds of commuters snack their way onto trains at the end of the workday. The most obvious and obviously enjoyed foods for their trips home are ice cream and frozen yogurt. Nothing could contrast more strongly with the nature and symbolic associations of morning foods.

The colder temperature of ice cream may well contribute to its going-home status. However, the very technique of eating ice cream forbids its association with "going to work." Morning Danishes and the like can be, and frequently are, consumed in a vigorous, hungry fashion, revealing our anxious gearing up to apply ourselves. Compared to ice cream, breakfast snacks are mere calories, quickly wolfed down to squelch stomach noises and obtain a sugar-propelled boost for the day. This is hardly the ice cream cone mentality. This snack virtually ensures a slower, more free-flowing, and far less utilitarian experience. At the very least, unlike breakfast foods, eating ice cream too fast results in a headache, while simultaneously defeating the entire pleasure-oriented, leisure point of its consumption.

In other words, the very act of eating, breakfasting, and homeward-bound snacking cues us in to the mentality shift under way. A bag of popcorn, another popular going-home snack, simply cannot be "inhaled" like a doughnut or Egg McMuffin, nor is it meant to be. Going-home foods reflect the winding down, leisure orientation associated with the direction of this commute.

The consumption of caffeinated and alcoholic beverages and a variety of snack foods plays an important role in bolstering our transitional activities. Our choice of food and drinks not only indicates which frame of mind we are in, but which frame of mind we want to adopt. These consumables signify the direction of our mental movement and physiologically help us achieve it. Through the drugs lacing our drinks, the kinds of snack foods we choose, and the temperatures at which we consume them, foodstuffs help us bridge realms in particular directions.

Clothes and Appearances Aside from eating and drinking, the transformative nature of commutes is also seen in the attention we give to our appearance at these times. During commutes, we frequently see people changing and finishing presentations of self. Changing or adjusting clothes, putting on make-up, styling hair and shaving while commuting simply continue the transitional activity of changing clothing at home or the workplace. During the commute, changing clothes and other aspects of one's looks is a fascinating, loaded sign of switching between realm-related selves. Driving hazards notwithstanding, mentally, commutes are quite a logical place and time for this type of boundary work.

The transitional reasons for changing clothes are tremendous and certainly are not negated by all the practical reasons we may have for wearing different clothes at home and work. Perhaps this is seen most clearly among people who change clothing despite no apparent practical need to do so. Marvin switches into and out of his blue, collared coveralls each workday, despite doing very similar tasks at home in the very same jeans, flannels, and T-shirts he wears underneath his coveralls. Steven changes from the casual jeans and sneakers he wears to work into sweat pants, often sans shoes, when he gets home. And Holly frequently wears a comfortable, wash-and-wear cotton/polyester shirt and slack set with roomy, flat shoes to work. She removes her make-up and changes into a functionally identical jogging suit and Keds sneakers immediately upon arriving home in the evening.

For these people and others like them, the transitional, symbolic activity of changing is what matters. Changing clothes is a logical, physical action that triggers and/or seals the mental transition between the realms and selves the clothes signify. Switching from one "uniform" to another is a highly significant form of boundary work. In the morning, getting dressed for work can be a crucial ritual for purely mental reasons, for this mentally launches us toward the realm of work. The physical acts involved concretize this mental transformation and help us achieve it. When we arrive home in the evening, changing clothes can be just as important, not simply to save on dry cleaning bills or protect furniture from the workday's dirt, but so we can fully adopt our home personae.

Of course, people need not change into and out of entire costumes to affect their transitions. For Mary and Melissa, the entire evening transition from work to home is embodied in single actions: kicking off shoes and removing a bra. On the train and in cars, the transition from work to home is also seen in such singular acts as loosening a tie or shirt collar, untucking a blouse, kicking off shoes, removing earrings, or disarraying hair. Morning transitions are revealed in singular acts that show the opposite transformation, from one's private, home-related self to a public, work-related one. Lipstick is carefully applied, electric razors remove the night's whiskers, ties are straightened, hair is brushed into place, and socks and sneakers are replaced with dress shoes. Any one of these transformational acts may be saved for the last minute, sealing the transition to a work self.

Frequently, clothes changing is preceded by showering, an extremely helpful transitional activity. Either at home in the morning or before leaving work, the act of showering before changing clothes is very effective for mentally dislocating us from one realm and preparing us for the next. Like a commute, but in a much more attenuated way, a shower also offers a liminal experience. If we're lucky, during a shower we also become relatively unaccountable and inaccessible to the people of both realms. For this reason, a shower encourages a relaxed, free flow of thoughts into whatever direction one wishes.[10] This gives

10. I have had the same experience as a number of my friends, who find that showers are so good at promoting the liminal, free-thinking experience, valuable solutions and strategies often result from them. We also share the frustrating experience of tending to lose these thoughts the moment we turn off the water and resume our place in the social world on the other side of the curtain. Soap crayons for scrawling notes before leaving this haven or pads of paper and pens left on the counter take the place of commuters' writing implements and tape recorders. They preserve the results of the empowering, cognitive freedom of liminality.

us a perfect opportunity to shed old selves and concerns and begin embracing new ones. Workplace and home expectations aside, the more we integrate, the less we feel any compulsion to change clothes, much less shower, in order to change realms/mentalities. We just don't need to rely so much on transitional tricks like getting into certain outfits to "get into" the "right" frame of mind for either realm.

The mental results of changing costumes accounts for a great deal of our clothes-changing behavior. We get dressed for a party just before we leave the house or guests arrive because it does such a wonderful job of putting us in the "party" and possibly "host" frame of mind. The effect caused by changing clothes can lead us to do so anytime we must change our social milieu, to help adopt a particular mentality. Even if it's as simple as putting on a fresh shirt, different pair of shoes, or more spectacular pair of earrings, we rely on the transitional, evocative power of changing clothing to help change into the sociocognitive outlooks associated with certain roles.

Murray Davis (1983, 58) has alluded to the transformative power of changing clothes in his analysis of the strip-tease. Part of the eroticism of "stripping," he argues, is that the stripper is engaged in a kind of role shedding. In my mind, this is only half the story, for the role-shedding (better, "self-shedding") is complemented by the stripper's simultaneous, visible adoption of a new role/self. When any of us sheds one socially and personally significant costume for another, we signify to ourselves and others that we are leaving one version of self and adopting another. This visible behavior helps induce in us a complementary, mental transformation. In the stripper's case, it's the depiction of this mental transformation that lends to her or his physical appeal.[11]

11. It is a strip "tease" because of its transitional nature. The element of transition is not sufficient to explain its appeal, however, for there is always Schutz's "transitional shock" as an alternative. Rather, in stripping, the everyday "frame" must not only be broken but broken slowly and intentionally while gradually replacing it with an erotic one. Of course, all the while it is surrounded by yet another frame, the one of fantasy. We seem mesmerized by transformations of all kinds in this culture, whether they turn us on or gross us out. The transformation of people is particularly riveting. Consider as evidence the popularity of "Transformers" toys, Power Rangers, the liquid-metal terminator in *Terminator 2,* the sparkling pointalism of Star Trek crew members "beaming up," and any creature who has the power to transform things, including witches (not to mention Halloween, generally), scientists, and computer graphics specialists, along with their products. These latter include the transformation of people's representations in movies, commercials, or computer programs (e.g., inserting Tom Hanks into old newsclips in *Forrest Gump* and dinosaurs into *Jurassic Park,*

One sure sign of "stripping" off one self and adopting another concerns wristwatches. If they change nothing else at the end of the day, numerous Lab workers remove their wristwatches (often along with emptying their pockets or removing jewelry). They do this almost as soon as they walk through the front door. Of all the ways to track the shedding and adopting of distinct mentalities, wristwatch-wearing behavior signifies one of the most interesting: the shedding and adopting of senses of time.

"Time work" is frequently part of Lab members' transition process, as they try to adopt a sense of time that's appropriate for the realm of destination. It is like "emotion work" (Hochschild 1983), done so we might adopt the correct feelings scripted into social settings. Once again, Murray Davis's work is suggestive of this process. He certainly provides evidence for the "time work" that sexual partners must do to adopt a more erotic reality. With all the other kinds of work necessary to trade everyday reality for this version, there must be some attention to one's sense of time, especially when it proves an obstacle.

The loss of a "common" sense of time (e.g., Flaherty 1987) may be a common element in many "scripts" (Gagnon and Simon 1974, 19) for sex. Is "great sex" possible when one is still aware of common time duration? No, certainly by some scripted definitions. And so, using Davis's argument, to have "great sex," it is customary at least at some point to eliminate awareness of the clock, as part of the everyday reality in which we normally operate. Indeed, I see Davis's depiction of being thrown back into everyday reality after satiation easily signified by suddenly wondering or realizing what time it is.[12]

or creating computer animated cartoons like *Reboot*), as well as the transformation of actual people, who may have been healed, wounded, or mutated as a result of occupational efforts.

12. One could imagine that prostitutes' professional mentality requires them to work at *not* adopting an erotic version of reality during sex. In the movie *Klute*, Jane Fonda's simple glance at the clock while having sex keyed us into her character's real frame of mind. In *Taxi Driver*, Jodie Foster also plays a prostitute. She lights a cigarette and tells Robert DeNiro he has until it burns out to have sex with her. This is a more erotic (if not poisonous) standard than a clock for some, but it's still a measuring device of common, real time. The exchange of money for anything (e.g., sports performances, baked goods, child care, singing, etcetera) is a powerful frame-breaker, making us approach and "see" this category of activity in an entirely different light. This is especially true regarding sexual activity. A prostitute's time work probably means *not* losing a sense of common time during sex, one indication that she or he is not engaged in erotic reality, but the reality of everyday wage labor.

Like Davis, Barbara Adam (1995), Michael Flaherty (1987, 1991, 1992), and Mihali Csikszentmihalyi (1975) suggest that one's sense of time is linked to ways of thinking and being associated with certain activities and places. E. P. Thompson's (1967) work on the process of sensitizing ex-agricultural workers to industrialists' awareness of the hour and minute is even more suggestive of the existence of a realm-specific sense of time. He argues that time clocks and punch cards were used to facilitate workers' growing awareness of the duration and exchange value of time. The move to segmentist, manufactory work thus added an additional, transitional dimension to these wage workers' days. They had to learn when to shed and adopt home- and work-specific treatments of time. To varying degrees, wage workers continue to face this task today.

More specifically, Thompson's agricultural-turned-manufacturing workers had to abandon what he called a "task" orientation to work. This is an independent, autonomous approach to work in which tasks are tended to within the constraints of the season and personal interests and demands for the day. In its place, early manufactory workers had to adopt a "time" orientation to work, in which the clock mandated the way workers approached and scheduled home and work tasks. For Thompson, this "task" versus "time" orientation is one of the most tenable points of distinction between new wage workers' pre- and post-manufactory experiences.

While Thompson explicitly equates a task orientation with the world of home and a time orientation with the world of (industrial) work, this realm-specific link is more variable among Lab workers. Alan and Marcia, for instance, are typical scientists in that they constantly get into trouble with their respective spouses for one reason. They're repeatedly late coming home in the evening. This is usually because they are simply unaware of the time of day, unlike their dinner-making spouses.

Whether they're working independently in offices or in a group on an experiment, Alan's and Marcia's days are largely task-driven. They do not need to know the time usually, having very few scheduled appointments in the year. And the time of day frequently has no bearing on whether "it's time" to start or stop a work task. The sequential demands of experimental work often require tending to a task until it's complete, however long that takes. The alternative is to risk losing all the effort already put into it. The window of time available either to make something work or to lose it and have to start all over again makes the precise time of day irrelevant. An emphasis on the classification of time during the workday promotes a keen awareness of the time for workers like machinists, however. Their work tasks also mean that they, like Personnel workers, generally can drop whatever they're doing more easily at, say, 12:30 P.M. to go to lunch, or at 5:00 P.M. to go home.

The realm-specific association of a "task" orientation with home is not necessary, either. Those of us with young children quickly discover that they (like us) do best when they're never too hungry or too tired. However, since children are incapable of regulating their eating and sleeping in the requisite manner, adults who operate in a scheduled world must develop and follow schedules for their children. We must start making dinner by a certain time, serve it by a certain time, get a bath ready and finished by a certain time, and finish dressing and playing and reading stories by a certain time. All this is to ensure that the child is in bed by a certain time so she or he gets up in the morning by yet another time. Any of our own "child-less" plans for the evening provide even more incentive for getting a child to bed "on time." Of course, even childless "couch potatoes" may adhere to a highly scheduled, time-conscious mentality at home. The beginning and ending of television programs schedule their evening hours.

Thus, many of us may well cast aside our watches when at home and do things in a more task-driven, unclocked fashion. However, others may just as easily rely more heavily on a scheduled, "time" orientation at home than at work. And at work, we may have a more task-driven rather than time-driven approach to the day, like some Lab scientists. In short, we may possess a more "task" or "time" orientation at home or work.

The precise, realm-specific sense of time we have at work and the one we have at home doesn't really matter. What matters is whether or not and how much these senses of time differ between home and work. Chances are, the more we segment, the more they do.

In fact, there is some evidence that suggests the more we segment, the more likely we are to experience time passing in different ways at home and work. This is regardless of whether our days and nights are more task- or time-oriented. The challenging nature and amount of activity going on (Csikszentmihalyi 1975), the desire to be there, the social ambience, the number of others with whom one is coordinating busy/empty schedules, and whether or not one is routinely waiting for something else to happen or someone else to appear, for example, contribute to the normative experience of time in any realm. Even others' levels of involvement and behaviors that create an image of busy-ness or laziness encourage us to adopt certain attitudes toward time. In other words, those of home and work may encourage us to frame time in particular ways—as "keyings" (Goffman 1974), perhaps, of a more common sense of duration. As we switch between these two social worlds, "house time" and "work time" may encourage us to speed up or slow down our pace and our experience of and attention to time.

Emma, for instance, who loves the time and spontaneous activities she shares with her two children and husband, says the time just seems to fly by in the evenings and on weekends. It tends to drag during the day, though. She works by herself in her own office most of the time and carefully, efficiently organizes and paces her work to minimize crises. Combined with her desire to be at home with her loved ones, the result is a different, slower perception of the hours she spends at the Lab.

Charles, on the other hand, loves the busy pace and interaction of his work day. Passing time at home is more problematic, for he lives by himself between one-day, weekend visits with his son. He frequently stalls going home with a trip to the golf course, or collects his clothes and quickly leaves for the gym just after arriving at home. He also watches a great deal of television at home and often goes back to the Lab on the weekends, lacking anything "better" to do at home, where time is "passed" more than "spent."

Emma's and Charles's more integrating counterparts make little distinction between time at work and home. They find that their pace, their interactions with others, and the extent to which they must coordinate schedules are about the same no matter where they are. For the most part, they don't seem to have "enough" time, whether at home or work.[13] But whether time seems to fly by or drag and become burdensome, it does so in both places, largely because both realms are so greatly intermingled. Success or failure, excitement or boredom in one "place" influences the experience of time in the other realm.

This is why the more we segment, the more pronounced are our patterns of when we do and do not wear wristwatches. Especially when one realm mentality includes an ever-present time/clock orientation

13. Csikszentmihalyi's (1975) work on the perception of time suggests that the fundamentally challenging but manageable nature of both realms may be an essential precondition for this particular sense of time across home and work.

but the other does not, putting on and taking off wristwatches becomes a highly significant sign of self-transformation. As we dress in the morning, for instance, putting on a watch may tell us where we're going, just like the clothes we put on. It induces us to adopt our destination's mind-set, for it symbolizes it. When we come home, removing this watch may symbolize and instigate a mental switch to another awareness of self and surroundings, including a specific sense of time. The more we segment, whether or not we change the rest of our clothing and accessories, the more pronounced watch-adopting and -shedding rituals may become.

The more we integrate, the less likely we may be to show distinct patterns in when we wear watches. We may wear them all the time except when we're asleep. Catherine and Marissa, highly integrating, powerful Laboratory employees, don't even take them off then. The only time they remove their watches is, interestingly, when they shower, normally a socially and therefore temporally liminal experience, to be sure. With so many waterproof watch styles available, they could easily choose to maintain time awareness in the shower too. Instead, this seems to be the one activity across both realms in which they are not required to keep track of time, by themselves or anyone else.

Another more integrating pattern is to wear watches randomly across both realms. We may put them on in the morning only when we
have a prescheduled appointment that day, for instance, an unusual event for a number of scientists and machinists. Or we may wear a watch at home when we have a scheduled engagement, but can't rely on a clock or significant other to know when we must stop, like when we cut the lawn, work on a car, paint a room, or drive somewhere. Whether we wear them all the time or only randomly, though, the more we integrate, the less likely we are to shed our watches the instant we step into the house at the end of the day or work week, as do our more segmenting counterparts.

Routes, Radios, and Rest Another way we encourage ourselves to make a specific transition is by changing the route we travel between home and work. Some of us choose different routes in the morning and the evening because of road traffic or crowding on different trains or buses. For those of us who drive cars, a stop at a favorite deli or store for coffee on the way to work can also call for a specific choice of roads in the morning than at night. Yet, in combination with other routine business, like stopping to buy a drink or food in the morning but not at night, varying trip routes may help us mentally orient toward our different destinations. Similarly, we may reflect work/home mentality switches through a weekly cycle of altering trips. For instance, we might take a different route home on each Friday only, in order to pick up a pizza, or each Monday morning to drop off dry cleaning. Here, again, the route (in combination with the task) helps trigger and prop up self-transformations.

But we may alter routes between the morning and evening or Mondays and Fridays even if there seems to be no practical reason to do so. It is common for Lab members to use two different routes between home and work: one for the morning and one at night. Moreover, the selection of this route seems to reflect and contribute to their wishes or needs to stall or speed up their mental transitions between realms.

People who want or need to switch into their work personae as soon as they leave the house tend to select an expressway or relatively major highway to get to work. Why? One reason is that its purely utilitarian connotations facilitate the orientation toward work. This is also why those who wish to forestall the work mode of mental operation inevitably select a tree-lined, windier, quieter or more local path to the workplace. For the journey home, similar desires to prolong or reject the work frame of mind influence route choice.

These choices simply reflect the kinds of associations we make with roadways, as described in Kenneth Jackson's (1985, 76) discussion about the design of suburban housing settlements. Historically, these areas were promoted as the antithesis of the city. As with every aspect of the suburban use of space and design, suburban architects and developers want to avoid invoking urban, utilitarian, work-oriented thoughts. These are signified by straight streets organized in square blocks. So, architects quite conscientiously design winding, tree-lined roads and parkways for suburban communities, promoting the perception of retreat into quiet, residential country life. When we choose between these different kinds of roads, we are choosing between the cultural, symbolic meaning of roadways. We use the resultant feel of the trip to help push us toward one end of the commute or the other.

A certain route also may contain personally special, meaningful buildings or spaces. Our choice to take it also may be shaped by the need or desire to direct our attention to the part of our self it evokes. Steve, for instance, chooses to drive through the middle of his small town some mornings, taking a slightly longer route to work because of the additional stoplights this entails. He does this on the days he's "obsessing" about his daughter's impending entry to kindergarten. The school is in the middle of town, visible from the road. Having just kissed her goodbye and still thinking about her and her "workday," he forestalls his by extending thoughts of her into his commute. On other days, he takes the quicker, more direct route to work, especially when he's eager to see someone there or begin a certain project.

In addition to specific routes signifying the direction of our transitions, a variety of other activities may change according to the direction of our trip. We switch between radio stations with different formats, for example. News radio is a popular choice for Lab members in the morning, especially for sports and traffic reports, but a music-oriented station is most popular in the evening. The former orients us toward the public, working world, the latter toward its private, leisure counterpart.

If we don't change our station, the station itself can signal the direction of the commute via its scheduled format features. For instance, in the New York City area, the controversial "Howard Stern Show" and its popular competitor "Imus in the Morning" are aired exclusively during the time when most people are heading in to work. The stations' features are quite different in the evening.

(On the other hand, some of the most integrating members of the Lab listen to National Public Radio [NPR] both in the morning and on the way home. Interestingly, the station features exactly the same type of programming [e.g., "All Things Considered"] at both times of the day. The lack of unidirectional, transitional support provided by this broadcast—or sought by its listeners—suggests that NPR's audience may be more integrating than most of the radio-listening world. However, even NPR offers distinct weekday and weekend programs.)

We also listen to CD and tape collections during our commutes but may change our choices according to where we're going. For instance, Debra is a scientist whose work demands bilingual skills. It's no wonder she listens to language tapes on the way to work but inevitably switches to classical music on the way home. Patty listens to combinations of news and country western music during the morning trip to work, but she watches soap operas on a small "watchman" television on the way back. The ways we use the technology available to us frequently differ according to which frame of mind we need to be in once we reach our destinations.

We may use our bodies differently too. On trains and in car pools, commuters often take advantage of the time out to close their eyes and rest. The more we segment, the more vital is the transitional function of sleep. Sleeping is private in nature, done in pockets of free time; it cannot be done while accommodating other status-related demands. It provides the most complete remission from the social structure and its demands (Schwartz 1970). Sleep also refreshes and puts distance between us and the activity in which we were engaged prior to sleeping (Davis 1983, 75–76). For these reasons, sleeping is a remarkably effective bridging activity between segmented worlds.[14]

Phone Calls

One phenomenon provides a striking contrast with commuting transitions. Cross-realm telephone calls do not allow us to slowly gear up or down into an other-realm sense of time or self. A child calling us at work or a supervisor calling us at home allows no "time out," no waiting period (Schwartz 1975) or nap to buffer our reorientation. These bridges between realms are the most brutal, for their instantaneous penetration into the recipient's realm requires an equally instantaneous mental gear-shifting. We must quickly reorient into the world of the caller when we answer the phone and hear her or him, repeating the process when we hang up and try to resume our tasks in the present realm. The moments in which we answer cross-realm phone calls are more like transitional "shocks" (Schutz 1973, 231) rather than the transitional "slides" allowed by commuting.

As we segment more, transitions generally become more difficult. This principle especially applies to cross-realm phone calls. And just as segmentation makes us want to limit other kinds of home-work transitions, so will we try to limit the number of cross-realm phone calls we make or receive. Rob, a machinist in his current shop for over 15 years, can list the five phone calls his wife has made to him at work during all that time. His older colleagues similarly describe infrequent phone calls from their wives, defending the legitimacy of these "intrusions" as rare, emergency situations.

When cross-realm phone calls occur, only two factors keep those of us who segment more from a disorienting, mental spin: (1) experience

14. Of course, sleeping on the train often is not the same as sleeping at home. Instead, people may take light naps, which are transitional by definition and from which they can quickly become aware of what's happening around them. Or they may simply close their eyes and rest while still awake, rather than forfeiting complete awareness of their surroundings. Because of its private, remissive nature, engaging in sleep while in public is a risky undertaking.

at making these instantaneous transitions, and (2) staving off full immersion into the caller's realm. Tom's younger colleagues talk to their wives more frequently than the older generation of machinists, for instance, but they use a few techniques that minimize their transitional stress.

First, several machinists talk to home each day during one or two of their breaks. A few wait for their wives to call while others line up to use the pay phone. Regardless of who initiates, though, machinists and their wives know these calls are coming, and these are the times they can discuss anything that needs attention.

Despite the ability to call or hear from their families at any time, many Lab employees talk to home at the same times each day. There is a very good reason for this. Predictability minimizes the transitional stress of cross-realm calls, just like routinizing morning and evening commuting transitions makes them easier. It lets us prepare for the cross-realm experience, placing ourselves in an appropriate mental state to receive or make a call.

Even better, talking during established breaks, especially lunch, provides the most transition time for switching into and out of a given frame of mind. Certainly, the pressure and/or need to immediately return to one's work during nonbreak time limits return transition time. By calling during a break, anyone can better accommodate and compensate for an inability to make transitions instantaneously.

Moreover, segmenting influences cause us to see breaks as relatively private time, so that we train ourselves into making mental switches at these times. Calling home during a break can be quite efficient, then, for we may have already made the requisite mental switch away from work and toward home. We can switch into and out of private, "break" time and take care of transition requirements for a cross-realm call, simultaneously. In a sense, we get two transitional activities for the mental price of one. Of course, it is precisely this mental price, not simply the temporal one, that makes us increasingly resist cross-realm calls as we increasingly segment realms.

Initiating rather than receiving phone calls also helps minimize transition problems. Like scheduling calls, this provides more control over when the switch into and out of an other-realm mentality is made. It allows us to optimize the timing of the transition, minimizing its impact on ourselves and our tasks at home or work. We have the best chances of adopting an appropriate mentality this way, as well as minimizing the call's interrupting effects. The more we segment, then, the more *we* insist on making the daily call home from work rather than letting spouses or children instigate the contact.

More powerful people utilize two additional strategies to minimize transitional stress from receiving phone calls. Both concern the screening of calls, allowing recipients to decide which calls deserve immediate responses and which ones can wait. First, the powerful use assistants to answer their calls at work, whether secretaries, receptionists, or junior researchers. These people buffer their superiors' needs to tend to the phone, including cross-realm calls. Even if standing orders are to "put through" family members' calls, the intermediary message from one's secretary that one's daughter is on the line gives a parent that much more time to switch gears before talking to her. And if one is deeply immersed in a realm-specific task, secretaries can always be told to hold all calls, preventing any kind of interruption and potential transitional problem.

At home, other family members can be used to screen our calls. If colleagues or clients have our home telephone numbers but we do not wish to speak to some or all of them at a given time, we can coerce family members to answer the phone. At the end of an exhausting day, already out of a bath, into a robe, and vegetating in front of the television, we simply may not be physically or mentally up to the transition required by an evening call from clients, students, or work mates.

Answering machines are the functional, inanimate equivalent to living assistants. Where employees are more autonomous and physically mobile, these allow messages to get through in the same way as handwritten ones. Some people at the Lab even keep their answering machines running while sitting next to them, screening calls in "real time." This lets them reserve the option of picking up the receiver or not, expanding or containing the interruption, and possibly demanding a cross-realm transition. Whether one uses live or electronic gatekeepers, tactics like these allow the better scheduling of cross-realm contacts, minimizing the occurrence and unpredictability of mental transitions.

Another way of reducing the transitional stress of cross-realm calls is to resist giving full attention to callers. While the caller might find this rude, terse conversations with a spouse while at work can be quite functional, especially for the extreme segmentor. Not only does this produce a deterrent effect, for a spouse will be less likely to call if repeatedly treated in an unreceptive fashion, but it also fends off full immersion into the home mentality while at work. It reduces the difficulty of the mental trip back again after hanging up. Conrad, a scientist who diagnoses and treats patients with terminal illnesses, has gotten extremely good at fending off immersion into his home self while at work. He is not only terse when his wife calls but frequently has no recollection at the end of the day of what their conversation was about.

As we integrate more, cross-realm phone calls have a less devastating effect. Calls are still interruptions, but they do not instigate transitional difficulties as regularly or as devastating as those of more segmenting counterparts. Only if a relative integrator is fully immersed in the distinctive, mental, essential core of realm territory will a cross-realm call result in a significant transitional problem. (Of course, an interruption from the *same* realm also may cause a serious problem in reacquiring one's concentration and bearings at these intense times.)

These easier transitions explain why, the more we integrate, the more frequently and randomly cross-realm calls are made and received. They wreak less havoc, so we don't need to minimize or schedule them as much. We'll receive as many or more cross-realm calls as we initiate, and the total number of these calls is greater than that of more segmenting counterparts. We're generally not so terse during these calls, either, welcoming chats and domestic news bulletins from family while at work and those from work mates when we're at home.

In addition, the content of cross-realm calls makes transitions easier for someone who integrates more. Whatever the origin of these calls, they tend to include talk about both ends of the connection. When extreme segmentors receive calls at work from their spouses, they tend to talk about only what's happening at home, with home-related others. The reverse is true on the rare occasions when they receive calls about work at home. There is more give and take about the topics of discussion for the extreme integrator, however. Thus, it is easier for these home-work negotiators to return to the realm of occupation after a cross-realm call because they haven't left it so far behind. The conversation, itself, is more likely to facilitate returning to the task that was interrupted.

Transitional Acts as Rituals

Just before leaving work in the evening, a number of Lab employees have made it a practice to call home. They have ritualized this act to the point where it is now an important part of their transition from work to home. Hellos and good-byes, drinking, eating, clothes-changing and appearance alterations, music listening, and napping all may assume a ritualized, highly predictable role in commuting transformations. At given points in our trips, we rely on these more or less heavily and more or less consciously. They remind us where we are, where we're going, who we must become, and who we must leave behind.

In *The Elementary Forms of the Religious Life* ([1912] 1965), Emile Durkheim offers a remarkable collection of insights on the transformational importance of ritual. He describes a "negative cult" of behaviors that separate the profane and sacred realms of social life. These behaviors stem from a variety of taboos and dictums about mixing the objects and classes of people who belong to these different, mutually exclusive and antagonistic realms. We follow these principles to segregate realm-specific elements into distinct spaces and times,[15] creating a mental, behavioral, and spatio-temporal "abyss" between worlds. This chasm maintains realm integrity by combating the "polluting" (Douglas [1966] 1985), intermingling of their elements.

Rituals, argues Durkheim, function to help people mentally transcend this boundary between sacred and profane ways of thinking and being. Through our actions and focus on the symbolic value of artifacts, we shed a given, realm-specific mentality and embrace another. Rituals, as "regularly repeated acts," are absolutely essential for us to "place ourselves within [a] sphere of action." Through their repetition, we renew the effects of being in either the sacred or profane states of mind, re-embracing our distanced selves. In other words, rituals help us make the transformations between everyday, profane selves and their special, sacred counterparts.

The segmentation of home and work leads us along a process with amazing parallels to the creation and maintenance of Durkheim's sacred and profane worlds. The boundary work of home and work creates and maintains these more or less distinct, everyday experiential realms just as religious rituals demarcate profane and sacred realms of being. For this reason, we also require visible, tangible, repeated actions to invoke and maintain either the home or work ways of being.

Commuting routines, for instance, bridge home and work. They allow us to leave one cognitive territory and enter another, transforming from one self to another. These often ritualized actions function as mental bridges between the mentalities that they help trigger and preserve.

15. See Eviatar Zerubavel's elaboration on the temporal dimension of separating the sacred from the profane in *Hidden Rhythms* (1985a).

In this sense, getting dressed in the morning and changing after work, or consuming certain beverages and foods at different times, are examples of highly significant boundary work. Their appearance during the liminal space and time of the commute is a logical manifestation of our transitional demands. Like the purifying rituals of Durkheim's priests and followers, these acts preserve the integrity of each realm, each territory of the self while allowing us to transcend them. As such, they play a significant role in solving the self-transformation problems posed by life in a highly segmentist culture. Their frequently ritualized enactment indicates just how important and useful these transformational acts can be, which is why we repeat them over and over again.

My primary concern in this work is with personal, ritual*ized,* or ritualistic, actions. These may or may not have the shared, collective meaning traditionally associated with the concept of "rituals." Nonetheless, I very much view ritualized action of this nature from the Durkheimian perspective.

Not only do I see such ritualized action as "a type of critical juncture wherein some pair of opposing social or cultural forces comes together" (Bell 1992, 16), but I specifically see it as a place where an *individual's* disparate social forces/realms of action come together and are made sensible. Moreover, a transitional, ritualized action accommodates the mental continuities *and* discontinuities of realms as we cross physical realm borders. It allows us to maintain a certain stability of these categories and self-juxtapositions even as it may help us create new ones.

(Routine behavior, for instance, is particularly important, for it triggers mentalities and reinforces well-established concepts, frameworks, and identities. New, spontaneous behavior, however, challenges understandings/categories/boundaries/selves. If it is repeated, conceptual boundaries may change, along with our understandings of these categories and selves. If a boundary-challenging behavior is immediately abandoned, however, realms and their relationship may remain intact, confirmed and strengthened by this behavioral test.)

Through symbolic activity, then, the combination of mental understandings and physical behavior becomes so much more powerful than either manifestation alone. Ritualized, transitional acts are a synergy of what is mental and physical, symbolic and practical. In fact, for me, any practical, physical, or physiological import these actions possess is superseded by (and is less interesting than) the mental, transcendent function they fulfill. Ritualized, transitional acts are one of the essential forms of boundary work, then, fusing what is cultural and personal, invisible and visible, as we create and maintain the realms of "home" and "work."

Conclusion

Boundary work may establish the extent of home and work or allow us to transcend categorical borders. Yet along each dimension of the home-work boundary, we find a continuum of options that let us set and reinforce our current position along the integration-segmentation continuum. The material I've presented in this and the preceding chapter, for instance, is summarized in Table 1.

But what causes us to make certain choices along each facet of personal boundary work? What encourages us to see and enact the home and work categories in certain ways, eventually resulting in the weight and number of our key chains or our commuting routines, for instance? To answer these questions, it is necessary to look at the structural characteristics and cultural assumptions of our home and work realms.

As a sociologist, I am most concerned with explaining individuals' views of categories and personal boundary work by looking outside the individual. Personal boundary work is not done in a vacuum, and it certainly does not reduce to some sort of biologically derived "personality" preference. However we currently think about home and work and their relationship along myriad dimensions, the situations we face in both realms continually constrain possible visions and practices. In both realms, we receive often quite specific mandates and suggestions about where and how we should place the home-work boundary.

These directives provide us with a certain amount of discretion in how we envision and delimit "home" and "work" along each boundary dimension. If we are given a relative lack of discretion by realm associates and ambiance in how we may approach the home-work boundary, it may mean we are forced to behave and eventually think in either more integrating or more segmenting ways than we might otherwise prefer. On the other hand, if we are given a great deal of discretion in how we go about our boundary work, we have more of a choice in how we behave and think, whether that is in a more segmenting or more integrating fashion.

A discussion of the workplace offers a first look at the remarkable influence of realm-specific people and artifacts on the places and ways in which we construct our boundaries.

Table 1

The Boundary Work of "Home" and "Work" along the Integration-Segmentation Continuum

INTEGRATION	SEGMENTATION
Calendars	
e.g., pocket calendar	two wall calendars, one at home, one at work place; no overlap in contents
Keys	
e.g., home and work keys on one ring	home and work keys on two rings; no overlap in contents
Clothes and Appearance	
e.g., one all-purpose home and work wardrobe; changing in morning and evening insignificant	distinct "uniforms" for home and work; changing in morning and evening crucial
many work- and home-related items in purse/ wallet	few work items in purse/ wallet
Eating and Drinking	
e.g., same foodstuffs and drinks consumed in same (un)routinized ways at home and work, throughout day and week	different foodstuffs and drinks consumed in distinctly different, (un)routinized ways at home and work throughout day and week

Table 1 continued

INTEGRATION	SEGMENTATION
|	|
Money	
e.g., same monies used for personal and work expenses, incurred at home and workplace	no overlap in accounts or uses of personal and work monies, places where they are spent, or their respective bills, receipts, and IRS forms
multipurpose bills, receipts, and tax forms	
Talk	
e.g., cross-realm talk within and about both realms	no talk about work at home; no talk about home at work
same style of talk used in both realms	realm-specific talk styles
People and Their Representations	
e.g., addresses and phone numbers for all acquaintances kept in one book	addresses and phone numbers for work and home acquaintances kept on separate lists in separate places
photographs of coworkers at home; photos of family kept at workplace	photos of coworkers kept in workplace; photos of family kept at home
coworkers come to house to socialize with family; family comes to workplace to socialize/work with co-workers	coworkers socialize together without families, in workplace during workday; family does not come to workplace

Table 1 continued

INTEGRATION		SEGMENTATION
|		|
	Reading	
e.g., "work"- and "home"-related material read and stored anywhere, anytime		"work" material read and stored only at workplace, during work time; "personal" material read only during "personal" time, away from workspace
	Breaks	
e.g., no distinction between worktime and personal time during day or year		distinct pockets of personal time during workday when no wage labor is done; distinct annual vacations when no wage labor is done
	Commutes	
e.g., "two-way bridges"; no transformative function		"one-way bridges"; crucial for achieving transformations between realm-specific selves
	Phone Calls	
e.g., frequent, random cross-realm calls; intra-realm calls include cross-realm subject matter		no cross-realm calls; intra-realm calls include only realm-specific subject matter

three

Structural Constraints and Personal Discretion: Work Stakes Its Claims

At home and work, discretion to do personal boundary work is offered or withheld in many forms. These forms may be quite specific to certain workplaces and families or more universally shared between them. More than anywhere else in this book, the observations, illustrations, and sources of discretion discussed here may be quite specific to the Lab. Other workplaces with different goals, organizational structures and work forces may have different policies, practices, environmental features, and reference groups that constrain personal boundary work.

What is not specific to the Lab, however, is the general dynamic in which these structural aspects of work provide a certain amount of discretion for personal boundary work. That is, personal boundary work occurs within greater or lesser margins of discretionary territory, which are set by the people and situations of work and home. These margins reflect others' ideas about where the home-work boundary should go, as well as physical possibilities for putting this border in certain places, in certain ways.

Throughout this chapter and the next, I explore how the margins of personal boundary discretion are set by social-structural, cultural, and interpersonal factors in quite specific and sometimes surprising ways.[1]

1. This means that after my analysis, there is still some variance in personal boundary work that is unaccounted for. This is because, within these margins of discretion, personal autonomy and biographies come into play. I shall leave that part of the analysis for another time, turning my attention instead to the places where sociology is most useful.

While the width of these discretionary margins may vary along each dimension of the home-work boundary, this is the space in which we must get the job done. Failing that, we may have to negotiate for even more room in which to place our idea of an acceptable border. In these cases, territorial disputes between realm associates and ourselves may be rife with the problems, compromises and power struggles that guide any territorial negotiations.

It's as if the people of home and work each form their own surveying team, marking out what they currently think of as the limits of their territories. Yet these surveying teams rarely establish their borders according to legal, pre-established monuments, subdivision property sizes, contracts, or deeds. Unionized labor with well-established contractual trajectories may be the only workers who have the clearly established, analogous borders that guide real estate surveyors' work. Rather, workplaces and households provide a range of mostly uncodified, customary expectations about where each realm begins and ends.

This leaves a lifelong potential for conflict, compromise, and change about where and how we place the actual dividing line. It also leaves the possibility, albeit a far less probable one, that we'll never experience any of this conflict and resolution. If the independently drawn borders of either realm neither meet nor overlap at any point in time, these margins may remain quite tacit and informal and the constraints guiding personal boundary work will remain largely unnoticed.

The discretion to do boundary work is analytically separate from mandates to do a specific kind of boundary work. It may be fairly obvious, for instance, that a boss or spouse who insists that we segment realms at building thresholds does not give us much discretion in how we do our boundary work. Yet discretion is not the same as the mandate to do more integrating work, either. If that same boss or spouse demands that we entertain colleagues in our home, talk about the work over dinner and through vacation, or bring our family along to corporate business meetings, they are not granting personal boundary discretion, either; they are only inverting more common kinds of mandates.

A closer look at "bureaucratic," "greedy," and "discretionary" workplaces makes this point clearer. So do the following discussions of various Lab policies, including time accounting procedures for employees, the sending and receiving of mail and telephone calls, and the assignment of different kinds of work space to different people. Different workplace reference groups also place brackets around Lab members' boundary discretion, all the while encouraging them to be more or less integrating. Finally, I explore the discretionary effect of the physical work environment and the nature of the work we do there, to see how this might bestow or withhold personal boundary discretion.

The "Bureaucratic," the "Greedy," and the "Discretionary" Workplace

The prototypical "bureaucratic" workplace is a segmentist norm against which all other discretionary allowances can be measured. It is an extreme case in which the workplace delimits its side of the home-work boundary so thoroughly that employees have very little discretion in how they do personal boundary work. Here, bureaucratic managers carefully consider and control the presence of virtually all their employees' cross-realm contents. Through stringent formal and informal rules about mixing realm contents, the bureaucratic workplace pushes us to distinguish between what is "ours" and "theirs," what is "private" and "public," what belongs to "home" and "work."

For instance, Gayle describes a former supervisor, who started sending out "antipollution" memos the day he joined her university department. Gayle and her colleagues were surrounded by faculty, classic occupational "professionals," who brought dogs and children to work, lectured in jeans and scruffy beards, seemingly came and went when they felt like it, and decorated their offices however they wished. When her new supervisor came on board, however, Gayle and her colleagues were repeatedly admonished in writing and in person for creating an "unprofessional" work environment.

By the second week of his tenure, Gayle's supervisor went so far as to undertake an inspection tour, pointing out all the "personal" items around their workspaces that "must go." He even declared the maximum size of the few personal items they were allowed to keep on their desks: small, "tasteful" photographs and plants. Violation of these rules and others, like putting artwork on the walls, making personal phone calls, and eating at one's desk, were now grounds for official reprimand.

It is ironic that this supervisor continued to couch his demands in the rubric of creating a "professional" work environment. As Gayle's story suggests, traditional, powerful, occupational professionals, like academics, lawyers, medical doctors, and architects, are likely to enjoy much more discretion than their administrative supporters in how they do their boundary work. (The burgeoning bureaucracies that increasingly employ lawyers and medical doctors may undermine professionals' customary power/discretion, however.) Whether self-employed or working in places like universities, professionals are more powerful than the administrative staff who support their work and institutions. Indeed, such professionals are more likely to demand and receive all kinds of opportunities that allow them to be more integrating than support staff, should they wish, including on-site day care and flexible schedules and workplaces.

Rather than a "professional" office, workplace policies like Gayle's supervisor's actually create a "bureaucratic" office consistent with Weber's ([1918] 1978, 2:956–58) analysis. The sense of self these policies create in employees is bureaucratic too. Workers are encouraged by policies like these to create compartmentalized worlds for home and work, moving sequentially between who they are and what they attend to over the course of the day and week.

The bureaucratic workplace is analytically countered by the "greedy" workplace. As Lewis Coser (1974) puts it, "greedy institutions" are those that demand the lion's share of our energy, loyalty, and commitment. My notion of the greedy workplace is based on this concept and manifested in the way it fundamentally redefines so much of our time and space, so many aspects of our selves according to its purposes. By extending its demands outside the time and space of the bureaucratic workplace, the greedy workplace also limits choice about the home-work nexus. Such workplaces demand that we be highly integrating, biasing that integration in favor of work.

For the greedy workplace employee, work is liable to be everywhere, all the time. It infiltrates so much of life that it may be consciously activated when the employee least expects it and when it would be unthinkable for the vast majority of us. Nearly everything one does, everyone one does it with reverberates from and through the workplace. Even one's family members become fundamentally shaped and defined by the spouse/parent's work. A wife becomes a "corporate wife," with her own corresponding career and a list of job responsibilities that directly support and allow the husband to proceed and succeed.[2] Children are present "at work" from a young age and are groomed to support a parent's work in myriad ways: from taking coats to passing around hors d'oeuvres, talking with, and otherwise enter-

2. See especially Kanter's chapter on corporate wives (1977a, 104–26) and Hochschild's "The Ambassador"s Wife" (1969).

taining guests; from learning to speak a special "language" to grading papers and stuffing envelopes; from learning to leave a parent alone so she or he can work to otherwise putting up with the emotional and physical leftovers of her or his work; from being shown off as a symbol of the parent's character and, therefore, her or his increased worth in the workplace to sacrificing material well-being and vacations without complaint; from running errands to working a cash machine, stocking shelves, politely waiting tables, acting as a professional surrogate, selecting a certain major in college, and eventually taking over the family business. Even the home itself may belong to the greedy workplace, granted temporarily to the employee and her or his family for the duration of their career here.

This kind of Orwellian workplace may not be so rare as our culture would like us to believe. Nor need it be so obviously "evil," given the way any U.S. citizen is taught to think. Consider, for instance, what we expect of the president of the United States, the average immigrant family living behind or above their restaurant, or even our clergy.

The following case is an extreme one, to be sure, but it illustrates how even an expectedly greedy workplace can push its employees too far. After graduation from seminary school, Mark moved his family to their new home in his Independent church's apartment complex. Fully

aware of and quite looking forward to the greediness of Mark's chosen career, he and his wife were soon taken back by the full extent of it in this particular church.

The couple had already resigned themselves to certain changes in the life they had envisioned. Ruth, for instance, had planned to continue "home schooling" their eldest child while taking care of the younger ones at home during the day. Their new church had a school attached to it, however, and they were told quite bluntly that it "wouldn't look good" if the assistant pastor didn't enroll his own children. In a short while, it became clear that home schooling would have been quite difficult anyway. Ruth found herself constantly baking, cleaning, entertaining, running errands, and visiting people, eager to fulfill the expectations of the congregation and her husband's boss.

Before long, the benefits of a more integrating workplace—such as a subsidized apartment to live in, a church car for errands, free school tuition, and free meals in the school cafeteria—no longer seemed adequate compensation. Mark was working sixteen-hour workdays, seven days a week. He had three days off in two years, each denied by the head minister but taken anyway. The family could never get away from the work. The sense of being always under scrutiny and never quite committed enough in the opinion of the head minister soon took a toll on the whole family. The couple became physically ill and lost unhealthy amounts of weight from the stress.

After two years in this position, Mark and Ruth left without even waiting for another job to appear, as had half a dozen of their predecessors. In fact, a classmate who had graduated at the same time and had also accepted a "calling" to Mark's church had left months earlier. The friend and his wife had reached their breaking point much earlier. (They had been able to, since they had no children to support.)

The final straw occurred when Mark and Ruth heard elements of their most private conversations, held in person in their apartment or over the telephone, repeated back to them. This happened just after they found out that, unknown to anyone else, the head minister had placed camera monitors and motion detectors throughout the church offices. Mark and Ruth could not help but wonder if he also had extended "work" into their phone and apartment even more than they had been aware of, through electronic eavesdropping devices.

Unlike the bureaucratic or the greedy workplace, the "discretionary" workplace leaves employees' boundary work up to them. There are countless dimensions along which specific workplaces may do this, as formal and informal policies support whatever choices an employee might make. The discretionary workplace offers options in terms of dress, whether or not one must use personal or work money for workplace expenses, the ways one can decorate one's office or home, make phone calls, take lunch or vacation, use workplace tools and resources, bring one's family into one's work, bring one's work mates into one's home, etcetera. There are no mandates.

The most discretionary workplaces offer options like telecommuting, for instance. (Again, it must be an option, not a mandate.) A telecommuting (or, better, "home-working") option gives employees an opportunity to mix home and work as they wish. They may choose to maintain a highly segmentist, traditional commuting relationship between realms. They may choose to simply shorten their commute, walking down the hall of their house to a separate office from "nine-to-five" while banishing children, spouse, and all domestic concerns for the duration. They may choose to work on the kitchen table and throughout the rest of the house, thoroughly intermixing traditionally domestic and wage work activities and people. They may choose to work neither "at work" nor "at home" nor during any set time of day or night, but at a separately maintained office space of their choice, in a community work center (generic office buildings or rooms wired for telephones and computers), or a privately owned or rented space somewhere else. Of course, to obtain the ultimate discretion in telecommuting, the option to engage in it or not must be flexible throughout the week, month, year, or even a given day.

The varying options presented by bureaucratic, greedy, and discretionary workplaces are easily seen in workplace child-care policies. Consider, for instance, the typically bureaucratic way of managing wage work and parenting identities. Segmentist beliefs generally result in resistance to on-site child care, eldercare, and flexible work time and workplace arrangements. This is at least partly because these practices allow home and work to be intermixed and better accommodated, ostensibly undermining employees' single-minded focus on work and a workplace identity. Such policies provide workers with much more discretion, which could be used to create a far more integrative arrangement than a bureaucrat would wish. A bureaucratic workplace limits employee discretion *and* ensures greater segmentation by refusing to adopt practices like these.

The greedy workplace is just as inflexible but in the opposite direction. As a precondition to working here, employees *must* enroll their children in on-site day-care centers or schools or keep them with them at their workspaces. Communes and close-knit religious communities, for instance, commonly expect that children will attend the independent schools they run. In a variety of ways, the children become a mechanism through which the group asserts increased social control over all its members. Indeed, one can imagine a situation in which an adult's employment hinges on their ability to present children who would also either work for the greedy workplace, themselves, or ensure that the parent would continue to do so.[3]

However, just as top-down workplace policies can demand a more segmenting or a more integrating approach to wage work and family, so can they allow for a much greater degree of choice. For instance, CMP Publications in Manhassset, New York, is a technical publications

3. In John Grisham's novel, *The Firm,* for instance, the law firm in question breaks into a new employee's house and replaces his wife's birth control pills with placebos. If she became pregnant, it would be financially more difficult for the lawyer to leave the firm. But, even more important, the child could be used as leverage to further ensure the father's loyalty and commitment should he contemplate leaving or turning in the firm because of their highly illegal and dangerous business.

company with the first private, on-site day-care center on Long Island. Lilo and Gerry Leeds, the company's founders and cochairpersons of the board of directors, are responsible for instigating the day-care center. It is their philosophy—and that of their son and company president, Michael Leeds—that underlies the center's goals, facilities, and activities.[4]

Nothing symbolizes the Leeds approach to home and work more succinctly than the immediate visibility of the day-care center. It is located on the ground floor of the office building, right next to the entrance. Through locked, glass doors and windows, employees' children—and, by proxy, their home identities—are visible to all who enter this "place of business."[5]

Space constraints originally led the Leeds to omit kitchen facilities for feeding the children. Parents supervised and fed their children at lunch time. However, the advantages to parents, children, and day-care staff that resulted from this approach led CMP to leave this arrangement alone. This is because each lunch time permits highly integrative activity at CMP, giving parents a chance to share stories, advice, and moral support and get to know each others' children firsthand. And, of course, the children get unique exposure to their parents' "work." They see at least some of the tasks and people important to Mommy or Daddy when they go to work. All of this occurs whether CMP parents take their children to the firm's cafeteria or choose to remain at the center for lunch.

Through their commitment to day care, the Leeds enable their workers to be more integrating *or* segmenting in their home and work. Em-

4. I am grateful to Ann Erbes, director of CMP's child-care center, for her insightful discussions and a visit to CMP's facilities.

5. During the last few days of my work on this book, the bombing of an Oklahoma federal office building that housed an on-site day-care center caused me to seriously rethink my position about on-site day-care facilities. It is apparent throughout this text that I am a strong advocate of these centers; the bombing shook me to the core. In my desire to see children looked after in a safe, happy, and developmentally supportive way while strengthening the parent-child relationship and increasing workplace productivity, it never occurred to me that my favorite solution could result in the horrifying deaths of those children and their parents. However, I have maintained my position as a strong advocate of on-site day care. A terrorist could target any day-care center located on or off the site of an adult's workplace. Moreover, the illegal, expensive, and risky system of child care provided in private homes by people who may or may not have appropriate training in the nurturing of children is an unacceptable, systemic alternative. Although it is decentralized and therefore not a logical target for terrorists, in the long run, this latter option is an even more risky, dangerous, and costly alternative for children, parents, and society.

ployees may put their children in the center, having lunch and talking with them and the other families each day. Or they may find and even pay a surrogate to sit with their children at lunch or refuse to talk to others even if they feed their children themselves. And, of course, they may keep their children out of the workplace altogether. At CMP, employees have the discretion to follow *any* of these paths.

CMP employees' opportunities for a more segmented or integrated approach to work and home are seen in other child-related policies too. While waiting for substitutes to arrive, sometimes there are staffing problems in the center. Because the Leeds allow all employees to juggle their schedules and be away from their desks during the day, parents can temporarily help supervise the children, if they wish. And although CMP also provides an on-site, "After-School-Care" program for older children, parents are free to keep their children with them in their offices. Older children are commonly seen doing homework, working on computers, and otherwise keeping busy in a variety of workspaces. Moreover, the Clinton Administration's Family Leave Act has no visible impact here. Years ago, the Leeds gave their staff four months' leave of absence after giving birth, holding their jobs and health insurance for the duration, should parents choose to stay home during this time.

Discretion-granting policies like these make it no wonder that hundreds of people apply for each job opening at CMP, from the most mundane to technically sophisticated positions. It's also no wonder that a standing joke has emerged: "CMP" stands for "Call Me Pregnant." Eligible to use the day-care center after one year of employment, newcomers commonly wait exactly three months, then launch into pre-natal parenthood.

Thus, CMP parents are structurally freed of much of the guilt and daily estrangement of many working parents, who have little choice in how their children may impinge on the workplace. The young mother, for instance, can simply take an elevator down to CMP's day-care center to nurse her infant. She efficiently returns to the mental world of her wage work and colleagues a little while later. None of the segmentists' bottles and breast pumps are necessary, although she could certainly use them if she wanted to. She has the *option* to alleviate whatever physical and mental discomfort might emerge from having to be either more integrating or more segmenting than she might wish.[6]

6. Apparently, providing parents with the discretion to manage their boundary work in this way isn't hurting the dedicated function of the workplace, either. Even

Consider the amazingly more common segmentist alternatives and implications for employees' child care in this country. The vast, vast majority of employers provide no child-care assistance or facilities. In 1990, less than 1 percent of all employers provided any kind of assistance with child care, including the most popular form of assistance: a small subsidy toward child-care expenses.[7] The glaring absence of even older children at work makes our culture's expectations in this matter quite clear. With such a predominant, bureaucratic approach, the discretion to be a "good worker" and a "good parent" in whatever way is best for one person does not exist in most workplaces, a direct function of segmentist beliefs in practice.

Policies that permit the selective use and minimal announcement of vacation days also create more flexibility in the juxtaposition of home and work. Lab employees may take their vacations in weekly lumps or in portions as small as a quarter of a day at a time. For primary parents, in particular, this policy is invaluable. It gives them the flexibility of using vacation days when children (or even aging parents) are ill, or even if someone simply needs a day off from the stress of both realms. And policies that ensure supervisors' receptivity to making part-time, flex-time, and flex-place work arrangements can be essential for valued employees trying to maintain work and home roles. Whether a worker is recovering from a heart attack; the onslaught of new parenthood; ongoing chemotherapy; a parent's, spouse's or child's illness; or the loss of a day-care provider, these policies help determine how segmenting and integrating workers can be.

In short, the workplace opportunities we provide and the practices we expect employees to adopt limit the amount of discretion each employee has for setting the home-work boundary. We increase the probability of a more segmenting experience, for instance, when we demand that workers take breaks at official times of the workday; wear clothing at work that is inappropriate or undesirable for home; spend different money on work and home expenses; not receive cross-realm visitors in person or on the phone; keep photos, mementos, decorations, and family fund-raising forms out of the workspace; keep work equipment and

during a recession, this company is far exceeding its projected earnings. For several years now, several times over the course of each year, this resulted in bonuses of equal amounts for each and every employee.

7. *SOS America: A Children's Defense Budget* (Washington, D.C.: Children's Defense Fund, 1990), 48.

materials in the workplace only; not talk about their "personal" lives during "work" time; seek social and athletic activities outside the workplace without the coordinating assistance of the organization; adhere to antinepotistic hiring practices and expectations; and be entirely absent from work for extended periods ranging from vacations to children's early years, because we give them no options to tend to home *and* work throughout the day, week, year, and life course.

One of the effects—and rationales—for bureaucratic and greedy workplace rules is to eliminate the range of scenarios that might emerge if boundary decisions were left up to individuals. Employers are sometimes afraid workers will take their work home only in the ways that cost the firm money and/or prestige, not in the ways that will make money or reflect well on it. They fear workers will bring home into the workplace in similarly selective ways. Where organizations can't or won't figure out who they can trust to do personal boundary work in acceptable ways, segmentist, bureaucratic policies aim to stop the flow of all realm contents between either place, for everyone. Integrating, greedy policies similarly aim to take choice away from the employee. And by encouraging the unrestricted flow of everything between both realms, it is also much easier for the greedy workplace to control where and when the line is drawn.

Privacy: Time, Mailboxes, Telephone, and Work Space

At work, the more we are trusted, the more privacy we are given. Privacy directly translates into how much discretion we have to do our boundary work. The more privacy we are given, the more opportunities we have to do boundary work as we wish. When employers restrict our privacy, however, they restrict the ways we construct the home-work boundary. The higher one's status at the Lab, the more privacy one receives, in all its many forms. This better allows workers to construct the home-work boundary as they need or wish.

Rosabeth Moss Kanter (1977a, 49–68) offers a useful framework to understand why this is the case. She argues that organizations need to trust workers more as they move up the organizational hierarchy, gaining increased status. Events and the job itself are not so cut and dry nor predictable at higher levels. At the Lab, this ambiguity includes unclear and variable definitions about a "proper" home-work boundary; a "proper" one seems to be whatever best gets the job done. Accordingly, higher-status, more trusted Lab employees receive more discretion to decide what a "proper" boundary is and what is the "proper" use of home and workplace resources.

Although many managers and scientists at the Lab are fairly integrating, quite a few take fairly segmentist approaches to their work. The point is, these latter workers have the *option* of taking more integrative ones, if they wish or need to. This is not the case for most lower-level workers, who are neither expected to take more integrative approaches nor trusted enough to be given the chance to do so.

There are quite a few dimensions to "privacy," yet at least one of these is a relative lack of accountability for our immediate whereabouts and actions. Not having to answer to others for where we are or what we're doing at a given time allows us to juggle commitments and concerns in ways that better suit personal realm situations. Accordingly, temporal and spatial accountability will be distributed unevenly in an organization wherever trust in workers' boundary decisions is also unevenly awarded.

For instance, as a group, Lab Personnel workers are trusted more than machinists, and scientists more than both of them. As a result, they each operate under policies where temporal and spatial accountability become less and less of a constraint on boundary work. Break policies illustrate this. So do the distributions of different kinds of mailboxes, telephone privileges, and work spaces at the Lab. These show (1) how privacy and, therefore, discretion, is used as a reward for those the organization most trusts and values, and (2) how this discretion may be used to support personal boundary work, whether individuals choose to be more integrating or more segmenting.

Consider, for instance, the varying segmentist and integrating workday break options available to management. At the Lab, break policies reflect the extent to which management thinks employees' vested interests are the same as theirs. The more management trusts workers, that is, the more they believe workers' "personal" agendas coincide with management's "work" agendas, the less management polices workers. So, as managerial trust increases, we see fewer temporal and spatial manifestations of enforced home and work segmentation, giving employees more discretion in how they manage the home-work boundary. Conversely, the less management trusts workers, the more breaks are formalized, to the point where breaks are taken collectively and timed. These latter arrangements betray the assumption that the full segmentation of home and work is both necessary and proper, since workers cannot be trusted to place appropriate boundaries, themselves. Thus, the formality of workday breaks and mechanisms to measure and enforce them is a useful, watershed test for how segmenting/integrating managerial assumptions are.

At the Lab, blue collar work groups often operate within strict, segmentist, authoritarian environments. Breaks frequently are taken collectively and timed, clearly marking the beginning and end of "personal" time. Machinist lunch rooms, for example, are vacant except for two precise, fifteen-minute coffee breaks and a thirty-minute lunch break. At these times, lounges fill and empty with almost cartoon-like speed.

This provides a brutal contrast to the use of Personnel and scientists' lounge areas. At the Lab, white collar and especially "professional" work groups take informal "breaks": personally initiated and ended and taken where they like. These workers are trusted to put in a "fair" day's work and, therefore, manage breaks as they see fit. As a result, these departmental lounges are utilized more randomly. They may have at least one person mulling about in them no matter what the time of day, but they rarely contain more than three or four people at a time.

Bureaucratically demanding that workers take breaks from work at particular times and places not only reflects segmentist views, but encourages workers to develop them. The machinists' break system, alone, for example, irrepressibly pushes both parties toward the segmentation pole. Peer pressure not to work through official breaks, employers' hands-off attitudes about break time activities, and their correspondingly autocratic attitudes over "work" time pursuits are the logical result of the Lab's designated breaks. Indeed, with a bureaucratic break structure and the attitudes and behaviors it promotes, newcomers quickly learn to distinguish between the time and space they and their bosses control.

Like break policies, other temporal practices at the Lab uncover a continuum of managerial boundary assumptions and employee discretion. First, any workplace time accounting procedures that hold us to the minute when we're resting, arriving, and departing make us extremely aware of which side of a number the clock hand is pointing to. Lab machinists' arrivals and departures are carefully scrutinized, for instance. They are verbally and sometimes financially chastised for skimming even one minute off the workday. Their extreme sensitivity to the clock is a logical result of this extremely bureaucratic policy about the classification of time.

Other approaches to temporal workplace accounting allow people at the Lab to come and go as they like, however, asking only that they get their jobs done. This approach encourages workers to focus more on the tasks they do, rather than the time of day. Lab scientists commonly enjoy this relative (non) orientation to time, where there are no official arrival, departure, or break times.

A middle-ground approach to time accounting, like that for Lab Personnel staff, may demand exact and reliable arrival and departure times but provide little surveillance throughout the day, with no official break times or durations. Even the timing and length of lunch breaks are juggled among work group members, trading off with and covering for each other to maintain phones and keep appointments. This kind of policy permits workers to develop a hybrid approach to time, a combination of an attenuated clock *and* task orientation while at work.

By heightening or downplaying the classification of chunks of time, temporal workplace policies encourage more segmenting or integrating approaches to home and work. An organization's insistence on a well-defined workday or a formal, collective break implicitly recognizes that there is a difference between its agenda and that of the worker. *Not* providing official, bureaucratic starting and stopping times, however, implicitly states management's belief that workers' interests are at least minimally the same as theirs. It simultaneously gives workers the chance to draw the home-work boundary as they see fit.

The privacy of mailboxes, phone calls, and work space constrains the intermixing of realms too. For instance, at first glance, a mailbox may seem an unimportant workplace accessory. Nonetheless, its presence or absence and its private or shared nature reflect as well as shape a particular mixing of items and selves at work.

At the Lab, scientists and top-level administrators have private mailboxes. Lower-level Personnel workers and machinists do not. Their mail is delivered to supervisors' mailboxes or desks and manually distributed to workers.

It takes relatively little physical space to provide pigeonhole mailboxes for workers. The failure to do so generally reflects managerial assumptions about two related phenomena. First, Laboratory mailboxes are distributed on the basis of workers' expected and actual correspondence patterns. Second, like temporal discretion, mail discretion is distributed according to how much management trusts workers to make their own decisions about how segmenting/integrating they will be.

Practically and symbolically, the sheer availability of a private, workplace mailbox encourages people to receive "personal" mail at work, just as the lack of a private mailbox discourages it. In the first place, unlike a collective mailbox, a personal mailbox symbolically emits the message that we're allowed, indeed, we're *expected,* to receive personally addressed correspondence. Private mailboxes are given to those who have (expected or proven) unique talents and roles in and outside the departmental community. It is expected that such "special" individuals will be known by name, perhaps even more than organizational title, and their mail will be addressed to them personally. For this reason, private workplace mailboxes actually are a sort of internal, organizational status symbol at the Lab.

But private mailboxes don't simply encourage internal, personally addressed mail. They encourage cross-realm mail too. At the very least, the anonymity of collecting mail from a private mailbox, rather than a collective one or someone's hand, quiets any hidden, segmentist discomforts about getting and using "personal" mail at "work" space, during "work" time. But, even more important, the organizational and occupational strata to which we belong may have historical, well-established patterns of cross-realm correspondence. New Lab members are automatically given or denied private mailboxes due to occupational affiliation, for instance, allowing and encouraging a given employee to adopt the preestablished norms of correspondence for similar workers.

Most fundamentally, though, the allocation of private or shared workplace mailboxes at the Lab reflects a certain degree of trust in how their holders place and maintain the home-work boundary. When someone cannot privately collect her or his workplace mail, it reflects a basic lack of trust in her or him to maintain an appropriate, that is, segmentist, home-work boundary. Handing out mail or lumping it in with other workers' items may be portrayed as a courtesy, a historically meaningless "default" practice, or an overt act of surveillance. But the upshot of these mail-handling policies is that boundary work via the mail is not left up to workers' discretion. Those who have private mailboxes are not only trusted to maintain their own views of an appropriate home-work boundary, however, but are implicitly invited to maintain far more integrative ones along this dimension.

Just as the handling of incoming mail gives more leeway to higher-status workers in how they handle the home-work boundary, so does the handling of outgoing mail. Here, too, access to Laboratory mail resources is distributed in a very uneven fashion. Lower-level workers, such as Lab machinists, for instance, typically do not mail items from the workplace using workplace postage and/or letterhead. In fact, cross-realm mail has acquired such a high level of contamination that many Lab machinists don't even drop their already-stamped mail into workplace receptacles. They send items strictly through a non–machine shop mailbox, visited during "personal" time. Workplace stationary is not available to them, either, tucked away as it is in supervisors' offices and desks.

Lab scientists, however, are free to use workplace postage and stationary as they wish, perhaps in part because the Lab could not enforce a segmentist mail policy with them even if it wished to do so. If a scientist writes a letter to her ex-boyfriend that spends most of its time catching up on what's happened lately but also includes a query about the conference he is coordinating, is the letter entitled to be written on official letterhead, posted with Lab stamps?

In fact, the Lab realizes there is a huge overlap between what's "personal" and what's "business" for its scientific staff. So the Lab simply has to trust the decisions each scientist makes in how to use Lab resources, including postage and supplies. (It is also quite common for scientists to use personal money to buy these items, though, so chances are, the Lab is coming out ahead in its mailing costs, anyway.) This is one of the ways in which the Lab's assumption of scientists' greater level of integration actually begets greater opportunities for scientists to pursue it. In return, of course, the Lab is acutely aware that it greatly benefits from the relative undifferentiation of scientists' "personal" and "workplace" information, contacts, money, time, and space.

In a similar way, the privacy of one's telephone calls and conversation space constrains the home-work boundary. Private telephone and conversation spaces at work give us more of an option to have cross-realm others call us there or not. More public space inhibits our desire and limits our opportunities for cross-realm calls.

When we know that others at work can hear and keep track of our home-related conversations, for instance, we tend to suppress them. First, there may be rules against these calls. In private space, we might feel fairly free to break these rules. But in more public space, we may fear the actions of supervisors who overhear us and feel compelled to correct us—or our conversants.

Andy, for instance, tells of taking a machinist's wife to task for calling her husband "too many times." He believed she was interfering with her husband's work and that her husband, too, was bothered by these calls but ineffective at stopping her. Andy answered the phone one time when she called and promptly took it upon himself to set her straight. Not surprisingly, she stopped calling. This kind of surveillance and interference might be seen as outrageous by (currently) more integrating people in more integrating workplaces. For Andy, it was simply a matter of doing his job: making sure one of his workers—and his worker's wife—kept the home-work boundary where it belonged.

Like time-accounting practices, workplace phone call monitoring shows how different assumptions about the relationship of home and work are implemented for different workers. Monitoring phone calls is a way of publicizing conversations, even if they take place in private offices. At the Lab, machinists have a more extreme form of monitoring than Personnel employees, who, in turn, are monitored more closely than scientific workers. Again, this betrays management's highly segmentist assumptions about machinists' time and space, mixed assumptions about Personnel workers and highly integrative views of scientists' territories.

Machinists' calling options suppress the making and receipt of cross-realm, "private" phone calls in several ways. Incoming calls are monitored through two phones at the heavy and light machine shops. In each place, multiple extension phones are answered by the shop super-

visor and tool crib attendant, whose work spaces are located in different areas on the floor. Recipients of calls are paged over a public address system. The effect of this arrangement is that everyone in the shop knows when a machinist receives a call. And the crib attendant and/or supervisor know exactly how long a call lasts, as well as one side of the conversation. (This is how Andy decided to intervene with his subordinate's bothersome wife.) Outgoing calls can be made during breaks on a pay phone located in plain sight within fifteen feet of the supervisor's office. The relative lack of privacy this affords is further attenuated as workers commonly congregate here during breaks and when they need to talk with the supervisor.

In the Personnel Division, calls made from the numerous offices are noted on a monthly printout, distributed to department supervisors. The frequent appearance of brief calls to check on children or touch base with spouses are not contested. Repeated lengthy or long-distance conversations are, however. Ostensibly, this is not because of the direct cost of a phone call but because a salary is being drawn for its duration. Of course, supervisors do not know the content of the calls, but because the call is to a home-related person, they assume "work" is not getting done at these times. Segmentist assumptions thus guide even this looser form of monitoring subordinates' calls.

The Laboratory's scientists and high-level managers experience little to no monitoring of calls. First of all, these individuals trust each other to decide what is the best way to use their time, wherever they are. These workers put in so much more time than they are technically contracted for that no one would dare ask them to account for how they spend their time each day. They also trust each other not to tax work budgets by charging long-distance, truly "personal" calls to the workplace, or at least to reciprocate by making long-distance work calls from home.

But scientists' and upper-management's lack of phone accountability also is grounded in the assumption that their "personal" and "work" interests overlap greatly. So much so that one cannot assume the "home-related" nature of phone calls even to friends or family. Amiable conversations with acquaintances, sometimes with no immediate agenda, are an important component of "work," no matter who they're with. "Chewing the fat" about an article, child, distributor, political rumor, job opening, or whatever helps establish and maintain good relations with people like past and present colleagues, suppliers, technicians, superiors, and secretaries. Any one of them could be an important future contact or resource and "you never know" when an important new idea or opportunity will result from a rather aimless chat.

In still other ways, a call home easily could be a "work" call for these employees. Of course, family members regularly provide detailed, work-related advice and assistance over the phone to Lab scientists and managers. But these workers also frequently push the temporal boundary of the workday or week into allegedly home territory. Work schedules often require a call to coordinate them with home schedules. And when a proposed work event interferes with domestic obligations, a "work" call may cover just about any conversational territory, as the transgressor tries to placate the transgressed. Accordingly, even monitoring scientists and upper management for workplace calls to a home phone number would be nonsensical. These calls are quite likely to be about work, directly or otherwise.

The availability of private workspace is a complementary constraint on the cross-fertilization of realms through phone calls. Whether in the case of a machinist, Personnel worker, or scientist, a lack of private workspace suppresses cross-realm calls, just as the lack of a private mailbox suppresses cross-realm mail. Those who share offices find telephone privacy violated when others answer the phone for them and/or overhear their sides of conversations. This alone may cause sensitive workers to tell cross-realm others not to call them at work or make them refrain from calling home during the day.

There are even more convoluted ways that a lack of phone privacy may cause us to alter our home-work boundary. The simple fact that our conversations occur in front of, but excluding coworkers makes some of us feel compelled to explain our calls. If our privacy isn't already totally violated by telephone and workspace allocations, we may finish the job through our own actions.

Lisa, for instance, is having marital troubles. She works in a small room with three other women who are, she says, very good friends. Nonetheless, confused and somewhat ashamed, she would prefer not to tell them the distressing details of her home life until she gets a better handle on them. Occasionally, though, she gets a troubling call from her husband or a family member or has to make inquiries about marriage counseling while at work. She then finds herself haltingly offering accounts of these conversations to her coworkers! The social imperative to ease the puzzlement and offense Lisa is sure she's caused by talking on the phone in front of them makes her repeatedly frustrate her own quest for privacy. (All three of her office mates, incidentally, are among the women who describe similar distress from a lack of telephone privacy.)

Americans generally believe it is rude to consciously exclude otherwise unoccupied people from conversations within their hearing range (Hall [1966] 1969). (This is why spouses, friends, neighbors, and roommates can make their displeasure with each other known by putting offenders under verbal siege.) So, given the kinds of workspaces they possess, gang office members frequently would rather not make or receive most cross-realm calls at work. More public space results in the undesirable broadcasting of calls to others, one way or another, possibly integrating realms far more than they might wish.

Private workspace allows us to better control our level of segmentation/integration in many ways. With more private space, people can visit in person or on the phone without us worrying so much about their impact on colleagues or coworkers' views of an appropriate boundary. We can decorate our offices and listen to music as we wish. We can tend to "personal" or "work" tasks as needed and/or desired throughout the workday. For instance, we can write anything we like—

a card, letter, poem, bank deposit slip, memo, article, or grant proposal—free from scrutiny and any voiced or implied accusations of "polluting" behavior. If we need a break or simply don't feel like tending to another item, we can read anything we like with the same freedom. Take away that freedom, and the home-work boundary reverts from a personal matter to an institutional one.

Boundary Reference Groups

Scientific work is the focus of the Laboratory, with scientists located in over a dozen scientific departments. After the university model, scientists mostly conduct independent research agendas in these departments, dedicated to each of the traditional natural sciences and a few subdisciplines. Some departments focus on the development of certain large-scale, collective projects too.

Within all of these departments, as well as in their own, department-like "divisions," hundreds of "nonscientific" personnel support scientists' efforts. They provide services like police and fire protection; custodial work; experimental and procedure safety assurance; food, library, and recreation services; uniform, equipment, housing, and travel requisitions; machining; carpentry; welding; plumbing; groundskeeping; child care; the accommodation of visiting researchers; and the hiring, firing, and retention of employees.

Accordingly, the Lab's workers are distributed across a variety of occupations, departments, work groups, and hierarchical strata. Employees are first split into "scientific staff" and "nonscientific staff." The scientific staff consists of scientists and scientific technicians; everyone else falls into the nonscientific category. For example, a biologist and her laboratory technician belong in the former group; their work group secretary, the department's administrative assistant, the librarian who maintains their subject collection, the janitor who cleans their laboratory and office floors, the women who handle their benefits packages, and the firefighters and police who provide protective services to them belong to the latter group.

Scientific staff members are distributed throughout numerous scientific departments, according to their fields of expertise. Each department—such as Physics, Biology, or Chemistry—is further broken down into work groups. Each work group focuses on a particular problem or set of problems, whether defined by methodology or substantive area of inquiry. In Physics, there might be Superconductivity, X-Ray, Chaos Theory, Geo-Physics, or Bio-Physics work groups, for instance. Of course, these work groups often become known as "Smith's group" or some equivalent, defined as they are by the interests and power of the principal investigator, who is the head scientist of a group or project.

Nonscientific staff members primarily occupy service divisions based on their occupational specialty. Service divisions include titles such as Fire and Safety, Personnel, Machining and Welding, Library and Information Services, and House and Groundskeeping. Nonscientific staff members also may be temporarily "farmed out" from the spaces in which they normally work. Typically, they may be sent to scientific departments to work in laboratories or offices on specific projects. A machinist could spend two years off the shop floor, for instance, working exclusively with a particular group of scientists on some well-defined project. Others, like secretaries, may be hired directly by a department or work group and report directly to the department chairperson or a principal investigator. Like scientists' departments, each nonscientific, service division is further broken down into work groups. In Personnel, for instance, people are assigned to "departments" that are work groups with names such as Employee Records, Salaries and Compensation, Recreation, Benefits, and Contracts and Grievances.

Across departments, divisions, and work groups, Lab workers are further divided by hierarchical position within each of these groupings. Scientific departments sport chairpersons, followed by associate chairpersons, who generally help with the administrative requirements of the chair. Below them are the principal investigators, who serve as work group leaders regardless of their seniority within the Lab itself. (A scientist's title and tenure at the Lab are generally independent of her or his present hierarchical position within the department.)

Nonscientific divisions have similar rankings, but title and tenure are more closely linked. A division's "top dog" may have a title such as general supervisor, general manager, head, or division director. They too may have a number of assistants to handle administrative or supervisory matters. These assistants (the division directors' personal staff) along with department (work group) managers, report to the division director. Department managers and division assistants are generally the most senior people within the work group or division. The rest of the employees report to the department (work group) leaders.

As a whole, the Lab is a tremendously conscientious and evermore family-friendly employer. Employees are well-paid, receiving tremendous benefits and job security. The Lab is constantly involved in introspective assessments of how well employees are treated. Management consistently pursues policies and programs that might increase the quality of employees' work and home lives, allowing them to recruit and retain a highly skilled, highly dedicated work force. Certain groups of workers are achieving evermore discretion in how they are permitted to do their boundary work as managers adopt flex-time, flex-place, and child-care programs.

Compared to many places they've worked, it is a relief, often a joy for people to work here. Many feel as if they're part of a treasured, hard-working, high-profile, and successful community. They proclaim a distinct loyalty to the Lab, if not their particular coworkers or supervisor.

Nonetheless, within the confines of broader workplace norms, rules, and guidelines about employee discretion in the use of workplace time, space, and resources come from a number of sources. The Lab's overall ambiance, policies, and resources exert distinct pressure on where and how all Lab employees draw the home-work boundary. But layered onto and in-between these constraints are those of occupational groups, departments, work groups, and organizational strata. For each employee, these are ever-smaller and more immediate, concentric circles of possibilities and expectations.

Some of these groups are more bureaucratic/segmenting. Some are more greedy/integrating in their expectations and policies. And some bestow great amounts of discretion on their members to handle the home-work boundary as they wish. All of them serve as reference groups for members, in Shibutani's (1955; 1962) sense of the term. Through their informal and formal expectations, these groups provide distinct perspectives on the home-work boundary, informing and constraining Lab members' choices even as individuals make them.

Occupations

At the Lab, the boundary expectations of an employee's occupational reference group often supersede department or work group guidelines. For instance, a department's technicians follow the sick day, vacation, and start, stop, and break times of their union, rather than the scientists' haphazard and often oblivious approach to these "entitlements." Although there is a range of segmentation/integration present among scientists, for example, as an occupational group, they clearly fall toward the integration pole of the continuum. Even when scientists try to keep most of their visible work artifacts and hands-on activity to the workplace, most of them socialize with colleagues at home, and all of them read, write, and/or think about their work at home. For this group, the time and space of home and work are truly the most interchangeable and malleable, exemplified best by all the spouses at the Lab who are also each others' scientific collaborators.

At the other end of the continuum, machinists take the prize for home-work segmentation. Again, there is a small range of variation here, but the majority of these workers are strict segmentors, unequivocally drawing a bold, indelible line between realms. The machinist who socializes with coworkers or regularly thinks about his work outside the shop is a glaring exception not the rule. In fact, machinists are fired and management demoted for failing to keep "personal" and "Laboratory" interests, equipment, time, and space distinct. Policies like these cannot result in anything *but* strict segmentors.

Occupational variations like these are not only due to employees' current workplace policies and norms. Pre-job and on-the-job training for our chosen occupations also provides us with clear messages about where we should expect the home-work boundary to be drawn. Scientists, for instance, learn early in their education to expect highly integrative lives during and after formal schooling. Their teachers' lifestyles provide role models for them, while patterns of undergraduate and graduate student life give them years of practice at becoming more integrative in how they see time, space, and self.

Just by adopting typical student behavior, scientists-in-training shatter the segmentist's "nine-to-five," five-day-a-week work schedule. For instance, students study and work late into the night, followed by late-morning risings. They work through weekends and fit in leisure pursuits whenever possible, throughout the day, night, or week, in-between the temporal cracks of school/work obligations. In fact, the malleability and freedom of the twenty-four hours in a college student's day can result in hard lessons for the undisciplined. For college freshmen, the freedom to pursue leisure or work whenever one likes also provides the freedom to "fail out." "ABD" graduate students, wallowing in unscheduled, post-course work and predissertation limbo, also may find out that a structured day and week can be quite desirable. Moreover, university students pursue leisure and develop friendships, sexual relations, political and religious affiliations, and living arrangements with the same people with whom they work, based on classroom, cohort, and other student group memberships.

Lab machinists, however, expect highly segmenting lives based on their early experiences as apprentices in the trade. From the beginning, they absorb management's and/or the union's stance about the incontestable difference between workers' and owners' spatial and temporal turf. On their first day, machinist apprentices typically clock in and out of work, beginning a lifetime of being sensitive to and held accountable for the classification of minutes. (As Thompson [1967] argues, time clocks were installed in early manufactories precisely to instill this sensitivity to time.) The way machinists take work breaks, the clothing they wear, the way they are paid, the personal provision of toolboxes, etcetera, all reinforce a clear division of time and space.

Colleagues' stories about machine shops all over the country also emphasize the public/private distinction in their lives and warn young machinists of accidentally or intentionally violating segmentist guidelines. For instance, Ed will not discuss any of his private life or his "private" tricks of the trade when he's at work. He adopted this stance early in his training, the result of a few things he saw in the workplace. To begin with, Ed knows machinists who were formally reprimanded and even fired when management found out they were "moonlighting" at other jobs. In his first place of work, Ed says management was always looking for an excuse to dock a worker's pay or to replace someone with a cheaper, younger guy. As reprehensible as he found his managers, the lesson for Ed was simple: a smart machinist keeps his mouth shut about *anything* he
does after working time, whether it's moonlighting, having a baby, managing a Little League team, or whatever. The less management knows, the less ammunition it has to use against you. If you don't let managers (or coworkers, who could accidentally betray you) know what you do on "your" time, management can't give you such a hard time about "their" time.

As an apprentice, Ed also learned to keep his machining logic and techniques to himself. Ed was trained by a smart, kindly man who taught him everything he could, based on thirty years of machining. Bright and personable himself, Ed eagerly listened and quickly picked up the trade, teasing out everything he could from his teacher.

Ed became quite a competent machinist in about a year's time, a result of his hard study and his teacher's excellent attention. He did not equal his tutor's skill, but he was quite an acceptable colleague and soon made about two-thirds of his teacher's salary. One day, his boss walked out of the office, approached Ed and his teacher, and fired the older gentleman on the spot. Ed, he informed the ex-employee, would take over his position as he was now a "better" machinist.

Now, Ed and his teacher both knew this was absurd. The only reason the older fellow was fired was because Ed reached an acceptable level of competence and could now replace his teacher for less money. Despite the offer of a substantial raise, Ed left this place of work three weeks later, once he found a position elsewhere.

Before he had even finished his apprenticeship, then, Ed learned at least one important lesson: don't tell anybody anything at work, unless you absolutely must. Whether the information is about home or work, your time or theirs, keep your mouth shut. This is essential to keep the line firmly drawn between "your" self and the one that "belongs" to them.

Dennis tells stories with similar morals from his years in the machining trade. One time (he doesn't know what came over him), he decided to throw a party for coworkers at his beautiful, spacious home. The events of that night only confirmed the error of his judgment and the segmentist principle he "should" have maintained. Several coworkers got drunk, embarrassing him and themselves with their behavior. That his family had to see this was unforgivable. One person even ran his car across the carefully tended lawn, leaving deep gashes in the yard as a souvenir. According to Dennis, the lesson of the evening was the same one he'd known since his apprenticeship: home and work don't, and won't ever, mix.

Dennis also tells of the time a supervisor was officially reprimanded and demoted. Rumor had it that this supervisor quietly turned his back when a worker repeatedly made an unforgivable infraction of workplace policy by lying on his time card. Rumor further had it that the reason the supervisor covered this up was because he and the worker socialized outside the workplace; they were friends.

As Dennis tells it, if the supervisor had not had the bad sense to become friendly with the machinist in the first place, none of this would have happened. This supervisor "deserved" his punishment for the same reason Dennis "deserved" the ruts in his yard: they both were "stupid enough" to violate a "correct"—that is, highly segmentist—home-work boundary. For Dennis, these later events simply reinforce the boundary lessons of his apprentice years.

When we move between specific jobs within an occupation, we may confirm or attenuate boundary expectations from pre-job, occupational training. When scientists move between positions, for example, they discover consistencies and slight variations in occupational boundary expectations. Many of the Lab's scientists possess international, multi-workplace careers, with experiences in the United States and West and East European countries. These workers provide surprisingly consistent descriptions of different boundary expectations between these places of work. Overall, they paint a picture in which American science institutions expect a greater degree of home-work integration from their members than their West and East European counterparts.

For instance, Lab scientists claim it is relatively common for European laboratories to actually prevent scientists from doing certain kinds of work on weekends. Although buildings and offices may be accessible, it may be impossible to obtain other necessary resources. Access to a mainframe computer may be denied. Scientists may not be able to refill liquid nitrogen and helium dewars, necessary to keep experiments going. Stock rooms and technical libraries may be closed. Institutional lights and hot water may be turned off. Technicians and other support staff may be unavailable.

During weekends, scientists working in the United States may very well choose to ignore the parts of their work that require these resources. However, Lab scientists say that in the United States, there is a relatively consistent availability of these resources, twenty-four hours a day, seven days a week. Thus, for scientists in the United States, the choice not to work at certain times is more of a personal boundary decision than an institutional one.

Naturally, there are many other work-related tasks that scientists working in highly constrained, European institutions could do over the weekends. Thinking about one's work, for instance, requires nothing in the way of institutional resources. In fact, some Lab scientists believe the relative scarcity of experimental and computational resources generally encourages European (and Asian) scientists to be very careful planners. They are forced to spend a great deal of time thinking about each experiment precisely because there are so few opportunities and resources to actually run experiments.

For example, scientists working in economically strapped countries sometimes are allotted only one or two weeks per every one or two years to use an experimental facility. In addition, the most fundamental stock room supplies may be scarce, like copper and glass tubing, stainless steel, and nuts and bolts. It may take six months to requisition and acquire a certain chemical or flange, or an entire year for a vacuum pump or titration system. For these reasons, careful planning is needed for each experimental component and theoretical contingency prior to requisitioning materials or beginning an experimental run.

In some countries, then, material constraints may mean that scientists have less control over when and where they do certain kinds of work activities. Even the ability to read scientific journals may have been and/or continues to be closely controlled in some countries. Original copies may be scarce and access to photocopiers may be routinely denied. Readers sometimes are limited to common rooms, where they may be observed. All of this obviously prohibits reading scientific articles at home. Personal computers at home are unheard-of for many European scientists, preventing computation, word-processing, and the controlling of experiments from home.

In contrast, consider Dave's delight when his work group first ran an experiment from a hotel room. Dave is a Lab scientist who regularly enters commands and reads experimental data from his family's computer at home. This time, however, he and his boss had to present papers at an important conference, halfway across the country from their experimental setup. With a laptop computer and modem, they adjusted the experiment's motors, read the output, entered new commands, and kept their experiment going despite being unable to physically touch it. The integration-friendly hardware, software, and telephone lines that this required remain unavailable in many countries, however, utterly preventing such a scenario in many parts of the world.

But the material constraints of European scientists are not the only influences on their differing approaches to the home-work boundary. Scientists who have worked in Europe suggest that culturally, European scientists have a more balanced approach to their home and work than American scientists. As they describe it, science is not quite as greedy a way of life in Europe. People reserve more time and energy for their families. (Perhaps this is the reason why European scientists do not display family photos at their workplace, in lieu of time spent with their subjects!) European scientists even follow the more customary, full-blown "vacation" patterns of Lab machinists and Personnel workers. European scientists apparently believe in taking well-defined lunch breaks with their colleagues, too, where they do not necessarily focus on work. One scientist even described the institution-wide practice of "knocking off early for a pint" while she was a post-doc in Germany, continuing the tradition she learned during her schooling in England and France. She is still somewhat shocked to see how utterly unthinkable this is for the scientists she's met at the Lab and throughout America.

The combined result of the different material resources and cultural expectations of American and European scientists suggests that there are overall differences in their boundary expectations and practices. American scientists are highly integrative, assuming that work will largely absorb and shape home. European scientists are also more integrating than segmenting. However, Lab scientists suggest that European scientists are less integrating than their American counterparts and more balanced in the weight given to distinct family and leisure commitments, on the one hand, and wage work, on the other.

There is also some evidence that boundary expectations differ for U.S. scientists according to whether they work in academic and academic-like settings or industrial ones within the United States. While too few Laboratory scientists have made this switch-over to tell if their experiences are representative of others', I find their observations quite plausible. Those who have "crossed over" suggest that industrial settings encourage them to be more segmenting than academic ones. These industrial positions were characteristically held in more segmentist institutions, with segmentist policies and supervisors. This, in combination with the secrecy mandated by uniformly proprietary research, led to scientists' clearer distinctions between home and work while holding jobs in industry. When the same scientists hold university and Laboratory jobs, though, that distinction lessens across multiple dimensions.

Machinists also describe some differences in segmentist boundary expectations when they move between "job shops" and prototype, scientific, or aerospace instrumentation work. Job shops are the most ruthless workplaces for machinists. If one was looking for evidence of Marx's and especially Braverman's (1974) views of modern wage labor, this kind of work and these places would do the trick. Here, machinists spend most of their time as machine-tenders, cranking out hundreds of copies of a single part, mostly using numerically controlled machines. Mistakes tend to be trivial in practice, but with exponentially worse results. Failure to watch a job during crucial times can result in dozens of ruined, irreparable pieces or even the destruction of an entire, extremely expensive machine. These accidents easily get a worker fired on the spot.

The epitome of alienating work situations, the only reason machinists work in job shops is for money. They're degrading, pressure-filled places, offering no job security, few or no benefits, and no opportunity for occupational growth. The rules are simple: show up on time, get your quota of work done in a certain amount of time, keep all personal matters out of the workplace, and receive cash or a paycheck in exchange. The machinist is treated as a mere extension of job shop machines and is expected to act that way.

Prototype machining and airplane instrumentation work require skill levels that are worlds away from job shop work. Here, the emphasis is on producing high quality work, often a single copy of a unique design. The close tolerances, intricate designs and unusual materials they work with define these machinists as trade "craftsmen" rather than machine-tenders.

Machinists enjoy higher levels of autonomy and pride in the more challenging, prototype work. Given more challenging work, more room to operate, and more respect by management here, machinists display a higher investment of self in prototype workplaces. This is key to their slightly more integrative outlooks here than when doing job-shop work. That is, even in scientific and aerospace workplaces, machinists have very segmentist approaches to their home-work boundaries. However, it is not uncommon for machinists who do hands-on, sophisticated tool-and-die work to have a certain level of personal identification with their work. Tool and instrument workers' unique work skills, the level of intelligence their work requires, their membership in the elite ranks of their trade, and the historical importance of their occupation encourages them to take a certain positive awareness of work selves home with them at the end of the day. In job shops, though, the very same men adopt an even more segmenting approach to home and work than when they're at the Lab, putting as much distance between their work and home selves as possible.

So, machinists and scientists experience some variation in boundary expectations when they move between work groups and organizations. However, these variations are never very far from the boundary expectations they internalize during occupational training. This suggests that by examining a given occupation's training programs and the contexts in which these programs occur, it is possible to get a sense of how occupational members will approach the home-work boundary throughout their careers.

The *lack* of such occupational training programs also shows the effect of occupation on the home-work nexus. In short, where systematic, pre-job, occupational training does not exist, the independent effect of occupation on boundary expectations becomes negligible. Local workplace norms become more important guidelines for personal boundary work.

The Lab's Personnel Division, for instance, is a kind of occupational microcosm. It includes salary and compensation specialists, medical insurance clerks, retirement counselors, grievance arbitrators, employee relations counselors, recruiters, records management clerks, immigration law specialists, receptionists, administrative assistants, affirmative action specialists, and recreational program employees and managers. Regardless of the occupation, most Personnel workers lack a formal credential that specifically prepared them for their jobs. Their on-the-job training is sometimes supplemented by a couple of workshops or courses on the "tools" of their fields. However, they uniformly lack the kind of formal, asituational, precareer, occupation-wide training of scientists and machinists.

For this reason, the independent influence of Personnel members' occupations on their home-work boundary is much more limited than machinists' or scientists'. Personnel workers' boundary expectations are quite protean, changing with the local norms of the departments and work groups in which they work. Their boundary expectations are embedded in the workplace itself in lieu of independently maintained, occupational traditions. This is why there may be such tremendous variation in these occupational members' boundary expectations and behaviors between work organizations. It's also why the move from one work organization to another may entail more of a boundary expectation shock for these workers than for scientists and machinists.

For instance, Lauren is a Personnel worker still happily reeling from the difference between the Lab and the manufacturer for whom she worked before. At the Lab, she does virtually the same job as before, with similar computer programs on similar databases. However, the Lab's more integration-friendly environment now makes "going to work" quite a different experience for Lauren.

In her last job, Lauren adopted the fairly high degree of segmentation that was expected of someone in her position. She had very little to do with her coworkers except for the workday and specific work tasks. Once she came to the Lab, however, she quickly realized that her new colleagues had different expectations. Most of them pursue more integrating options from the Lab's offerings, even if these are limited to neutral space, leisure-oriented activities. When her new coworkers invited her to join them in these activities, Lauren quickly accepted and began replacing her old, segmentist boundary practices with more integrating ones. Now, along with several colleagues, she participates in the Lab's ballroom dance club, her departmental volleyball team, post-workday medical seminars on healthier lifestyles, tennis, and lunchtime "power walks," exploring the local grounds while talking about so many different "home" and "work" things.

Other integration-friendly practices also changed Lauren's plans for the home-work boundary. She is stunned by her work group's practice of letting her take daily breaks and vacation time as needed/desired. With a husband on shift work, sometimes unseen for days, the ability to create long weekends or a two-day "weekend" in the middle of the week is priceless. She was similarly shocked to know that, should an occasional lunchtime break last longer than anticipated, she is trusted to make up the time on her own. Her new manager doesn't even want to hear about it.

Lauren was also surprised to see how people in her new work group talk about family and leisure concerns whenever they like. Brief phone calls to cross-realm others are assumed, and, careful to keep conversations short, Lauren now feels freer to make and receive such calls. Between this and the expectation that she'll talk with coworkers about her outside interests, Lauren's previous feeling of estrangement in the workplace is abating. Although she prefers to remain more private than some people with whom she now works, Lauren is delighted to have the option to integrate more and does so along several dimensions.

Other than direct, occupational idiosyncrasies learned in formal and informal training, our occupation influences where and how we expect to draw the home-work boundary in another way. In general, one's position on the integration-segmentation continuum is associated with one's occupational status within a work organization. The lower a worker's occupational status, the more segmentist that worker is expected to be, by her- or himself *and* others.

The Lab's janitors, lawn mowers, file clerks, and machinists' and carpenters' helpers, for example, are absolutely essential. However, they have relatively low statuses within their departments and across the Lab's occupational matrix. The result is that the Lab expects highly segmentist practices from them and structures their opportunities for boundary work accordingly. Workers in higher-status occupations, like scientists, are associated with more integrating expectations and opportunities. This pattern is present within Laboratory work groups and departments as well as within the overall organization.

Departments, Work Groups, and Organizational Strata

Some Lab departments are comprised primarily of members of a single occupation, such as chemists or machinists. Each exhibits general expectations for the home-work boundary that are consistent with the occupation around which the department is built. Yet, as the Lab's scientific departments show, the feel of any department may differ from others, even within a single occupational category. Departments' effects on members' home-work boundaries differ accordingly.

Regardless of occupation or departmental purpose, unhappy, oppressive, meanly competitive workplaces encourage us to segment more, just as unhappy, oppressive, meanly competitive families do. They make us want to mentally and emotionally leave them behind as we physically depart from them, restricting them to the times and spaces in which we absolutely must engage them. They make us hide out in offices and bedrooms whenever possible, relying on inner strength to keep our heads above a sea of unhappy turmoil.

Cheerful, respectful, and resource-plenty departments invite us to invest our total selves in them, however. They encourage us to thoroughly identify with them, embracing our families and personal goals from within their walls, and departmental missions and membership from within our homes. They encourage our extrovertive sides, virtually asking us to dive in and join the fun, bringing along all other-realm contents.

One Laboratory science department is the epitome of the former kind of department. An oppressive, somber place, it produces the feel of an abandoned building, even in the middle of the week. At all times, the vast majority of office and laboratory doors remain closed in this building, and rarely do colleagues engage each other even in more public places. Here, there is a complete absence of hallway humor and the chaotic, hustle-bustle that defines other departments. Residents even walk between rooms furtively, hugging the walls and avoiding eye contact, much less bodily contact, with other transients. Outside of lectures, the only public conversations I witnessed were brief, functional exchanges of information in front of mailboxes.

Cut-throat competition for resources and recognition and a history of authoritarian administrations have left this department's work groups pitted against each other. As a result, the entire building seems infused with unhappy history. Détente, with senior staff snubbing each other's staffs, work, and persons, seems to be the best anyone can achieve here. It's as if everyone is always wondering when, not if, the next attack will come, and who the enemy will be. It's no wonder that some of the bubbliest, friendliest people I met at the Lab quickly learned to tone down and hide their enjoyment of life when they joined this place.

The contrast of walking into one of the other scientific departments is like a breath of fresh air. The hallways of this second department reverberate with laughter and conversation, and one must carefully negotiate the clusters of conversants scattered throughout halls and stairwells. Office doors here are closed only when someone truly needs privacy for a discussion or analytical session. By keeping doors open, occupants signify their accessibility and amenability to their colleagues and administrators. Even the administrative offices are set up in a way that invites queries and chatting among staff and passers-by. Here, there is enough scientific and individual success for all and a community devoted to ensuring it continues for all, as a community.

Not surprisingly, scientific members of this department are uniformly more integrating than those in the first department, but in very specific ways. Although members of the first, "Unhappy" department are more likely to be married to their collaborators, their "socializing" with department members stops there. Most have nothing to do with their colleagues outside of the workday and place.

On the other hand, members of the second, "Happy" department actively seek occasional social activities with colleagues. These range from dinners together after guest lectures and attending out-of-town conferences together, to departmental parties and small, same-age gatherings at each others' houses. These scientists are also more likely to eat lunch together at the Lab cafeteria, several in large groups of a half-dozen or more. Aside from married scientists, staff in the Unhappy department rarely lunch together; only a few temporary, postdoctoral research fellows gather together on a regular basis, frequently talking about their plans to leave this place.

Members of the Happy department are much more likely to do wage work at home too. It's not that they do more work than members of the Unhappy department, but they do it in more places; they bring it into their homes in the evenings and weekends. Unhappy department members tend to keep their work in the workplace, spending longer hours there, rather than bringing it home with them. Unhappy department members prefer staying behind a closed door at the Lab rather than pollute their homes with relatively undesirable work mind-sets and artifacts.

In other words, members of the Unhappy department adopt more segmenting practices than the second department scientists for some of the same reasons machinists do. They insulate themselves and their families from the unhappiness of their department as a means of survival. They try to bring home only those aspects of their work selves and plans in which they have pride and to which they look forward. For the second, "Happy" department, this includes departmental colleagues, issues, and administrative work. For the Unhappy department scientists, these are precisely the things left behind when they go home each day.

The same principle also guides the practice of bringing home contents into work. Where work and coworkers are unpleasant, we may have no wish to let them see the objects of our more sacred realm, living or otherwise. The Unhappy department scientists, for instance, have markedly less of a tendency to decorate their offices with personally meaningful objects. Family photos, if there are any, face the scientist not visitors. And a step into their offices generally betrays little about the other side of their commutes, certainly not when compared to the Happy department scientists. For the latter, each office displays almost all of the following: collages of family and work photos, posters and photographs of leisure activities, artwork from travels, sculptures made of laboratory bits and pieces, cards from colleagues, and calendars of favorite subjects and places.

In our culture, the invitation, the option, to integrate realms more must be overtly given in order to counter broader, segmentist assumptions. Departments are a key organizational level in which this happens, where we get the message of whether colleagues care about all of us or just our work selves. And these messages are made just as clear through the social environment of a department as through any memos that might be written on the subject.

Where our departments are broken down into even smaller units, that is, work groups, these messages are further reinforced and challenged in a variety of more overt and covert ways. Laboratory work groups frequently develop their own styles of interaction and boundary expectations. While staying true to any formal organizational, departmental, and occupational guidelines, these even more "subcultural" norms further clarify boundary options in formal and informal ways.

Because of their immediacy and our feeling of direct accountability within our close work groups, these reference groups may be the most important for us. They directly determine how we enact the broader guidelines of organization, occupation, and department. This is the level where many bureaucratic policies are either supported or challenged, where departmental ambiance can be intensified or rejected, and where occupational norms take on more tangible, idiosyncratic meaning. As a result, even if we stay within the same organization, occupation, and department, the move to a different work group can demand a new approach to personal boundary work.

For instance, within the same scientific department, there are work groups who eat lunch together every day at the Lab cafeteria. Other work groups have nothing to do with each other at this time. There are work groups who regularly socialize outside the Lab, and those who have virtually nothing to do with each other in the outside world. There are groups whose members regularly give themselves "assignments" for the evening, taking work home and talking to each other about it on the phone at night or when they come in the next morning. Some work groups regularly join each other in their labs on weekends. Others treat the collaborative part of their science as a nine-to-six job and have no contact outside the workday or -week. And there are those whose families form a regular, important part of the work group's conversations and plans, while other groups know almost nothing but demographic information about their members' home lives.

Norms about work clothing and grooming produce the telltale "looks" of different work groups, too, reinforcing more integrated or segmented experiences between group members. Different work groups show different standards for the pronounced display of family photos and memorabilia within workspace, as well. And certainly our work groups provide us with normative guidance about whether or not we host and/or attend baby and wedding showers; birthday, retirement, and holiday parties; and funerals and picnics with our coworkers and families.

When a work group is formed, one or two individuals can be crucial in sorting out and promoting a certain vision of space and time, home and work. Once established, newcomers, eager to discern and follow the practices of their new reference group, generally pick up on these traditions. Continuity is maintained or lost as the work group evolves. New members join or replace old ones, and everyone moves along the life course, facing new constraints and expectations at home and work.

Life course position has a visible effect on scientists' extra-workplace socializing, for instance. Scientists who share similar positions in the life course are more likely to socialize with each other than with those who do not. Over the life course, we are constrained and concerned by factors such as the presence of young children, the absence of grown children, household budgets, the health problems of parents, offspring and selves, and generation-specific leisure pursuits. For this reason, a socializing schism, based on shared life course constraints and interests, sometimes occurs within and across the Lab's scientific work groups.

In some groups, for instance, this schism has the appearance of being based on seniority and hierarchical rank. Yet this is simply because seniority and rank among Lab scientists is strongly associated with life course position. Where relatively young scientists share the rank of older scientists but the life course statuses typical of their biological age group, they almost always socialize with the younger crowd.

Of course, a hierarchical strata within or across a department may well serve as the work group with which an employee most clearly identifies. At the Lab, this is frequently the case in the Personnel and Machining Divisions, where management lunches with each other, rather than subordinates. Because higher-ups within Lab departments assume and receive more flexibility in how they establish their boundaries, these upper level strata frequently exhibit more integrating practices than other members of their departments, with their colleagues' blessings.

For instance, higher-ranking Laboratory members typically enjoy the privilege of later starting times. They may work away from their desks and even at home. They may take longer lunches and other workday breaks. They may bring family members to work and make personal phone calls as they wish. They receive larger, private offices that may be decorated and used as they wish and possess reimbursement options for personal money spent on "work" expenses.

Of course, higher-status Lab members' work frequently, practically demands more flexible work arrangements. They are constantly taken away from their desks, attending meetings, supervising projects, and otherwise executing their jobs. They sometimes need to get away from phones and subordinates to concentrate on important tasks, and may stay home or hide out in a library as a result. They often are up late at night taking care of work problems or returning from a business trip, earning the right to later-than-usual starting times. And the expected purchase of guests' meals, their own per diem expenses, and monetary outlays for projects often require that they use personal money for work expenditures, with or without later reimbursement.

Nonetheless, the underlying rational for the boundary practice options afforded to higher-status workers may be compensation for something less immediate. In the past, higher-status workers generally have shown that they are fully dedicated to their work. In one way or another, these individuals earned the trust of a series of superiors. Not only have they shown great respect for the territorial boundaries of their work, but they have gone above and beyond strict segmentist principles, showing a willingness to usurp "home" time, space, money and/or self for "work." Higher-ups at least partly receive more flexible boundary options as a reward for their dedication and willingness to devote themselves to their work. They can offer themselves more flexible, integrating options, whether or not they take them, because as proven loyalists, they are unlikely to "abuse" them.

In short, when broader workplace norms are silent, vague, or negotiable, the work group is where they are most directly interpreted. Here is where we find out if cross-realm calls are really acceptable. Work groups let us know if we really can bring our pets, spouses, and children to work with us. They tell us if we're actually expected to invite colleagues to our homes, if we must remain accessible to our work mates twenty-four hours a day, if we actually have flexible working hours and places, or if we're expected to be at our desks or work benches at certain times, everyday. They let us know if it's possible for collective resources to be brought home, or if they must be left at the workplace. Our work groups commonly are the ones who tell us if we can follow maternity leaves with six additional weeks of part-time work. Most directly, then, our work groups set and bend institutional rules along a multitude of dimensions. These immediately and practically establish many of our boundary options.

In general, Laboratory management has concluded that practices that keep workers satisfied in their ability to balance the rewards and obligations of work and home seem to be what's best for the organization. This unquestionably requires an on-going flexibility in the kinds of segmenting and integrating options the Lab is willing to consider. It requires an open-minded quest to tease out just how much and along what dimensions the Lab must fundamentally trust its workers to use their judgment about the home-work boundary and where it wishes to draw the line for them.

Probably like many workplaces, the Lab is a mixed breed with bureaucratic, greedy, and discretionary elements. For the most part, and given a certain, bureaucratic baseline present throughout the Lab, this organization takes a relatively decentralized approach to establishing home-work boundary options. Department managers and work groups possess most of the onus and freedom to set boundary guidelines, largely according to how much they trust their subordinates. This is why such wide variation is found in the boundary options available to workers throughout the Lab. It is also why membership in these different boundary reference groups is so important in determining how much boundary-setting discretion each Laboratory worker possesses.

The Physical Environment

There are other aspects of the places in which we work and live that constrain personal boundary work. The extent to which each place feels different from the other forms more conscious and unconscious impressions about the character of each realm. More similar realm environments downplay a segmentist view of home and work; more different environments enhance it.

For instance, consider the different kinds of mailboxes we have at work than at home and the kinds of telephones we use in each place, and where they are located. Consider the availability and kinds of more private space in either realm. Even bathrooms, some of the most private spaces in our culture, are most frequently designed for one occupant, or at least, one person per activity at home, while those at work commonly accommodate several people at once. The fixtures, themselves, are remarkably different too. The physical features of our workplace and home contribute to our personal experiences and meanings of home and work in what are sometimes the most undeniable but taken-for-granted ways.

At the Lab, for instance, experimental scientists work in surroundings remarkably different from their homes. The shells of individual laboratories commonly house fluorescent lighting, cinder brick walls, linoleum floors, and slate-covered cabinets and shelves. These are filled with stainless steel, glass, sinks, rows and rows of bottled chemicals, refrigerators for biological and chemical samples, and myriad equipment set-ups, ranging from counter-top titration systems and plant growing stations to large floor appliances. Typical wall decorations include white-boards with schedules and assigned work shifts, the Periodic Table of the Elements, DNA and gene mapping information, yellow radiation hazard notices, photographs of projects and printouts of calculations, and notices for first aid and emergency procedures.

Just the doors on individual laboratories remind people where they are. Regular, office-like versions are plastered with access and safety restriction announcements. Some include punch code security alarms, to protect innocents from their own naïveté. Forbidding, submarinelike doors further announce bacterial and viral hazards and completely prohibit all but the most insistent from entering.

One of the large, collective facilities at the Lab is a breathtakingly huge conglomerate of sputnik-like shapes made from thousands of steel flanges, glass windows, and nuts and bolts. Steel and copper tubing is everywhere. Aluminum foil is plastered on everything, with racks and racks of electronics modules, miles of multicolored wires and hundreds of computers and telephones cluttered on tiny tables. Large tanks of various gasses, small preparation spaces cluttered with electronics and cleaning solvents, journal articles and reference books, and steel storage cabinets surround experimental stations. Hundreds of notices about electronics and radiation safety procedures, take-out menus for local restaurants, "Far Side" cartoons of nerdy scientists, white-boards filled with diagrams and equations, researchers' home phone numbers and poster displays of work groups' findings cover the cabinets and walls.

Without watches, workers are quite unable to tell what time of day it is here. The lighting, climate, and sounds in this glaringly white, almost windowless, clicking, chugging and whirring environment remain constant, twenty-four hours a day. Only periodic announcements over the public address system and the ringing of nearby telephones break up the relentless background noises of this place. Like moles, scientists sometimes emerge from the maze-like interior squinting up into the sun or visibly taken back by the lack of it. They scan the outdoor horizon to see what kind of a day or night it has been for the rest of the world; the weather itself is often a bit of a shock. It is ironic that a workplace so dedicated to discovering nature denies it so effectively.

It is also no wonder these scientists sometimes find such difficulty adjusting to their families' pace, routines, and conversation levels when they go to their suburban homes, usually a ten- to twenty-five minute trip from the Lab. A workplace like this contrasts vividly with residences, from the furniture, lighting, background sounds, and kinds of conversations heard there to the kinds of people encountered. The physicality of this workplace alone cannot help but inhibit a more continuous, integrative experience of realms, even for the most integrating members of the Lab.

Even the flow of traffic contributes to a certain degree of experiential shock when scientists arrive at work or go home. Access is carefully controlled in the Lab's large scientific facilities. Security systems are designed to keep out those who are unwary, untrained, and physically at risk. Because there are few visitors in these buildings, there are few opportunities to keep scientists in touch with anyone other than scientists concerned with similar things. This and a lack of windows so that even viewing the outside world requires a separate, purposeful endeavor, keep scientists focused on what's going on inside their buildings, rather than the rest of the world. Of course, this only adds to the possibility of disorientation when they rejoin their families at home.

The amount of danger associated with a workplace is an especially important way in which personal choices to integrate/segment realms are constrained. Dangerous workplaces may prohibit visits from spouses and especially children. Lab machinists, for instance, would be ill-advised to bring their children and unwary and inappropriately dressed spouses onto shop floors. Scientists who work in radiation environments or toxic chemical laboratories are flat-out forbidden to do so. Likewise, consider those who work in building and road construction, in "clean rooms" where machinery or silicon products are made, in fields infested with Lyme Disease–carrying ticks and where pesticides and dangerous harvesting equipment are used, in meat-packing factories, steel and chemical plants, coal mines and hundreds of other hazardous work environments. Whatever the federal and workplace regulations, common sense rules out children's and spouses' integrating presence in any of these places.

Work Accessibility

Of course, what we actually do each day when we go to work also has a great impact on our ability to segment/integrate realms. The way we do our work and the work tasks, themselves, is a synergistic outcome of the nature and goals of our work organization, our occupation, the department and work group in which we work, our hierarchical position within the organization, and the physical environment in which we do our work. These elements combine to produce the one general dimension of work with which I am concerned here: its accessibility. This is the extent to which we and others are able to access our work from outside the workplace, conceptually and physically. According to its accessibility, the nature of our work itself may encourage or inhibit us from taking it elsewhere, may give us more or less discretion in our boundary placement.

Most obviously, our work varies in the degree to which it can be physically moved out of a dedicated workplace. The tools we use and the things we produce may mean that parts of our work simply cannot be taken home with us or accessed from home computers and with home machinery. Items may be too heavy or bulky. They may serve as collective resources, prohibiting us from removing them for personal use. They may be confidential and we may be forbidden to remove them from file cabinets or safes. Distrust of workers may mean some items are simply off-limits and must be kept to the workplace under threat of "termination." (Visions of Arnold Schwarzenegger bursting into supervisors' offices throughout the country come to mind.)

Much of our work may be location-specific, so that, for example, file clerks, custodians, plumbers, and road construction workers simply can't pick up their work and do it anywhere else. Even if we could purchase it, the technology simply may not exist to let us do some things from other locations. (In fact, the less our work tasks are tied up in "things," the more we are able to do them somewhere else. The greater degree of integration shown by scientists and upper management, for instance, is at least partly possible because a good portion of their work is "thinking," a highly portable activity.) And, of course, our work may be part of such a collective endeavor that we cannot do it without, say, the rest of the assembly-line workers.

The accessibility of our work depends on its less tangible characteristics, too. The extent to which other people can understand our work severely constrains our chances of "taking it elsewhere." As Lab scientists and machinists commonly observe, people may have a hard time understanding what we do. It may be some time before even our own children are capable of grasping what we do each day, severely limiting our ability to include them in it. Even married scientists who specialize in different techniques or disciplines sometimes cannot "talk" to each other about the subtleties or most taken-for-granted assumptions of their fields. Likewise, those who must keep information confidential may find it so frustrating to effectively explain what's going on at work, they and their listeners may give up even trying to talk about it. In fact, if we think in a different conceptual language at work than at home, possessing information and tools there that cannot be communicated to outsiders, the line between home and work is almost automatically drawn along this dimension.

In addition to work's accessibility, even something as mundane but ever-so-important as the size of our workload constrains the way we place the home-work boundary. Our workload can be effectively or actually increased in numerous ways. For instance, two people with the same job title can find themselves handling it in entirely different ways depending on the number of interruptions they receive. By placing one person in a receptionist's desk in the middle of a lobby, and the other in a private office at the end of the hall, the first person's increased accessibility results in more interruptions. People who are highly interrupted in the workplace may well resort to taking work tasks home with them in order to get them done (notably women, at the Lab) (Nippert-Eng 1992b).

Lab Personnel workers are also subject to seasonal and project-specific increases in their interruptions and workloads. Increased telephone queries, drop-in appointments or annual report-writing and contract deadlines may cause temporary adjustments in their home-work boundaries in order to handle increased workloads. Moreover, economic recessions, organizational and/or industry-wide downsizing, war, new occupational scarcities, and even brief periods before we replace lost members of our work groups may increase our workloads when we're the ones who stay. At these times, we arrive earlier and stay later at the workplace, come in on weekends, bring work home for the evenings, and generally think about our wage labor activities a lot more, no matter where we are. If nothing else, the stress of trying to handle a too-heavy workload comes home with us at the end of the day.

Whatever workplace events might perturb our previous realm borders, our families usually tell us pretty quickly if they'll accommodate a newly drawn line or not—and for how long. In general, the power of the workplace to insist on its version of a territorial border is in direct relation to how badly we must rely on that workplace for income. The more we need our income and the more we need it from that particular place, the greater the power our workplace has over our families in deciding where and how the home-work boundary will be drawn. Our families may be more amenable to negotiating some points along the boundary than others, just as workplace members may be. But it is up to each family member/wage worker to straddle the demands of both realms, however even or lopsided their influence might be.

four

Be It Ever So Humble, There Are Also Surveyors at Home

Just as the workplace delimits how much discretion we have in doing our personal boundary work, so do our households. The rewards, threats, and admonishments for "toeing the line" may be based on different motives and desires in each realm. However, like our wage work affiliations, if we wish to continue those with our families, we must accommodate residential constraints, our family's and our culture's views of where "home" and "work" begin and end.

From Explicit Permission to Tacit Omission: Spouses and Our Realms' Reach

Within the marital relationship, the more powerful our spouses and spouse-equivalents are, the more significant is their impact on our boundary options. Spouses' attitudes toward our wage work, workplace relationships with spouses, if any, their views of our domestic responsibilities, their own work and domestic roles, and any psychological or physical problems they're having are all important constraints on our mixtures of home and work.

For instance, from the beginning of their relationship, Elaine realized how tremendously important Joe's scientific work is to him. Over the years, her efforts have ranged from those of a facilitator, enabling Joe to do his work better, to actually doing parts of "his" work. Their combined efforts have inextricably interwoven Joe's home and work together, creating an almost seamless, highly integrative existence.

Elaine has framed and hung photos of Joe's work in their home and even decorated one of his birthday party cakes from a photograph of a work project. She hosts and cooks for numerous parties with Joe's colleagues, talking about guests' work and family concerns as easily as her own. At these times, Elaine not only manages food, drink, and conversation but runs interference with their child so that Joe is free to interact with company. And at these times and others, she accommodates any visiting colleagues who wish to stay with them overnight. Elaine also suggests and organizes events with Joe's coworkers outside their house, often to celebrate Joe's professional achievements. The social invitations Elaine and Joe receive are entirely from family or Joe's coworkers.

At home, Elaine takes work-related phone messages for Joe and sees that he gets them. She frequently can supply the information callers need, especially on the status of experiments, papers, and talks and on Joe's location and plans for a given day. This is partly because Elaine actively encourages discussions of Joe's work over the breakfast and dinner table, on the phone throughout the day, and in the car. At these times and others, she translates Joe's endeavors into lay persons' terms for their child and extended family. She also shares this information in correspondence of the most mundane and special kinds, including the family's Christmas card letters. Elaine can explain his work so well because she also types and edits Joe's manuscripts at home and at his office.

As a result of her efforts, Elaine has a very good feel for the way Joe's work gets done. This makes her a valued adviser about his schedule, encounters with colleagues, and career trajectory. Elaine even plans to accommodate that trajectory by molding her own career around his job opportunities and geographic possibilities.

Joe's high level of home and work integration is also seen in the couple's household artifacts. Like her own work-related books, papers, mail, and implements, Elaine allows Joe to strew his work articles freely about their home, never demanding that he contain them to a certain place. She sees them not as clutter, but as evidence of their shared hard work and the centrality of these endeavors in their lives. Rather than "pollution," these artifacts are more like trophies of their integrating life choices, efforts, and successes. The frequent presence of their young son in Joe's office serves the same function.

On the other hand, Steve's wife insists that any work items that come home, like inscribed pens, electronics, journals, computer equipment, etcetera are kept in his home office. She never goes into this room and it is the one room in the house she refuses to clean. Moreover, it's only after their child is in bed and all the daily chores are done that Barbara permits Steve to go in there. Colleagues are not invited home, and when Steve must occasionally attend a dinner following a speaker's address, Barbara never goes along. Steve's work-related comments are often greeted with terse, resentful remarks, effectively squelching further conversation. Barbara also refuses to take phone messages for Steve, telling callers to phone him at the office, during work time. And if Steve is home when a coworker calls, Barbara tells him to take the call on his office phone with the door shut.

Much of what Elaine does for Joe would be inconceivable for Barbara. Barbara sees Steve's work self in direct conflict with his home self, competing with her and the children for his loyalty, attention, and energy. As a result, she insists on spatially, temporally, and socially separating his work and home lives. As she sees it, her job is to enforce, rather than blur these boundaries, as a way of containing Steve's greedy, ever-threatening work.

Hank, too, describes a wife who shares a desire to keep his work life to the workplace and their home life to themselves. In all ways but one, she's been remarkably successful. Hank has virtually no work-related artifacts in the house and never invites colleagues into their home. As a rule, his family does not visit or phone him at work and he dislikes discussing their endeavors with coworkers. However, the presence of a single, cross-realm artifact is a real sore spot in Hank's and Gloria's life: after declaring he was looking forward to retirement, Hank's next comment was, "I won't have dirt under my fingernails any more."

Hank believes that dirt is a "trademark" of a good machinist, which he knows he is. The problem is that Hank and his wife are embarrassed by his occupation. This is undoubtedly one of the main reasons they are such relatively staunch segmentors. In this context, both of them are continually frustrated that no matter what he does, Hank cannot get the dirt out from under his fingernails. His hands betray his machinist identity and Gloria continually makes it known how disappointed she is with this one failure at containment. For all their success segmenting along other points of the home-work boundary, Hank's fingernails let his work self constantly intrude on who he is, "contaminating" nonwork situations everywhere he goes. Retirement will finally restrict his occupational identity to a set time and place, pushing it out of the present altogether.

Anybody who has one knows that the attitudes of spouses and spouse-equivalents may be quite important for where and how we draw the line between home and work. We can usually count on our significant others to let us know exactly when, if not why, we're pushing the boundary too far in either direction. Sometimes, though, a spouse's impact extends beyond the actions and beliefs she or he consciously directs toward us.

Paul's wife, Jasmine, for instance, is at a low point in her life. The daughter of a wealthy, influential family in the Middle East, she grew up with a healthy ego, domestic servants, and plenty of money to spare. After an excellent education and graduate degree, she began an exciting career in Chicago as a junior reporter for a major news magazine, reporting on the land of her birth. She and Paul were married soon after and began their long-distance, dual-career marriage.

Within a year, Jasmine was laid off. Shocked, she joined Paul in the Northeast. It took weeks before accepting the fact that her only choice was to become a housewife; no other acceptable job opportunities or sources of income appeared. Worse, she was unable to cook, drive, or shop, living in an isolated, suburban area with no friends, no family, no mass transit and a scientist's limited salary.

Jasmine's quiet misery and disappointment placed new constraints on Paul's workday. She began frequently phoning Paul at the office for reassurance and contact during the day. She wanted him to go to work later and return home earlier each day. Jasmine's need for intellectual stimulation, ego-boosting, and companionship fell entirely on Paul, no matter what the place or time of day. These interruptions made it evermore difficult for Paul to immerse himself in his work. Whittled back to an eight-hour workday from his usual eleven or twelve hours, his wife's wish to talk and work side-by-side on domestic projects led Paul to give up his custom of working within domestic space, too.

Paul does not believe his wife understands the effect she is having on his work and chances for tenure. Nor does he try to explain it to her. He loves Jasmine and believes that if he does his best to help her through these rough times, she'll soon become more independent. He does not mind her intrusions as completely as he might either. Her present reliance on him often makes Paul feel like a better, more giving person and a more needed husband than in the past. As a result, he silently resigns himself to the new configuration of work and home his loved one seems to require, but which he hopes will be temporary.

Greg's wife does not intend for her difficulties to bleed over into his workday either. Yet the systematic destruction of Greg's previous boundary between home and work is a logical result of her problems. Greg has long looked forward to going to work each day; it is a reprieve from his family. It's not that he's crazy about machining; he's ambivalent about it, at best. He likes the most challenging parts of it, but probably because they best allow him to forget about home for a while.

Greg's children consistently cause problems for him and his wife. The children's drug addictions and associated moral and financial irresponsibility have long punctuated the family's malaise, which results at least partly from the unpredictable, on-again-off-again nature of their children's difficulties. In his wallet, Greg even carries a note his son wrote to him years ago, apologizing for his behavior and promising to try to do better. There are occasions at work when Greg takes this note out and simply stares at it, hoping that this time, this side of his son will come through.

Most often, Greg can handle the long-standing problems with his kids, keeping them where they belong, that is, at home. But Greg's wife has begun treatment for a serious psychological problem. She recently disclosed that she "made a deal with the Devil" when her sister was seriously wounded in a car accident. She "offered Him her soul" in return for her sister's life. Her sister fully recovered. Now Greg's wife is no longer able to contain the absolute fear she feels as a result of this episode, kept secret for so many years. She is terrified of death and of what she did. She is not very cooperative in working with a therapist, for she doesn't believe there's anything anyone can do about the situation. And her understandable obsession with her situation translates into Greg's constant worry about her. He does his best to ease her mind and take care of everyday things when she sometimes cannot.

Surely, neither Greg's children nor his wife consciously intend to reshape his "home-work boundary." Yet their personal situations have unquestionably caused Greg to increase his level of integration between home and work. As undesirable as this is for him, thoughts about home, evoking his home mentality, are now ever present at work, too. This man, visibly aged beyond his years, seems tired and beaten-up at work now, too, as his workplace self is slowly consumed by who and what he is at home.

Joy's husband does not seem to understand the constraints he places on the way she manages her home and work lives either. Both Ph.D. scientists, George reserves long hours for himself at work and at home.

He expects Joy to fit her work responsibilities into an eight-and-a-half-hour day, though, and take full responsibility for rearing their two preschool children as well as managing the chores at home.

Joy is astonishingly good at handling this. She is a self-described whirlwind in both places, and even her work group supervisor notes how difficult it is to keep up with her pace. By sacrificing all the "private" time her colleagues and husband reserve for themselves, she has been glowingly successful in both realms.

Joy obviously adores her work and her family. Yet she now faces the decision of where her career will go from here. She would love to pursue a prestigious appointment at another institution. But her husband's attitudes and practices pose two problems. First, she seriously doubts if George would follow her to another job for ego reasons, if nothing else. He is very interested in leaving his own institution, but apparently not if Joy is the reason. Joy is fairly sure that at least one of the universities courting her might arrange for George's appointment in another department. George, however, remains uninterested in even discussing the possibility.

Even more important, Joy has serious doubts about her ability to keep managing their children and home and also have enough energy and time to set up a research program and laboratory and oversee students' careers. George steadfastly refuses to do more around the house. He supports his "inability" to do more by leaving early and coming home late. He insists that he needs longer days at work and rest when he's home so he can "think." As a scientist who has to make a name for himself, he says, he needs a lot of time for thinking. As a result, from the time the children get up in the morning until they go to bed at night, they are entirely Joy's responsibility.

George's absence not only results in Joy's share of the work at home but in her share of the labor at work too. Her supervisor selects and plans their experiments. She carries them out. Here is where George's claim that he needs thinking time is not as absurd as it might seem. The more intellectual tasks of the scientific professions really do require such time, at least in small amounts. Unlike her husband, though, Joy simply has no quiet thinking time at home or work. While George enjoys a long, solo commute, a quiet, solitary office and laboratory, and the freedom to ignore domestic demands, Joy crams her science into a relatively short workday in a shared office and shared laboratory with a seven-minute car ride home. And while George has a wife at home to take care of his children and creature needs, Joy does not. As a result, Joy does not engage in the critical, definitive, agenda-setting aspects of her work, even though she knows her professional life depends on it.

As a result, no matter which realm she's in, Joy feels she must constantly struggle to accomplish minimally satisfactory goals. And she is convinced this won't get any better in the near future. Her husband has made no move to change his ways and she simply cannot get any more efficient in either realm. Moreover, Joy loves George and her children. She does not intend to leave them or lower her standards for the care she thinks her children deserve. For these reasons, Joy knows that her husband's attitudes and practices will continue to limit her choices. And she has no idea what to do about several pending job offers that would clearly benefit her professionally. In an occupation where work is greedy and a relatively high level of integration is expected, George permits and supports a far more segmenting experience than Joy knows she can afford.

Now consider what would happen if Joy and George worked together, collaborating on the same projects. Whether they're at home or in their laboratory, James and Chloe find their relationship an empowering cornerstone for the activity at hand. Not only are they married, but they are scientific collaborators. As a result, James cannot help but understand the demands Chloe's work and their family have on her, for he shares them. And his immediate, shared interest in Chloe's success in both realms encourages him to adopt practices that support her highly integrating life, just as she supports his.

The purpose of time and space varies constantly throughout almost all of James's and Chloe's days. James discusses Chloe's work at home, in their laboratory, or in either of their offices. He discusses domestic issues in any of these places. He covers for her in their lab when she needs to travel or attend a meeting and adjusts their work schedule when she must tend to her aging parents. And he provides dinner and shops for them when she must concentrate on her writing. James's and Chloe's vacations often are intermixed with professional talks and visits to colleagues. They freely delve out their salaries for work-related travel, photocopying, books, and office and laboratory supplies, as well as domestic expenses. These "workplace" expenses are even declared on their personal, joint income tax return.

As rewarding as James's supportive role and their highly integrative lifestyle is, however, Chloe has paid a dear price in her career because she is married to her collaborator. James's department chairperson was a long-time adversary of his when James and Chloe received their first joint, prestigious research grant. The chair offered Chloe nothing more than a technician's appointment to carry out this work at the Lab. This position was clearly insulting and well below what her credentials demanded. The couple believes it was an act designed to encourage James to leave the department, that is, an attempt to manipulate James through Chloe. They dug in, however, and two years later, a new administration finally gave Chloe a more respectful yet still temporary position. Her opportunities for future employment, not to mention her institutional retirement funds, almost certainly will be affected by this.

In short, Chloe's work life at the Lab largely has been shaped by her connection with James outside of it. A scientist of her stature, with a Ph.D. and numerous publications and grants under her belt, would not have received such degrading treatment if she and her collaborator were not so obviously connected outside the Lab. Of course, Chloe could not have won her present position without James's willingness to throw around his far heavier political weight, a result of his longer tenure and higher profile at the Lab. It took months of public fighting, especially on his part, to get past Chloe's initial appointment. But there's a very good chance that none of this would have happened to Chloe in the first place had they not been married.

After talking with their colleagues and noting how couples throughout academia are treated, I have the impression that the chairperson's behavior was tolerated by the rest of the department as the logical price James and Chloe should have expected for violating segmentist principles. It's as if people who have the "bad sense" to collaborate with their spouses should expect to pay a price for it; they should expect to be offered and accept second-class status within the workplace. Other married collaborators at the Lab incredulously tell stories about job offers from universities and research institutions demanding that they and their spouses share an office (unlike other department members of their ranking); share a single appointment (with one salary, one person's benefits, one vote within a department, and one staff member's worth of teaching and resources shared between them, etcetera); or, with a similar effect, accept one appointment for one spouse, with the other spouse informally granted separate office space, a telephone, photocopying, and the use of institutional letterhead, but no salary, no departmental vote, and no other support.

The idea that departments would suggest such arrangements to unmarried collaborators is absurd. These proposals, and their absence for unmarried collaborators, are direct, telling signs of a segmentist culture. They send a message to everyone that, like industrial plants that admittedly spew noxious fumes into the air, married collaborators may choose to contaminate a segmentist workplace but they should expect to pay a fine for it.

Of course, when departmental politics affect our collaborators, they also affect us. But when collaborators are also our spouses, workplace goings-on reverberate even more loudly in our homes and are taken even more personally than usual. For James and Chloe, happiness at home, as a couple, absolutely depends on their joint efforts, successes and rewards at their lab. One could speculate at length about the reverse: how much their happiness as a couple will affect their successes in the lab.

Thus, spouses' constraints on our home and work juxtapositions include a variety of attitudes, practices, and understandings that support or inhibit specific views and uses of the workday and -place. If our spouse provides us with a desk in her or his office, types, entertains coworkers, bakes workplace goodies, purchases our computer and installs the software, photocopies and/or mails things for us, it increases our level of home-work integration. If she or he patiently listens to and offers advice about workplace problems or puts up with and even shares our self-congratulations for workplace successes, it does the same. And if she or he flat out refuses to do anything like this, it encourages a more segmenting experience. But the constraints our spouses place on home-work juxtapositions also include less overt, "default" attitudes and practices. As Joy's case intimated, some of the most powerful of these have to do with raising our children.

The Sacredness of Children and the Primacy of Parenting: Kids and the Polluting and Purifying of Realms

The children of Laboratory employees exert a range of segmenting and integrating influences on their parents' boundary work. Young children are extremely segmenting influences along some aspects of Laboratory parents' realms. Their parents are much less likely to take wage work home with them or socialize with colleagues outside the workplace. But young children lead to greater integration along other dimensions. For instance, Laboratory parents talk about young children a great deal in the workplace. They bring photographs of and objects made by and for children into work spaces. Children visit in the workplace on Christmas Eve and whenever a parent takes time off from work but feels like showing off a child to those still working. They are regularly brought to sports and cultural events on-site. Lab employees have daily cross-realm conversations on work telephones about and with their young children. The effect of young children on Laboratory mothers' boundaries is more visible than fathers', however.

As they grow older, children's effects on their parents' home-work boundaries lessen along these dimensions. Laboratory parents begin to take wage work home with them again and join coworkers for dinner and outings. Yet the integration of home into the workplace lessens: parents do not talk about their children as much, nor do they continue to bring in and show off objects for, by, and of their children. Conversations about children dwindle, except for brief phone calls *with* the children to check that they made it home from school all right or to remind them of a domestic chore, etcetera. Again, though, this lessening effect of children on parents' boundaries and boundary work is not true for all parents; it is more visible for mothers than fathers.

Children's greater and lesser effects on Lab workers largely stem from two, often interrelated factors: the "sacredness" of Laboratory workers' children and the "primariness" of Lab workers' parenting. Of course, boundary-related policies in both realms and others' less formalized attitudes about children and the appropriate relationship between home and work are extremely important here. Yet one's parenting mentality and relationship are important theoretical bridges between these kinds of contextual elements in explaining the varying effects of children on parents' boundary work.

Parenting the "Sacred" versus "Profane" Child

Viviana Zelizer has beautifully argued the evolution of our current cultural view of children as relatively "sacred," precious entities entrusted to adults' care, deserving the very best from us. In the last hundred years, a number of cultural and legal changes reflect this transformation. The advent of criminal prosecution for parents who neglect their children, community safety programs, mandatory school attendance, the provision of city playgrounds, and giving children separate bedrooms and playrooms within the house are at least partly a result of seeing children in a more sacred light than before (Zelizer 1985).

Zelizer's historical continuum is even more powerful when placed perpendicular to and over top of itself at any point in time. That is, one view of contemporary (or any other historical moment of) parenting is to see it spread out along a continuum of how "sacred"/"profane" children are for individual members of a society. Such a continuum covers a range in which "sacred" views of children direct us to cherish and protect them at all costs, while "profane" views of children see them as totally ordinary beings, just like adults, unremarkable and unworthy of extraordinary attention or care.

In its extreme form, "sacred-child parenting" places children (especially infants) on a pedestal of the highest magnitude. Here, a parent's life is utterly devoted to a child's needs and desires, subordinating all other goals, actions, claims, and people to the child. "Profane-child parenting," however, keeps the child at a commitment and attention level even with everyone and everything else. The child deserves no "special" treatment, evoking no "special" ways of thinking or being.

The more parents adhere to the "sacred child" model, the more their parenting is defined by a special mentality, a special way of thinking and being, readily invoked by the mental or physical presence of the child. This mentality hinges on "taking the role of the other" (Mead 1934), that is, the child, anticipating what she or he is thinking, and helping her or him to cultivate her or his potential. Thus, this is a highly exclusionary mentality, precluding other ways of being within the parent. It especially forbids the kinds of profane mentalities and activities that might be perfectly appropriate, even expected, among adults.

This single-minded, mental devotion is not only absolutely necessary to "properly" care for a sacred child, it is the definitive aspect of this kind of parenting. Anything except the child and child-related matters may be seen as threats to this little sacred being, including events and people who challenge the parental mentality that the child evokes and "deserves." If forced to choose, extremely sacred-child parents protect a child and the relationship with a child at the expense of all other people, creatures, and relationships. But, even more important, sacred-child views make parents feel as if they must always, constantly, make such choices.

On the other hand, the more parents adhere to the profane-child model, the less their parenting assumes that the child is entitled to or will actually receive exceptional treatment. The profane-child mentality centers more on preserving the role of the self *in spite of* the role of the other, that is, the child. This means that the impact of a child's presence on more profane-child parents is no greater than any adult's presence: limited to sudden, undeniable intrusions on the parent's agenda. The child's presence and demands assume the same meaning as anyone else's and may be ignored, deflected to someone else, or forestalled as long as possible in deference to the parent's or the entire family's agenda. The child is left to fend for and amuse her- or himself as much as any adult, and is expected to modify her or his demands and selfish expectations likewise.

In terms of a parenting mentality, then, a profane child does not evoke any special (even ridiculous) way of behaving or thinking, or prohibit parents from mentally tending to other matters in the child's presence. The child is just another person in the house, no more or less privileged, no more or less treasured than anyone else. The child has no greater, and perhaps even a great deal less status, than any other member of society. The child and her or his demands simply queue up with everyone and everything else, receiving attention according to standard rules that are not based on age or the "specialness" of a parent-child relationship.[1]

The mental impact of children's profanity/sacredness is what primarily accounts for however "greedy" a hold they have on parents. Historically and personally, the more sacred we view our children, the more greedy they are. They become little embodiments of an institution (i.e., childhood) demanding our total energy, loyalty, commitment and self. The more profanely we view our children, though, the less "greedy" they are, freeing us to think and act in ways that do not place the child at the forefront of consciousness.

To illustrate these different approaches, consider some currently popular parenting advice. In the last several years, children's advocates and child development experts suggest a new trick to ensure the well-being of (sacred) children. New and expectant parents are advised to crawl or walk on their knees across the floors of their homes, anticipating safety hazards as they try to literally see things from their infants' and toddlers' points of view.

This exercise not only reflects but symbolically summarizes the sacred-child mentality. The parent of a sacred-child is constantly trying to better see the world from her or his child's perspective. This not only helps protect the child from harm, but allows the parent to best complete her or his task of providing the best possible developmental support, proof of how much the child is cherished. By immersing one's self

1. On the kinds of considerations that typically guide queuing behavior and the provision of attention, see Barry Schwartz, *Queuing and Waiting* (1975).

in the child's viewpoint, the parent hopes to better adopt a good sacred-child parenting mentality, using parental abilities to compensate for any the child may currently lack.

However, even if they know of this trick to help ensure an infant's safety, profane-child parents are more likely to remain standing or sitting in their chairs, never bothering to see the house from floor level. They may even watch from there, as someone with a more sacred viewpoint crawls around and does the troubleshooting.[2] Basically, the (pending) appearance of a more profane child gives a parent little reason to alter her or his viewpoint or surroundings. Indeed, for as long as she or he chooses to remain in an adult-level field of view, the extremely profane-child parent may begin a lifetime of being fairly uninterested in or perhaps surprised and annoyed by what her or his child grabs, falls over, and gets into each day.

The profanity/sacredness of a child varies tremendously according to a number of factors. As a whole, our culture may see children more sacred now than before. However, there is still variation among the present population as to just how sacred, how valued and demanding our children are and should be. Individual parents may differ in their views of how sacred a child is, just as sets of parents might. One person may see her or his own child as more—or less—sacred than somebody else's, for instance. Moreover, any given parent may differ in her or his view of and behavior with a child depending on whether the child is a girl or a boy; a first, second, third, or ninth child; healthy or sickly; cuddly or standoffish; even smaller or larger than usual for her or his age.

In addition, the sacredness of a child generally diminishes in our culture as children grow older. No one can deny that there is a distinct lessening of our propensity to "oooh" and "aaah" over children as they grow up. Logically, then, as our growing children assume less sacred and more profane status, so do our approaches to parenting. We alter

2. I am aware that the primary responsibility for chasing around after small children and otherwise ensuring their safety is frequently based on a sexual division of labor at home. Lab machinists especially describe their wives' responsibility for this kind of immediate supervision, whether or not husbands/fathers are at home. Thus, in addition to differences between parents' views of how sacred children are, the household, sexual division of labor also may be important in determining who does and does not get down on the floor and/or remove dangerous objects from children's hands. My discussion is meant to be metaphorical more than a complete listing of why parents do and do not check out their children's field of view.

ourselves less in children's presence, ignore them more, discuss the "proper" way of doing things for and with them less, and generally treat our relationships with them as less remarkable aspects of life.

"Primary" and "Secondary" Parenting

Models of parenting also may be placed along a continuum of how "primary"/"secondary" the activity is. This aspect of parenting refers to how much any given person is directly responsible for looking after and taking care of a child.[3] Assuming a two-parent household, one parent usually functions as a "primary" parent, the other as a "secondary" parent, although these roles may be repeatedly switched over time.

A primary parent is the person who is most constantly accessible and attentive to a child and most accountable for the child's behavior and well-being. She or he is the "default" care giver, providing most of the "continuous coverage" (Zerubavel 1979; LaRossa and LaRossa 1981) demanded by our society. The secondary parent is less responsible for looking after the child. However, relative to the primary parent, her or his amount of caretaking may vary tremendously. The secondary parent's activities may be only slightly less than those of the primary parent. Or she or he may "help out" relatively rarely, when it is explicitly agreed upon, for a specific period of time.

Across all parents, "primary" and "secondary" parenting become even more relative terms. A continuum approach to these terms seems even more appropriate at this level, especially if we compare any parent to a broader standard. It is not only possible for a child to possess two more "primary" parents but to have two more "secondary" parents. In the first case, both parents assume a great deal of "hands-on" responsibility for taking care of the child. In the second, neither parent takes much responsibility for the child's supervision and care. It is also quite possible for a single parent to be qualitatively more like a "secondary" parent although she or he is technically, quantitatively, the primary parent. Likewise, a grandparent or paid care giver may be more of a child's "primary parent," even when two legal parents are present within the home.

Compared to secondary parents, primary parents find their children

3. I use the terms "primary parent" and "secondary parent" in the sense that Arlie Hochschild ([1989] 1990) does. Although she does not explicitly define the term in any one place, it is clear that we use it in similar ways, at least regarding coupled parents.

more mental and physical work. (*How* much more work depends on the difference in the amount of responsibility each party takes for the child.) An extremely primary parent is constantly engaged in the surveillance and supervision of her or his children whenever they're together. This responsibility may be invoked over the telephone at any time, too, if child and parent are separated. Primary parents are not only more ready to notice if something goes awry, but they're also the ones who intervene most often when it does. They're not only more frequently cleaning up after the child, but laying the groundwork for the child's next activity or need. And her or his accessibility and/or attentiveness means that the primary parent is the person a child most often goes to if she or he needs something or simply wants to share some discovery or feeling.

(During infancy and the toddler years, this attentiveness also means the primary parent will understand a young child's language best, acting as translator for a secondary parent as well as others. It is precisely the sharing of so many of the child's experiences, of learning what she or he finds interesting, that gives the primary parent the advantage in acquiring this skill. Relying on shared, contextual clues, the primary parent pieces together the child's language, matching sounds with objects and actions more often than the less attentive, secondary parent.)

Like the extent to which their children are sacred/profane, the degree to which parents are primary/secondary in their responsibilities determines how "greedy" a child is for them. This also happens for mental and physical reasons. A child may demand more "primary" attention (LaRossa and LaRossa 1981) from a primary parent simply because this parent is around more often. (If this parent also views the child as more sacred, she or he will be more likely to actually provide the requested attention, even giving it before the child actually requests it. The extremely sacred child's mere existence is a constant request for attention.) In addition, the more primary a parent is, the more time and physical energy she or he devotes to the kinds of chores and planning necessary for the child's upkeep.

Parenting and the Home-Work Boundary

However primary/secondary our parenting is, it is predicated on relatively sacred/profane views of children. It's this compounding effect of the sacredness of children and the primariness of parenting that helps explain the effects of children on Laboratory parents' boundary work. The effects of children on their parents' home-work boundary are most pronounced when parents combine a view of children as highly sacred with pronounced, primary parenting responsibilities. Children have the least impact on extremely secondary parents with very profane views of children. It is the combination of mental *and* physical demands of seeing children as highly sacred and as one's special caretaking responsibility, or not, that helps account for children's effects on their parents' boundary work.

The mentality and activity of the sacred-child primary parent virtually prohibit thinking about and/or doing wage work while in the presence of children. Parents are encouraged to keep the child and parenting relationship at the forefront of consciousness, even when the child is absent and wage work is supposed to be the focus. The profane-child/secondary-parent mentality creates no such effect, however, so that wage work may be done within the profane child's presence, perhaps blocking out her or him altogether. This is especially likely when wage work itself is greedy and demands its own sacred, highly exclusive mentality. In fact, some children could not possibly compete successfully with wage work demands for their parents' attention without the cultural imperatives associated with sacred children and primary parenting.

The sociological "role" and "role conflict" literature rather neglects the mental, experiential dimension of "roles." Instead, it focuses on the logistical and triage-like demands of *physical* role-related dilemmas. It repeatedly portrays role conflict as the demand to be in two places at one time, or to do two things at one time, each associated with a different social role and/or role-related other. In this light, role conflict is conceptualized primarily in its visible forms, drawing attention away from its invisible roots.

However, the inability to *think* with two different mentalities at the same time is at least as big a source of role and "self" conflict. Where it is possible to think in one role-specific mentality and act in accordance with other-role expectations, role conflict dwindles away to insignificance. One can think about a report that must be written by a certain deadline, for instance, and still fix dinner, assuming some competency in the kitchen. But where two tasks must be done that require full immersion in mutually exclusive mentalities, role requirements cannot get any more conflicting.

In fact, many of us could take tasks home with us if we had to leave work to care for a sick child at home. However, the more sacred we see that child, and the more mentally demanding our work tasks, the less capable we will be of actually getting any work done under these circumstances. We worry, comfort, and watch, not even trying to open our briefcase. We simply cannot be in two mental places at once; we must alternate between them. As home and work mentalities become less exclusive, however, "role conflict" also lessens, for we can "think/do two things at once."

For the wage-earning family member, role conflict frequently comes down to demands to think from home and work mentalities at the same time. It is metaphorically impossible to simultaneously "see" the same things from the floor (as a sacred-child parent might) *and* from an adult's standing height (as a personnel manager might). Not only do we see the same objects from different perspectives, one of which may be irrelevant for a given the situation, but our fields of view include different objects.

This is why, when they have the option to do so, sacred-child parents contain work to the places and times when children are absent, yet more profane-child parents continue to do wage work in their children's presence. When a child is more sacred, Lab workers retract wage work into the childless workplace and -day, just as they may retract husband-hood or wife-hood into the childless portions of the day. Practical demands notwithstanding, it is only after they arrive at the Lab that parents of sacred children turn to work, just as only after the kids have gone to bed might they give undivided attention to their spouses. Location in time and space becomes the easiest, most convenient way of managing different "foci of attention" and the daily "paradigmatic shifts" (Kuhn 1970) between them.

As these parents show, then, a sequential solution is one of the most logical ways to resolve (mental) role (better, "self") conflict. One of the side effects of this is acquiring a certain degree of mental agility and versatility. We learn to alternate between viewpoints, becoming adept at adopting and shedding mentalities as we switch between them. This is the underlying dynamic of Rose Coser's (1991) astute observation, for instance: people who experience (and, I will add, resolve) role conflict become more cosmopolitan, intelligent, and well-defined individuals. Such people learn to fully embrace different mentalities *and* develop the skills of switching between them.

Consider the mental foundations of Joy's segmentist day, for instance. At work, she sees the world from an adult scientist's metaphorical height of about 5 feet 4 inches. At home, she's mentally operating at about a three-foot-high perspective as she tries to adopt and accommodate her children's views of the world and the domestic work they require. It's no wonder that Joy finds it inappropriate, as well as virtually impossible, to do any wage work at home while her children are awake and only slightly less so when they're asleep. The house demands her attention on the children's behalf, even when they're asleep. Nonetheless, Joy reaps an intellectual flexibility from the requisite skill she has developed in adopting and shedding multiple mentalities throughout the day.

George, however, her scientist husband, has no problem sitting in the living room and reading a journal article while the kids are around. Because he rarely attempts to mentally leave his world and enter theirs, he has no problem ignoring his children. He is certainly not scientifically incapacitated by their presence. In addition, the children have learned to direct themselves toward Joy when they want something, minimizing any intrusions they might make on George's agenda. The undone chores of the house have a similar noneffect on his ability to focus on wage work at home; they, like his children, are not classified as his immediate, primary, mental, or physical responsibility. As a result of this more mentally singular and continuous day, George simply is not pressed to develop the intellectual flexibility and agility of his wife.

Joy is an example of someone who combines a relatively sacred-child view with her role as primary parent. Children cannot get any greedier than they are for parents like her. Accordingly, these are the parents whose children exert the most segmenting influence on their lives in terms of when and where they do their wage work. As living realm "contents," Joy's sacred children trigger a way of thinking that precludes others.

Compounding this mental block against wage work in their presence is the physical energy and time more primary parenting demands. First, there is the energy expended on direct interactions with her children and analysis of those interactions. But there are also many tasks that Joy must do to prepare the way for her sacred children's development. This form of parenting cannot be done without the completion of mundane, household chores. These let precious children crawl and sit on clean floors, eat healthy, nutritious food, wear clean, functional clothing, not choke on or stumble over objects, etcetera.

Where no one else will do the "grunt" work of the house, the sacred-child primary parent must, for her or his parenting is predicated on it. And if these parents will not or cannot rely on others to do this preparatory work (either professionals or other family members), sacred-child primary parents will have little energy and time left to tend to anything else within the home, including work tasks. Even after a child has gone to bed and the direct interaction of the day is done (however temporarily), more sacred-child primary parents at the Lab commonly turn to domestic chores.

Contrast this with a situation in which children are no longer so sacred/greedy. Recall Penelope, whose large family prohibits her from taking vacations away from home. She quits wage work *and* domestic work during her annual vacation time, despite remaining at home. This is time for herself, not her coworkers or her family. Her children are teenagers and, she believes, quite capable of fending for themselves in the kitchen and laundry room. They know how to "open a can of Spaghettios," "call out for pizza," or "wash their own jeans."

Penelope never would have left her children to fend for themselves when they were young. In the process of growing up to be normal, healthy teenagers, however, her children have lost some of the sacredness they possessed as babies. Even though Penelope remains their primary parent, their greedy reach into her life has lessened. And she not only takes an annual vacation from tending to their creature needs now, but she can bring wage work home with her throughout the year and even do it when her kids are awake.

The greedy reach of sacred children doesn't stop at more primary parents' workplace walls, though. This view of children and parenting encourages Lab members to not only push wage work back into the confines of workplace walls but to extend "home" right through them. Workspaces are infused with the presence of cross-realm talk about sacred children, artifacts that remind parents of them, occasional visits from children to show them off, and, as the children get older, cross-realm phone conversations with them. And the more sacred Lab children are, the more they come into employees' workplaces whether things are going well or poorly.

Annie, for instance, was told that she must return to work after her six-week maternity leave or lose her perfect, three-day-a-week job. A new, highly touted day-care center was scheduled to open in September, three months after Annie's scheduled return to work. She was assured there would be room for her baby there, at the same time that the older child would start kindergarten. So, enjoying her job and needing the income, Annie found a local woman who would watch her children until the Fall and she returned to work on time.

Unfortunately, the only baby-sitter Annie could find supervised five other children in the baby-sitter's home. Annie's two became the youngest in a group of seven. After a few days, her older daughter started having nightmares and sometimes night terrors, eyes wide, screaming and crying in bed while still unconscious. Annie was certain it was from the highly stressful day-care situation, but could find no alternative. She could find no one else with space available who would consider watching the infant, too. She grit her teeth, reminded herself over and over of the temporariness of their situation, did her best to assuage her daughter's fears, and prayed for the day-care center's opening day. Every minute of every day—at home and at work—was a struggle over whether to quit her job or wait just a little longer.

Coworkers commiserated and offered suggestions as Annie tried to focus on the tasks piling up on her desk. She finally used her vacation time to buy herself out of a few workdays, keeping her children home with her. Not until the beautiful new day-care center opened could Annie mentally return to the far more segmentist approach to home and work she had enjoyed before the baby's arrival.

At the Lab, mothers- and fathers-to-be commonly begin the pattern of infusing their workplaces with sacred-child-related concerns and artifacts during pregnancy. Within certain socially approved contexts, the expected arrival of a child is one of the most talked-about and collectively treasured events in our culture, due to babies' highly sacred status. Wherever mothers and mothers-to-be have a strong workplace presence at the Lab, this event is an important focus of workplace conversations, as well as talk at home. Even where women are scarce, actively interested and aware Laboratory husbands regularly exchange information about wives' pregnancies and their post-birth plans. A visibly interested and supportive audience of either sex can give the arrival of children a major role in the integration of home and work.

It is hard to imagine anything more fundamentally, undeniably integrating than a visibly pregnant worker. A pregnancy is a powerful souvenir of home life. It brings the very essence of home into the workplace in its most sacred form. Pregnant women's presence in more integrating workplaces enhances an already family-friendly environment. Here, they are a visible confirmation of the "correct" relationship between home and work and the priority of selves we locate there.

For instance, when Carol, Kim, and Samantha became pregnant at almost the same time, Personnel fairly buzzed with excitement. Inbetween work tasks, the three expectant mothers constantly talked about their pregnancies, the babies, the fathers, their plans, their purchases, clothes, and doctors' visits. Previously amiable, the three women increased their extra-workplace socializing, going to restaurants, stores, and each other's houses together. Everyone around them got into the act, asking after their well-being and plans, offering advice about new motherhood and how to take care of little ones. In her kitchen, Kim still displays a picture of the three women wearing the same maternity dress (in different colors, of course.)

The three children now attend the same day-care center, and even as they grow older, their antics form a treasured part of departmental chats. Their pictures are proudly displayed in each woman's office, and they each have photos of the others' children in their wallets and/or on their desks. Other workers also carry around the children's pictures. All of this intensified others' talk about their own children. Beginning with a male coworker's launch into fatherhood, the three women's pregnancies further formed a sort of "critical mass," setting off a chain reaction in all adoring parents.

The integrating symbolism of a pregnant woman confirms the general approach to the home-work boundary in places like Personnel. Yet it seriously, undeniably challenges that of more segmentist groups. More than anything else, the varying treatment of pregnant women in the workplace shows that "pollution" is in the eye of the beholder. Strict

segmentors may try to avoid hiring women in the first place, fearing their mere potential for future pollution of this sort. Of course, even women professionals, the most powerful, autonomous, and respected of women workers, continue to be judged in and excluded from the workplace by what they are assumed to do and be at home (Aisenberg and Harrington 1988).

Short of being fired or not hired (illegal practices but logical ones for extremely segmenting, rigid-thinking employers), pregnant workers may find themselves the target of more segmenting bosses and coworkers' stigmatizing actions. These may be unspoken and utterly without hostile intent, yet they still result from the pregnant worker's polluting condition. After all, a pregnancy quietly challenges assumptions colleagues may not even know they have.

For example, just after having her second child, Carly, a scientist, met with a therapist to explore her colleagues' bewildering treatment of her. Not a single department member commented on her pregnancy throughout her pre- and postnatal months. Not one. Most avoided her altogether. Stunned and shaken by their behavior, Carly began questioning the very foundations of her life: who she was and what her place was in the scientific community. Carly's therapist quickly retorted that Carly wasn't the one with the problem, her colleagues were. Yet this did little to change Carly's earth-shattering realization that maybe her family and her identity as a mother had little place in her new work community.

Carly already had a child when she was hired by the Lab, as did most of her colleagues. So, she reasoned, the idea of her as a parent could not account for her colleagues' reaction. In fact, her treatment here was so shocking largely because her prior pregnancy was met with the hearty cheers, continuous inquiries, and gifts from colleagues in two previous institutions. This was what she had come to expect of a workplace and constituted quite an acceptable home-work boundary for her.

One interpretation of Carly's situation is that in her new department, it is perfectly all right to have a home life and children as long as one doesn't seriously violate the "myth of separate spheres" that Kanter (1977b) describes so adeptly. This is precisely what a worker challenges when she becomes visibly pregnant, however. It is quite possible that the mere sight of Carly caused her colleagues to be uncomfortable. Through her growing belly, her home symbolically, directly intruded on and threatened a more segmentist vision of their workplace, its function and boundary. At the very least, her pregnancy, so clearly a "home-related" matter, was not proper subject matter for their workplace conversations.

Carly's new colleagues are, and can be, much more segmenting than her. First, they are almost entirely men and will never face the biological necessity of "polluting" realms in order to have children waiting for them at home. Second, at the time, the vast majority of Carly's colleagues were clearly more secondary parents, if they had children at all. Almost all of her colleagues had wives at home who basically raised their husbands' children for them. These two factors alone easily allowed Carly's coworkers to better preserve the segmentist feel of the workplace that she so directly challenged with her pregnancy. Even Carly's own prior practices maintained the illusion of this boundary. She did not bring her child or husband to work, rarely socialized with her colleagues and rarely interrupted regular workday arrivals and departures, five days a week.

Only after the baby is born and the visible signs of integration subside can more segmenting colleagues remove from their minds a new mother's polluting effect. Of course, this assumes the no-longer pregnant boundary violator keeps quiet about her new baby, offering an illusion that nothing happened over the last forty weeks (forty-six, if she took the Lab's maternity leave, like Carly.) Even then, some coworkers may be incapable of "forgiving and forgetting," and the mother may be treated as something of an oddity for the rest of her tenure. This is how the mere fact that women physically bear our society's children may cause an unfair disadvantage to them in a largely segmenting culture, whether or not they also become primary parents after birth. No story better confirms Mary Douglas's ([1966] 1985) observations:

> A polluting person is always in the wrong. He has developed some wrong condition or simply crossed some line which should not have been crossed and this displacement unleashes danger for someone. . . . Pollution can be committed intentionally, but intention is irrelevant to its effect—it is more likely to happen inadvertently (113). . . . The only question is whether a forbidden contact has taken place or not. (130)

In short, the effects of children on parents' home-work boundaries depend on several factors. Certainly, the social milieu of our workplace and the boundary assumptions and policies of employers and colleagues are important constraints. But on the home side of our commutes, the kind of parental role we assume also is quite important. More profane-child and secondary parenting permits wage work to extend its greedy reach into our homes, just as sacred-child primary parenting extends home into the workplace, via children's greedy reach.

However, as even the most sacred of children grow, they lose a certain degree of their sacredness and parenting may change. As children lose some of their preciousness, moving from the center of our consciousness toward the periphery, home can better accommodate work again. But this is not only because offsprings' increasingly profane status lets us disattend them more readily. Practically, older children also require less energy. Even a primary parent doesn't need to do so many things for and as a result of them. We don't need to immediately supervise and anticipate older children so much, as their own common sense takes over (we hope). We expect our kids to start taking more and more responsibility for their actions and needs. This allows us to begin substituting work and work-related activities in place of the time, space, and activities that were previously dedicated to the child.

Growing children's decreasing sacredness also results in a lessening of their reach into work realms via cross-realm talk and artifacts. As children get older, Lab employees talk less about them at the workplace. The most essential and rudimentary parenting skills have been acquired, parental relationships are better worked out, and children's characters and antics are more taken for granted. Lab workers carry few current photographs of growing and grown children in their wallets, and they display fewer and fewer current photos of them on desks. Hand-made, lovingly mangled paperweights and scribbled drawings disappear from desk tops, walls, and toolboxes. The ebbing of the greediness that first brings stories and representations of babies into a well-contained workplace and day lets workers gradually remove child-related artifacts and talk from it, as well as expand it into the home. Only when growing children fail to maintain normal, reliable levels of maturity and health may parents continue or revert back to the protective, more obsessive parenting patterns of their offsprings' infancies.

The impact of children also lessens considerably if both parents assume and/or share aspects of primary parenthood. If someone else actively shares an identity as primary parent, sacred children perturb and constrain home-work boundaries less. That is, "co-parents" rather than extremely primary and secondary parents mean sacred-child parents can alternate with each other at no perceived cost to the child. The child's needs compromise both parents but incapacitate neither. Parents simply take turns thinking about and doing wage work at home as well as at the workplace, and both reap the emotional rewards and mental versatility of sacred-child primary parenting.

For instance, as much as Carly's colleagues do not support her desired level of home and work integration, her husband does. He takes responsibility for a great deal of the direct interactions with his children, working at home in the mornings to take care of the baby or when either of his children are sick, driving them to after-school functions, and overseeing, playing with, and teaching them during evenings and weekends. He grocery shops for the family and does a good share of the housecleaning. Although Carly does most of the everyday chores at home, at least Phil's more primary version of parenting lessens the demands on hers.

Carly and Joy, the scientist whose husband takes little responsibility for anything at home, are especially good examples of the "default" effect our spouses can have on the ability to segment/integrate home and work. Through our spouses' demands and practices, we may be left filling certain parenting and domestic labor roles by default. Phil's role at home allows Carly to have a more integrative existence when she's there. George's role at home permits only a more segmenting experience for Joy. Thus, while they share similar views of their children, parenting, and work, each scientist's husband provides a different amount of discretion in how these women do their boundary work.

In our society, women traditionally are the parents responsible for child-rearing and upholders of family religious life. Both roles, especially via the Judeo-Christian religions, lead to women's heightened beliefs in the sacredness of childhood and their assumption of primary parenthood. Commonsense definitions of "mothering" rather than "fathering" children, for instance, reflect the fact that children have been most sacred and most greedy for women in our culture. More "mothering fathers" (who act as sacred-child primary parents), secondary-parenting women (who, in lieu of a "mothering" spouse, may pay female surrogates to look after their children), and "fathering mothers" (who voluntarily cut all ties to their children when their biological contribution to life is severed) are becoming visible. However, I see no reason to expect that the preponderant pattern of women assuming more sacred-child/primary-parenting roles will significantly change in the near future.

These gendered attitudes about children and the gendered division of domestic labor are the main reasons that the work of so many women at the Lab is so visibly affected by having children. Laboratory women in a variety of occupations largely segment home and work and manage mutually exclusive, dual commitments by keeping wage work to the workplace. Only when children are in bed or grown and/or husbands are "helpful around the house" and "understanding" do they engage in wage work at home. At the same time, though, Laboratory women describe patterns of integrating more than men in terms of cross-realm thoughts, artifacts, and talk about their families while at the workplace.

This is why there is a pronounced, jarringly visible and then increasingly invisible effect of children on Laboratory mothers' home-work boundaries as children grow older. If women are the ones who see children as most sacred and who take the most responsibility for children's care, then women will be most alleviated by growing children's decreasing sacredness and practical demands. Laboratory men, especially those now entering grandparenthood, describe little change in the effects of growing children on their home-work boundaries. If anything, there is a constricting, rather than expanding of the time and effort spent on wage work as children grow, largely due to their wives assuming more of the family's economic burden.

These dynamics also explain the experience of the few Laboratory women whose husbands assume more of a primary parenting model.

The impact of children differs over the life course of these women too, but it is consistently lessened, as the immediate and domestic work responsibilities of children are shared. And these dynamics also explain why primary parenting men at the Laboratory experience the same effects on their home-work boundaries as their female counterparts.

The pronounced effect of infants on the home-work boundary seems to be most devastating to Laboratory women who previously had highly integrative lives, but biased in favor of their work realm. All scientists, these women's lives centered on their work prior to the arrival of a child. Afterward, however, the clash between two extremely greedy and traditionally gendered institutions began in earnest: science and motherhood started their tug-of-war.

Because of their work, scientists usually leave the geographic regions in which their families and friends are located. This begins when they leave home to acquire the education needed for their work. Job opportunities uproot them again. Over the years, scientists frequently socialize almost exclusively with colleagues and often marry them. By the time they're ready to have babies, women scientists' identities, their entire self images (like their male coworkers') are wrapped up in their work and their circle of colleagues.

Enter the baby and the physically exhausting and relentlessly unpredictable needs of an infant for attention twenty-four hours a day. As if all the logistical concerns of feeding, cleaning, and otherwise handling babies weren't enough, new parents must also handle the emotional intensity of trying to ascertain and juggle the child's needs and likes with their own. They must decide just how sacred/profane this baby is and, therefore, how tumultuous is the baby's impact. A new biological mother must also deal with physical recovery from episiotomies, rectal damage, constant vaginal bleeding, and perhaps major surgery.

All of this happens in the harshest of physical conditions, chronic sleep deprivation. For women used to defining themselves as intelligent, analytical people, the mental debilitation from constantly interrupted sleep can be as bad as its physical effects—worse, really, in terms of instilling doubt about who one really is now. Unable to think clearly or even to develop a reliable sense of diurnal time, life and her own character as she's previously known it may be gone for the new mother. And while fatigue creates the inability to distance herself from the situation, culture actually directs her to embrace it so utterly that motherhood becomes the definitive aspect of her being.

Nursing may add another dimension to a new mother's physical concern and anxiety. Again, the logistics of the activity can be difficult enough. But for highly independent women used to coming and going as they please, the need to be constantly available and fundamentally defined by their milk-producing function can be a traumatic dimension of life with baby. And by virtually ensuring that the nursing mother loses more freedom and control over her schedule than the father, the choice to breast feed may challenge the most previously egalitarian marriages and partners in unexpected ways.

To say this is difficult for any mother is quite an understatement. But it may be worst for women who have defined themselves so thoroughly by their work before the baby arrives. Suddenly cut off from the previous focal point of their existence, women professionals may find the loss of their work-based lifestyle thoroughly traumatic. Of course, men professionals would feel the same if they were suddenly yanked out of their daily lives and asked to completely redefine themselves and their priorities, as a sacred-child culture demands of women. (This is at least partly what happened to air traffic controllers in PATCO and, to a less extent, many middle-aged managers during the early 1970s recession, according to Katherine Newman [1988].)

Despite the double shift of a highly segmented day that motherhood may pose for women after a maternity leave (i.e., a day of wage work preceded and followed by an additional shift of primary parenting and domestic work) this return may nonetheless be a mental, identity-related reprieve for those used to integrating more. This is at least one of the reasons why workplace policies that permit new mothers to return to work more gently, on a part-time basis, are desirable. Such policies not only mean welcoming women back to work on a two- or three-day-a-week, or five-day, half-day basis, but providing on-site, quality day-care that supports temporary and part-time schedules.

These resources permit women to balance what may be an acute desire to return to their previous, work-based lives while adjusting to the relationships and demands of their newly emerging ones. They can maintain some sense of continuity in who they are and the roles work and home have had for them before, while negotiating the discontinuities and new mentality that may be mandated by a baby's arrival. And, if they're especially lucky, this gentle return to work sooner, rather than later, can give new, tentative parents valuable access to insights and support from coworkers. For professionals who are also primary parents and isolated from family and neighbors, this may be the only reliable place to find daily, "sanity-saving" advice and commiseration.

In time, as the child (and parents) mature, new skills are acquired and new routines take hold. The family members adjust to each others' presence and integration along numerous, new dimensions can make up for the loss of old forms. Rather than prebaby realm juxtapositions skewed toward work, more balanced forms of integration may emerge from the postbaby rubble.

First, parents may become much more efficient in how they work, achieving at least as much and as high quality work now in less time than they took before. A number of academic women I've met say they became vastly more productive after becoming mothers, for instance. Knowing that time is no longer an infinite resource, they are more disciplined, more serious about doing their work whenever they can.

But those who seek integration also may invite colleagues into their homes now, instead of meeting elsewhere. New workplace friends come over for dinner or embark on child-friendly outings simply because they have children too and share the same constraints and interests. And the children's antics and problems give good cause to talk far more about home while at work and to far more people. The common ground of parenthood encourages a higher level of home-work integration even across generations as differently aged employees' share stories, insights, and maybe some new-found respect for each other.

In short, the biological fact that someone has a child has no predictable effect on the parent's home-work boundary, whether he or she contributes sperm or an egg and ten months' gestation. Children's effects on the home-work boundary stem from purely social facts. These are primarily the cultural view one has of children, the kind of parenting role one assumes, and the attitudes, policies, and practices of others at home, work, and child-oriented institutions. All these factors tend to vary between parents and over each parent's life course. This variation is what largely accounts for the varying impact of offspring along different dimensions of parents' home-work boundaries.

House and Home: The Possibilities and Probabilities of Space

The physical layout of our homes, the ways we feel about them and our neighborhoods, and the distance they are from our workplace have a distinct impact on the home-work boundary. Our home's layout is important because space constrains the amount and types of things we can keep, use, and display there; the house itself limits our discretion to do boundary work. A large, floor-level garage, for instance, allows for a milling machine, a lathe, and a drill press. Without space for these things, a machinist cannot do certain kinds of work at home, whether or not she or he wants to; these activities *must* stay elsewhere.

Even when work artifacts are not so heavy and cumbersome, domestic space constrains their presence. It may determine, for instance, whether we can have a separate office or if we must use the kitchen table for wage work. In this respect, home space helps determine (1) our interruptability and, therefore, the probability of trying to do wage work and keep wage work items at home, and (2) the visibility of work-related artifacts.

Children and spouses can interrupt us no matter how big our house or apartment. But they *must* interrupt us if we have too little or inadequately partitioned space. (This is why Virginia Woolf places such importance on having "a room of one's own" [1929].) Just the probability of interruptions due to working on the kitchen table or phone can make us relegate important wage work to a distinct workplace. For instance, Ginny regularly used her kitchen phone to make post-"regular work day" business calls to people in different time zones. The last time she did this, however, she yelped at a client when her infant son bit her toe. After that, Ginny decided to keep all work calls to the workplace.

Moreover, the need to control others' access to work-related materials can make us keep them at a separate workplace. Confidential and otherwise important work papers must be kept at work if there is no safe place to secret them from others at home. Ginny, for instance, not only keeps her work papers at the office, but now keeps her important domestic papers there too, a function of her son's attraction to her home desk and shelves. Having given up trying to keep him from scattering them about, she moved these items to a place where she need not worry about their safety nor about being interrupted while tending to them. At home, her sacred son, coupled with her lack of "sacred" space, encourages her to segment realms more by keeping work to the workplace. But she's been encouraged to integrate more by keeping domestic papers there too.

If we don't remove them altogether, too little or too public domestic space also increases integration through the corresponding visibility of cross-realm items. Whether items are being used or stored, cramped domestic quarters with mostly common space mean everyone sees what we're working on and where we do it. If we rent rather than own our homes or have little money to spend on new furnishings or modifying old furniture and storage spaces, we may also be limited in our ability to conceal artifacts. We may *have* to integrate more as we read and write work-related material on our beds or kitchen tables, store books and materials on all-purpose shelves, or do piece work on the counter where family meals are prepared.

Domestic space also affects whether or not we'll invite cross-realm others into our homes. The nature of home space, itself, does not really determine whether we have people over. Rather, these decisions are influenced by social norms and feelings about whether or not our domicile is adequate or appropriate for certain people and events. A spare sleeping bag and empty floor space may be fine for a young cousin staying overnight, for example, but totally inadequate for the boss. Indeed, the higher a potential guest's social status, the more likely we are to question the adequacy of whatever space and furnishings we possess. And if we think highly enough of even the lowest-status member of our workplace, but lowly enough of our abode (however objectively humble or stately it may be,) we will probably refuse to have cross-realm members in our homes.

We not only question the adequacy of *our* domestic space, but that which surrounds us. If we feel intimidated, embarrassed, or annoyed by our neighbors' endeavors and belongings, we may well choose to exclude cross-realm others from our homes or certain kinds of domestic events. Angelika and Roberta provide good examples of this point, the former changing her preferred form of cross-realm socializing and the latter eliminating it altogether because of changes in their neighborhoods.

Angelika's small backyard shares part of a boundary with her neighbor's narrow, rectangular backyard. When her new neighbors moved in, they decided to use their yard as kennel space for their eight dogs: six pit bulls and two rottweilers. The space is not cleaned regularly, nor are the dogs supervised to quiet their barking and bickering during fence-running patrols. These are undeniably vicious creatures, and Angelika and her husband are genuinely frightened to go in their own backyard. On top of this, the smell and noise in the hot summer months is overpowering.

The couple still have their colleagues over, but the delightfully terraced and delicately gardened backyard is off-limits for entertaining. Not only would Angelika's guests be in harm's way otherwise, but the house must be kept closed due to the smell and noise. Thus, the neighbors have ended Angelika's airy, open house parties, altering her cross-realm entertaining.

Roberta has similarly stopped going into her backyard and no longer holds her popular barbecues on their self-made, year-old patio and deck. Just after completing and starting to use their outdoor entertaining area, the house next door began to be used as a boarding home for recently released ex-convicts. The transient, seedy, male population and resident landlady constantly yell at each other, usually about money. Roberta's family, so active in their local church, is bombarded with the foulest language day and night. They are strongly suspicious and fearful of drug activity too, yet the police lack evidence to justify their interference. As a result, and despite their recent completion of long-awaited renovations in- and outside of their home, Roberta and her husband have placed it on the market. They feel as if they have lost the choice to go outside their own home, and that includes the option of having people over to the house. They don't want guests to see what's going on even if company simply walks from the car into the house.

Just as the nature of our home space contributes to, but does not determine whether or not we have coworkers over or for what kinds of events, so does domestic space constrain the extent to which work

comes into our homes via the amount of upkeep it requires. Again, standards of "acceptable" landscaping, repair, and cleanliness vary tremendously, especially according to who is going to see it. So, the actual space of our home contributes to, but does not determine how much upkeep it requires. Nonetheless, time spent cleaning and repairing our home is time we cannot spend on wage work or entertaining colleagues, at home or anywhere else. Moreover, if we feel the house does not meet an acceptable standard of internal and external presentation, we may not invite cross-realm others over until it does. Of course, if we're unwilling or unable to do or pay for this work or if we cannot solve the deterring problem, cross-realm others may never be invited to visit. An embarrassing septic system, slovenly housekeeping, or a house built on "the wrong side of the tracks" all affect pride in our homes. This, like pride in the families they house, plays an important role in encouraging or discouraging us from bringing cross-realm others there.

Our homes constrain the home-work boundary in still another respect: their distance from the workplace. Long distances between realm locations may inhibit the cross-fertilization of realms because of the relative inaccessibility of each realm's contents, including people. Along other dimensions, however, long distances between home and work actually can encourage integration.

First, long commutes encourage a certain amount of experiential discontinuity between realms. When realm locations are separated by so much time, such great and varied geographic space, and even multiple modes of travel, we experience a greater sense of difference in who we are and what we do at each point. (Of course, these long distances also give us a better opportunity to achieve the transition mandated by largely different realms and selves.)

Second, long commutes make it undesirable to make multiple trips between home and work in any given day. This deterrent effect encourages us to classify the tasks, interactions and aspects of self that can be attended to in either location and those that can be addressed only in one place. We identify and reserve for the workplace whatever absolutely requires the living and inanimate resources there, identifying and reserving for home the things that are only available or possible there.

However, even as a long commute encourages a certain experience of discontinuity in who we are and what we do in each realm, it also may encourage us to create a sense of constancy across realms. This is because the deterrent effect of the long trip and the classifying activity it promotes also encourages the multiple use of times and spaces. For instance, we may want or need to work some more on a given day, but also wish to go home at a certain time for a family dinner. If the trip back to the office is a long one, we will probably identify and bring home mobile wage work tasks for the late evening and dining room table. Likewise, if we know we won't get home until after normal business hours because we have such a long trip, we may well take care of "personal" phone calls and domestic errands during the workday, from the workplace.

Just as the distance between home and work deters us from making the trip, it deters others from doing so too. If we like entertaining coworkers in the evenings and seeing family during the day, the long distance may result in undesirable segmentation. But if we don't like this kind of realm intermingling, a long distance between home and work is beneficial. With a long commute, no one expects us to volunteer to pop by the lab and write down a few numbers later in the evening. Our colleagues don't expect us to entertain them at our home very often, either, or to visit them at their houses. And if we feel obliged to extend invitations to coworkers, we may be fairly certain that only the most friendly and dedicated colleagues will travel the long distance to visit us. The distance, itself, sifts out the socially obligatory from the socially desirable. It insulates us from the distasteful parts of entertaining, just as it insulates us from "postworkday" tasks at the workplace.

Like the layouts and surroundings of our homes, then, long commutes place constraints on our boundary work, although they do not determine it. While long commutes have certain segmenting impacts, these may be offset by their integrating influences. All of these may be used to a home-work negotiator's advantage.

Gary's commute, for instance, not only reflects but contributes to the desirable segmentation of parts of his life but to the integration of others. A powerful, insightful, easy, and extremely courteous scientist, his home is about an hour and a quarter away from the Lab. His wife is a lawyer who began her practice when they lived about half an hour west of their present home. Years ago, when Gary landed his job at the Lab, they decided on their present location as a middle-ground compromise. It would let Gary's wife retain her clientele while lessening his drive to work. Now her clients come from the area more directly around their home. With the same logic, they could move even farther east if they wanted to, lessening Gary's commute even more. They have no intentions of doing this, however.

The fact is, Gary enjoys his life outside the Lab. He relishes the time spent with his children on various activities and family trips to nearby sports arenas, theaters, and music halls. He spends a lot of time playing and teaching golf and enjoys seasonal obligations as a counselor for high-school students aspiring to his occupation. Moreover, Gary often prefers to socialize with his wife's colleagues rather than his own. He learns from them and finds them a stimulating, welcome alternative to his weekday associates and discussions. While old school chums, teachers, and long-time collaborators occasionally visit at his home, he mostly keeps work-realm people and activities to the Lab. In fact, he invites these select few to his home precisely because they are insulated there from the numerous interruptions of the workplace and the people with whom he would prefer not to socialize. Thus, Gary's choice to continue living so far from work helps structurally reinforce his visions of home and work and what is a desirable boundary between them.

Conclusion

Of all the constraints that limit personal discretion in boundary work, the amount of privacy we are afforded at home is one of the most important, just as it is in our workplaces. Although dependent on the physical layout of a residence and neighborhood, privacy at home is largely awarded or withheld by the people (and creatures) who live with us and cultural norms about how accessible we should be to them.

Like workplace privacy, privacy at home is important because it gives us options about whether and how much we wish to infuse one realm with the other. For instance, consider the options of more sacred-child primary parents in small apartments with small children. These are quite different from the choices of more secondary parents with large homes, dedicated domestic workspace, and teenagers in residence.

The structural aspects of each realm lead to more phenomenological constraints on the home-work boundary. The amount of privacy one experiences not only bequeaths boundary discretion but is an important dimension along which realms might be compared. Each realm *feels* a certain way, evoking an emotional and sensory state of being that grows out of what we do, how we do it, with whom and under what conditions. The home-work boundary feels weaker or stronger, depending on experiential continuity/discontinuity as we move between realms.

Discontinuity sometimes results from an undesirable sense of self and activity in one realm and a more desirable, or even simply a different but equally (un)desirable sense of self in the other. In these cases, we may conscientiously develop segmenting practices to contain the undesirable, keeping it only to the place and time we must bring it forth. Otherwise, interrealm discontinuity may have no negative roots or connotation. Some Lab employees who largely segment do not find either realm distasteful, only different. Their containment practices seem to emerge as the natural, unconscious accompaniments to "Okay, that was fun. Now let's see what's happening over here with this part of me and my life." Realm containment does not seem to be such an overt quest for them.

This feeling of continuity/discontinuity between realms emerges from numerous sources, all having to do some way or another with the structural, intersubjective characteristics of realm involvement.The following are among the most important points of comparison:

- the physical environment of a realm;
- the social ambiance of realms;
- one's orientation toward time and perception of time within realms;

- an individual's sense of the rewards sought within each realm and how well rewarded one is;
- the sense of commitment to others in each realm;
- how well an individual feels she or he is treated in each realm;
- whether or not there are good friends/confidants in each realm and whether this is important or not;
- how challenging one's efforts are in either realm;
- whether or not one seeks and/or achieves a sense of immortality or tries to carry on important traditions through one's efforts in each realm;
- whether or not one has the sense of making unique contributions in each realm (how "irreplaceable" one feels);
- the sense of belonging in either realm;
- the moral frameworks used in either realm to interpret others' actions and guide one's own;
- the amount of direction and interruptions one experiences in either realm (the ability to set an agenda of one's own and carry it out unimpeded);
- the privateness/publicness of one's activities and mind-set in either realm.

So, the people, activities, and environmental characteristics of home and work encourage us to learn, feel and respect the differences between these territories. These differences become most apparent during transitions between realms. Here, worlds and ways of being demand resolution in a most immediate sense, whether they are more similar or different.

When we have trouble with transitions, for instance, the problem probably is one of an unsuccessful or difficult self-transformation, due to the nature of the realms and selves that must be bridged. The more we segment realms/selves, then, the more likely this trouble is. We may be pressed to simply cope with it if we can't come up with ways to get rid of it.

On the other hand, where realms are so similar, and especially if one is extremely greedy, the problem of transitions recedes into the background. Instead, home-work negotiators may find themselves trying to fabricate or strengthen a more tenable boundary between realms. A closer look at "Jimmy" and "Eleanor" lets me explore the ways these aspects of the boundary process manifest in the course of real people's everyday lives.

five

Jimmy, Eleanor, and the Logic of Boundary Work

Each of us has some ideas about what home and work are and how they relate. We perceive certain themes and aspects of self as more continuous and some as more discontinuous across realms. These ideas and perceptions are grounded in others' ideas about what realms mean and what they expect us to do and be within each realm. Regardless of how successful we are, boundary work emerges as practical attempts to resolve all of these perceptions and demands. We accept and accommodate some of these constraints while resisting others, and experience various levels of success in developing practices that let us do both.

Jimmy and Eleanor are two Lab employees whose realm constraints are quite different. As a result, their boundary work differs markedly. Jimmy, for instance, engages in the same, full range of boundary work as Eleanor. However, the parts of it that he finds most problematic focus on transcending the boundary. In fact, he provides a perfect opportunity to explore the kinds of structural and cultural considerations on both sides of the commute that are likely to result in boundary transitional problems.

I selected Jimmy for this chapter not because he was uniquely bothered by transitions, but because he had a unique, sincere desire to reflect on the problem. It became apparent early in our conversation that he had a troubled heart. His attempts to handle the juxtaposition of two wildly different worlds seemed to underlie much of his concern.

Jimmy was looking for someone to talk to about this, as he tried to make sense of it. Since I appeared to be interested in these things, he let go, and I listened. Only occasionally, when he had clearly stopped talking and was looking expectantly at me, did I offer a comment or ask another question. There was an air of therapy about this interview, to be sure, which I adopted on several other occasions when this seemed to be the best way to get people talking about what I wanted to discuss.[1]

Eleanor, on the other hand, required quite a different style of interview, which worked very nicely given the aspects of boundary work that she was uniquely good at elaborating. The most problematic aspect of Eleanor's boundary work is the setting, not the transcending of her home-work boundary. Again, I don't think she is unique in facing this problem, but she was unique in her ability to reflect on and verbalize the extensive, detailed way in which she tackles this problem. She too was an interviewer's dream, like Jimmy but in a different way, about different things.

Eleanor relished a kind of mental repartee as we talked. She wanted the questions quick and she wanted them as detailed as possible, so she could answer as precisely as she preferred to be questioned. She greatly enjoyed anticipating me, following the clues I'd given from as early as my first contact letter to see if she could beat me to my punch on any line of thought. She was very good at it. I thoroughly enjoyed myself, as I think, did she.

Accordingly, the sections of Jimmy's and Eleanor's interviews that follow are a result of both how I played my role as an interviewer with them, grounded in their unique expectations and needs on the day we spoke, and my interest in the parts of their boundary work that seemed most problematic. In narrating each of their stories, I include both Jimmy's and Eleanor's interruption-riddled material as it emerged during the interview. However, in order to best understand the import of his observations, Jimmy's transitional problems call for me to set up the cultural and structural constraints that set up his boundary problem—that is, establish the walls that he must eventually scale. He describes the different points along the wall where he most acutely feels the problems of trying to get over it. Of course, Eleanor's problematic and more interesting boundary work is in building those walls. I realized this early in my interview with her and quickly defined my role as one in which I would try my best to get her to show how this is done, brick by brick. The result is less work for me in narrating her story now, for I spent

1. Different people need different interview structures, which may vary even according to the timing of the interview. I vary my style according to the cues I pick up early in the conversation.

much more time interrupting, clarifying, and prompting her during our original conversation.

In short, my conversations with Jimmy and Eleanor had a very different feel, and I narrate their stories a bit differently, too. Yet the forms of both the conversations and the stories are a direct result of the point I wish to make here: different juxtapositions of home and work not only encourage us to be more segmenting or integrating, but they also result in our differing problems with and attention to boundary transcendence or placement work.

Jimmy's Homecoming

> When I come home from work, I'm usually tired and— **You just get there and—** Yeah, as soon as I get there my wife might be yellin' at either one of 'em [the kids]. Or my wife says, "It only happens when you walk in the door." She keeps on sayin' that. As soon as I walk in the door, they go wild. They run around, you know, and they don't listen to me. I'll say, "Calm down in here. Give me a kiss, give me a kiss," and I'll just take off again. And they'll just scream and go crazy and I, I don't want to come home to this. You know, I want to come home to a, a quieter household. But my wife says, "Well, they're kids. They only do it with you. You don't see 'em too much, so they get wild."
>
> . . . My wife, she knows how to handle them. But right away, I start yelling at 'em. And then, I tell you, I kick myself in the ass, 'cause I resent it. 'Cause they're only kids. And I, and I— See, during the day, I think, like if it was a nice day, and it was nice and warm outside, I say well, how about I take them to the beach. And I think about that, you know. It would be nice to take them down to the park. You know. But as soon as I get home, like, I'm tired and the night before, I didn't get enough sleep, or whatever.

A 30-year-old machinist and married father of three children, Jimmy finds that his problems extend through dinner, occurring within minutes after his arrival.

> We go to sit and eat dinner. We were eating dinner [one] particular night and I was so used to just talking to my wife and communicating with her, and that basically came to a halt. I'd just want to eat—"[Carrie], just please eat your dinner. Eat your dinner. Stop talking"—you know. And I just, it just, it annoyed the hell out of me. **Why?** Because I, I just, I don't

> know, I— To me, I took it as, what is the big deal? Just eat your dinner, and let me and Mommy talk. To me, it's just a very simple thing to do. And they just wouldn't, just couldn't do it. They still don't do it. But things are getting better 'cause they're getting older and I'm dealing with it better. After a while, you cope with situations. We talk— We say we'll talk about it later, when they go to bed.

Like the period just after arriving in the workplace, homecomings, frequently overlapping with dinnertime, logically serve as transitional periods. For Jimmy, this is the crucial period when he must adjust between two totally different worlds, trying to put one behind him so he can more fully participate in the other. Quiet decompression time is what he wants and just about the last thing he gets. *This* is the time he wants to discuss what and when *he* wants, so he can complete his transition and get on with his home life. Putting such a conversation off until the kids are asleep defeats the whole purpose of it. He wants to stop being a machinist and resume his identity as a happy, supportive father and husband *before* they go to bed.

Ironically, but not uncommonly, Jimmy's unmet desire for making the transition into a happy father makes him resent his children's participation in his homecoming. Jimmy's daughters do not need the kind of transition he does; they haven't left or arrived anywhere. He, however, needs a long "hello" of the quiet, relaxing variety. He wants to be a joyful and stimulating parent, but work, the kids' relentless immediacy, and concerns with the rest of the evening just don't let him shift gears in the speed and direction he'd like.

To understand why this transition period is so important and, accordingly, so unsatisfying to him, we need to know more about Jimmy's work and home lives. In the process, the logic of at least some of his personal boundary work becomes apparent. As Jimmy describes his feelings and concerns, the sociocognitive and social-structural constraints of both realms come together. This lets us better appreciate the phenomenological roots of his—and others'—daily homecomings.

> I enjoy what I do. . . . I like the working atmosphere here. The way the Lab is set up. First of all, I like the scenery. I like, you might call it a campus situation. I do like what I do. I do like my job. The benefits are good. The shop is clean. I worked in small job shops that were filthy. I made a lot of nice friends. The only gripe I have is with management. Like I says, you can't have everything. And overall, I like it. . . . I enjoy machining, I'm proud of my work. . . . People come up to me, friends and

> that, and [say], "Is that what you want to do? Wouldn't you want to be in management?" I say no, I'm happy where I am. I'm happy being a machinist, a laborer. That's all I want in life. I'm happy with what I do here [at work]. I'm happy here and I'm also happy at home.

Despite similar levels of content (and, as will be apparent later, discontent) in both realms, work and home are two very different worlds for Jimmy. Jimmy and his colleagues see theirs as the very best situation possible for a machinist. Nonetheless, they have a rather unpleasant work world, physically and socially. They enjoy a far less friendly and supportive environment than many people at the Lab and work within a far ruder physical setting.

Jimmy's workplace is a loud, dangerous, institutional environment—a great huge room filled with machines and supplies and men. In a brightly lit, non-air-conditioned, and crowded workspace, dozens of noisy and potentially life-threatening machines operate simultaneously. The air is sometimes suffocatingly hot and always filled with the screeing, whirring, and chunking sounds that overwhelm any large machine shop. On top of this, Lab machinists use substances every day that are so toxic, they take special safety courses and wear special clothing, ear and eye protection, and even respirators.

I experienced an acute, healthy sensation of fear that dampened but never quite left me during interviews with some of the machinists. To reach one of the lofts where we talked, I had to walk across the expansive shop floor. It was an exciting jaunt that made me feel wonderfully "in the field" but extremely wary too. Mandatory goggles protected my eyes, but my ears would sometimes ring for several minutes after completing the trip. Before I traded my respectful business pumps for more practical sneakers, I slipped a couple of times on floors repeatedly and fastidiously cleaned but always respeckled with the lubricant or metal shavings of a job in progress.

My biggest concern was that I never knew quite what to watch out for, or what sound might betray an accident about to happen. Everything looked and sounded threatening. As part of their wealth of experience, machinists know which sounds are normal background noise, which ones indicate a certain machine is being used, and which ones mean something is wrong. It seems that their ears, even more than their eyes, provide crucial information essential for their well-being. If a part suddenly loosens, they can respond instantly because of the sound it makes just prior to flinging off in a Frisbee-like fashion. They know what the five-ton crane sounds like coming across the room on its track. I didn't, of course, and suddenly realized how important sound could be to staying alive, or at least in one piece, in a place like this.

This is a stereotypical "man's" world: dirty, machine-oriented, and physically demanding.[2] Only one woman, a "helper" who systematically, visibly suppresses traditional signs of femininity, works among dozens of men on one of the shop floors. These places are a far cry from the cozy suburban homes these workers return to each day, where a feminine touch, the presence of healthy, happy children, and the order of a well-cut and landscaped lawn is treasured.

Jimmy finds work at the Lab far more alienating than places where he worked previously. In small family businesses, he and the owner machined side-by-side. Amiability and interest in each other and their families were the rule. Now working for this much larger, far more bureaucratic operation, Jimmy's had several run-ins with management. The theme that runs through all these encounters is management's dissatisfaction with Jimmy's slow acceptance of their supreme authority in the workplace and their highly segmentist views about "work" time and tasks versus "personal" ones. From his first tangle with management over an expected promotion to later conflicts about the use of time and space, he's had a tough time adjusting.

> I worked in shops with four or five people tops, counting the boss, and [at] a very personal level, which I like. And, when I came here, it was a total adjustment for me. 'Cause I never worked in a big place. I never worked in a union. And I had a lot of problems. With management. Just getting adjusted to it. . . . It affected my marriage. 'Cause I just didn't understand. I would go home in a real bad mood, saying I can't believe what they did to me today. I can't believe what's going on. I don't deserve this. I can't believe the way they lied to me. . . . Everything I do seems to be wrong. Either the set-up is wrong, or I take too long on the job, I go to the bathroom too long. One time, they were telling the inspectors to reject my work. And I was going in there and arguing with them. Show me what's wrong with it, I can't find—And they were like, on the cuff, saying well, we were told to give you a hard time, basically. And this is, this is ridiculous! And, like I says, this is because I got the union involved [over a denied promotion]. I got 'em pissed off. So, from day one. And then one supervisor tells the other. It doesn't stop. . . . And my wife was like,

2. See David Halle's *America's Working Man* (1984) for a discussion of the centrality of these attributes in the work and identities of other affluent, blue-collar men.

> "I can't believe this is happening to you. You've never had any problems with anybody." "I know," I says. "Yeah, I know, I can't believe this is going on." . . . It's just that tension, that friction that annoyed the hell out of me.

Jimmy is still coming to terms with the disappointing realization that to Lab management, he is nobody special, a "nonperson." Numerous colleagues echo this perception. "If I had a heart attack and died today, they'd replace me tomorrow and they'd never give me another thought. Never," says Harold, Jimmy's colleague. Management sees him only as a machinist, says Jimmy, and they couldn't care less about his life outside the lab. They're only interested in two things: how quickly, carefully, and reliably he finishes one job and returns it to collect another, and how closely he follows the rules about the use of Lab time, space, and materials. He struggles with the idea that other people can and want to treat him like this.

Perhaps the most striking aspects of Jimmy's workplace are the elementary school-like policies and encounters that permeate his day. These stem from a fundamentally antagonistic relationship between the union-protected machinists and their managers. Highly intelligent, grown men, Lab machinists frequently are treated like children. It is ironic and puzzling that those who do such sophisticated and essential work in such a demanding place are simultaneously treated as if, like children, they cannot be trusted.

For instance, consider the collective, timed breaks Jimmy and his coworkers take, usually in a cafeteria-like room. Like "lunch time" and "recess" for school children, this arrangement permits maximum control over machinists' schedules and close scrutiny of their activities. Moreover, leaving the immediate vicinity of the building during work time is grounds for reprimand and/or suspension, much as it is for students.

Close supervision is also expected while machinists are working. Supervisors, like teachers in the classroom, feel free to roam the shop floor, reminding people to get back to work or checking on underlings' progress. Traditionally, Lab machinists are reprimanded both publicly and privately with great gusto and lost tempers. Supervisors allegedly act more like irate, irrational parents of adolescents than colleagues. According to their own stories, workers sometimes respond in kind, playing out their roles as childish, defiant resistors to authority and management's "unprofessional" behavior.

Workers' expectations for demeaning and arbitrary managerial behavior are based on personal experience and a collection of everyone's personal stories. These stories constitute a kind of shop floor folklore. They portray a string of authoritarian, self-interested supervisors and the naive, well-meaning and hard-working machinists who fall prey to them. Even the more relaxed approach of Jimmy's present supervisor cannot counteract the effects of these historically grounded warnings about how the work world works. Here is one of Jimmy's contributions:

> We work overtime. And one of the guy's wife calls up and says—I know her, her name's Carol—and she says, "My refrigerator's sparking and it's arcing." I says, "Well, Carol, pull out the plug." "I don't know where it is." So I says, "Well, the fire department's right across the street." I'm friends with them, so I said go. So she says, "You've gotta get Paul, you've gotta." So she's hysterical. At the time, Paul's playing softball at the league. So I said to one of the guys at work, "Do me a favor. Go in and tell John [supervisor] I'm gonna get Paul. His wife's on the phone and she's getting hysterical." So I go get Paul with my car, I bring him right back, I drive right up. I'm walking inside and I hear my name being yelled over the loudspeaker. This is about six at night. "Jimmy to the office *now.*" So I go in the office and I says, "John, what's, what's wrong?" "Where were you?" I said, "Well, I had to step out of the building." He says, "What, you left the building?!" And I says, "Well, didn't this person tell you?" He says "Nobody told me anything." I said, "Well, look, let me explain." "No," he goes, "you left on company time, you're gonna be written up as such." I said, "Wait a minute, can't I explain?" He says, "I don't want to hear it, never leave without—" So he wouldn't listen to me. So, next morning, I tell my shop steward, and we went at it again. Saying that theft of services, you shouldn't've left the building and— My, my union took the stance that well, first of all, you informed somebody and, second of all, it was an emergency. And you didn't leave Lab property. And given the situation and what he did, we have, we will recognize this as a—requiring only a warning. . . . See, each supervisor handles the shop different and has his own personality. I mean, some have the personality that they don't care, some have the personality that they [say], you know, "I'm gonna make a name for myself. I don't care what happens to you or anybody else."

In addition to the over-the-shoulder supervision of their first-line managers, Jimmy and his colleagues are easily viewed by upper management from the reception area of private, glassed-in, balcony offices. Like classmates summoned to the principal's office, machinists dread being "called upstairs." As Jimmy's story indicates, their presence is even summoned over a public address system, like those connecting principals' offices and children's classrooms throughout this country.

Even the way Jimmy and his coworkers are assigned to and carry out their work seems more appropriate to handling children than adults. These men are given a good deal of latitude in the execution of their work but not in the selection or scheduling of it. They work by themselves most of the time. Jimmy especially finds this appealing, given his children's noisy, unpredictable, interrupting presence at home. However, the jobs they do at any given time are not up to machinists.

Unfortunately, the lack of autonomy in scheduling their work may be even more frustrating than not letting Lab machinists choose their cutting and polishing sequences. Machining can require a great deal of set-up time and utter concentration in following through a planned series of tasks. From a single machinist's perspective, it can be infuriating and highly inefficient to be forced to turn one's attention to another task in the middle of something else. This is especially true if the second job requires the break-down and later reestablishment of the first set-up.

Jimmy's and his coworkers' opinions are rarely sought about how the designs they're working on could be improved. In fact, they are formally forbidden to contact the designer whose job they are executing. Questions and suggestions must be channeled through their supervisors, although some senior machinists who refuse to follow this particular rule do so with few repercussions. Forbidding feedback between designers and machinists gives the latter the message that their input is not desired or valued by their managers or the rest of the Lab community who requisition their services.

These feelings are compounded by management's apparent failure to personally congratulate and thank machinists for their efforts. Typically, Lab machinists perceive management's view of their work as merely what they are expected to do in exchange for a paycheck. They describe a management that generally fails to see their tasks as personal challenges, opportunities for creativity, or chances to sharpen and build pride in one's skills. Praise for a job well-done is rare, in their eyes, which makes workers feel quality work is unappreciated and, perhaps, unnecessary.

For the most part, Jimmy and his coworkers seem to resist any perceived lack of appreciation for their work. They are uniformly smart people, gifted in mathematics and the perception of space relations, with a flare for design engineering. Working on scientific prototypes, Lab machinists are among the "cream of the crop" for machinists. They see themselves as hard workers (certainly harder workers than many of the scientists they see jogging or chatting outside their buildings each day) giving the Lab a fair day's work for a fair day's pay. A few even see it as their explicit obligation to work hard and carefully in order to carry on the distinctive tradition of the machining occupation.

Mostly, then, Lab machinists take pride in the work they do, in spite of the way they see it thrust upon them. It is a visible struggle, one which sometimes is lost, for these men to balance managerial messages about their personal value with occupational and personal pride. Here is Jimmy's account of the situation:

> My reward [at work] is just to do my job and get paid. Everything used to be on a more personal level and that you worked next to your boss, and you knew what was going on in his life, and you tried to do your best. And it was rewarding in the sense that (beside, as they say, there's always the bonus) but besides that, throughout the years it was "thanks a lot, I really appreciate you staying late to get that job done." That makes me feel awful good. I'm always doing favors and I very rarely, I very rarely ask for anything back. But I like that thank you. I like that, "Hey, look, man, you really helped me out." And as soon as somebody doesn't do that, doesn't appreciate it, that's when I stop. That's what it does to me.
>
> Here, I just look at it as, well, that's just the way it is now. That's the way management's set up. So, I never got a thank you. I never got a "Hey, you did a good job." That never happened. And I'm not the only one. So I just take it as that's just the way this atmosphere is. So I do my job, I do it right, and I get paid for it. . . . It bothers me, but not like it did. I mean, they can do what they want. 'Cause I know that I'm doing the right thing. And I know that what I do is right.

Management's and machinists' fundamental distrust and antagonism toward each other is reflected in a peculiar, downward spiral of each party holding the other "to the letter" of the Lab's union contract. Jimmy has experienced a range of these picky, petty confrontations. He never belonged to a union before, settling what minor disagreements he had with his boss "man to man." But now he has joined the ranks of his coworkers who keep a copy of the union contract in their tool boxes for instant verification of management's right to do something. In fact, contract negotiations tend to thoroughly exhaust management and union representatives, as each tries to obtain maximum discretion in handling unforeseen situations with Jimmy and his colleagues.

Jimmy has made increasingly liberal use of the shop steward during his tenure as well. These union officials serve as machinists' parent-like advocates whenever they or management allegedly commits an infraction of the many rules. The shop steward, like a school child's parent, is both an interpreter of management's viewpoint and a machinist's way of countering the complete discretion of institutional authorities.

As Jimmy sheds his coveralls and goggles and scrubs the grime from his fingernails in the locker room, the process of trying to put this world behind him begins. He enjoys his work and his work mates but not the tension between workers and management. In this emotionally unsupportive, segmentist workplace, everyone seems perpetually poised to fight.

Nonetheless, at the end of the day, this regimented, restrictive, and sometimes degrading world of milling machines, thousandth-of-an-inch tolerances, and flying bits of metal must be traded for an entirely different realm. It's no wonder Jimmy's daily return to his home is a bit of a shock, no matter how much he looks forward to it, and why it signals the need for an important change in manner and focus.

> I do my eight to ten hours and I like to go home to, to see my wife's day. Who did what, how ya' doin', who called, what's happenin'? . . . And I like my kiss and my hug from my children. . . . To me, it's not a job where I really, I carry my work home with me. You know, I work, I machine the part from wherever it stands, I pick it up tomorrow and I continue working.
>
> . . . My personal life is a lot different than my working life. . . . See, I'm the type of person— I like to, I kid around a lot. But, when it comes to certain things, I take my job, I'm very serious. . . . That's like, when people see me when I'm not here [at work], they say: "wow, you're so much different. You know, you're kidding around, you're always a clown. At work you're so serious." That's just the person I am, that's just the difference.
>
> . . . In the beginning, I would bring home the personality problems. I would bring that home and it'd put me in a, a bad mood or a different mood. But that just doesn't exist anymore.

Even today, though, it takes Jimmy a while to re-embrace the mindset needs to carry out his home-based relationships as he would like. He relies on the family he loves so much to love and cherish him, at least partly making up for the lack of humanity and recognition at work. But walking into the house at the end of the day is not always a pleasant experience. Much of the time, it simply means trading an environment in which he is, amazingly, quite comfortable and fairly free of distractions, for one in which he feels two distinct sources of pressure. First, there are the incessant interruptions and commotion of the kids. Second, there are his unrelenting concerns with evening wage and domestic work.

Jimmy relished going home before the children arrived. He and his wife would quietly discuss their work days and thoughts over the meal she prepared, symbolic of her love for him (DeVault 1987) and embracing him back into his home and home sense of self. Now, however, Jimmy is the family's primary wage earner. He must work long, hard hours. Not only does he often miss dinner with the family, but when he does make it, the kids are liable to make it a chaotic, hardly relaxing event.

> I'll tell you, I'm with my kids for a couple hours and they get on my nerves. I dread that. That's towards the end of the day. I get home, I'm tired. The kids are strung. They had their day. So if I sit down to eat, well, I usually don't eat with the family if I work overtime, 'cause I don't get home until seven. So if I get something to eat they'll be like, you know, they'll be like— I like to sit down with privacy. It really bugs me 'cause during the day I say to myself I can't wait to get home but then, they're kids, then they don't listen to me. That annoys me. And my wife gets upset.

In short, the tension caused by Jimmy's supervisors at the Lab is replaced by an even greater tension due to his kids' presence.

Arriving at home also promotes an increased, unpleasant focus on how Jimmy's going to bring in further income that evening or weekend, when he does handyman "side jobs." As he eats dinner, he's thinking about these things too—what he'll do after dinner as well as what he did before.

> You see, I'm very, very pressured. My wife tells me we need so much this month for the car payment, that for the insurance bill. So right away my mind wanders, to get this amount of money I can— I'm going to work overtime so we can expect this to come in.

Occasionally, Jimmy's wife works in the evenings, hosting parties. It "gives her a break" and makes her feel like she's contributing to the household finances. It also means an evening necessarily free of wage work for Jimmy, but one that's filled with domestic work instead. He likes what this does for his marital relationship, but it's hardly a reprieve from the rest of the day.

> Right now she's doing the parties, so I'm cutting down on my side jobs after work. So I've been watching the kids and that, 'cause that's the deal we made. So I, I sympathize with her and I do little things and she appreciates that. Like, I vacuum and do the dishes and give the kids a bath and I put them to bed. And it makes me feel good, 'cause I'm helping her.

When he comes home from work, then, Jimmy is pretty much substituting one set of tiring demands for another. Emotionally and physically, his wage work utterly exhausts him, whether at the Lab or in other people's houses and garages. And an evening with the kids, no matter how much he loves them, can be even more exasperating. Jimmy reflects the fairly even balance he feels between the advantages and disadvantages of being at home and at work in his response to the question, "If you had your choice, would you rather spend your time at home, at work, or somewhere else?"

> [Chuckles] Gee, my wife asks that question a lot. I like keeping busy. My wife thinks I'm a workaholic. Either I'm doing something somewhere or for myself. You know, I have a little workshop. You know, I don't— [long pause]. It's strange. I say I like to be with my family, but like I said, after an amount of time, with the commotion with the kids—At the same token, I like my own time, my own peace and quiet. So. The only thing I resent is working the extra time. If there was a happy medium that if I spent time with [both things]—

Yet the family for whom he does all of this and the sense of self he maintains with it are all worth it. The only time he regrets the work is when it prohibits him from enjoying his family. Home, after all, is where and why Jimmy does the things he does. He wants to because it is morally correct and it makes him feel good about himself. Here, he describes his sense of commitment at home, with his wife and children.

> If she ever needs me, I'm there. You know, I'm always there. . . . I knew what I was getting myself into. We planned our life, we saved for a down payment. So there were a lot of changes that first year [I worked at the Lab], but they were planned. And now, our plans for the future now are [that] my wife raises the kids and I, which is her job, and my job is to be the supplier. My daughter just started kindergarten, and when the youn-

gest goes to school, she'll go back to work. So that end was planned. What I didn't see happening was things happening here that affected the other half. Being, quote, the trouble-maker, you know. . . .

. . . If I could just work a forty hour week, I feel, me, personally, my life would be ideal. To me, it would be like, the ultimate. I'd be very, very happy. I'd be home with my kids. Like, my daughter started soccer. And I can't meet the practices. And, I hate to say it, but she sucks. Well, my wife takes it very personally. Like, she says to me: "You don't spend the time with her. You've got to teach her." I only could a couple times 'cause it gets dark and you've gotta go home.

. . . Like last week, I pulled seventy-seven, seventy-six hours. I work side jobs. I do cars, home improvements. I used to work two jobs. I worked in a machine shop at night for two years. But that, machining for fourteen hours a day, really, I just, I couldn't handle it anymore. I'd go from here, and I'd go straight to my other job. And I'd work 'til eleven. And at night it just got to be, it got to be too much. So I just started doing things on the side. Every weekend I'm working.

I just keep saying to myself, this is a commitment I made and I'm gonna work and do it. But I guess, after a while, you just get tired. Physically. Like on break time, a lot of times I'll sleep through break time. **For fifteen minutes?** Oh, it helps a lot. Yeah, I do it right on my bench. That's another thing that used to piss them off, management. As well as any other thing. They used to say, "When I walk around the shop during break time and see you sleeping, bad impression." It was like, to be honest with you, it's my own time. And you know, I do things on the outside, which I don't bring in here, but I do get tired and I do it because of a reason.

So, so, I'm happy and content really in home and the job. It's just the extra pressure and the extra jobs get to me. And, it affects me here, 'cause, as I said, I am definitely a little tired, and it affects me with my patience with my kids at home. I don't have the patience to share with them. And it upsets me and I see that. It really bothers me.

What kind of rewards do you expect for your efforts at home? Well, I, I, being, quote, the provider. That's all I want, is the appreciation. Which I get.

Jimmy's desire to do his best in fulfilling all these expectations—his, his coworkers' and managers', his wife's and his children's—largely explains his transitional problems. It's not so easy to put his work world behind him. It takes a little extra time, beyond that of his fifteen-minute trip home, to mentally catch up with his new physical location. The next set of demands just come too soon. Physical exhaustion enhances his problem of mental, transformational lag. Fatigue generally inhibits the ability and desire to do necessary transition work. Like most realm inhabitants, though, his family equates his physical presence with his mental presence. They expect him to fully participate in his home realm, to be mentally and behaviorally up to speed with the rest of the household the moment he arrives there.

In fact, Jimmy's description of the way personal fatigue reflects and actually inhibits carrying out his sense of familial commitment raises an additional point about boundary work. No matter how much any of us try to keep realms separate, one undeniable factor inhibits our efforts. One body, one mind occupies both the "private" and "public" spatio-temporal territories of "home" and "work." No matter how clearly his Lab contract distinguishes between work time and personal time, no matter how clearly he tries to distinguish between these times and places, Jimmy's one body and mind occupies both. What he does in one realm affects what he does in the other. Working side jobs affects his performance at the Lab, just as working at the Lab affects his performance with his children. It is impossible to physically distinguish between time and space, and therefore to segment between home and work to the extent that Jimmy's manager, and maybe Jimmy, wants him to. Our mental capacity to segment and transform is intimately linked to and limited by our physicality.

At least in one respect, Jimmy's transition to work in the morning is a little easier. Jimmy does not feel it necessary or appropriate to adopt the kind of emotionally supportive, interested role at work that he does with his family or "outside," "personal" friends. This becomes apparent in the way he describes his sense of commitment to the people with whom he works.

> The commitment at work is, if somebody asks me to do something, I say yes. Matter of fact, the first time was last week [that] I said no to somebody. But in my commitment, if they needed something from me, I would do it. No matter what it is. If it's not personal. **What does that mean, if it's not personal?** People having problems with their marriage or something like that. I just feel uncomfortable because I'm very personal about it. First of all, I feel like I can't be very much of a help. But then people say, well, just lending the ear is help. But I just, I feel uncomfortable just— Like I said, especially if I'm not that friendly with him, I don't relate

> to him *on the outside*. So, like I said, I feel uncomfortable when someone starts talking about the problems they have. Especially when it's, I don't know, marriage or something like that.
>
> For instance, a guy I work with right now is going through a divorce. And he happens to live about a mile away from my house. And I was friends with his wife and I was friends with him. And I go jogging. And sometimes I run past his house and the commotion and all's I do is break it up. And they'd want me to take sides and I never did. But one of 'em believed that I did and I got involved, and the other one wanted me to go to court and testify. And I wouldn't do it. So, like I said, I really don't— First of all, I feel helpless. 'Cause like I said, I really don't know how to do it because they're *a worker friend, not a personal friend,* so I really don't know what to do to help him to begin with. You know, I don't know what to do for him. I really don't. And that's why it makes me uncomfortable. Second of all, I work with this guy all day long. I don't want to get him upset. So I leave it as, if I can help you, I'll help you. But in a sense. Like I was helping him fix his house 'cause he was destroying it. She, he had knocked the front door off. So I went over there the next day and put the door back on for her. You know, in that sense, I tried to do that. But I wouldn't, in a sense— You know, they asked me for information and I wouldn't do it. "Is he sleeping around? What's he doing after work?" And basically, I don't want to know. And I don't want to get involved to begin with. And I was very uncomfortable with that, very uncomfortable. [Emphasis added.]

Jimmy very much sees himself as sharing the same basic traits across realms, that is, "I'm friendly. I care about people." Yet this is an interesting story because here, the classic problems of anyone caught in the middle of a divorcing, antagonistic couple were compounded by Jimmy's segmentist view of home and work. He grounds his sense of helplessness and the desire to remain as uninvolved as possible in the view of his coworker as a "work friend" not a "personal friend."

Jimmy's rules of friendship—of listening, of getting involved—are different for these two groups of people. He doesn't think it's appropriate to interact with a coworker on a "personal" level. Instead, relationships with "work friends" are rooted in the basic human courtesy and compassion he shows to anyone: in stopping two people before they physically hurt each other, fixing something for them because he knows how, or in listening if he can't avoid it, because he doesn't want to be rude.

So, Jimmy's senses of commitment to those of home and work are not only different, but built on a classic segmentist approach to viewing cross-realm relationships and protecting realm territories. Cross-realm relationships are threats to the integrity and purpose of each realm and the selves associated with them. They are to be discouraged, or at least handled very carefully. Getting more involved in the situation he describes—by spying, offering advice, or testifying in court—would make at least two aspects of a segmentist existence more difficult. First, it would threaten the distinction Jimmy makes between his two worlds and the associated ways he views and interacts with people. Second, it might well make it more difficult to maintain a reasonably trouble-free, professional relationship with his coworker in the workplace. Indeed, these are reasons many Lab employees make distinctions between "work friends" and "personal friends" and the different kinds of moral commitment to which each is entitled.

The distinction between these two groups of friends reflects the same logic that explains why people like Jimmy find transitions into the emotionally greedier realm of home more difficult. Coming home is tougher than arriving at work because home is a place where Jimmy's sense of commitment is at its fullest and most demanding level. And it's even more important to him to live up to it there than at work.

Like other aspects of transitions, then, the amount of transitional stress we feel is a result of two realms coming together. Jimmy's homecoming difficulties are not a result of what happens at home, only, but what happens in *both* realms, especially given their extreme, phenomenological disparities. Facing situations in which the home-work boundary is largely, clearly established for him by others, Jimmy's case illustrates how this translates into his need to tend far more to transitional rather than placement boundary work.

But what happens to boundary work when the structural and phenomenological elements of both sides of the commute provide (1) a great deal of discretion for personal boundary work within (2) situations and activities that are far more similar across realms? Eleanor's case lets us look at the aspects of boundary work that tend to be more problematic for people who fall closer to the integration pole, that is, placement work. Eleanor is a powerful Personnel manager, accountable to hundreds of "clients" as well as her own supervisor and office staff. She's forty-five years old, the mother of a teenage son, and wife of a local businessman.

ELEANOR'S ESCHER

> Work is my life. It's my existence. You know, I don't consider it to be separate or distinct. It's not a chore; it's not a burden. It's my existence. . . . They're so fused for me. I don't see this is work and this is home. There's such a fusion there, in my life. . . . It's a good family. It's a comfortable environment. I like being there. I like being there, and I like being at work. It's interchangeable.

Eleanor's story is one that undoubtedly emphasizes continuity between realms. Compared to Jimmy, Eleanor has a highly integrating life, biased in favor of work. This results in boundary work that is rich with efforts to impose some sort of distinction between the time, space, and manner dedicated to each realm, even though these distinctions may be quite subtle.

Consider, for instance, Eleanor's response when I asked early in her interview whether or not she'd be interested in more flexible work times and places:

> Well, I think my job really transcends these kinds of arrangements. I mean my job is borderless. I may be in at eight in the morning. It would be very rare, but I may if the circumstances warranted it. And as I already said, I may be here at seven at night. And that is not infrequent, because the circumstances warrant it. I may take lunch. I may not take lunch. I may take two hours for lunch, such as I'm doing today, to go off so I can have a luncheon, or I may work right through. I may go and play badminton one lunch hour, then I may work through lunch for the next three days. I have a flexible schedule, but the net result is that the Lab gets about sixty hours of me a week. And they're fortunate they get sixty hours, and the time of day at which they get it is really very secondary. So I'm in control of my schedule. I think that's the most important thing to note. It's odd and it's up and down and there's no absolute consistency to it, but I have the latitude. So it's not necessarily really germane to ask if I'd like seven through five or whatever, because I can work seven through five on a given day if I want to.
>
> **When you say, "my job is borderless," the reference is purely temporal.** I think so. **Do you have any spatial sense of that as well?** How do you define spatial? **A distinction between a workplace and a home, a residence versus work?** Place is less significant to me. I

don't associate with the space so much; I associate with the task. So I don't. It's secondary.

Do you bring work home with you and work on it there? Yes. **Where?** Well, it's not really an office; it's an anteroom off the bedroom. I have a desk there. Yes.

Do you carry a briefcase or something like it? I do have a briefcase, right. It's not, I do not work at home regularly. I work at home, I'm always working at home inasmuch that Lab business is never far from my mind. I might get up early in the morning and because I've thought about an issue and I've had some ideas I might jot them down. I'll bring paperwork home if it's very backlogged and certain things have to be signed off on. Then I'll sit down and have a couple of an hour, say a two-hour session signing off on things. It's not constant, though. I don't, I don't bring work home constantly by design. I would prefer to do it here and stay later. I don't blur the line that way as much as Richard [Eleanor's husband] does. He uses his [home] office on a daily basis for the business of his firm. And I prefer not to. . . . I feel that the pressures here are significant, and I guess I really try to break the pace. If I simply carted stuff home, it would be a continuation, so I do try to break the pace. But I am going to sound a little bit distorted because at the same time I can say to you my work never leaves me in terms of my thinking process. It may leave me in terms of I don't have a pile of papers here to deal with, but it never leaves me in terms of my activity, thinking, thinking process. **So while you're at home, puttering around the house, you're thinking about it all the time.** Exactly, yes. Oh gosh [snaps fingers], let's do that or must do that. Yes. And I make notes. I live with these little yellow sticky things [Post-it notes]. **Is there a pattern to the stuff you bring home to work on, other than thinking things?** No. Well, I'll tell you. Next week I plan to work at home in the afternoons because we're putting out a new manual, a new policy manual. . . . I have do to some final editing and get it in the form that it can go to the typesetters. . . . But I'm going to work at home because it's—I could do it in the library too, conversely, but I think I'll do it at home next week, because Thomas [Eleanor's high-school-age son] will be writing exams next week. He'll be home early in the day, he'll have an irregular schedule. . . . So, well, it's very task-dependent. The decisions that I make as to what to do at home and what not are very task-dependent. As I said before, I will take a stack of papers home if it's just review and sign it, if I'm back-logged. You know, that is something that I've done quite regularly. And I will make calls from home. I make calls from home. I normally don't get into the office at nine o'clock, until nine-thirty. But invariably I put out a couple of business-related calls before that time by my home. So I guess basically I try to keep it separate, but there's an inevitable overflow.

Are home and work really interchangeable, or is there something special about each place? In terms of my being comfortable in the environment and happy, they're not interchangeable. It's just a continuous feeling. But the environment is totally different. **Could you describe that difference a little more?** No. **Are there things you can do at home you can't do here?** Yes, probably, because the phone isn't ringing off the hook. I mean I can put my feet up and be a lazy slob if I want. I can pour myself a drink and watch television and I can cook and do the household chores. We do have household assistants. We have a maid and we have a gardener, but I do clean up and pick up and I enjoy that. And I, I enjoy that pottering around the house. So I like doing things at home that don't have timetables. I guess that's the difference. That is *a* difference.

People are always wanting a piece of you in your work life. There's always half-a-dozen people wanting a piece of you at any one time. Wanting something from you, needing a result. That is not the same at home, or if it is, if it does exist at home, it's not quite so obvious. I mean, I have to say my son will occasionally want a piece of me to do something for him. My husband will occasionally want a piece of me. But it's different. The timetables are different. The pressures, the demands are different, and it tends to happen more naturally. If you've got six scientists and all want an outcome and all want it tomorrow, it's something that you have to track. You have to start off, you have to go about it in a rational way. At home, the structure for dealing with things, for existing, is not the same.

. . . The things at home are generally being done to my own design. . . . It's dependent on the mood, I guess. But I don't, I'm not structured at home. I'm always running around doing half a dozen things at once. **Then how is it different from here?** Probably not. It's juggling again. Well, the deadlines are self-imposed.

In general, how much are you aware of the time at home? The hour of the day? Am I aware of the hour of the day? **Yes.** On the weekends, not at all. No, I'm not. **Are you aware of it at work?** Yes, all the time. Because one has to be on time for appointments. Yes, no, I'm very aware of the—Well, I'm—It's interesting. I'm aware of, in the office I'm aware of the time only if I have appointments throughout the day. I have to stay alert to what's going on. On afternoons when I may be appointment-free, which wouldn't happen very often, but I do lose track of time. I mean, it could be six o'clock and I would know only because people are gone. So there're differences, but certainly at home I don't watch the clock at all. **But you never take your watch off.** Right. Never take it off.

. . . I don't feel like two different people [at home and work], but the objects of my focus are very, very different. **What do you think about at home, for instance?** Well, I'm thinking about what lies ahead, in terms of the family activity. Trying to be prepared for what needs to be done. Again, planning, always planning. Always thinking ahead. **Household maintenance, grocery shopping, bill paying?** Mm-hmm, right, right. Watering the plants, etcetera. **When you're at work, how does that differ from the kinds of concerns there?** Well, it doesn't. I don't, as I say— I think the nature of the business changes, but I don't think the thought processes themselves are different. Because at work it's the same way, always thinking ahead. What are we confronting next week? Where is this leading? What is important? What can lie? Etcetera, etcetera. I think the subjects are different, but I don't think the thought processes are different.

Eleanor's physical surroundings also encourage a more integrating experience of home and work. Although her workplace includes institutional versions of carpet, lights, and furniture, Eleanor works in a pleasant suite of offices, cheery, clean, and functional. Surely, this is one of the benefits of this kind of white collar work, no matter how stressful, challenging, exploitive, or rewarding it may be in other ways. She put effort into decorating her own office, displaying a number of artifacts that include gifts and photos from family and colleagues. The same effort is seen in Eleanor's home, which combines functionality and a worldly awareness of various cultures and family roots in an airy, large, well-lit, and well-kept house. It contains a great deal of common space inside and out, with a large patio area and backyard gazebo. Although they are different, then, both home and workplace are comfortable, tasteful, and quiet (certainly compared to machinists' shops and scientists' labs), virtually interchangeable in these respects. Even the cheerful sociability of each atmosphere is similar.

Continuity between realms is also partly due to the cross-realm presence of people in either place. Nonetheless, there are some distinctions in who makes these cross-realm visits and how often they do so.

Do you ever have people from the Lab over to your house? Yes. Dinner parties, maybe four or five times a year. **Who comes? Are you**

> **obligated to have them over or are they friends?** No, they're people that we want to see. They happen to be colleagues and friends whom we've made at the Laboratory. The office staff, we get together socially, intermittently. We have had a tradition of meeting at my house at Christmas and exchanging gifts, as something we have done as a tradition. We took off yesterday, or was it the day before? The day was Tuesday. We took off, I had suggested that we take some time to go to the park before school broke. . . . We picked up deli sandwiches on the way down and we went wading and we took blankets and towels and sunscreen lotion and all of this, and fortunately the place was busy. . . . We like to do things together really, but we do it, but we don't encroach on each other because I think each of us respects that we all have personal lives, and that's the way it is. . . . Oh we have lunches, of course, we have birthdays, so they happen half a dozen times a year. We celebrate those. So we do have occasion to be social together, but it's not at my home. It's only maybe once a year at my home. So they're not in my circle of friends with whom I would normally exchange dinner parties and things like that. They are distinct and separate.

Eleanor's coworkers are present by way of photographs of them that she keeps at home too, although they are not exhibited. These are stored "shoe box style along with everything else that comes off the camera." The collection especially includes pictures taken of them at her home, at Christmas time. She keeps all of the gifts they have given her at work, though, and has no other promotional items or knick-knacks from work at home. Of course, cross-realm phone calls to and from her coworkers and work-realm others occur on a daily basis.

Eleanor has several reminders of her family within her office space.

> **Do you keep any photographs of family and friends on your desk at work?** Yes. It's a photo of Thomas, a school photo. It's about two by one inches. You know, it's small. I have a shelf of papers and books right above my desk and it's there. It's not that visible, but it's there. And I have no photo of Richard.
>
> . . . On my wall I have a poster, an Escher painting, poster, which Richard obtained. It's a print. . . . He obtained a collection of them and I framed one, and it's mounted in my office. And that came from him. It wasn't a gift, but it was acquired through him. I think another item must've come from him too. I have a photo on my wall of a monument. And I believe that photo came from Richard. Again, it wasn't a gift, but it was acquired through him.

Only occasionally does her family make workplace visits or does Eleanor evoke them in workplace conversations. Mostly, her family's presence is evoked through brief, daily phone calls.

> **Do you have problems with interruptions at work from Thomas and Richard?** Never. No, rare. We don't talk, we don't converse very much, really, during the day. We'll reissue for later. We would never ever call just to say what's up. Thomas has occasionally called to say what's up. But he used to do that when he was younger. But that doesn't happen so much now because he has an agenda of his own.
>
> . . . We talk a lot on the phone. Well, we don't talk a lot, but we have brief conversations on the phone. But there's a direct, that's really the linkage.
>
> **Do you talk about your friends and family at work very much?** No. Not much. From time to time, but not much, because we're all too busy doing what we've got to do. I'm not a gossipy person. Well, I'm not interested. But I'll stop and have a private conversation. It's not that I won't, but I don't. It's not my habit. We talk about, we share, we share family matters, but it's not a preoccupation.
>
> My husband comes here regularly for business, of course, because he does business with the scientists at the Lab. Oh, he probably comes about once a month, I would think. **Does he stop in to visit you when he comes?** Mm-hmm, occasionally, not regularly. He wouldn't make it a regular pattern, but he has, yes. **Does he call when he's here?** No, no. He's here for business. **What about Thomas, does he visit here?** He's, he likes to use the swimming pool and he likes to use the tennis courts, so we come here for that. I bring him for that [on] weekends. And he would not be in a position where he could pop into the office, because he doesn't drive. So, no, visitations are rare for him. **Do you wish there were more?** No. Because I see enough of him at home.

Her son's independence due to age, maturity, and a separate "agenda" keep him from encroaching any further on Eleanor's work world. Thomas's maturity and independence keep him from overly constraining Eleanor's home life too. He simply doesn't present the incessant, noisy, physical, and emotional demands that Jimmy's young offspring do, for instance.

Moreover, Eleanor's husband has a busy life of his own, and this largely keeps him away from her workplace and day and from taxing her with too many demands at home. Richard is a scientist by training and also in upper management, at another institution. He works even longer hours than Eleanor, in a similarly challenging position.

Interestingly, Richard's similar work has both integrating *and* segmenting effects on her realms. Their workplace worlds and experiences create a shared, if sometimes unspoken understanding of their daily lives. It also adds to the overall effect of their home being absorbed by work, since both of them are so preoccupied by their wage work and the people associated with it. But Richard's work also *prevents* Eleanor from talking more about her work than she otherwise might.

For a while, Eleanor and Richard were employed in different departments at the Lab. When Richard left, Eleanor stayed at the Lab and soon leaped up the ladder to her current position. Now, she handles numerous tasks for all departments, all dealing with scientists' work. Eleanor's job also demands that she maintain a high degree of confidentiality. Because Richard has been part of the Lab and still knows many of the people and projects found there, his ability to understand Eleanor's work could prove hazardous.

Do you talk about your work much with your family and friends? No, not really. Occasionally, not regularly. It's not that germane. **To what?** To their interests. I mean what goes on— **How do you know that?** I assume they don't ask about it, so—I don't venture much. I mean, I really am quite compartmentalized. I don't venture—I prefer not to get into regular discussions about business-related events outside of the office, because then I think you'd have to be more cautious. What I mean by that is I deal with a lot of— My friends are also in the Lab circle, so I would have to be very, very cautious about how I discussed issues. So I try not to crossover into a situation in which I might compromise a situation or be compromised.

Could you compromise it by telling your son or husband about it? I wouldn't tell either of them about something that was particularly sensitive. No, I wouldn't. Now remember when I first joined the Lab, Richard was a staff member. He was a post-doc. So from the very beginning, we just absolutely avoided discussing— Because I had, of course, access to confidential records of people's salaries and status, etcetera. So we just made it a practice. We didn't discuss Laboratory business. So maybe, maybe the practice has evolved from that. But I still feel very responsible to those whom I administer here at the Lab. I mean, I'm not talking about the staff, I'm talking— I mean, I'm not talking about my office staff. I'm talking about the people whose appointments we administer, and their affairs that we administer. I keep that very close to the chest when I'm outside the Laboratory. Yes, I have to. I can't, I can't afford to be gossipy even in, in the slightest way.

Now that doesn't mean that I go mum all the time. I have, we have many family friends with whom we socialize who are staff members at the Lab. So when issues come up, I have to be very discrete. And I will tend to talk about issues objectively rather than divulge anything that I happen to know. So I can talk about things. It's not that I have to go silent and behave ridiculously about it. But it's, it's the purest form of discretion that I've ever encountered. So I'm saying discussion is not out of the question, but it has to be couched in terms that are objective. And you have to be cautious not to divulge information that's not anybody else's business. **Is there a certain amount of discomfort when you have to watch yourself like that?** Not really, because it's a practiced art by now.

It's one thing for Eleanor to feel this among their circle of friends. At least friends go home at the end of an evening. But when you must censure yourself in front of your spouse too, this part of the home-work boundary requires constant patrolling. It seems a bit like walking a tightrope. It gets easier with practice, but because the consequences are so dire, the fact that one is walking a tightrope is never far from one's mind. It's easiest just to keep potentially dangerous conversational turf to a place and time when spouses and friends are not present.

Of course, if Richard had been, say, a medical doctor or a cook (with no Lab affiliation), or even Eleanor's full collaborator, she could probably talk much more freely. Instead, Eleanor stops short of an even higher level of integration in her life, because of her husband's wage work. It overlaps greatly with hers, but not entirely, causing her conversations at home and work to do the same.

The nature of Eleanor's work also has kept her from bringing her family into her workspace more than she does. Her short, functional phone calls and her failure to bring personal reading material to work partly result because she has no time to do otherwise. But Eleanor expects her subordinates to "put work first" while they're *at* work, and unity among staff is an important goal for her. Therefore, Eleanor carefully considers the example she sets for her staff. Her supervisory capacity never seems far from her mind in this respect, as seen in her explanation of why she does not bring things like school sales items to work on behalf of her son.

> It's an issue of authority. If I brought in items such as you describe on behalf of Thomas and presented them to my staff, they would be— They may perceive an obligation on their part and I wouldn't want to put them in that position. So I, I wouldn't do it. In earlier years, I might have brought in Cub Scout candy. I don't remember. I mean, I wouldn't have had a reason not to in earlier years. But even if I was of a mind to now, I certainly have a reason not to. And therefore, it doesn't happen.

Nonetheless, Eleanor gains further continuity between realms because her "personal" interests coincide greatly with her wage work demands. Recall that she is the person who reads the *New York Times* at home each morning:

> I don't come in until nine-thirty, and what I'm doing is reading the *Times*. That's very important to me, at breakfast, [to] read the *Times*.
>
> **Is that important for your work?** I think it is important for my work. . . . I need to. I like to stay— I happen to like international politics. I mean I'm fascinated by it. But it also does spill over into the job. Dealing with an international community here, it's very helpful to be able to talk knowledgeably about what's going on around the world. And within the United States, within the domestic agenda of government. It's of great value to me to be able to talk knowledgeably and stay current with what's going on in this country, socially and politically.

In fact, Eleanor generally enjoys problem-solving when the difficulties have a "large human component." This further guides her interests, activities, and focus at home and work, including her multipurpose newspaper reading.

Eleanor's realms are connected further through two additional factors: (1) her sense of being well-treated in either place and the importance this has for her, and (2) the sense of commitment she feels to the people of each realm. This similarity ends, however, when it comes to the rewards/recognition she seeks in both places.

> **How well do people treat you at home?** Pretty well, I think. **Does it matter to you how well you are treated there?** Yes. You mean, would I not care if I were not treated well? Oh, yes. **What about at work?** Yes. **Does that matter to you?** Yes, it matters a lot. I wouldn't allow myself to be in an environment where I were not treated properly.
>
> **What kinds of obligations or commitment do you have to the people you work with? Where might your commitment to them stop?** I don't know where it would stop. My commitment is to give them

a— I want to provide them with an environment in which they can flourish and to which they want to return every day and where they can grow personally and where they can do useful things. That's the challenge. To be the best that they can be.

What about at home? Do I want my husband to be the best that he can be? [Laughs.] **How would you describe your commitment there and where it might end?** Oh, I have a lot of obligations and commitment to them. **Is it different?** No, I don't think it's— I want the best for them too. I want my husband to do the best business that he can do. I want my child to be good in school, and to the extent that I can assist him in that way, you know, I would do so. I generally want people to be happy and productive and have a purpose. And I think again, the concepts, we're talking different people and different occasions, but the concepts might not be so terribly distinct.

What kinds of rewards do you expect for your efforts at work? Professional respect. I expect to be given a lot of latitude. You're talking about from my superiors, now. **And from your coworkers.** Well, from my superiors, I expect the better I am, the more latitude I want. I *expect* that from my superiors. What do I expect from coworkers? I expect us to have a sense of unanimity.

What about at home—what kinds of rewards do you expect for your efforts there? I expect to be [sighs]; it doesn't happen. . . . I would like him [her husband] to recognize more often and more fully the contribution that is involved in managing the household. . . . Like I know he recognizes that it happens, but I guess I would like the recognition to be more task-specific, instead of him simply saying occasionally you're great, you take care of everything. You know, I would like it to be more regular and more on a task-specific basis.

As her comments above indicate, *dis*continuity, a distinction between realms and selves, at least partly comes from the extent to which Eleanor feels rewarded in each realm. This is an experiential point of distinction for every woman I interviewed at the Laboratory. And while the grounds on which they feel justly rewarded at work vary between women, the grounds on which they feel unjustly rewarded at home are the same. This includes women who bear much more of the domestic burden than Eleanor does, due to the presence of small children and no housekeeper or landscape service. No one articulated it better than Eleanor, though.

Do you feel justly rewarded for your efforts at work? Do I feel I'm justly rewarded? I think one would always say they'd like to earn a little bit more money or—I mean, maybe that's intrinsic in human nature. I don't think we ever think we're overvalued. I've never felt I was ever overvalued in monetary terms. But I have a lot of rewards. I really have a long leash here. Nobody, I don't have to deal with any managerial hassles in my job. And that's very important, not only to my ability to do well, but to function happily. So I have a pretty good professional life. I really do. There's a big distance between me and my superiors, and I have a lot of latitude, and so I don't have any interactive pressures that I know many people suffer.

What about at home—what kinds of rewards do you expect for your efforts there? I expect to be [sighs], it doesn't happen. [Short laugh.] I'm getting back to the household management tasks. My husband has a professional career, I have a professional career. I do all the household management. I pay the bills. I do the grocery shopping. I plan the meals. I arrange all the maintenance that has to be done. Matters, instances where my husband is not able to do the maintenance, where it's a chore beyond his— We're having a new driveway put in. I'm dealing with the contractor. We've had the kitchen done. I've dealt with the contractor for over a year. I'm still dealing with the contractor. I do family correspondence, and Richard'll put a footnote at the end: "Hi there. Pleased you're well. Bye." But I'll do the family correspondence. I write all the Christmas cards. I organize everything.

And the source of contention is that, well, . . . I guess I would like that to be recognized more by Richard. He has taken it for granted so long. I make the bed every morning. I may sleep downstairs some nights because it's very hot or because he's snoring badly, so I go down to the guest bedroom. So I have to make the guest bedroom. I go upstairs and he hasn't made the bed. You know, he'll get out of it, and he knows I've slept downstairs 'cause I'm not in the bed. He won't make the bed. And this is peanuts, but it would be nice if he, if his thought process was directed towards all the day-to-day things that I do, that he no longer recognizes because they've been done by me for so long. If I were to give him a list of all the things I did, it would probably surprise him, because these are things that he's taken for granted for so long. I've always done them. You see, I've done them since we were married, but I've continued to do them even though I now have a comparable professional life to his own.

. . . I'm also a corporate wife. He's a president of a company. We have to do corporate entertaining. I organize the dinners. We may have them catered, and I may only do some of the cooking, but I have many, many types of existence. The corporate wife, the mother, the businesswoman. You know? And he is free to look only at his business mission because I make it possible for him to do that.

Now I'm not saying he's not sensitive and he's not aware of everything that I do. But you asked me what I would like to be rewarded [for], so I'm getting back to the same point. . . . Whereas he waltzes through his life, he's directed towards his business. Everything else is unperturbed and taken care of.

And what does aggravate me is when he delays taking care of things. Sometimes things can go— We needed new tubes in the fluorescent lights in the television room. And it needed to put new, well, new wires and new tubes. And we waited six weeks until it was done. And when he did do it, it took him half an hour. But it involved going to the store and actually doing it. So things like that aggravate me. Because if I'm going to take control and make sure everything ticks, then when that light needs fixing, I want it fixed now. I don't want it fixed six weeks from now. Especially because you're not doing any of these things anyway. Therefore, when they need doing, I want them done within at least two weeks. That's my source of aggravation, when the few things he is expected to do or can do around the house don't get done.

But again he's focused, you see. That's a big distinction, I think, in the sexes. The women still— We talk about doing it all, having it all. Hell, forget about having it all. Doing it all, I think is the phrase at the moment. [Laughs.]

So, that's contentious. But it doesn't eat at me, and it doesn't affect our relationship. But if you ask me deep, deep, deep down under my skin, what gets me going occasionally, it's this. It's that. It's that. So, I think that's worth sharing. In this, you know, "doing it all" framework, if I'm going to be the manager of the household, if I'm going to be the corporate wife, if I'm going to bring home half the bacon, I want the recognition from time to time. You know, you don't have to fall on your face and kiss my feet, but, just a general awareness of all the time of what I am doing.

And yet if you asked me would I like the reverse to be true? Would I like to be free to focus solely on my work here at the Lab? And I would say no. I don't want to have a life revolving— So I mean there's an intrinsic conflict there. I'm telling you how I'd like to be recognized, but if the tables were flipped, would I want him to be doing all of this and me to be focused only on my life at the Lab? Not at all. So, you see, I'm happy, but there is a slight grizzle. . . .

Eleanor's distinctions between home and work are even more apparent in her descriptions of the routines she follows in the morning and evening and those during the week versus the weekend.

Do you have a prework, morning routine? Richard has made breakfast. Yes, tea and toast. And so, the first thing that happens is I go downstairs and have breakfast with him. I go to the toilet and I go downstairs and, right. During breakfast we will read the paper. He will leave for work shortly afterwards. I will continue reading the paper. . . . I'm still reading until eight-thirty. I'll clear up the breakfast dishes, and then I'll take a shower, and then I'll get dressed and make the bed and that's pretty much it.

Does this routine help you mentally prepare yourself for work, in any way? Yes, I think about things, that little list with everybody's names on it. I think about things. [Refers to list in pocket book that has co-worker's names and things to check on for each of them.] **So you're kind of getting ready throughout the routine for what's going to happen.** I am, yes. And it's not that I say to myself, okay, I'm going to think about the office now. It just enters into the consciousness. I could be reading an article in the *Times* and all of a sudden, it will drift in, so I make a note of that. Yes, no, it's not ordered up, you understand, it just presents itself.

Do you have a routine when you get to work? No. The only routine is to hit the business of the day. **Do you start as soon as you get here?** I normally pour coffee within the first half-hour. That would be a routine, all right. Not necessarily immediately, but within the first half hour. **Are there any particular feelings you usually experience when you arrive at work?** No. No, I say hello to everyone and just waltz on in. I never, I don't know what other participants have said. It never enters my head that I'd rather not be here, for example. Never, ever. I'm just continuing on in my world.

Do you have a specific routine at the end of the work day? You said at some point you start to think about Thomas and what's for dinner. Yes, right, and that again is a secondary thought process. But it does occur, it tends to occur towards the end of the day. No, I don't have a set routine because as I mentioned last night, I didn't get home 'til seven-thirty and Richard and Thomas had made dinner. So it's not as though I can say I'm there at six-thirty every night and I'm doing dinner. I do the grocery shopping, I do take care of that. And again, it's as needed. And we have a grocery store in the village where I live. And I tend to duck in several nights and buy a few things. **On the way home?**

Yes, on the way home. So maybe two nights a week on average I will duck in and get things, rather than do a mammoth grocery shopping.

Are there any particular feelings you have when you arrive at home? It depends. I could be turned off if the kitchen's a mess. But no, again, it's the same natural evolution. Now I'm home, how nice. But no, I don't have—I don't have the feeling that I'm checking in or checking out of anything. It's just a progression from one physical location to another, but I don't have a mood change. Right.

What do you usually do when you get home? Pour myself a drink. No, the first thing I do is look at the mail. I shouldn't skip. I first of all see if Thomas's home and find out how his day was and say hello and at least get acquainted. Right. Look at the mail. Unpack, maybe I've got sweaty sports clothes. 'Cause I maybe have exercised at lunch time, so I make sure I've put them in the washing machine. So I'll sort of do all of that basic stuff. And then I'll think about what we're gonna have for dinner, if I'm home first. And I will pour myself a drink. I have a drink, usually every night. I would say, I would have it more often than not. **Is that an important part of the "end of the day?"** I think just sitting down and reading the mail and just sort of blanking out is an important part of the day.

Do you like your trip between home and work? Mm-hmm. I usually have public radio on. So, I enjoy the public commentary that you hear, and I enjoy the classical music. It's very relaxing. I do a lot of thinking in the car, actually. But I do not do make-up in the car. I'm not one of those. But I do thinking, I do think. **Is it mostly about work or—** Yes, yes, mostly, what the day's going to bring. **On the way home, too?** No, less likely, less likely to be work related. I'll probably be thinking about what we're gonna have for dinner, that sort of thing. So, my thoughts relate to where I'm headed. **Do you drink or eat during either trip?** No. **And you only listen to Public Radio?** Yes.

Some people break their trip down into different segments. They use a certain exit ramp or stop light to tell themselves they should start to think about or do something at that point. Do you do this? Is there a point where you usually start to think about your work concerns in the morning/your family concerns at night? [Shakes head "no" during question.] **It just all flows for you?** Right.

What are the good points to making that trip? I don't think there are advantages or disadvantages. If I were making a trip that were an hour and a half long, I'd certainly have a whole host of disadvantages to share with you, but twenty minutes is really neither here nor there. I don't—

It's not a cooling off period, anything like that. It doesn't serve me in any way. I may use it for thinking and relaxing, but it's not a tool that I need to break up the home and the business. I don't need to, it, for that. It's a transition.

Do you have a weekend routine? Yes, we do, actually. Saturday is normally running around, taking care of household needs. And maybe working around the house, doing odds and ends. I don't mean housework 'cause I've already explained that the bulk of that's already taken care of. Just catching up and taking care of things, odds and sods. Normally Saturday.

We always, we have a tradition in our family, we always have lunch together on Saturdays. And this has been going on as long as I can remember. And we always go into town and get cold cuts either from the Italian deli or the German pork store. We buy fresh bread, we buy Italian pastries for dessert, and lunch is the time of the week. . . . To the extent that we're normally around, it has become the key point. Even more so than Saturday dinner, although we have Saturday dinner together too.

And Sunday breakfast is also traditional. My husband plays racquetball at seven in the morning. And he always brings home bagels and lox. And that has been a fifteen-year tradition, also. So, I guess Saturday lunch and Sunday breakfast. And of course we have the Sunday edition of the *New York Times.* We're really in hog's heaven! With bagels and lox and the *New York Times,* what more could one want? And we don't surface. **You just need a good cup of coffee.** Yes, we grind the beans and we do it properly on Sunday morning. And we don't really surface from that routine on Sunday morning until nearly midday.

Are you concerned with your appearance at home? No. No. **Do you dress any differently for work than if you're home for the day?** Well, it depends. On Saturday, on Sunday morning I'm, I'm a real slob. Because as I mentioned to you yesterday, we have bagels and lox and we read the *New York Times.* So I get up. I wear contact lenses, 'cause I can't see a thing. I have to grope my way to the bathroom. So on Sunday mornings, Richard comes home from racquetball, and I get up and I put a sweatshirt on, not necessarily any shorts, it depends how long the sweatshirt is. If it covers me up, then I'm decent. No, no, no footwear whatsoever, no make-up. I brush my hair into this sort of thing, you know with a rubber band. Don't have a shower, just go downstairs, have coffee, read the paper. And then about twelve o'clock I'll hit the shower. And that's what I consider a real slob. [Laughs.] But I do do it. Yes. On the other hand, Saturday morning tends to be a chores day. I have to go out and do shopping, and do bits and pieces. So I tend to get up on Saturdays, shower as usual and then put make-up on. I may wear jeans, though, as opposed to this kind of garb. [Indicates dress.] But Sunday is a real let-yourself-go day. At least morning, until midday.

Eleanor's distinctions between work and home result in different mental orientations depending on whether she's going to work or home. But overall, she finds a great deal of overlap between realms, and her boundary work reflects and enhances this. Although she dresses differently during the week and the weekends, for instance, she does not change clothes when she gets home each day.

As a matter of fact, what she wears during the week is, in itself, a further source of continuity for Eleanor. At home, Eleanor enjoys sewing, and a dress or suit for work is likely to be the task at hand. She has dedicated the large room outside her bedroom to both pursuits, featuring a desk for paperwork at one end and her sewing machine and ironing board at the other. Like model airplanes hanging in an office, or dozens of children's photos on an office table, Eleanor's sewing encourages a certain level of realm penetration through cross-realm talk.

Do you ever tell people that you've made the dress that you're wearing? If they ask. Yes. **Do they know that you sew?** Yes. And sometimes people will say, "You know, that's lovely. Did you, by the way, make it?" And it'll be a yes or no.

Not only does Eleanor fail to change her clothes when she gets home from work, but she maintains the same style of talk, too.

Some people speak the same way, no matter where they are. On the other hand, some people do change the way they talk to others, depending on where they are. Do you talk any differently at home and at work? You mean their syntax? **Style of talk, which can mean lots of things. It can mean having jargon. It can mean expletives.** Oh. **It can mean tone of voice.** Mm-hmm. **It can mean formality, informality.** Mm-hmm. **It can mean lots of things.** Mm-hmm. **Do you see yourself changing at all?** No, no.

Consider also, for instance, the ways Eleanor manages her calendars and her purse and wallet contents, which include her keys and credit cards.

Where do you keep information about social occasions? We have a calendar. By one of our phones. **Where is it?** In the breakfast room.

And it's rather central. We have a calendar where we scribble things of what's coming up. **Work-related events?** No, these are social. They could be work-related too. If I'm going to be out of town, for example, it will be on the calendar because we have to coordinate our travel schedules. But anything significant that's going to involve the family goes on that calendar.

How many calendars do you personally use? I use two, Richard uses two. He has a calendar that he carries with him. I have my desk calendar here and the one at home. I do not carry one with me. . . . There are some times I wish I had a calendar in my purse, too, but I'd rather suffer the inconvenience of having to look it up elsewhere and then get back to the person who cares about my schedule. Because maintaining three calendars is mad.

Is there a difference between what goes on the calendar at home and what goes on the one here? Not necessarily, no, no. I will have personal events on this calendar. I maintain two calendars that have things that I really need to be aware are coming down the pike. **So both may have the same things on them.** There is an overlap. Yes. The calendar at work will not have things such as a change in day that the housekeeper's coming, for example. I won't put that here. But it will be on the home calendar. So there is some subtle difference, but they do overlap, yes.

Eleanor's purse and wallet contents:
cash
paychecks
credit cards:
  two for gas, used for own car, personal use
  Visa, American Express used for work and personal expenses

business cards:
  venetian blinds appointment (for home)
  own, used for home and work contacts

notes with phone numbers:
  contractor for kitchen
  towing company
  shoe repair

two car registrations
  driver's license

calling card, used for personal calls only
  Lab employee card/badge

prescription plan card
ATM cash card
library card
check cashing card

keys (all on one key chain):
first car, second car, house, office building, office door

stamps
pens
calculator used in restaurants to divvy up bills
comb, brush
dental floss
sewing supplies
scissors
cosmetics
tissues
hand cream
perfume
toothbrush and toothpaste
contact lenses
extra earrings for sports activities

medicines:
Immodium—used mostly for business travel
other kinds—used anywhere
Band-Aids—for paper cuts at work
cough lozenges
gum, candy

locker combination
small notebook with perforated pages for writing notes to self or others

photo of son

note made that morning while reading *Times* on stuff to do at work
note of what to buy on the weekend

As these last, more integrating strategies show, the selves and uses of time and space at home and work are not so far apart for Eleanor. She certainly does not find transitions problematic—or even noticeable. True, she has enough time by herself during her trip between realms to make any necessary adjustments. But this is at least partly because these adjustments, that is, self transformations, are not as great as Jimmy's.

The self in either realm waiting to be adopted by Eleanor is not so different from the other, nor so pressing in its demand to be adopted by a certain time.

In short, Eleanor has the option to suppress or enhance the differentiation of her territories. She is structurally capable of pursuing a more "fused" or "fissured" existence and the practices that support either. She could contain all her work to the Lab, thinking about it, making phone calls, reading the *Times* and discussing Lab matters only there. She could refuse to have coworkers over or choose to store their photos in separate albums left at work. She could sew only weekend clothing and domestic artifacts, like quilts. She could have married someone unconnected with the Lab, could suppress her family's phone calls during the day, and could remove their gifts and facsimiles from her office.

Instead, Eleanor's life remains well depicted by the Escher print that hangs in her office. The fact that it represents her home within her workspace is symbolic enough, as it was originally her husband's acquisition. But the choice to display an Escher, rather than some other piece of art, is simply poetic.

M. C. Escher's fame lies in the creation of works that depict the transformation of various recognizable things into other, sometimes quite different but equally recognizable things. An Escher utilizes what

are often multiple, minute transformations across the full span of a picture, showing remarkably subtle changes at the points where individual objects meet. Each object shares at least one drawn boundary with another, but, to either side of that line, the slight differences in a pair of objects are fascinating when their cumulative effect is noticed. Objects flow out of others, transforming into still others and creating an impression of all matter as malleable, able to turn itself inside out and become almost anything.

With an Escher, it's the incremental process of transformation, the similarities between objects and the endless potential to create something new by slightly distorting a line here or there that catches the viewer's interest. Once we've seen what's in the middle of the picture, our understanding of what's at the left and the right, or top and bottom of it, is firmly embedded in the knowledge that these things are distinguished only as a matter of degree. This is one of the reasons that an Escher is such a clever piece of work, sort of a visual stream of consciousness.

Eleanor's relatively integrating juxtaposition of home and work is beautifully symbolized by Escher's attention to subtle transformations and the continuity and flow between objects. During her physical movement from home to work and back again, Eleanor moves from one slight variation of self and world to another. These transformations feel like the gradual, almost unnoticed changes that Escher depicts: a gentle, almost imperceptible move across time and space in which the self transforms from one familiar form into another, certain aspects of self unfolding while others temporarily tuck back in on themselves.

That is, Eleanor simply does not have the kind of jarring, mental adjustment to make between her home and workplace doors that Jimmy does.[3] Jimmy's transformations compress the minute, gradual, fluid transformations of Escher into one shocking, fell swoop. He not only has a far more radical transformation between worlds and selves to achieve, but he simply doesn't have enough time or energy to make it in a one-step-at-a-time, gentle fashion. The subtleties of an Escher are not part of his life. Hard lines separating abruptly well-defined and widely dissimilar entities better represent Jimmy's daily worlds and selves. And since similar lines and shapes are not imposed on Eleanor, it is up to her to draw them in, should she desire a similar work of art.

Like the rest of the Laboratory staff, Eleanor's socialization about the home-work boundary began during childhood. Her father was a career military man and the first to show her the expectations and practices of fairly intertwined realms. While he "never practiced tactics at home," she experienced trips to the base, coworkers visiting their home, and frequent conversations about her father's work. She saw how their family life was clearly defined by one member's occupational position and job location. Eleanor's mother, on the other hand, was a homemaker for most of Eleanor's childhood and only later worked part-time as a forewoman in a factory. Eleanor does not recall discussing her mother's wage work or meeting her coworkers. Through her parents' examples, then, even as a child Eleanor was already aware of a range of ways in which home and work might meet. Not surprisingly, though, she most clearly identified with her father's home-work nexus, seeing his more integrating career as more exciting and challenging.

Messages from her young adult years emphasized this preference. Eleanor, herself, has only some college education. Yet for years she has

3. See Simmel's essay "The Bridge and the Door" (1985, 32–37), Van Gennep's *The Rites of Passage* (1960), and Bourdieu's essay "The Berber House" (1973) for some interesting reflections on the symbolic value of the door and its role in framing experience.

worked with and for Ph.D. scientists almost exclusively in an environment dedicated to them and their lifestyles. These scientists generally have remarkably flexible views of time and space, acquired during lengthy professional socialization. Eleanor's husband, of course, is also a Ph.D. scientist. She met him while he was in graduate school and helped financially and morally support him through it and his postdoctoral work at the Lab. His present, highly integrative views of home and work, time and space, simply continue the views he developed earlier and help support Eleanor's similar outlook.

All of these sources provide Eleanor with clear alternatives to the more segmentist principles that sometimes guide other people's ways of thinking about these realms and their relationship. Even more important, the discretion she receives from home and work allows her to enact and emphasize these more integrating views and the specific boundary practices that reinforce them. Her realms, their physicality, her peers, significant others, and the practical demands she faces, all of these give her more integrating ideas about what home and work mean as well as provide her with the option to set up territories as she wishes.

As Eleanor's case suggests, we probably begin internalizing models of "appropriate" home-work juxtapositions as soon as we become aware of our surroundings. Sometimes we see these models in rather indirect but extremely effective ways. For example, training in the possible and probable relationships between home and work begins in early years through the home-school nexus. From the moment we begin kindergarten (or even earlier, via home/day-care arrangements,) children's daily lives offer lessons about future home-work boundaries and the ways we should think about each category.

In many respects, the prototypical experience of the elementary school child prepares her or him for the mostly segmenting expectations of the adult home/work world. Just like the home and work categories, the integration-segmentation continuum applies to the possible conceptualizations and juxtapositions of "home" and "school." What we might think of as the typical, public school experience in this country appears closer to the extremely segmenting end of this continuum. What is now known as "home schooling," however, appears toward the integrating pole. In the former case, the people, activities and mentalities associated with each realm are relatively distinct, with little overlap in those of home and work. In the latter case, there is a great deal of overlap, with time, space, people, and self appearing in the more multipurpose fashion of more integrating home-work negotiators. Midpoints along the continuum are well-represented by those whose parents are also teachers in the same school, or whose siblings share classes.

Our expectations of home and work are shaped by a range of possible home-school arrangements, then. We also receive messages from the home-work arrangements of our adult care givers, household members, and acquaintances, as well as those portrayed through mass media. Like Eleanor, we can each point to the threads of constraints and possibilities that influenced our views of home and work in the past, as well as those that do so now.

Art Appreciation

Despite all the logical reasons there are for home and work to meet in different ways for different people, and for each of us to pay more attention to placing or crossing the home-work boundary, whenever I have discussed this project, people have asked me one question: which is better, integration or segmentation? There are undoubtedly a few interesting dynamics that promote this question, as well as questioners' quick offerings of their own opinions. My best answer is that neither approach is innately "better." Probably the only thing "better" for everyone is more discretion to use elements from both ends of the continuum to create a personal home-work boundary. This is the only way to handle the widely disparate, different constraints and desires each of us has for specific relationships between home and work.

Sometimes people ask me this question in a sort of "is the grass really greener over there?" frame of mind. The question arises from a certain envy of those who currently occupy whichever end of the continuum the questioner does not. There are those at the Lab whose work and home lives sometimes feel suffocatingly seamless, for instance. Aspects of the segmentist lifestyle clearly appeal to them. It would be nice, they muse, to get away for at least half a day each day from the same group of people to whom they are currently accountable all the time, to "take a real vacation," or intensely focus on domestic chores *or* wage work at a given time. Likewise, more segmenting Lab members sometimes are envious of highly integrating acquaintances and the ways they interweave home and work. It must be nice, they think, to shed the pressures of an almost split personality, two distinct shifts of thinking and acting each day, especially when they are in constant conflict with each other.

The first group may lack the discretion to put boundaries around greedy occupations as they wish. The second may wish to bring more of home into the workplace or vice versa. For whatever reason, though, each group can only imagine that the other must possess a better life, a better home-work nexus.

The question about which end of the continuum is better sometimes implies another question too. Which end of the continuum, I've been asked, is a more "natural" and therefore "better" juxtaposition of thoughts, activities, and relationships? I'm not sure if it's possible to answer this question from a historical, biological perspective, but I'm not sure it is a terribly productive enterprise, either. Clearly, the various distinctions we make now between home and work are artifacts, and these must be continually, institutionally supported in order to exist. Any distinction between home and work is not "natural," therefore, except in the sense that human beings have a "natural," hard-wired tendency to make distinctions of all sorts.

But is the artificial distinction between home and work, however large or small it is, good or bad? Does it matter? Not if workplaces and groups and families are unwilling to consider the arbitrariness of the assumptions they make. Telecommuting options are intriguing, for instance, because these technologies, combined with the need to reduce traffic and car emissions and workplace overhead, provide a real opportunity to make this question salient for at least a few workers, employers, and families.

In the long run, I know that I equivocate on this question of what is "better." But there are good things and bad things about the extreme segmentation of home and work, just as there are about the extreme integration of these realms. Just as no given juxtaposition of home and school is inherently "right" or "wrong," neither is any juxtaposition of home and work. Rather, different positions along either continuum have different consequences. By sorting out the consequences, we can decide if we must or want to live with them, or not. But the ultimate issue along which we can decide if any specific configuration of realms is appropriate is far more practical and immediate. Does it work for a given person at this point in her or his life, given a specific set of goals and constraints?

In spite of this, I have noticed a distinct tendency among people I've met to rather vehemently point out what is wrong with others' home-work juxtapositions, with little understanding of what might be guiding such choices. Overall, the normative standard of segmentation means that we easily recognize the daily life of those who segment more, for it takes classic forms we have come to expect. The life of the more integrating home-work negotiator, however, is more unconventional. It is less easily understood outside a small, closed circle of like-minded individuals sharing similar constraints. And just as the conventionally trained museum visitor finds difficulty with avant-garde displays, so too do conventionally trained home-work negotiators seem to find difficulty with a more integrating person's unusual home-work life. Indeed, in our segmenting society, it is the relatively integrating who receive the brunt of the criticism I've heard.

For instance, some of the more segmenting people at the Lab declare more integrating people deviants in a number of ways. They are "workaholics," pathetically lacking a life outside of their work. They are "disrespectful," especially because they do not wear suits, dresses, and nice shoes to work, but all-purpose clothing, even shorts with sneakers and sandals. They are "dishonest," because they jog during nonlunchtime "work hours" and sometimes do not appear until 10:00 A.M. or later in the day. (The fact that they were probably wage working until 2:00 or 3:00 A.M. the night before, may have been writing or reading at an interruption-free home since 7:00 A.M., or take no lunch break or vacation goes unnoticed.) I also have heard and heard of the condemning of children's presence, personal phone calls, and personal artwork at designated workplaces within the Lab, all signs of allegedly "unprofessional" people.

Of course, more integrating Lab employees sometimes level criticisms similar to those of avant-garde artists at their more conventional counterparts. They see more traditional "sculptures" as technically good, maybe, but sadly lacking in meaning. They see more segmenting workers as unquestioningly accepting an "unnatural" and "undesirable" separation between home and work. The channeling of so much time and energy into their workplace appearance is "inappropriate," if not pathetic. It's an attempt to substitute form for content, reflecting their lack of meaningful endeavor and significant life goals. More integrating conversants refer to more segmenting people as regimented "worker ants," "estranged," "alienated," or simply "bored and boring." To work with people whom one would not have to dinner in one's own home is a shocking and sad commentary on one's life choices and success.

More integrating people trying to wage work at their residences also sometimes complain about others' "rudeness," and "stupidity" for interrupting them at home. Simply, when more segmenting employees are home, they are not working. For them, social visits and phone calls during these times (at least) are welcome. Of course it is difficult for more segmenting people to understand that these intrusions may not be welcome for others who may be concentrating on wage work, even though they're at home.

Of course, boundaries between home and work are composites of segmenting and integrating practices and viewpoints. As a result, others predictably respond differently to the parts of one's boundary work that make sense to them than to those that do not. In accord with each viewer's expectations, certain decisions we make about how and where we do and do not draw the line are more troubling than others. And these are likely to change with each member of the audience.

Family members' and workers' criticisms of those who have opposing, or more extreme approaches to the home-work boundary are just as logical as the boundary work that leads to them. These criticisms may be just as functional as personal boundary work too. In a Durkheimian sense, pointing out deviant cases from one's own home-work configuration helps reinforce the "rightness" of one's own situation and choices. However, these criticisms do not negate the equal validity and logical foundation of all the possible positions on the integration/segmentation continuum. These different and emergent ways of seeing the world are simply more or less appropriate for a given person, embedded as she or he is in the social structure.

Nonetheless, we seem predisposed to judge others' boundary work and views of these categories according to our own, passing positive or negative evaluations according to how much they differ. The results of this are varied. The unconventional sculptor, for instance, may be forced to devote a large part of her life to convincing others that her creation is indeed art, despite its lack of conventionally bounded space. This is necessary simply because her "boundary work" shatters others' expectations, which inhibit her own visions and practices. In the more traditional forms of sculpting, however, boundaries result from internalizing conventional ideas of where they belong and mastering traditional techniques of enacting them. Because these borders accord with others' views of "proper" boundary work, little energy must be spent convincing others this is art. Little conceptual conflict occurs between producer and audience because conventional kinds of sculpture are easily identified/classified with conventional wisdom.

Similarly, while the extreme integrator primarily works to inhibit the imposition of boundaries within her free-flowing life, the extreme segmentor works daily to enhance segmentist norms for the home-work boundary. These two negotiators use the same tools to do their different boundary work but employ them in diametrically opposed ways. Of course, those of us falling in-between these extremes use some tools in one way and some in another to construct "hybrid" versions of the home-work boundary and categories.

There are important, real ramifications of the tendency to critique and fault alternate juxtapositions of home and work. Especially among Lab employees who have little discretion in how they personally set the home-work boundary, the variety of boundary work they see across the organization generates a tangible level of animosity, resentment, really. The apparent ability of others to come and go as they please, take lunch, tackle work tasks or whatever they like, when they like, for as long as they like, even to dress in a disrespectful fashion when they're at the Lab are real sore spots for those who "must" do otherwise. In the reverse direction, it is also a problem when people interpret other employees' rigid schedules, dress styles, anti-socializing patterns, and sometimes antagonist views toward their work as a reflection of inferior values and an unacceptable work ethic, rather than the result of far less institutional discretion to handle these matters.

This cannot be functional for the organization. Any time groups of workers that must depend on each other are pitted against each other—perhaps without even realizing they are—work will suffer. Perhaps individuals will too.

For instance, a colleague once told me of her difficulty, caught between a more integrating department Chairman and a more segmenting Dean. The Chair could usually be found in his office, three or four days a week, in the mornings only. A well-published scholar, he was at home the rest of the time writing. He wore jeans and comfortable sweaters to work in either place and always had an easy mix of "home" and "work" present in any of his conversations. Obviously, he was a more integrating person, at that time. My colleague was a perfect disciple, emulating his patterns of integration. She wrote at home two days each week and in the mornings on the other three days, leaving her teaching and committee work for the afternoons.

The Dean, however, was not noted for his publications or teaching but for his abilities to secure resources for his powerful home department, oversee and contain the expenditures of all other departments under his control, and attend meetings with upper-level administration and job candidates. As was his habit, he strolled through the halls of the college several times a day, occasionally stopping in offices to chat with the occupants. He was a very sharp, very carefully dressed and groomed person, clothes perfectly tailored, usually suits, and, only rarely, an obviously expensive wool sweater (complete with pristine leather patches on the elbows) and slacks.

The Dean made my friend nervous, although she could never figure out why. One day, the reason became much clearer. Flying through the hallway on her way to class, she encountered the Dean. The second term had just begun, and, for the first time in her life, she was teaching four classes at once. Out of breath, she smiled and said, "This is so difficult! I don't know how anyone has ever managed to teach so many classes and get any work done!" The Dean lifted one eyebrow, continued to walk and said, "Maybe you should try spending a little more time around here."

My friend says she truly could not make sense of this comment for some time. How could that possibly be a solution? How could the length of time she spent in the building help? If anything, it would make matters worse, for this was no place to get work done. And why would he even care where she was or for how long? The logic of segmentation finally asserted itself and translated the comment for her. The Dean must have thought she was not working hard enough, since he did not see her often enough during corridor patrols. That was the last time she initiated conversation with her Dean. If that's the kind of creature he was, she reasoned, communication was not only dangerous but pointless.

Since my friend comes up for tenure review next year, I must wait to see if the relatively segmenting Dean uses his position to penalize her different home-work juxtaposition. I wonder if she would do the same, if their roles were reversed. And I can only guess what might happen if she had chosen to follow in the Dean's footsteps, rather than her Chair's. The Chair dislikes much of what the Dean stands for, probably including the Dean's segmentist approach; it symbolizes much of the life choices and approaches to work that the Chair finds distasteful to begin with. Worse, in the Chairman's mind, the Dean is not a "real" academic, for this is not how a "real" academic lives.

The potential for this kind of situation is present throughout all kinds of workplaces, throughout organizations devoted to all kinds of things. How often do the very things that symbolize more segmenting and more integrating approaches to home and work influence superiors', coworkers' and underlings' assessments of each other? Do they even know that these things count in how they measure up? And how much marital conflict, resolution, or dissolution is also a product of different visions of home and work coming together?

At the very least, we should be careful of leveling criticisms at those with different views of home and work, whether via a job performance review or living room philosophizing. It's difficult to say whether or not we might become more like any of our targets in the future. Everything that contributes to one's position on the home-work boundary is subject to change. In fact, we *expect* these things to change, across our careers and across the life course. When they do, the only real alternative to moving one way or the other along the continuum is to withdraw from boundary negotiations altogether.

My final response to the "which end of the continuum is better?" question is, therefore, the proverbial sociological retort. It is an answer that can be quite frustrating to members of an impatient and dichotomous society so used to expecting a "thumbs up or down" response. But a close look at a place like the Lab shows how so many factors like occupation, organizational position, the domestic division of labor, and one's family composition create such different demands on home-work negotiators. In fact, it provides a book full of reasons why this question can only be answered with a firm "it depends."

Older Dogs and Newer Tricks

Carly and Edith illustrate my point. They show how people with changing social-structural constraints and boundary expectations seek alternatives to old views and practices. As they pursue new understandings of what constitutes a "work of art," these women invent and borrow tools other than those of their pasts. As a result, they are creating new, previously unexpected configurations of home and work with a range of subtle and not-so-subtle changes in their boundary work.

Carly, for instance, is the scientist whose colleagues' reactions to her pregnancy caused her such consternation. The lesson she took away from the incident was that her family is welcome at work only in the most limited and abstract ways. Desk photos and brief conversations about kids are one thing. Asking colleagues to deal with her as a scientist when she is also visibly, relentlessly a mother(-to-be) is quite another.

As a result of what happened, Carly has backed off from her department. Its rejection of such an important part of her encouraged her to modify her boundary expectations, at least where it was concerned. She has decided that it is impossible to elicit the happy integration of home and work of her previous two jobs. So she has become a more conscientious segmentor, arriving at and leaving work at standard times and keeping her involvement with colleagues to this pocket of time and space. She has developed a new sense of "work" too, decoupled from her workplace, and now sees her interests as fairly distinct from her department's.

Carly's department is now merely an acceptable place of work. It offers her the paycheck and other necessary resources she cannot obtain by herself and probably could not find elsewhere. She reserves her dynamic, friendly, humorous side for those who reciprocate and simply goes about her business the rest of the time.

Carly's desire for integration remains unabated, though. This is a woman who grew up in a highly integrating family, continued all her adult life. Accordingly, Carly counterbalances divestitures in some areas with increased investments in others. She relies more heavily now on her extended family, past colleagues, and her scientist husband's colleagues to keep her integration levels up and affirm a more holistic sense of self. They, rather than her departmental colleagues, now infuse home with work. She tirelessly discusses her work with all these people, an endless stream of dinner and living-room-couch guests.

Carly has invested more heavily in home in another way too. Not long after imposing a new order on the boundary chaos her second pregnancy precipitated, Carly had another child. This too confirms her newly clarified sense of who she is and the roles she will allow each realm-specific identity to have in her life, given the roles she believes work will let her family have there.

Edith is an example of someone who's had to replace her previous mental framework and visible practices even more than Carly. In fact, if anyone knows that understandings and juxtapositions of home and work should be seen as "works-in-progress," it's Edith. For most of her life, she was one of the most highly integrating people I've met. Now Edith confirms the adage of what we risk when we "carry all our eggs in one basket": we can lose them all.

Edith was married to her professional collaborator for forty years. She bore their six children, ran the house, and got her Ph.D. from a tough, prestigious institution at the same time. Smart, no-nonsense (she had no time for it), they landed their first jobs together and quickly established a name for themselves. Their collaboration became legendary, for their work was ground-breaking and good and is still part of the disciplinary canon. Edith has been honored repeatedly as an international, highly respected scientist. National agencies and committees continue to seek her leadership and input.

Like most women, Edith not only put in the same day at the office as her husband, but when she went home, she was entirely responsible for the house. Nonetheless, and despite the extra work for her, Edith relished the intellectual stimulation and informal camaraderie of the many visitors she and her husband invited into their home. Edith's children are all consummate professionals in different fields now and she at least partly attributes this to the diverse, smart people they met over the dinner and breakfast table while growing up.

Several years ago, however, Edith's husband announced he was leaving her for a technician thirty years younger than her (and him). For Edith, shocked and numb with disbelief, what would have felt like a bad dream for anyone was also a professional nightmare. At the time, her husband was not only her collaborator but also her administrative superior. He soon cut off her institutional funds, leaving her with no money for laboratory supplies or assistants. In a short time, with the exception of one or two senior departmental colleagues, the whole department seemed to avoid her. Whether from fear of retribution or embarrassment for Edith at the way her husband treated her, they stayed away. Indeed, the entire department seemed shaken by the impact of Edith's marital/work situation. The details of splitting up property and friends in a failed marriage can be nasty and devastating enough. But this is exponentially worse when the friends and intellectual and material property of a work collaboration must be divided up too.

In only a couple of weeks, Edith went from the sure knowledge of her brilliance, worth, and life choices to not wanting to live another day. Why? In one unexpected turn, Edith didn't simply lose her foothold as a wife, she also lost her grounding as a collaborator. The assumptions of her life on both ends of the commute were challenged all at once, for they were so inextricably woven together. This is exactly the kind of risk we take when we integrate home and work as thoroughly as Edith did.

A therapist helped Edith buy some time to sort things out. The children sided with her, which bolstered her ego. She began collaborating with one of them, which brings her great joy as well as intellectual stimulation. *This* is something she knows, familiar turf on which she can rebuild both sides of her daily trip to work. Her ex-husband was relocated through the offer of a promotion. And a new administrator secured some temporary institutional funds until she secures her own grant.

Edith spends a lot of time now figuring out how to handle all the dimensions that once made up her home-work boundary. She simply cannot integrate realms as she did once, for the person and departmental friendships her identity was built on are gone. Even the issue of having colleagues stay over at the house is problematic, for she feels awkward without her husband's and children's presence there. Faced with the sheer impossibility of keeping home and work as they once were, she now tries to create and accept more segmenting understandings of her self and realms and practices that will support this view.

For instance, she's developed an extensive routine at the end of the day, including the use of alcohol to take her from work to home mentalities. Rather than linger at home in the mornings, she has changed showering and breakfasting routines to let herself fairly bolt out the door. And at work, she relies more on herself to find excitement in her profession, keeping mostly to herself in a quiet little office. She works on acquiring the resources to hire at least a postdoctoral student to work with her and share the joy of this part of her life.

As Edith reconstructs a healthy self-image and home life as a single woman, so does she try to construct a work life and mentality as a lone scientist. She is building an entirely new classificatory model of "home," "work" and self, partly through new boundary practices. Is either model intrinsically "better" than the other? I don't think so. Much like the rest of the Laboratory staff, her new practices simply help Edith get through the day. In the process, they experientially help formulate new understandings of home and work and self, reinforcing those understandings that still work for her and replacing those that do not. The only important issue is whether or not the new model will help this home-work negotiator as well as the old one did, while it was appropriate.

conclusion

Beyond Home and Work: Boundary Theory

When I began this project, I wanted to further what I think of as "boundary theory." What kinds of structural characteristics do cultural boundaries possess, and what might be the implications for our thinking and behavior as these boundary structures vary? The following observations and illustrations have driven much of this project.

If we think about the structural aspects of classificatory boundaries, perhaps the most immediate thing that comes to mind is a boundary's *placement*. First, what is the sheer size of the conceptual territory included within a boundary? Categories may be larger or smaller, and expanded or contracted over time.

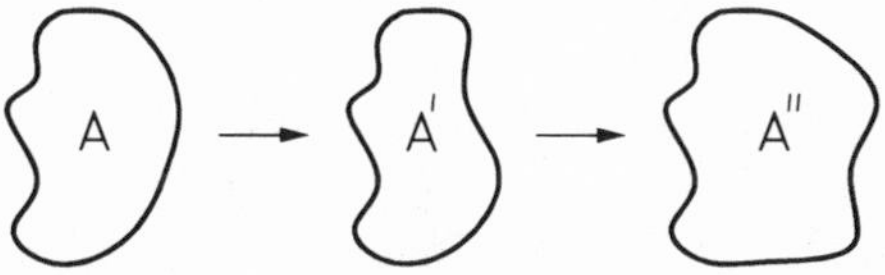

A → A′ → A″

Consider the expansion and contraction of the following categories: "home" and "work," what we think of as "language," "sociology," a "family," "mental illness," "amateur" athletes, "suitable" mates, or "enough" income. As we mature, moving between jobs, organizations, and households, or wage working in and out of our houses; as scientists find out more about primates, dolphins, and whales; as a discipline progresses into "autoethnographies" and "block modeling"; as social norms and economic institutions support nontraditional groupings within households and biological parents increasingly forsake their moral and economic obligations; as the ranks of Prozac users and "Attention Deficit Disorder" children swell; as we continue the quest for a national identity as international "winners"; as we forge our way through the life course, becoming less or even more picky over who is acceptable coupling material; or as we have more or less of a bank balance to meet our expenses, how do categorical turfs reflect the changes in how we think?

These examples also imply that, in addition to the overall extent of a boundary (i.e., the size of the area it encompasses), we may also think about the exact placement of that boundary at each point along its length, about the location of each specific boundary point or section. What leads to these kinds of changes? What sorts of influences and constraints differ over time so that a boundary is repeatedly redrawn to include and exclude and perhaps even re-include a variety of elements?

At one time, for instance, my extended family consisted of German ethnics living in two small, neighboring towns in Yugoslavia. Although they never moved house, in the period between World War I and World War II, their citizenship changed four times. They learned two national anthems as school children and, depending on their ages and the location of their particular villages, one of two official languages in addition to "Hoch Deutsch" and the German dialect spoken at home. They were included in this political entity now, that one later, as the lines around their homes, their businesses, and their progeny were drawn and redrawn.

Later, the national boundaries surrounding my eventual in-laws would continue to change. First, despite their nationality and due to their ethnicity, the men were drafted at gun point by Hitler's army. Their villages and homes were claimed by the invading Russians. Eventually, the family ended up in a refugee camp in Austria run by the French. The United States, via the Rainbow Division, next assumed responsibility for the camp. Within a few years, my in-laws-to-be would see the Parachute Drop at Coney Island on the horizon, from the bow of a transport ship. Brooklyn would be their new home and the United States, the final country to encircle them.

Just by looking at my adopted family, then, and over a span of only about thirty years, no less than seven national boundaries were redrawn to include and exclude different categorical contents. Similarly, we may well ask when it is that loved ones are included as part of one's work world or that wage work objects become part of the home environment; that ketchup is defined as a "vegetable" for school lunches; that gays are considered "fit parents"; that an individual with a lifetime of poor classroom performance becomes "college material"; that soldiers are encouraged by universities to enroll in and parade across their campuses; that neighbors become subhuman and subject to slaughter; that a body of water is no longer drinkable, fishable or swimmable; or that a polar bear, a whale, or a doe becomes "fair game."

Over time, categorical borders loop in and out, sections are filled in and erased. Social conditions, priorities and goals provide the categorical qualifiers. The process and the changes themselves are fascinating, especially if we look closely at which categorical contents remain relatively constant over long periods of time and which ones are more peripheral, more easily shed or adopted, and why.

Focusing our attention on boundary placement also allows us to note the extent to which categorical boundaries overlap. There is a large range of potential overlap between culturally linked boundaries, so that the amount of shared contents may be larger or smaller at any given time. Each categorical boundary is firmly, thoroughly drawn, but their juxtaposition means certain elements belong to both classes, others are exclusively located in one. How much they overlap may be one of the crucial ways in which linked categories change over time.

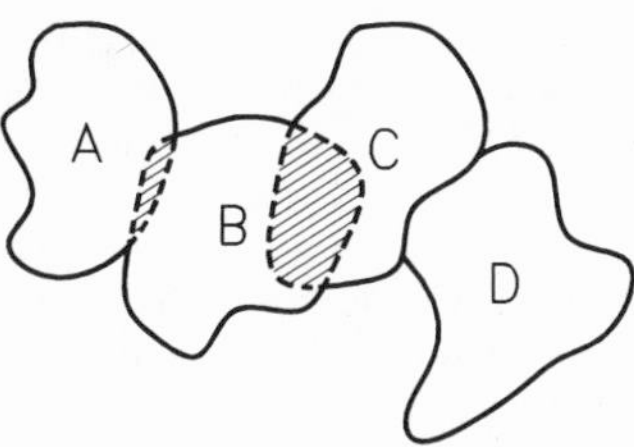

It is this overlapping dimension of boundaries that has been sorely neglected in the study of home and work, for instance. If we fundamentally conceive of any two categories as oppositional, inversely defined classes of things, and especially if we further locate them in distinct times and spaces, we virtually force ourselves to ignore their overlapping potential. In the case of home and work, these assumptions have been compounded by a tendency to consider and treat each category separately. The study of both these things becomes far richer if we simply acknowledge the potential for categorical overlap. At the very least, this allows us to dissociate the mental categories from their physical locations, freeing us to see the more essential categorical boundaries, the constraints that place them, and the work that sustains them.

For what other categories do we unfairly make these assumptions, ignoring the potential for infinite degrees of overlap and producing unrepresentative, inaccurate scholarship as a result? Of course, exploring such overlap also means being extremely sensitive to the myriad points at which categorical boundaries are placed. Therefore, a sensitivity to boundary overlap also forces scholars to become much more sensitive to the multitudinous dimensions of categories, the many, many points where decisions are made about who or what belongs where and the boundary work that reflects this.

The *permeability* of a boundary, or a given section of it, is also part of a boundary's structural profile. This aspect of a cultural boundary makes it relatively easier or harder to mentally move across categorical borders.[1] Boundary permeability is a function of at least two elements: how different the divided categories are from each other and how well we do our boundary work. Initially, it's the juxtaposition of two relatively similar or dissimilar categories that helps determine boundary permeability. The more similar the categories are, the more permeable is their shared border. Yet we also may become adept at mentally moving be-

1. Joseph Pleck's use of the word "permeability" is fairly well known among work-family role researchers. It is quite different from mine. (See Joseph H. Pleck, "The Work-Family Role System," in Patricia Voydanoff, ed., *Work and Family: Changing Roles of Men and Women* (Palo Alto, Cal.: Mayfield, 1984), 8–19. His image of this process and his idea of "asymmetrically permeable boundaries" concerns "work-family roles." In practice, Pleck's argument is based on the assignment of conventional boundaries of time and space to "work" and "family" roles. Permeability refers to the extent to which home or work roles intrude on the time and space that is equated with the opposite realm's roles. His notion of asymmetric permeability is the extent to which individuals violate the dedicated time and space of work or home in order to attend to things that belong to the other place. Moreover, Pleck is not interested in this process or ratio for an individual, as much as he is for sets of individuals. He is interested in making a gendered argument, noting that the asymmetry is in one direction for men, another for women. Culture more often causes women to place their commitments and responsibilities to the family over top of their work commitments and responsibilities, so that family usurps some of work's territory. Culture more often causes men to place their work roles over top of those at home, usurping some of the family's territory. So, for Pleck, permeability does not refer to the ability of people to make mental transitions between realms, but to the ease with which one pre-defined and oppositional role can invade and assume the territory that he associates with the other.

tween the most dissimilar categories and/or resisting the movement between very similar ones. Although we might not make the boundary itself more or less porous, through practice we may compensate for any structured permeability or lack thereof.

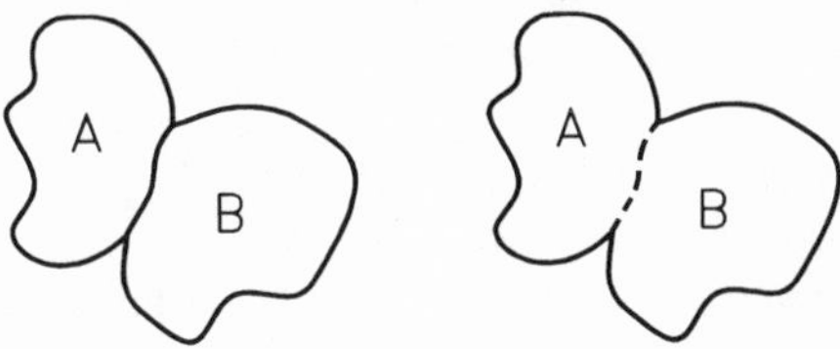

First, consider permeability as a function of categorical similarity/dissimilarity. Again, what are the implications for our thought and behavior as this aspect of a boundary changes? For instance, how does the permeability of a boundary affect individuals' mental and behavioral *transitions* between the divided categories, especially when the categories are experiential realms or some other existential pocket of distinction?

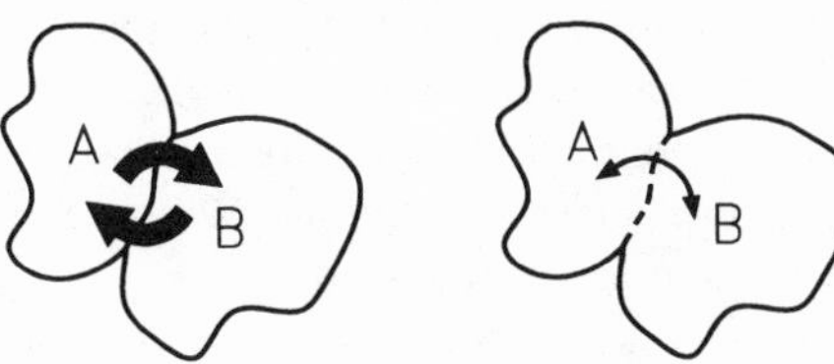

Impregnable borders that divide two very dissimilar categories imply one-way transitions between categories. Mental (possibly physical and social) movement over the boundary and into one side is a radically different enterprise from movement into the opposite category/destination. More permeable boundaries, however, resulting from the juxtapositions of two more similar categories, allow for less distinctive, less direction-linked transitions. The similarity of categories makes their transcendence a more two-way endeavor. The more we segment, for instance, the more our commuting routines depend on the direction of the commute. The more we integrate, the more irrelevant direction becomes and the less our commuting routines are a good prediction of where we're going.

Boundary permeability gets even more interesting. It may be more symmetrical or asymmetrical depending on the direction of movement. The attempt to pass through a boundary from one side may be a much harder or easier endeavor than trying to pass through it from the other side (i.e., the direction of the transition may be more or less relevant in terms of its difficulty). We may have a much tougher time mentally moving from home to work, than from work to home, for instance. Of course, the multidimensional nature of categorical boundaries means that permeability may be more/less symmetrical in some places than others too.

Indeed, boundary permeability may actually prevent multiple trips between categories. Highly permeable from one side, there are some boundaries that are so impregnable from the other, they absolutely prohibit any return. Once we have sex, we no longer can be "virgins." Once we cannot be resuscitated, we can no longer be alive. Once we defect (and assuming the political regime in the country we've left doesn't change), we cannot return and resume our lives in the place we were born. Once the ball has dropped in Times Square, the New Year begins and the old one is over for good. Once we truly accept Copernicus's, Newton's, Darwin's, and Heisenberg's claims, we can never go back to prior notions of how things work and are related to each other.

For this reason, boundary permeability also helps determine which kind will be the most demanding boundary work for us. Where boundaries are more permeable, making transitions quite easy, our boundary

work focuses more on placement activities. Where a boundary is more impregnable, we focus more on transcending it.

Thus, if the home-work boundary is less permeable from the home side (meaning it is relatively difficult to make the move into the work realm), our morning focuses on transitional boundary work. If, however, we find it quite easy to make the transition from work to home in the afternoon (for we are always eager and more able to quickly resume our distinct home self and activities), our afternoon activities may focus more on placing and maintaining the boundary between realms. (The same pattern holds true for distinct sections of the boundaries too, of course, whenever permeability varies.)

Remember Jimmy and Eleanor. Jimmy's home-work boundary is virtually pre-set for him, making transitions the more difficult aspect of his boundary work. Eleanor's transitions are much less problematic. Her effort is more focused on making distinctions between home and work and keeping that tenuous boundary in place.

Think of a different example: the ease with which we make the transition from life to death. Because of its ease of accomplishment (and along with the assumption that this is an undesirable transition), we have developed a huge array of boundary placement work to prevent this transition from happening. The reverse transition, however, from death to life, is more difficult to achieve. This is a much more impregnable boundary (although not as impregnable as we once thought), and its placement work is almost done for us. Accordingly (again, given our assumptions that being alive is better than being dead), our work for this boundary focuses on transcending it, on bringing back to life those who are technically dead and on reversing the process of death (dying) itself.

Moreover, now imagine that we can reliably move between life and death, at will: the transition in either direction is quite easy. Imagine that we are so good at this that we find ourselves slipping between these two conditions at any moment, without prior notice. All of a sudden, cultural obsessions with transcending this boundary—in either direction—might well abate. With transitional skills mastered and phenomenological questions answered, our new obsession might well be the quest for ways to contain ourselves to one or the other conditions. In short, the easier it is to repeatedly jump across a boundary, the harder we have to work not to do so.

Consider another example. Without serious, costly medical procedures (and maybe not even with them), think of the terrible time had by hirsute, large, and well-muscled men trying to maintain their masculinity by day and become deceptive transvestites at night. Their ability to cross over into the gendered behaviors and areas usually associated with women is severely impaired. Their ascribed attributes place a real boundary on their achieved ones. Put them on the Internet, however, take away the normal, appearance-related impediments to crossing that boundary, and they might have a very hard time resisting the urge to feminize themselves whenever they log on. The ease of pursuing one's boundary-crossing obsession could now make boundary maintenance—between real and virtual reality, masculine and feminine forms of self—the new, more demanding challenge for such a person.

This trade-off between boundary permeability and the kind of boundary work required is seen in interactions between individuals and institutions, too. Consider for instance, a situation in which transitions are so difficult or easy for individuals that institutions are forced to spend a great deal of effort on transitional or placement work, respectively. If Thomas Kuhn ([1962] 1970) and Ludwig Fleck ([1935] 1981) are right, science is driven by the ways scientists think about things. Accordingly, it becomes very important for scientific "paradigms" (pervasive, interpretive frameworks that guide present research and help reconstruct what came before) to have distinct, strong boundaries between them.

The problem is that it is difficult for an individual to learn to think in such a distinctive manner. And even after this is accomplished, it is relatively easy for someone constantly looking for what's new and different to slip into an institutionally "pathological" frame of mind.[2] Thus, scientific communities become known for their long periods of occupational training, when intense, paradigmatic indoctrination takes place. This helps individuals make the difficult transition over the boundary that separates the ways scientists think from everyone else (including scientists in other disciplines). However, scientific communities also become known for resisting the individual scientist's work. The peer review process is specifically designed to hold suspect any given scientist's work, particularly that which is most threatening to the current thoughtstyle. Reactions to experimental anomalies, new theories, and unconventional, "undisciplined" questions and methods may be understood in this light.

In short, for the individual, entry into the well-marked mental territory of science is a difficult transition to make, while exit out of it is much easier, to the point that it might be done accidentally. So, science as an institution must help individuals achieve the transition over the rather impermeable border leading into it. At the same time, it tries to reinforce its boundary at the scientific forefront, where the paradigm is most easily transcended and, therefore, most seriously threatened.

Alcoholics Anonymous (AA) also provides a neat case of how an institution tries to counteract the varying ease of members' transitions. AA members believe it is difficult to make the switch from being a drunk to being sober, yet quite easy to cross the boundary in the other direction, from sobriety to drunkenness. As a result, a whole list of behaviors, rules, and supportive endeavors try to help potential members over the first boundary, yet strengthen and keep the second one in place. In the first case, AA works to downplay the difficulty of beginning a sober life, while recognizing that this is indeed a long process, a diffi-

2. Here, I mean "pathological" in the sense of using an unusual, alternate interpretive framework. It could belong more properly to another culture or discipline, for instance, or it might be one that belongs to one's own discipline but is specific to another historical period, past or future.

cult transition into being a "reformed alcoholic."[3] In the second case, AA works to make the boundary between sobriety and back into drunkenness more real, more important, and less readily transgressed than it is.

I find these latter, boundary strengthening activities of the group particularly fascinating, those strategies that aim to keep reformed alcoholics "on the wagon." AA is very limited in the kinds of boundary work it can use to counter the ease of members' transitions to drunkenness. So, the group embraces and emphasizes the fragility of this boundary, perhaps representing it as even more tenuous than it is. Members are taught that the transition from a sober self and lifestyle to a drunken one is so easy that as little as one drink can make them cross the line. In essence, one drink, imbued with almost supernatural powers, becomes the entire boundary separating the two worlds. By emphasizing all this one drink stands for, AA makes it mentally more difficult to consume it and thus begin the "slide" into another experiential realm.

One more example shows what happens when transitions are so easy that they require difficult placement work from us. In the United States, we have a bit of a political paradox. We demand and we justifiably pride ourselves on peaceful, easy transitions from one political administration to another. But the same mechanisms that permit this easy transition also make it quite difficult for politicians and administrations to truly distinguish themselves. That would not be a problem except for one thing: in order to be elected (or reelected), any administration, any politician, must possess a distinct, positive identity.

On the one hand, our system requires us to vote for specific candidates. This means we must make distinctions between politicians. Ostensibly, job performance is one of the overriding factors that should guide our choice. By looking at what politicians have and have not accomplished, we are supposed to select the candidates who have uniquely impressed us in this regard.

On the other hand, the same sorts of constraints that provide options and guide behavior, the same bureaucrats who really do the vast majority of the work continue to be in place before and after voters have their

3. In fact, the complete transition back to pre-alcoholic sobriety is impossible, according to AA, which is why members believe they cannot become "ex-alcoholics." Once you are an alcoholic, the most you can achieve is sobriety; the propensity for alcohol dependence will always be with you.

say every two or four years. This not only keeps business as usual and makes the quest for real, noticeable change a bit difficult, but it means that any administration will have a hard time establishing a distinctive identity through its accomplishments. In practice, a new administration has far more in common with the one that preceded it than it could possibly have distinct from it. In fact, it is obligated to do so.

I wonder if it is a structural need for boundary work in spite of structural demands that forbid it that almost forces us to uniquely identify candidates (and decide whether or not to elect/reelect them) according to their party membership and their unique media images? Party affiliation distinguishes a candidate in two ways. First, it separates her or him from other- or nonparty members. Second, it aligns the candidate with a long string of others' recognizable accomplishments. Since any one candidate cannot hope to accomplish much within her or his term, it makes perfect sense to seek distinction by aligning oneself with one's political allies over a much longer period of time.

Of course, the second way in which we uniquely identify candidates by something other than their distinctive accomplishments is through candidates' looks and their abilities to talk well about things, rather than actually do them. Thus, candidates' distinctive charismatic elements rather than distinctive accomplishments become incredibly important to both them and us. So important, in fact, that we might vote out an incumbent who has done a fine job on a day-to-day basis but who has done so without as much "distinction" as a challenger exhibited throughout her or his campaign. (Of course, an important qualifier is that this distinction must be achieved on socially acceptable grounds.)

Is this paradox also one of the reasons why war (even more than the proverbial tax break) is a politically desirable event? War heroes and wartime administrations frequently receive a healthy reward at the polls. Is it just their sacrifice and military success that accounts for this? Or could it be that war imposes a uniquely meaningful boundary point in a world where these are inevitably hard to come by? It virtually forces the polity to distinguish between the administrations and individuals involved before, after, and especially during the conflict, allowing us to vote with a degree of confidence that may be lacking at other times.

Our political system does a good job in assuring easy transitions, then. But that same system, in promoting the interchangeability of administrations, also requires us to distinguish between them. In short, our politicians and our voters may be torn between structures that inhibit our attention to boundary placement work, on the one hand, and those that demand it, on the other.

We may also ask what leads to change in boundary permeability, eventually affecting the kind of boundary work we do. For instance, what leads an individual to become more segmenting or more integrating in her or his relationship between "home" and "work," not just once but repeatedly over the life course? What kinds of political and practical reasons guide a new communist regime to impose a more impregnable boundary between a State's present and past? And why is it that after this regime "falls," the border between past and present becomes more permeable again? (Why, that is, did "St. Petersburg" become "Leningrad," only to become "St. Petersburg" again, several decades later?) What might make us increase the permeability between "family" and "strangers" along some dimensions but decrease it significantly along others? (Perhaps, for instance, we might suddenly become serious about treating "family" who assault, batter, and torture children, women, and men like "strangers" who did the same thing. Along other dimensions, however, countless factors may cause us to place ever greater emphasis on the difference between those whom we meet in public and those whom we have known since birth.) Similarly, we might also ask why, long ago, different ethnicities, religious affiliations, and skin pigments became significant sources of distinction between people? And why are we now moving away from the unmitigated reservation of distinct jobs, housing, neighborhoods, schools, and bathroom facilities for people possessing distinct ancestries or sets of X and Y chromosomes?[4] Is it economics, the Constitution, the New Testament,

4. Some days, I wonder if the "Politically Correct" (PC) movement will take us so far in the quest for integration that acknowledging any differences between categories of people will be off limits. (Indeed, in the PC climate, we seem to be losing the right to use the very words that might let us do this, for, as PC people know, such words not only reflect but encourage boundaries between people.) Aside from the more obvious question of whether or not this is a good goal, there seems to be a danger here. By removing certain words and subject matters from the table, the quest for totally permeable, indeed, nonexistent, boundaries between people may prevent us from doing the very work that needs to be done to really achieve this goal. If I cannot talk about the real differences between groups, how can I educate myself or anyone else about which differences we should respect and which ones we need to overcome, or how to go about doing either? Even losing the ability to joke about these boundaries (in ways that are acceptable to those who are the butt of the joke, of course) threatens to affect the process by taking away the good humor we need to get the job done. For instance, watching the news one night, I was appalled when

Liberal ideology, the Weltgeist? For sure, the result is an increasingly permeable boundary between classically divided categories of people, at least along certain dimensions, at least within the United States.

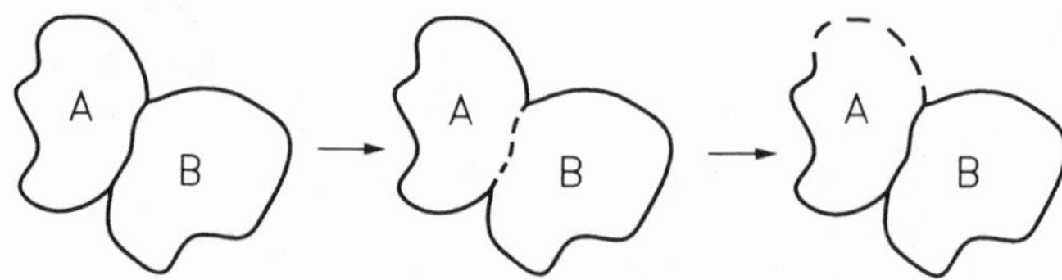

Other than increasing or decreasing the degree of similarity between categories, we also may influence boundary permeability through practice, practice in making the transition between categories more easily or in setting the boundary more strongly. The more successful we are in doing our transition work, the more permeable we make the boundary. The more successful we are in doing our placement work, the less permeable we make the boundary. Failure in either of these endeavors affects boundary permeability in the reverse direction. Of course, we may have varying success in our boundary work at different points along any one boundary too, differentially affecting permeability along the length of the boundary.

More generally, this means that the future study of boundaries should also focus on the ways behavior can transform boundary structures. Boundary structures influence our thinking and our visible behavior in so many ways. But is the reverse also possible? Forcing some-

---

network news aired a story of Bill Clinton's alleged faux pas while surrounded by his staff at an exhibit of Lego creations. Clinton joked that the castle they were looking at was almost big enough for one of his unusually short cabinet members to live in. In the clip, Lloyd Bentson starts to laugh along with the others, then catches himself. He turns to Clinton, eyebrows in his hairline, shaking his head and waving his finger back and forth in the classic "no, no, no" gesture. I appreciate Bentson's extraordinary sensitivity to the plight of those quite unlike him, but as one of the "vertically challenged," even PC advocates would allow me to say that there was nothing wrong with this joke. My more general point, however, is that the day we lose our ability to spontaneously laugh about things as harmless as this is the day our culture moves that much closer to becoming another Yugoslavia, another Rwanda. Negotiations over the boundary between what's funny and what's not, what's in "good" taste and what's in "bad" continue to attract my attention. Murray Davis's *What's So Funny?* (Chicago: University of Chicago Press, 1993) is a good source on this subject.

one to clock in and out of work, prohibiting the movement of wage work objects out of the workplace, demanding that wage work be taken home and done there, or that colleagues be entertained there, are constraints that not only affect our behavior, but eventually fashion the very structures of our mental home and work categories: their size, their exact contents and their permeability.

Likewise, as Kai Erikson asks, how does an individual engaging in acts of war, alone, encourage her or him to see people, objects, and the world in new ways, ways that support evermore hate and violence?[5] How do the following affect the ways we think: the burning of crosses on the lawns of interracially married couples; the increasingly similar yet still different dress codes for women and men; the busing of school children; the coeducational practices of schools; the experience of employment in places where the highest ranks of workers run the melanin and gender gamuts; placing "Women's Studies" or "African American Studies" in university departments of their own; being permitted to watch extremely violent programs on television or in the movies throughout the day, from a very young age, but being forbidden to see nudity until the very late hours of the day or after we turn eighteen years old; listening to and singing along with children's songs and television programming emphasizing the commonalties among people with different languages, genitalia, and skin pigment; or seeing the very young, the very old, or the mentally or physically sick in only isolated places and times?[6] Boundary work on these categories and countless others completely surrounds us and infiltrates every aspect of our existence, since it is such a fundamental aspect of society. And it fundamentally shapes the ways we view these categories and their relationships, via the boundaries that separate them.

As all of these examples intimate, the ability to recognize boundary work and explore how it affects the ways we think depends on one of the main themes of this work: mental, categorical boundaries are reflected in the boundaries we place around space and time. This is an essential dimension of boundary work and therefore provides a wonderful point of entry into identifying boundary work and the cultural

5. Kai Erikson, "War and Ethnic Boundaries: The Destruction of a Croatian Village," plenary session address given at Midwest Sociological Society 1995 annual meeting, Chicago.

6. On the social construction of gender, ethnicity, "race," age, death and dying, for instance, see Christine Williams (1989), Richard Williams (1990), Betty Friedan (1993), and Robert Zussman (1993).

boundaries it reflects and encourages. How do the different attributes of a boundary's structure manifest in different uses and meanings of space and time? If a category grows larger or smaller, what kinds of temporal or spatial evidence might we see of its change? If categories begin to overlap or the degree of overlap changes, how is that represented in the ways space and time are used, before and after the change? If a categorical boundary becomes more or less permeable, how might this be manifested in the ways categorical contents move or are moved through time and space? And how might changes in the ways we divide time and space, alone, encourage us to change the way we think about categories and their contents?

This is one of the reasons why it makes so much sense to take an ethnographic approach to the study of self and identity. Mental sources of and changes in identity require practical boundary work to prop them up, if not stimulate them altogether. Look at the boundary work and you'll see the selves and the transformations it supports. In particular, the ways in which the self appears over time and through space reveal the ways in which different aspects of self are enacted, supported, demarcated, and transformed. This is because practical boundary work is the Modern self's clever response to transformational demands over the course of the day and life. With mental changes, habits change, ways of interacting and dressing change, traveling and working props change, residence and travel and sleep patterns change, the people with whom we socialize change, what we eat and drink, the music we listen to changes, and so on. By noticing these, throughout the day, the year, the marriage or wage work career, we may be most quickly, most accurately alerted to an individual's sources of identity and any self-transformations under way.

The link between the ways we divide time and space and how we might subsequently adjust our ways of thinking is also one of the reasons why subjects like "homeworkers" and "telecommuting" are interesting. Telecommunications technologies, for instance, give workers the opportunity to break with older uses of space and time in delineating realms. But they also provide extraordinary pressures to come up with new ways of using these tools if employees/family members wish to maintain distinct categories of existence. The technology can encourage us to rethink what home and work mean and how they should be related, developing new ways of enacting these realms, accordingly. Or, we may not take advantage of/not succumb to the effects of these conventional boundary-attenuating technologies. We may continue to impose older notions of these categories but simply shorten our commutes. Management's and family members' expectations about what constitutes "work," when and where telecommuters are allowed/expected to do it at home, and whether or not sanctions and rewards in either realm are linked to one's physical presence will play a large part in unfolding these possibilities. Telecommuters' abilities to create and substitute new transitional activities for their previous, physical journeys to and from work will also affect the success of this increasingly popular concept of home and work.

Sociology, not to mention the work of other social scientists and analysts, hinges on the existence and implications of categorical boundaries. It is my intent to add to our understanding of these socially constructed phenomena with this analysis of "home" and "work." And I do so from a most "microsociological" angle, consciously neglecting much of the historical context and broader political-economic structures from which the more immediate, micro-level manifestations I discuss emerge and which they then support and/or challenge. One book can only hold so much, after all.

Nonetheless, I hope it is apparent that this book on "home" and "work" is firmly rooted in my theoretical interest in all boundaries, their characteristics, and the classification systems that result from them. It is for this reason that, in addition to earning a place among other well-established substantive and theoretical literatures, I hope this study will be placed squarely in the heart of a newly emerging field within sociology. This is the field Eviatar Zerubavel calls "cognitive sociology."

Cognitive sociology is the sociology of thinking, the study of the social, cultural influences on how we think about everything that is around us. As evidenced in *Social Mindscapes: An Invitation to Cognitive Sociology* (1996), Zerubavel's approach draws on many traditional areas of inquiry both within and outside of sociology. From such diversity, what Zerubavel gives us is what I think of as a "theoretical method." It is a way of focusing on the cultural cornerstones of thinking, the specific points where society most heavily influences personal thought. This includes the mandate to pay acute attention to the kinds of relationships that exist (and might exist) between thought-objects. This strategy is extremely helpful for exploring the social meaning and connectedness of things, and even the historical processes, values, and norms that help shape these meanings. In fact, this is what enabled me to begin my own work in the field, exploring the link between the things that encourage us to think a certain way and the visible ways we enact them. Cognitive sociology provides a lovely "foot in the door" for any sociologist, then, but especially for someone interested in the study of everyday life.

At its most fundamental level, this book is about a subject at the cornerstone of cognitive sociology, namely, classification: its cultural foundations, its structural-situational influences, its personal variations and enactments. If there is one, general sociological question that I have asked myself throughout this text, it is, "What are the mental and behavioral implications of the cultural and social-structural foundations of classification for an individual member of society?" I have tackled this question by focusing on a specific process: "boundary work" (which is my two-word answer to the question just stated), why we do it, what it is, what influences it, and what it means for a given person.

As two of the most important categories of everyday life, "home" and "work" have provided me with an especially good opportunity to study how historical, cultural, and structural constraints translate into personal, mental boundaries. They further show how these mental boundaries translate into existential ones, and vice versa. These territories of the self show how we use time, space, and slews of artifacts, activities, and associates to enhance and manage more similar or different mental distinctions. By looking at the boundary work of home and work, we see how innovation and accommodation appear in what is mental *and* practical. What we see is nothing less than the joining of the cultural, the structural, and the personal to make the categorical.

Whether I've succeeded in my goal of answering these questions is obviously up to readers. Yet I hope this work will be useful not only as an illustration of an especially sociological process and a certain way of exploring it but also as an analytical tool. I found myself better understanding my own life and behavior while working on this problem. I hope my efforts serve a similar purpose for others who also are trying to understand the processes in which we are engaged and the constraints that affect us. Ultimately, it is in the explanation of these processes that the power of the "sociological imagination" (Mills 1956)—and any sociologist—lies.

Appendix

Interview Questionnaire for *Home and Work*

Introduction to Respondents and Consent-to-Be-Interviewed Form

Thank you once again for agreeing to do this interview with me. Your cooperation is very much appreciated.

You are being asked to be a volunteer in a research study for my Ph.D. dissertation research. The questions I'm going to ask you today are about your home and work activities. The purpose of this study is to explore the ways in which people manage their home and work activities, both practically and mentally.

As you already know, your part in this study will involve an interview, during the time(s) we have agreed. The length of the interview varies tremendously, although pretests have shown that people take between one and a quarter and two and a half hours to complete the questions. In the event that we have not finished the interview at the end of today's session, I will ask you if we may continue it at another time, at your convenience. This could be done on site during a work break, perhaps by meeting elsewhere in person, or, if it's better for you, over the phone in the evening.

In order to give you my undivided attention during the interview, I will be recording our conversation. Let me assure you that all your responses are absolutely confidential; I will be the only person to know what you have said during this interview. The tapes of our discussion will be kept off-site and locked up, with only an identification number on them. Likewise, any paperwork for this interview will be identified only by interview number. The master sheet matching interview numbers and respondents' names is also kept in a locked file cabinet off-site.

When the results of this research are made public, none of the actual names of any individuals will appear in it. For the most part, your answers will be combined with others' and appear as aggregated data. An especially insightful comment of yours may be quoted, however, attributed to you only through a pseudonym (made-up name) or descriptive phrase. For instance, the dissertation will read "Mary, a research group leader and mother of two, stated the following: . . ." "Mary," of course, will not be the individual's real name. With this in mind, I hope that you'll try to be as honest with me as possible throughout the course of this interview. Your actual thoughts, experiences and feelings are the responses I'm looking for.

You should also know that I have been asked to make a presentation of my findings to members of [the Lab's] Personnel Department. Again, as with any publications and talks on this project, individual respondents will remain anonymous within this presentation. The purpose of the talk I give will be to present an overview of my research, as well as specifically address some of [the Lab's] recruiting and retention concerns.

All of these steps are designed to carefully ensure the confidentiality of your remarks. For this reason, I do not anticipate any risks to you associated with this research. Nor do I expect that there will be much cause for you to feel uncomfortable during this interview. However, if any of the issues we discuss is particularly problematic for you, this is a possibility. You do, of course, have the right to refuse to answer a question if you find it too troubling to discuss at this time. It is my experience, however, that most people find discussions about their home and work are enjoyable events, sometimes even therapeutic in nature.

In a more general sense, your responses will help me gain further insight into why people see home and work the way they do. It will be my job to convey this understanding to others, perhaps showing that any given way of seeing home and work is not so much better or worse than any other, but simply logical and practical, given certain experiences.

At this time, then, I'm going to ask you to sign two copies of this document which I am required to obtain by the Committee on Research Involving Human Subjects (CORIHS), an ethics panel overseeing all pertinent research projects at SUNY Stony Brook. Once you have done that, stating that you have consented to be interviewed by me, we can get started with the interview.

Please note that according to CORIHS guidelines:

You do not have to be in this study if you don't want to be.

You have to right to leave the study at any time without giving any reason and without penalty.

If you have any questions about the study, you may contact me, telephone # 929-6290 (home) or 632-7700 (office).

If you have any questions about your rights as a research subject, you may contact Dr. Robert Schneider, Committee on Research Involving Human Subjects, (516) 632-6960.

Any new information that may make you change your mind about being in this study will be given to you. You will get a copy of this consent form to keep. If you sign below, it means that you have read (or have had read to you) and have understood all of the information given in this consent form, and you would like to be a volunteer in this study.

I consent to be interviewed by Christena Nippert-Eng for her Ph.D. dissertation research, as outlined above:

(name) (date)

Interview Schedule

I. Background Information on Work and Home

These first few questions will provide a little background about your family and your job and how you feel each of them.

1. Briefly describe your job. Do you usually look forward to going to work each day? Why? What do you like most/least about what you do?

2. Would you say your job is a very important source of identity for you? Why?

3. Describe your family (who's there, how often, how much time spent together). If children: Where are they during the day, who picks them up, drops them off for day care, school, activities, or play with friends? Do you have any pets?

4. Do you usually look forward to going home and being around your family each day? Why or why not?

5. Would you say your family is a very important source of identity for you? Why?

6. If you had your choice, would you rather spend time at home, at work or somewhere else? Why?

7. Do you do any chores at home? Do you think of any of them as work? Why?

Checklist:

child care (specify demands), pet care
laundry
finances/bills
ironing
cleaning
dinner dishes
shopping—grocery, gifts, house repairs, clothes
car work
lawn and grounds maintenance
garbage

8. Do you have enough time for yourself—enough free time to do what you like? How do you feel about that? Do you think it's important to have time for yourself? Why?

9. Are you happy with your house or apartment? What do you like about it? What do you dislike about it?

Checklist:

location: work- v. family-related v. leisure-related

finances: unit price, taxes, commuting costs
house itself—specify attractive features: work- v. family-related v. other
other

10. When you chose your house or apartment, or if you've done any remodeling since then, did you consider a need for space to do your work at home? Did you consider a need for space to entertain guests?

11a. How many telephone lines do you have?
If one: Have you considered getting an additional line? Why?
If two or more: Why so many? What are they used for?

11b. Do you have call waiting or any other special features like conference calling? Why?

II. The Boundary—Ways in which It Is Established and Crossed

This next set of questions addresses the many ways in which the worlds of home and work may intersect. For some people, home and work are kept quite separate, yet for others, they are closely interwoven and sometimes quite difficult to distinguish. This part of the interview will explore the ways in which your home and work lives intersect.

12. Do any of your relatives work at [the Lab]? If yes: Do you see much of them while you're at work? Do you like the fact that you work with them?

13. Do any of your friends, people you met outside the workplace, now work at [the Lab]? If yes: Do you see much of them at work? Do you like this?

14. Have you ever brought your family or friends to your work place? If no: Why not? If yes: Who did you bring? Why did you bring them? How often has this happened? Would you like to bring them more often?

15. While you're at work, do you often think about your home, family, and friends? Is it possible for you to take care of your work activities while thinking about other things, like your family, running errands, or a hobby? Would you say that most of your workload requires your undivided attention, or can you be thinking about one thing and doing another most of the time?

16. Would you generally say that having to deal with family and home-related matters during the day has been a problem for you with this job, in particular? Why is that?

17. Are you allowed to make personal phone calls at work? Do you? To whom? How often? How do you feel when you have to make a personal call at work? Why is that? How do you feel when your coworkers make personal calls?

18a. Are you allowed to receive personal phone calls from family and friends or about personal business at work? Do you? Who calls you? How often? How do you feel when you get a personal call at work? Why is that? What do you do when this happens? Say you're talking with a coworker and she or he gets a call from their spouse, what do you do?

18b. Have you ever had a problem with a worker who didn't seem to be showing the right level of commitment or responsibility toward (their) work? What happened? What seemed to be the problem? How did you resolve this?

19. Some people have a problem being interrupted by family and friends at work. Either they call or drop by too frequently or at inconvenient times. Has this ever been a problem for you? Have you ever had a talk with them about being interrupted at work? Have you developed particular working techniques, ways of scheduling your workload, or sets of rules about others contacting you at work to keep thoughts about home from interfering with your work?

20. Does the nature of your job mean that you are frequently interrupted at work? Who's usually doing the interrupting? Do you mind this? Would you say this is a problem for you? Have you developed any techniques to discourage coworkers from interrupting you?

21. Do you talk about your family and friends at work? How often? Who do you talk to about your personal life? Is this something you enjoy doing? Do your coworkers seem to feel the same way?

22. Have you ever been uncomfortable because a coworker started to tell you about (their) personal life? What happened? Why did you feel this way?

23. Do you ever have people from [the Lab] over to your house? Who? Are they good friends? When? What do you do? Do you enjoy it or do you think it's kind of a burden?

24. Do you ever get together with your coworkers in a neutral, social place, like a restaurant, bar, or athletic field? Where do you go? When do you go? Who's there? Is this something you enjoy?

25. Are there ever any social occasions that you go to as part of your work? Is it required that you go? Do you consider these occasion and events to be "work"? Does your family go along? Are they expected to? Do you enjoy these occasions? Are there any social occasions that you don't go to? Why?

26. Some people choose an occupation or job in order to accommodate the demands of a family. Has this been true for you with this particular job? Are there any special family constraints you have on your work?

27. Do you have a sense of what's fair to (others) re: the time you spend on work? How has this affected the kind of job you've taken?

28. Have you ever had to take part-time rather than full-time work on account of your family? How did you feel about that? What were the circumstances at the time? What job did you take? Did you enjoy the work? Would you have preferred to work full-time? Was your spouse working full-time at the time? Why didn't she/he take the part-time work?

29. Do you ever have to leave work early, go to work late, or stay home from work on account of your family or home-related business? (Specify.) How often has this happened? What sorts of circumstances were involved? How do you feel when this happens? How does your boss feel when this happens? What about your coworkers? How do they feel about you coming late, leaving early, or staying home altogether because of personal business?

30. Some employers have a system in which all employees are at work during the middle of the day, but individuals have some choice about the time they start their workday. Some people contract to start at 7 A.M. and finish at 3 P.M., others might choose the more traditional hours of 9 to 5. Would you be interested in this kind of option if it were available? Why?

31. Could you bring your work home if you wanted to? If yes: Does your boss expect you to bring it home? Do your coworkers expect you to bring it home? Do you expect them to bring work home?

32. Do you, in fact, bring your work home? What kinds of work tasks do you bring home (reading, writing materials)? Why do you bring these particular things home and not something else? (Look for physical constraints, probability of interruption, inability to think "correctly" at home.) Where do you read/use it? Why there?

33. In addition to what you've already mentioned, do you bring home any other supplies or materials from work to use at home? If yes: Are they all over your house or do you have a separate room where you keep these materials, like a study or workroom? Both?

34. How often do you find yourself thinking about work while doing home-related things? What kinds of tasks let you do this more easily? In what situations do you find it most difficult to think about your work and still do your home activities?

35. Altogether, then, about how much time during the day/week do you spend on work activities at home? Would you say that the amount of time you spend on your job while at home is just about right, too much or too little for you? Why do you feel this way?

36. Are you often interrupted at home? Who's interrupting you and for what kinds of reasons? Do you mind? Have you developed any ways of handling this?

37. If respondent works at home: What if you're working at home and a family member or friend interrupts you? Is this disorienting? Would you say it's more or less disorienting than when you get interrupted at [the Lab]? Why is that? What do you do when this happens? If not mentioned previously: Do you adjust the kinds of work you bring home because of the probability of being interrupted? In what way? (Look for kind of interruption v. frequency.)

38. Where do you keep information on work-related matters like health insurance and other benefits, union membership, social occasions, and recreation?

39. How many calendars do you use? Where are they? What's on them? If more than one: How do they differ? (If pocket calendar, check for distributional equity between home, work, leisure.)

40. Do you keep any personal paperwork at work? What? Why?

41. Do you have a computer at home? Do you use it for work-related activities? What, specifically, do you use it for? How often? Where do you keep it? Why there? Do you like the idea of having a computer at home for your personal use?

42. If applicable: Does your spouse bring work home? Why? How much? How do you feel about the amount of work s/he brings home? What about the amount of time s/he works, in general?

43. Do you ever talk about your work with your family and friends? How often? With whom? What kinds of things do you talk about? What do you rarely talk about? Why don't you mention these things to them?

44. How does your family seem to feel about the work that you do? Are they proud of what you do?

45. How do they feel about the amount of time you spend at work? If you bring your work home, how do they feel about that? Do they expect it? Has anyone in your family purposefully tried to keep you from doing your work? Who is or was it? What have they done? Why do you think they did or do this?

46. Do you ever get calls about work at home? How often? How do you feel about that? Do you ever have to go back into work as a result of a call to handle problems?

47. Do you ever have to be away overnight from your home and family on work-related business? How often? How long? How do you feel about that? Can your family go along? How do you feel about that? How do they feel about that?

48. Some people have a problem keeping work from infringing on their attention to family and nonwork interests. Is this generally a problem for you? (When is it most problematic?) Have you developed any techniques or rules to keep work from interfering with your home life?

49. Do you bring a lunch from home to work with you? If yes: How often? Why is that? Who makes it? Do you ever get any messages in it? Do you generally take a lunch break or do you usually work while eating? Do you eat your bag lunch at your desk or leave your workspace to eat it?

50. Are there official hours when you are expected to be at work? How strict is your employer or supervisor about showing up on time and staying until the official quitting time? How are these rules enforced? What happens if you don't show up on time or if you leave early?

51. Are you expected to be at home at a specific times during the day? If yes:

When is that? What happens if you leave early in the morning or don't show up on time in the evening?]

52. Do you usually take breaks during the day from your work? Why or why not? Official policy? What kind of breaks do you take? (How many; how long; where do you go; what do you do; who do you take them with?) Do your boss and coworkers refrain from approaching you during your breaks?

53. What if you want a break from whatever you're doing at home—can you take a break whenever you feel like it? What do you have to do if you want a break? If you are taking a break from whatever's going on at home, how do you relax—what do you do during your break? How long would this last?

54. Do you carry a briefcase or something like it between work and home? Why? What's in it? Where do you keep it at home? Why a (briefcase) or (whatever and not a briefcase)?

55. Do you subscribe to any magazines or journals? Which ones? Are they mailed to your home or office? Why there?

56. Do you ever take personal reading material to work, such as a novel or hobby-related magazine? If yes: How often? Why? Where do you read it? Does anybody seem to mind? If no: Why not? Do you think other people would mind if you did? Would you mind if your coworkers read these things at work?

57. Do you ever bring craft or hobby materials from home to work, either to work on or to show other workers? What are they? Why bring it there? How often do you do this?

58. Do you ever bring things to work on behalf of your spouse or children, such as school sales items or walk-a-thon sponsor sheets? Why or why not? Do you enjoy doing that?

59. Do you keep any photographs of family and friends on your desk or in your locker at work? Why or why not? What are they? Where do you keep them?

60. Do you have any photographs of your coworkers at home? Where are they? (Displayed, in photo albums, or stored away somewhere?)

61. Do you have any knickknacks, conversation pieces, family art work or gifts from home at work? Why or why not? What? Where are they? Are there any gifts from coworkers here?

62. Do you have any knickknacks, gifts, or promotional items from work at home? What? Where do you keep them? (Probe: pens, buttons, bumper stickers, products, mugs, T-shirts, posters.) How did you acquire these? (Purchase, gifts, awards.)

This next group of questions concerns some of the more negative ways that home and work can impinge on each other. They address the worries and anxiety that can be associated with our activities and how this might influence our participation in either realm.

63. Have you ever experienced any significant work-related stress or worries? Why do you think that is? If yes: Do you find that you bring work-related stress and worries home with you? Do you think this has a significant impact on your family and your activities there? About how often would you say this happens?

64. Do you ever experience any significant home-related stress or worries? Why do you think that is? If yes: Do you find that you bring your home-related stress and worries to the workplace? Do you think this has a significant impact on your work and your fellow workers? About how often would you say this happens?

65. Are there ever times when you feel torn between what you think you should be doing for work and what you think you should be doing for you family? Would you say that you have had to work at balancing you work and home-related responsibilities? Are there any special arrangements or strategies that you haven't mentioned yet that enable you to accommodate both your family demands and your work demands?

66. Have you ever received medical treatment for a stress-related illness or condition? If yes: Did you ever see a counselor or therapist because of this kind of stress? What was the source of your stress? Did it have anything to do with the demands being made on you at home and/or at work?

67. The next thing I'm going to ask may seem a bit unusual, but it's usually a lot of fun too. I'm going to ask you to take a look in your wallet, purse, and pockets and tell me what you find. This may reveal some rather interesting things about who you are, what's important in your life, and the different roles you play.

Checklist:

cash
paychecks
checkbook
savings book

business cards (specify personal or business)

phone numbers: # of business; # of personal

car registration
driver's license
car insurance card

Social Security card/numbers
frequent flyer cards (business) (personal)
health insurance cards

credit cards: # of business; # of personal

calling card (used for business, personal, or both?)
cash card

check cashing cards
credit union card

[Lab] employee card
[Lab] savings and annuities card
[Lab recreation] card
blood donor card

auto club
car rental card
investment broker card
video rental card
library card
union membership card

other leisure passes and membership cards—specify

calendars

keys: how many key chains? why separated as they are?
(specify keys on each key chain)

receipts, returns
food coupons

rain checks, rebates (home-ownership, consumables for family, gifts?)

stamps
pens, pencils
calculator (used where?)
pocket knife (used where?)

comb, brush
cosmetics
Chap Stick
dental floss
mirror
emery boards
tissues
feminine supplies
nail clipper
handkerchiefs
lint brush
matches, lighter
safety pins
sewing supplies
stockings

sunglasses/glasses/contact lens care

birth control
aspirin
medication
antacids
Band-Aids
(Why do you carry these?)

gum, candy

nostalgic items—specify

photos—kept where? specify relationship to individual. (Ask why none of obvious possibilities.)

other

III. Transitions and Gear-Switching

This next group of questions is about routines. Some people have little routine to their day, while others have quite specific routines scattered throughout their day. These questions focus on the existence and nature of any routines you may have.

68. Do you have a pre-work, morning routine? Is there anything that you have to do besides getting yourself ready to go to work? If yes: Do you mind having to do these things? Why or why not? What do you think about while you're doing this routine? Does this routine help you mentally prepare yourself for work in any way?

69. Do you wear a wristwatch? If no: Why not? If yes: When do you put it on and take it off? Where do you keep it?

70. Do you have a routine when you get to work? Do you have to start work right away, or do you pretty much start whenever you feel like it? Are there any particular feelings you usually experience when you arrive at work?

71. Do your boss or any of your coworkers seem to have routines upon arriving at work? Pick one that comes to mind and describe it.

72. Do you have a specific routine at the end of the work day? Do you have to work right up until the official quitting time, or can you stop a little early if you feel like it? What do you usually do? Why do you do this?

73. Do your boss or any of your coworkers seem to have routines at the end of the day? Pick one that comes to mind and describe it.

74. Are there any particular feelings you have when you arrive at home?

75. Do you have a typical routine when you get home? If yes: What is it?
Do you have to start taking care of things right away, or do you get to relax for a while, first?

Right away: Why does it have to be done right away? Do you mind having to take care of things immediately? Why or why not?
Relax: Is relaxing a bit when you get home important for you? Why?

76. Do you have a weekend routine? What kinds of things do you usually do during the weekend?

This next set of questions concerns your trips to and from work.

77. First of all, describe your trip to work: how long (time, miles); method of transportation. Any other options? Why this type of transit? Solo or car pool? Ever consider the other option? Why this one? Route/kinds of roads taken; why did you pick this route?

78. Now describe the trip home: Do you take the same route both ways? Why or why not?

79. Would you call your journey to work a "commute?" Why?

80. Do you like your trip between home and work? Why?

81. What do you think about or do during your morning trip to work? What about your evening trip home?

(Look for: drink/eat—what; when; why; same both ways?; shave/make-up; phone, CB, TV, tapes, radio (which? what format? same both ways?); think about work/home; future plans—specify identity/fantasy/daydream.)

82. Some people break their trip down into different segments. They use a certain station stop, exit ramp, or stop light to tell themselves they should start to think about or do something at that point. Do you do this? Is there a point where you usually start to think about your work concerns in the morning/ your family concerns at night?

83. Do you think there are any specific advantages or disadvantages to the kind of trip you make between home and work?

IV. Comparison between the Mentalities of Home and Work: Dimensions along which They Might Differ

What I want you to think about now are the similarities and differences between how you think and act at work and at home. Some people find that they have pretty much the same frame of mind whether they're at home or at work. On the other hand, some people find that they have to mentally switch gears when they turn their attention from work to home activities and vice versa. These questions are designed to compare your particular home and work experiences.

84. Some people feel like they're almost two different people when they're at home and at work. Is this true for you? Why do you say that?

85. When you're at home, what kinds of things do you usually think about?

86. When you're at work, what sorts of things are usually on your mind?

87. Is your activity at home meaningful and important to you? Is it challenging? Are you proud of what you do there? What about at work? Meaningful? Important? Challenging?

88. How well do people treat you at home? Does it matter to you how well you are treated there? What about at work—do people treat you well there? Does that matter to you?

89. When you tell people about your job, is it something you're proud of? When you tell people about your home life and family, is it something you're proud of?

90. What kinds of obligations or commitment do you have to the people you work with? Where might your commitment to them stop? What about at home—how would you describe your commitment there and where it might end?

91. What kinds of rewards do you expect for your efforts at work? Do you feel that you are justly rewarded or recognized for your effort at work? What about at home—what kinds of rewards do you expect for your efforts there? Are you justly rewarded for your effort at home?

92. Do you feel needed at home? Would you say you are indispensable? Do you like this? What about at work—do you feel needed and indispensable there? Do you like this?

93. In general, how much are you aware of the time at home? At work? Why is that? Would you say you're usually in a rush at work? At home?

94. Do you feel you can be yourself at work? Why? What about at home—can you be yourself there?

95. Is there a friendly, happy atmosphere at home? Do people joke and laugh much? Do you, personally, make an effort to make things cheerful at home?

What about at work? Is there a cheerful atmosphere there? Do people joke and laugh much? Do you, personally, make an effort to make things cheerful at work?

96. Do you have good friends at work? Is this important to you? Why? What about when you're at home—do you have any good friends you talk with there? Do they live nearby, or visit fairly frequently? Is it important to you to have good friends that you see at home? Why?

97. Do you have a sense of carrying on a tradition or contributing to history at home? Do you ever think about whether your activity, in some sense, makes you immortal? Is this important? What about at work—do you feel as if you are carrying on a tradition there? Is it one that might in some way make you immortal? Is this important to you?

98. Are you concerned with your appearance at home? At work? Do you dress any differently for work than if you're home for the day? How?

99. Do you follow the same grooming routine whether you're going to work or staying home for the day? Is there anything you do differently? (Look for showering; hairstyling; for women especially, make-up; for men especially, shaving.)

100. Some people speak the same way, no matter where they are. On the other hand, some people do change the way they talk to others, depending on where they are. Do you use the same language at home and at work? In what ways does it differ? Do you have to conscientiously change your language when you get to work or when you go home?

V. Parental Socialization on Boundary

We're just about finished. These last few questions are about the way your parents' home and work activities might have intersected.

101. What did your parents do for a living? Did either of them work for a wage out of their home? If no: Did they bring work home with them very often? Did they seem to like their work? Did they talk much about their work at home? Did they ever get calls about work at home? Did they take you to work with them? How well do you think you understand their work?

102. Did your parents participate in any union activities? Were you ever introduced to their customers or coworkers? Did they ever have people from work over for dinner? Do you know if they considered any of the people they worked with to be their friends?

103. Do you think your parents' views and practices have had any impact on your ideas about mixing home and work? Is there anyone else, or any experience you've had, in particular, that's affected your views of mixing home and work?

That concludes the interview. Thank you so very much for your time and insight.

REFERENCES

Abbott, Andrew. 1988. *The System of Professions: An Essay on the Division of Expert Labor.* Chicago: University of Chicago Press.

Adler, Patricia A., and Peter Adler. 1991. *Backboards and Blackboards: College Athletes and Role Engulfment.* New York: Columbia University Press.

Aisenberg, Nadya, and Mona Harrington. 1988. *Women of Academe: Outsiders in the Sacred Grove.* Amherst: University of Massachussetts Press.

Alt, John. 1976. "Beyond Class: The Decline of Labor and Leisure," *Telos* no. 28:55–80.

Bateson, Gregory. [1955] 1972. *Steps to an Ecology of Mind.* New York: Ballantine.

Bateson, Mary Catherine. 1989. *Composing a Life.* New York: Atlantic Monthly Press.

Beach, Betty. 1989. *Integrating Work and Family Life.* New York: SUNY Press.

Becker, Howard S. 1986. *Writing for Social Scientists.* Chicago: University of Chicago Press.

Bell, Catharine. 1992. *Ritual Theory, Ritual Practice.* New York: Oxford University Press.

Berger, Bennett, ed. 1990. *Authors of Their Own Lives: Intellectual Autobiographies by Twenty American Sociologists.* Berkeley: University of California Press.

Berger, Peter L., and Thomas Luckmann. 1968. *The Social Construction of Reality.* Garden City, N.Y.: Anchor Press.

Binford, Henry C. 1985. *The First Suburbs.* Chicago: University of Chicago Press.

Bourdieu, Pierre. 1973. "The Berber House." In *Rules and Meanings,* edited by Mary Douglas, 98–110. Harmondsworth: Penguin Books.

Bourdieu, Pierre, and Loic Wacquant. 1992. *An Invitation to Reflexive Sociology.* Chicago: University of Chicago Press.

Braverman, Harry. 1974. *Labor and Monopoly Capital: The Degradation of Work in the Twentieth Century.* New York: Monthly Review Press.

Christensen, Kathleen. 1987. "Women, Families and Home-Based Employment." In Gerstel and Gross 1987, 478–90.

Cohen, Stanley, and Laurie Taylor. 1978. *Escape Attempts.* New York: Pelican Books.

Cole, Stephen. 1983. "A Hierarchy of the Sciences?" *American Journal of Sociology* 89:111–19.

Coser, Lewis. 1974. *Greedy Institutions: Patterns of Undivided Commitment.* New York: Free Press.

Coser, Rose Laub. 1991. *In Defense of Modernity.* Stanford: Stanford University Press.

Cott, Nancy F. 1977. *The Bonds of Womanhood: "Women's Sphere" in New England, 1780–1835.* New Haven: Yale University Press.

Cowen, Ruth Schwarz. 1983. *More Work for Mother: The Ironies of Household Technology from the Open Hearth to the Microwave.* New York: Basic Books.

Csikszentmihalyi, Mihaly. 1975. *Beyond Boredom and Anxiety.* San Francisco: Jossey-Bass.

Csikszentmihalyi, Mihaly, and Eugene Rochberg-Halton. 1981. *The Meaning of Things.* Cambridge: Cambridge University Press.

Davis, Fred. 1992. *Fashion, Culture and Identity.* Chicago: University of Chicago Press.

Davis, Murray S. 1983. *Smut.* Chicago: University of Chicago Press.

de Saussure, Ferdinand. [1919] 1959. *A General Course in Linguistics.* New York: Philosophical Library.

Delaney, Kevin J. 1992. *Strategic Bankruptcy.* Berkeley: University of California Press.

DeVault, Marjorie L. 1987. "Doing Housework: Feeding and Family Life." In Gerstel and Gross 1987, 178–91.

Douglas, Mary. [1966] 1985. *Purity and Danger.* ARK ed. London: Routledge and Kegan Paul.

———. 1975. *Implicit Meanings: Essays in Anthropology.* London: Routledge and Paul.

Dubin, Robert. 1956. "Industrial Workers' Worlds: A Study of the 'Central Life Interests' of Industrial Workers." *Social Problems* 3:131–42.

Durkheim, Emile. [1912] 1965. *The Elementary Forms of the Religious Life.* New York: Free Press.

Durkheim, Emile, and Marcel Mauss. [1903] 1963. *Primitive Classification.* Translated and edited by Rodney Needham. Chicago: University of Chicago Press.

Edwards, Richard. 1979. *Contested Terrain: The Transformation of the Workplace in the Twentieth Century.* New York: Basic Books.

Ellis, Carolyn. 1994. *Final Negotiations.* Philadelphia: Temple University Press.

Elshtain, Jean Bethke. 1981. *Public Man, Private Woman: Women in Social and Political Thought.* Princeton: Princeton University Press.

Epstein, Cynthia Fuchs. 1988. *Deceptive Differences.* New York: Russell Sage Foundation.

Flaherty, Michael G. 1987. "Multiple Realities and the Experience of Duration." *The Sociological Quarterly* 28, no. 3:313–26.

———. 1991. "The Perception of Time and Situated Engrossment." *Social Psychology Quarterly* 54, no. 1:76–85.

———. 1992. "The Erotics and Hermaneutics of Temporality." In *Investigating Subjectivity: Research on Lived Experience,* edited by Carolyn Ellis and Michael G. Flaherty. Newbury Park, Cal.: Sage.

Fleck, Ludwig. (1935) 1981. *Genesis and Development of a Scientific Fact.* Chicago: University of Chicago Press.

Folbre, Nancy, and Heidi Hartmann. 1988. "The Rhetoric of Self-Interest: Selfishness, Altruism, and Gender in Economic Theory." In *The Consequences of Economic Rhetoric,* edited by Arjo Klamer and Donald McCloskey, 184–203. New York: Cambridge University Press.

Foucault, Michel. [1966] 1973. *The Order of Things.* New York: Vintage Books.

Fowlkes, Martha. 1987. "The Myth of Merit and Male Professional Careers." In Gerstel and Gross 1987, 347–60.

Freud, Sigmund. [1917] 1966. *Psychopathology of Everyday Life.* New York: Norton.

Friedan, Betty. 1993. *The Fountain of Age.* New York: Simon and Schuster.

Gagnon, John H., and William Simon. 1974. *Sexual Conduct.* Chicago: Aldine.

Gergen, Kenneth. 1991. *The Saturated Self: Dilemmas of Identity in Contemporary Life.* New York: Basic Books.

Gerstel, Naomi, and Harriet Gross, eds. 1987. *Families and Work.* Philadelphia: Temple University Press.

Goffman, Erving. 1959. *The Presentation of Self in Everyday Life.* Garden City, N.Y.: Doubleday Books.

———. 1963a. *Behavior in Public Places.* New York: Free Press.

———. 1963b. *Stigma: Notes on the Management of Spoiled Identity.* Englewood Cliffs, N.J.: Prentice-Hall.

———. 1971. *Relations in Public.* New York: Basic Books.

———. 1974. *Frame Analysis.* Cambridge: Harvard University Press.

Gorz, Andre. [1980] 1982. *Farewell to the Working Class.* New York: South End Press.

Hall, Edward T. [1966] 1969. *The Hidden Dimension.* Garden City, N.Y.: Anchor Books.

Halle, David. 1984. *America's Working Man.* Chicago: University of Chicago Press.

Harper, Douglas. 1987. *Working Knowledge: Skill and Community in a Small Shop.* Chicago: University of Chicago Press.

Hochschild, Arlie Russell. 1969. "The Ambassador's Wife." *Journal of Marriage and Family* 31:73–87.

———. 1983. *The Managed Heart: Commercialization of Human Feeling.* Berkeley: University of California Press.

———. [1989] 1990. *The Second Shift.* New York: Avon Books.

Jackson, Kenneth. 1985. *Crabgrass Frontier.* New York: Oxford University Press.

Kanter, Rosabeth Moss. 1977a. *Men and Women of the Corporation.* New York: Basic Books.

———. 1977b. *Work and Family in the United States: A Critical Review and Agenda for Research and Policy.* New York: Russell Sage Foundation.

Kessler-Harris, Alice. 1982. *Out to Work: A History of Wage-Earning Women in the United States.* New York: Oxford University Press.

Klass, Perri. 1990. *Other Women's Children.* New York: Random House.

Kuhn, Thomas S. [1962] 1970. *The Structure of Scientific Revolutions.* Chicago: University of Chicago Press.

Lamont, Michele. 1992. *Money, Morals and Manners.* Chicago: University of Chicago Press.

Lamont, Michele, and Marcel Fournier, eds. 1992. *Cultivating Differences: Symbolic Boundaries and the Making of Inequality.*

LaRossa, Ralph, and Maureen Mulligan LaRossa. 1981. *Transition to Parenthood: How Infants Change Families.* Beverly Hills, Cal.: Sage.

Larson, Magali Sarfatti. [1977] 1979. *The Rise of Professionalism: A Sociological Analysis.* Berkeley: University of California Press.

Lasch, Christopher. 1977. *Haven in a Heartless World: The Family Besieged.* New York: Basic Books.

Levi-Strauss, Claude. [1968] 1978. *The Origin of Table Manners.* New York: Harper and Row.

Levine, Donald N. [1985] 1988. *The Flight from Ambiguity.* Chicago: University of Chicago Press.

Lifton, Robert J. 1993. *The Protean Man: Human Resilience in an Age of Fragmentation.* New York: Basic Books.

Lopata, Helena. 1993. "The Interweave of Public and Private: Women's Challenge to American Society." *Journal of Marriage and the Family* 55, no. 1:76–90.

Lukes, Steven. 1974. *Power: A Radical View.* London: Macmillan.

Mannheim, Karl. [1936] 1985. *Ideology and Utopia.* San Diego: Harvest/HBL.

———. 1972. *Essays on the Sociology of Knowledge,* 5th ed. London: Routledge, Kegan Paul.

———. 1982. *Structures of Thinking.* London: Routledge, Kegan Paul.

Mauss, Marcel. 1967. *The Gift: Forms and Functions of Exchange in Archaic Societies,* translated by Ian Cunnison. New York: Norton.

McLellan, David, ed. 1977. *Karl Marx: Selected Writings.* Oxford: Oxford University Press.

Mead, George Herbert. 1934. *Mind, Self and Society,* edited by Charles W. Morris. Chicago: University of Chicago Press.

Mills, C. Wright. 1956. *White Collar.* New York: Oxford University Press.

Newman, Katherine S. 1988. *Falling from Grace: The Experience of Downward Mobility in the American Middle Class.* New York: Free Press.

Nippert-Eng, Christena. 1988. "Liminality in Everyday Life: Commuting and the Transition from Home to Work." Paper presented at the American Sociological Association meeting in Atlanta, Georgia.

———. 1991. "Constructing the Home/Work Boundary: Mental Categories in Everyday Life." Paper presented at the Society for the Study of Symbolic Interaction meeting in Cincinnati, Ohio.

———. 1992a. "Identity Kits: A View of Your Self from Your Wallet or Purse." Paper presented at the Society for the Study of Symbolic Interaction meeting in Pittsburgh, Pennsylvania.

———. 1992b. "'Mommy, Mommy,' or 'Excuse Me, Ma'am,': Gender and Interruptions at Home and Work." Paper presented at the American Sociological Association meeting in Pittsburgh, Pennsylvania.

———. 1993. "From Home to Work and Back Again: Commuting and the Transformation of Self." Paper presented at the Society for the Study of Symbolic Interaction meeting and the American Sociological Association meeting in Miami, Florida.

Reskin, Barbara F., and Patricia A. Roos. 1990. *Job Queues, Gender Queues.* Philadelphia: Temple University Press.

Ryan, Mary P. 1981. *The Cradle of the Middle Class: The Family in Oneida County, NY, 1790–1865.* New York: Cambridge University Press.

Salaman, Graeme. 1974. *Community and Occupation: An Exploration of Work/Leisure Relationships.* Cambridge, Mass.: Cambridge University Press.

Schutz, Alfred. 1973. "On Multiple Realities." In *Collected Papers,* 4th ed., 1:207–59. The Hague: Martinus Nijhoff.

Schutz, Alfred, and Thomas Luckmann. 1973. *The Structures of the Life World.* Evanston: Northwestern University Press.

Schwartz, Barry. 1968. "The Social Psychology of Privacy." *American Journal of Sociology* 73:741–52.

———. 1970. "Notes on the Sociology of Sleep." *Sociological Quarterly* 11:485–99.

———. 1975. *Queuing and Waiting.* Chicago: University of Chicago Press.

———, ed. 1976. *The Changing Face of the Suburbs.* Chicago: University of Chicago Press.

———. 1981. *Vertical Classification.* Chicago: University of Chicago Press.

Sennett, Richard. 1977. *The Fall of Public Man: The Social Psychology of Capitalism.* New York: Random House.

Shibutani, Tamotsu. 1955. "Reference Groups as Perspectives." *American Journal of Sociology* 60:562–69.

———. 1962. "Reference Groups and Social Control." In *Human Behavior and Social Processes,* edited by A. Rose, 128–47. Boston: Houghton Mifflin.

Simmel, Georg. 1955. "The Web of Group-Affiliations." In *Conflict and the Web of Group-Affiliations,* edited and translated by R. Bendix. New York: Free Press.

———. 1985. "The Bridge and the Door." In *George Simmel's Sociology of Als-ob,* edited and translated by Michael Kaern. Pittsburgh: University of Pittsburgh.

Stone, Gregory P. 1962. "Appearance and the Self." In *Human Behavior and Social Processes,* edited by Arnold M. Rose, 86–113. Boston: Houghton Mifflin.

Terkel, Studs. 1972. *Working.* New York: Avon Books.

Thompson, E. P. 1967. "Time, Work-Discipline, and Industrial Capitalism." *Past and Present* 38:56–97.

Tuan, Yi-Fu. 1982. *Segmented Worlds and Self.* Minneapolis: University of Minnesota Press.

Turner, Ralph H. 1976. "The Real Self: From Institution to Impulse." *American Journal of Sociology* 81 (March):989–1016.

Turner, Victor. 1967. *The Forest of Symbols.* Ithaca: Cornell University Press.

———. 1974. *The Ritual Process.* New York: Pelican Books.

Van Gennep, Arnold. 1960. *The Rites of Passage.* Chicago: University of Chicago Press.

Waugh, Linda R. 1982. "Marked and Unmarked: A Choice between Unequals in Semiotic Structure," *Semiotica* 38:299–316.

Weber, Max. [1904] 1976. *The Protestant Ethic and the Spirit of Capitalism.* New York: Charles Scribner's Sons.

———. [1918] 1978. *Economy and Society.* Vols. 1 and 2. Edited by Guenther Roth and Claus Wittich. Berkeley: University of California Press.

Weiner, Lynn K. 1985. *From Working Girl to Working Mother.* Chapel Hill: University of North Carolina Press.

West, Candace. 1984. "When the Doctor Is a 'Lady': Power, Status and Gender in Physician-Patient Encounters." *Symbolic Interaction* 7, no. 1:87–106.

Weston, Kathleen, and Lisa Rofel. 1987. "Sexuality, Class, and Conflict in a Lesbian Workplace." In Gerstel and Gross 1987, 434–35.

Whyte, William. [1956] 1957. *The Organization Man* Garden City, N.Y.: Doubleday Anchor.

Williams, Christine L. 1989. *Gender Differences at Work.* Berkeley: University of California Press.

Williams, Raymond. [1976] 1985. *Keywords.* New York: Oxford University Press.

Williams, Richard E. 1990. *Hierarchical Structures and Social Value: The Creation of Black and Irish Identities in the United States.* Cambridge: Cambridge University Press.

Wood, Robert C. 1958. *Suburbia: Its People and Their Politics.* Boston: Houghton Mifflin.

Woolf, Virginia. 1929. *A Room of One's Own.* New York: Hartcourt Brace.

Zelizer, Viviana A. 1985. *Pricing the Priceless Child: The Changing Social Value of Children.* New York: Basic Books.

Zerubavel, Eviatar. 1979. *Patterns of Time in Hospital Life.* Chicago: University of Chicago Press.

———. [1981] 1985a. *Hidden Rhythms.* Berkeley: University of California Press.

———. 1985b. *The Seven-Day Circle.* New York: Free Press.

———. 1987. "The Language of Time: Toward a Semiotics of Temporality." *Sociological Quarterly* 28:343–54.

———. 1991. *The Fine Line.* New York: Free Press.

———. 1996. *Social Mindscapes: An Invitation to Cognitive Sociology.* Cambridge: Harvard University Press. (forthcoming)

Zussman, Robert. 1985. *Mechanics of the Middle Class.* Berkeley: University of California Press.

———. 1987. "Work and Family in the New Middle Class." In Gerstel and Gross 1987, 338–46.

———. 1993. *Intensive Care: Medical Ethics and the Medical Profession.* Chicago: University of Chicago Press.

INDEX

Abbott, Andrew, 67
Adam, Barbara, 135
Adler, Patricia and Peter, xiv, 83
Alt, John, xvi, 23
Aristotle, xii
Attewell, Paul, xvii

Bateson, Gregory, 24
Bateson, Mary Catharine, 83
Beach, Betty, 5
Becker, Howard, 111
Bell, Catharine, 147
Berger, Peter, 13, 26, 122
Binford, Henry, 23
boundaries (categorical)
and boundaries around space and time, 289–290
and classification, xii–xiii, 277–292
and conceptual frameworks, xiii, 277–292
cultural versus personal, xiii, 13, 17
emergence and transformation of, xii, 277–292
individuals and, xii–xiii,10–16
and humor, 287–288
overlap between, 152–153, 279–280
permeability of, 280–289
placement of, xii, 277–292
and interpersonal conflict, xiii
political, 278–279, 285–287, 289
social construction of, xi, 1–28, 277–292
symmetry of, 281–287
theory of, 277–292
mental versus physical forms xi, xiii, 34–36, 277–292
boundary placement work, 8, 11–12, 27–28, 228–230, 245–264, 277–292
boundary transcendence work. *See* transitions
boundary work
and classification, 6–8, 10–28, 277–292
constraints on, xiii, 12–18, 253
defined, xiii, 7–8, 33, 42–43, 292
of home and work
constraints on, 12–18, 28–29, 38–42, 51–53, 148
defined, 7–8
dimensions of, summary, 28–29, 43, 149–151
kinds of, 8, 11–12, 27
as link between self and society, 17
nature of boundary between, 277–282, 287–292
and personal discretion. *See* home-work boundary, and personal discretion
and personal innovation, 17, 37–38
and position along integration/segmentation continuum, 8–9, 27, 90
practical and symbolic value of, 44, 47, 48, 50, 52–55, 58–59, 68, 88, 95–96, 127
as a process, 7
relationship between mental and physical forms of, 7–8, 10, 27–28, 34–36, 40, 42–43, 106, 110, 147–148, 277–282, 287–292
as sculpting, 10–17, 28–29, 50
and self. *See* self; transitions

boundary work (*continued*)
See also classification; home-work boundary
sculpting as, 10–17, 28
types of, 8, 229- 231, 245, 282–287, 290–291 (*see also* boundary placement work; transitions)
violence as, xii
Bourdieu, Pierre, 110
breaks. *See* home-work boundary, key dimensions of, breaks
bridges, 105, 108–110, 117, 148, 228
building thresholds, 40–41, 72, 77, 79, 106, 265

calendars, xi, 43–47, 100–101, 261–262
categories
change in, 277–279, 282–284, 287–290
characteristics of, 277–292
and conceptual borders, xi
cultural versus personal, 25, 38–42, 99, 100–101
home and work as, xi, 28
movement between, 107–117 (*see also* boundaries, permeability of; transitions)
and order, 99–102
purity/pollution of, 99–102
size of, 277–279
Christensen, Kathleen, 5
childcare policies, 158–162, 173, 212–213, 220
children. *See* "home"-related constraints on home-work boundary, children
Christensen, Kathleen, 62
classification
and boundaries, xi–xii, 29–30, 277–292
and boundary work, 6–8, 10–28
change in, xi–xiii, 277–292
due to behavior, 288–291
and conceptual or categorical territories, xi, 25, 28
and culture/group membership, xi, 18, 25, 99–102
and meaning, xi, 276–292
mental and physical manifestations, 28, 34, 40, 42–43, 85–87,99–102, 100–102, 127, 277–292, 147–148, 276–292
and social science, xi
and socialization, xi–xii, 17–18, 265–267
See also categories; cognitive sociology; time, classification of; space, classification of
CMP Publications, 76, 158–161
coffee. *See* transitions, eating and drinking, coffee and caffeine
cognitive engineering, 105, 108
cognitive sociology, xiv, 30, 291–292
Cohen, Ira, xvii
Cohen, Stanley, 108, 122
commitment, sense of, home versus work, 228, 241–245, 254–255
commuting. *See* home-work boundary, key dimensions of, commuting; transitions, commuting
constraints. *See* "home"-related constraints on home-work boundary; "work"-related constraints on home-work boundary
contamination. *See* pollution
Coser, Lewis, 25, 155
Coser, Rose, 210
Cott, Nancy F., 18
Cowen, Ruth Schwarz, 18
coworkers
divorce, 116, 243–244, 273–276
and home-work boundary, 2, 67–68, 73–76, 116

Index

Csikszentmihalyi, Mihaly, 35, 71, 129, 136–138

Davis, Fred, 50, 54
Davis, Murray, 26, 35, 80–82, 86, 111, 134, 135, 142
Delaney, Kevin, xvi, 67
Devault, Marjorie, 20, 240
dirt, 99–102, 196
discretion. *See* home-work boundary, personal discretion and
divorce: and coworkers, 116, 243–244, 273–276
Douglas, Mary, 99, 120, 146, 216
Dubin, Robert, 4
Durkheim, Emile, xi, 13, 18, 35, 44, 108, 110, 146–147, 270

Edwards, Richard, 23
Eleanor, 29, 33, 63, 86–87, 228–231, 245–266
Ellis, Carolyn, xvi, 83
Elshtain, Jean Bethke, 18
Epstein, Cynthia Fuchs, xvi, 24
Erikson, Kai, 289
Escher, M. C., 246, 264
Evans-Pritchard, 129
"everyday" and "erotic" realities, 26, 35, 80–82, 111, 135
experiential realms
  continuity/discontinuity between, causes of, 227–228, 245–246, 263–265
  defined, 25–26, 28

family
  and boundary work, 2, 14, 73–76
  sample interviewed, 31–32
  as coworkers, 69, 158, 200–202, 273–276, 251–253, 274–276
family businesses, 67
  See also self-employed; home-workers
Flaherty, Michael, xvi, 136
Fleck, Ludwig, 13, 26, 283
Folbre, Nancy, 18
Foucault, Michel, xi, 13
Fowlkes, Martha, 4
frames/framing, 24–26
  home and work as, 24–26, 138
  and mentalities, 26–27
free area, 122
Freud, Sigmund, 48
Friedan, Betty, 289
friends, "personal" versus "work," 243–245, 249–250, 252–253

Gagnon, John, xvi, 58
gender, 14
  and appearance, 53–57
  and domestic division of labor, 101, 240–242, 256–257
  and effects of children, 218–219, 221
  and interruptability at work, 193
  rewards and, home versus work, 255–257
  segmentation, according to, 53–57
  and workspace, 38
Gergen, Kenneth, 105
Gerstel, Naomi, xvii
Gieryn, Thomas F., 7
Goffman, Erving, 24, 26, 84, 121, 124, 138
Gorz, Andre, 23
greedy institutions, 155
Grisham, John, 158

Hall, Edward T., 170
Halle, David, xvi, 4, 20
Harper, Douglas, 83
Hartmann, Heidi, 18
Hochschild, Arlie Russell, 4, 20, 83, 135, 155, 207
home
  as boundary-constraining, physical space, 14–15, 22–25, 221–227

home (*continued*)
creation of, 10
defined, 3, 18–28
as an experiential realm, 25–26
as a frame, 24–26
personal versus historical images, 24–25
phenomenology of, versus that of work, 18–28, 227–228, 231–264
as private endeavor, 20–21, 81–83, 154
as semiotically linked with work, 4, 21–24, 116, 154
See also work
homecomings. *See* transitions, hellos and good-byes, homecomings
"home"-related constraints on home-work boundary, 6–7, 14, 100, 194–228
children, 75–76, 187, 198–200, 222, 231–232, 239–242, 247, 251, 273–274
as coworkers, 69, 158, 275
as pollution, 202–203, 208–221
profanity/sacredness of, 202–207, 209–221; and greediness, 205; variation in, 206–207
responsibility for, 207–221; biology and, 221
parenting, 14
co-, 217
gendered, 218
models of, 203–211, 217–218
primary/secondary, 203, 207–208
of profane/sacred child, 203–207
parents, 69, 265, 267
privacy, 226–227, 240–241
residence, 221–227
distance from workplace, 221, 224–226
feelings about, 221, 223–224
neighbors, 223–224, 244
physical layout, 221–223
spouses, 194–202
attitudes toward domestic division of labor, 197, 240–242, 256–257
attitudes toward wage work, 194–202, 265–266
and confidentiality of work, 252–253
as coworkers, 69, 200–202, 273–276, 251–253, 274–276
default practices, 202, 211–212, 217–218, 251–253
and divorce, 116, 243–244, 273–276
domestic division of labor, 197–212, 216–219, 221, 231, 240–242, 256–257
as pollution, 201–202
problems of, 197–202
workplace relationships with, 200–202, 251–253, 265
See also home-work boundary, personal discretion and
home-work boundary
change in, 15–16, 277–279, 282–284, 287–290
characteristics of, 277–282, 287–292
defined, xiv, 42
key dimensions of
address and phone books, 68–70
breaks, xi, 2, 40–41, 61, 91–98 (*see also* home-work boundary, personal discretion and; lunch; vacations; "work"-related constraints on home-work boundary, break policies; work, breaks from, daily)
calendars, xi, 43–47, 100–101, 261–262
clothes and appearance, 50–57, 100, 186, 259–261 (*see also*

transitions, clothes and appearance-changing)
commuting, xi, 105–148 (*see also* transitions; transitions, commuting)
eating and drinking, xi, 60–63 (*see also* lunch; transitions, eating and drinking)
gifts, 72–73
keys, xi, 48–50, 100–101, 263
money, 2, 63–67, 85
people, xi, 67–68, 73–76, 100 (*see also, in present entry,* address and phone books; gifts; photographs)
phone calls, 41, 75, 80, 94, 99, 251 (*see also* transitions, phone calls; "work"-related constraints on home-work boundary, phone calls)
photographs, xi, 2, 3, 70–72, 185, 263
reading, xi, 63, 78, 83–91, 115 (*see also* "work"-related constraints on home-work boundary, mail and mailboxes; newspapers; storage of realm-specific and cross-realm items)
summary, 149–151
talk, 76–83, 93–94, 144–145, 169, 231–232, 251–253, 261
wallets and purses, xi, 55–60, 262–263
personal discretion and, 10, 16–17, 27, 148, 152–193, 194–228, 240–241, 245, 264, 266
sex and, 1–4, 39–40, 80–82, 85, 86, 135
social construction of, xi, 1–28, 268
socialization for, 3, 14, 17–18, 265–268 (*see also* "work"-related constraints on home-work boundary, occupations, training for and boundary expectations)
tools for, 6–7
variations in, 1–6, 14–16, 277–282, 284–292
See also "home"-related constraints on home-work boundary; "work"-related constraints on home-work boundary
homeworkers (and boundary work)
eating, 62
home office, 88–89
mail, 85
transitions, 106, 117–118
See also family businesses; self-employed; telecommuting

integration
as "craftsman" model of home and work, 22
criticism of, 267–273
through cross-realm items, 34–38
defined, 5–6, 11, 17, 22, 26
direction of, 9–10, 25, 55, 58, 72, 81–82, 220–221
as a "finite province of meaning," 26
and Politically Correct movement, 287–288
and self, 5–6, 8, 11, 17, 20, 23, 34–38, 102–107
through time and space, 23–24, 38–42, 66
and time awareness, 138–139
and transformations, 103, 107
integration-segmentation continuum (of home and work)
in academics' work, 82–83
defined, 5
individual positions along, 6, 8–9, 24, 26, 148
change in, 15–18, 36, 98, 273–276

integration-segmentation continuum (*continued*)
criticisms of, 267–273
and difficulty with boundary work, 27, 107, 229–231, 245–246, 263–265
identified through key boundary dimensions (summary), 149–151
organizational conflict due to, 268–273; among academics, 271–272
and more problematic type of boundary work, 27, 28–29, 107, 229–231, 245–246, 263–265
social influences on, 14, 148, 152–154, 186, 194, 226–228 (*see also* "work"-related constraints on home-work boundary; "home"-related constraints on home-work boundary)
interviews for this study
confidentiality of, 32, 293–294
described, 30–33
questionnaire used for, 293–306
use of material from, 32–33

Jackson, Kenneth, 23, 140
Jimmy, 29, 33, 228–246, 251, 265
journey to work. *See* home-work boundary, key dimensions of, commuting; transitions, commuting

Kanter, Rosabeth Moss, 4, 58, 155, 162, 215
Kessler-Harris, Alice, 18
keys, xi, 48–50, 100–101, 263
Klass, Perri, 5
Kuhn, Thomas, 13, 26, 210, 283

Lab, the: described, 30–32, 171–173, 188–189, 233–240
Larossa, Ralph and Maureen M., 53, 208
Larson, Magali Sarfatti, xvi, 67
Lasch, Christopher, 18, 23
leisure, 16, 22, 40, 74–75, 93, 114, 132
Levi-Strauss, Claude, 62, 131
Levine, Donald, 5
Lifton, Robert J., 105
liminality, 79–80
commuting as, 119–123
defined, 119–120
showering as, 133–134
See also transitions, hellos and goodbyes, homecomings
Lopata, Helena, xvi, 24
Luckmann, Thomas, 13, 26, 122
Lukes, Steven, 12
lunch, xi, 91, 93–96, 159, 187, 246
bag lunches, 94–96

machinists
boundary expectations
job shop versus prototype work, 179–180
training and, 3, 174–180
breaks, 92, 164
calendars, 46
clothes and appearance, 40–41, 53
discretion/trust, 163
folklore, 3, 175–176, 236
job/work descriptions, 1–3, 41–42, 164, 171–176, 179–180, 233–240
mail and mailboxes, 165, 167
money, 2–3, 63–64
phone calls, 98, 142–143
privacy of, 167–168
photographs, 2–3, 38, 72
as relative segmentors, 2–3, 174, 175–176

sample interviewed, 31–32
spouses, effect on home-work boundary, 196–198
supervision of, 234–239
talk, 78–79
time accounting, 164–165
time awareness, 137
vacations, 96, 98
wallets, 58–60
work accessibility, 192
work space, privacy of, 3, 233–234
See also commitment, sense of, home versus work; Jimmy; personal treatment, home versus work; rewards, home versus work; work, union
mail and mailboxes. *See* "work"-related constraints on home-work boundary, mail and mailboxes
managers: and boundary discretion, 163, 169, 253–254
See also Eleanor; home-work boundary, personal discretion and
Mannheim, Karl, xi, 13, 26
Marx, Karl, 13, 91–92
Mauss, Marcel, 18, 72
Mead, Herbert, 67–68, 204
mental agility, 210–211
mental gear-shifting. *See* transitions, as mental gear-shifting
mentalities
conflict between, 209–211
defined, 26
parenting, 204–207, 209–211
and selves, 26–27
Mills, C. Wright, 4, 22, 91, 292
Modernity
and home and work, xv, 1, 25, 91
and money, 67
and self, 57
"multiphrenic personality," 105
neighbors. *See* "home"-related constraints on home-work boundary, neighbors
Newman, Katherine, 220
newspapers, 63, 84, 86–87, 115, 254
and classification, 87, 254
North, Oliver, 64–65

objects and identity, 34–38, 68
See also self
occupations
and importance of earnings, 2, 63–66
and position along integration/segmentation continuum, 14, 18
socialization for, 3

paradigm, 13, 26, 210, 283–284
parents and parenting. *See* "home"-related constraints on home-work boundary, parenting
parties, 79–80, 176, 186, 223–224
good-bye and welcome home, 125
as liminal time and space, 79–80
Personnel workers
boundary expectations, 180–182
breaks, 164
calendars, 44–47
children, 212–214, 222
clothes and appearance, 55–57
discretion/trust, 163
job/work descriptions, 171–173, 181
keys, 49–50
mail and mailboxes, 165
phone calls, privacy of, 168–169
photographs, 71–72, 76
purses, 55–57
sample interviewed, 31
time accounting, 164–165
time awareness, 137
vacations, 96–97, 212
work accessibility, 192

Personnel workers (*continued*)
work load, 192–193
workspace, privacy of, 38, 170, 249
See also commitment, sense of, home versus work; Eleanor; personal treatment, home versus work; rewards, home versus work
personal treatment, home versus work, 228, 234–244, 254
pets, 38, 52, 72, 76, 154
phone calls. *See* home-work boundary, key dimensions of; machinists; Personnel workers; scientists; transitions; "work"-related constraints on home-work boundary
photographs, xi, 2, 3, 70–72, 185, 263
Pleck, Joseph, 280
Polis, xii
pollution
and anti-pollution activities, 64, 154
and border patrols, 99–100
children as, 202–203, 208–221
defined, 99–102
as dirt, 99–102, 196
and housecleaning, 99, 101
and intentionality, 216
married workers as, 201–202
pregnant women as, 213–216
of realms, 75
privacy
and discretion, 162–163, 226–228, 240–241
See also "work"-related constraints on home-work boundary: break policies, mail and mailboxes, phone calls, time accounting procedures, work space
"protean man," 105
"public" and "private" space. *See* space, "public" and "private"
"public" and "private" time. *See* time, "public" and "private"
purification/purity. *See* pollution

reference groups. *See* "work"-related constraints on home-work boundary, boundary reference groups
Reskin, Barbara, 20
residence. *See* "home"-related constraints on home-work boundary, residence
rewards, home versus work, 228, 238, 242, 255–257
gendered, 255–257
rituals. *See* transitions, as ritual activity
Rochberg-Halton, 35, 71, 129
role conflict
and mental agility, 210–211
mental versus physical foundations of, 209–211
Roos, Patricia, xvi, 20
Roth, Julius, 122
routines. *See* transitions, routines
Ryan, Mary P., 18

sacred and profane realms, 35, 108, 146
Salaman, Graeme, 4
Saussure, Ferdinand de, 21
school, and socialization for home-work boundary, 266–268
Schutz, Alfred, 13, 26, 142
Schwartz, Barry, xvii, 23, 121, 142, 205
Schwarzenegger, Arnold, 192
scientists
address and phone books, 69
and boundary discretion, 163
boundary expectations

academic versus industrial, 179
change in, 273–276
training and, 3, 174, 176–179, 214–216, 266, 273–274
United States versus other countries, 176–179
breaks, 164
calendars, 43, 69
children, effect on home-work boundary, 186–187, 198–199, 210–211, 214–217, 219–221
clothes and appearance, 53–57
discretion/trust, 163, 176–179
"Happy" versus "Unhappy" departments, 183–185
as relative integrators, 1–3
job/work descriptions, 1–3, 171–172, 174, 176–179, 183–185
keys, 48–49
life course position, 186–187
mail and mailboxes, 165, 167
money, 2, 64–66
phone calls, privacy of, 169
photographs, 70–71
purses and wallets, 55–60
sample interviewed, 32
spouses, effect on home-work boundary, 194–196, 198–202, 266
talk, 169
time accounting, 164–165
time awareness, 136–137
vacations, 97–98
work accessibility, 192
work attitudes, 2–3, 30
workspace, 2–3, 189–191
privacy of, 2–3, 38
sculpting: boundary work as, 10–17, 28–29, 50
segmentation
and antipollution activity, 99–100
and alienation, 92
criticism of, 267–273
defined, 5–6, 11, 17, 22–23, 26
as a dichotomy, 24
direction of, 58
as dual "provinces of meaning," 26
and group membership, 124–126
historical emergence of, 18–24
implications of, 34–36, 102–104, 105–106, 147
and need for transitions/transformations, 27, 124–126
prevalence of, 18, 24
and self, 6, 8, 11, 17, 20, 23, 27, 34–38, 102–104
and suburban living, 23–24
through realm-specific items, 34–36
through time and space, 23–24, 38–42
and time awareness, 137–139
as "utilitarian" model of home and work, 22
self
asituational, 6
creation of, through boundary work, 20, 34–38,98–99
defined, 34
ethnographic approach to, 290
evocation/support of, 35–38, 42–44, 47–48, 51, 59–60, 67–68, 70–71, 73–75, 98–99, 100, 105–106, 110–117, 123–127, 134–135, 146–148, 185, 228, 231–232 (*see also* transitions)
"institutional," 57
as a mentality, 26–27
modern, 57
as a negative cult, 146
public versus private, 20, 22, 62, 77, 79, 81–83, 83–91, 89–90, 94–96, 154, 239, 243–245
"real," 57

self (*continued*)
realm-specific, 6
threats to, 34–35, 68, 72, 99–102, 108–110, 142–143, 183–185, 196, 245
through time and space, 34–38, 42–44, 55, 60, 72, 105–148, 239–240, 243, 246–249, 273–276
work-related, 2–3
See also objects and identity; self-consciousness; territories of the self; transitions
self-consciousness, 73–75
self-employed, 65, 89
See also homeworkers; family businesses
self-identity. *See* self
semiotics, 21
Sennett, Richard, 18
Shibutani, Tomatsu, 173
Simmel, Georg, 57, 108
sleep. *See* transitions, and fatigue; transitions, sleep
social territories, 38, 40
defined, 38
sociology
and everyday life, xiv
integration-segmentation in works of, 82–83
and study of boundaries, xi, 291
theory and practice in, xiv
See also cognitive sociology
space
as a boundary tool, xiv, 2, 5–6, 11, 22–24, 110
classification of, 38–43
contentious, 42
employers' versus employees', 3
neutral, 16, 74, 79–80, 93–97
"public" and "private," 38–42, 62, 83–91, 93–97, 222–223, 162–171
variability of, 38–39
residential, 221–227
suburban versus urban, 23–24, 140
See also home-work boundary, key dimensions of, keys; liminality; storage of realm-specific and cross-realm items
spatio-temporal benchmarks, 122, 259
spouses. *See* "home"-related constraints on home-work boundary, spouses
Stone, Gregory, 50
storage of realm-specific and cross-realm items, 87–91
suburban living, 23–24, 140

talk. *See* home-work boundary, key dimensions of, talk
Taylor, Laurie, 108, 122
telecommuting, 157–158, 268, 290–291
Terkel, Studs, 4
territories of the self, 28, 34, 68, 73, 77, 99, 147
Thompson, E. P., 136, 175
thoughtstyle, 13
thresholds, constructing, 40–41, 72, 77, 79, 106, 265
time
accounting procedures, 153
awareness of, 135–139, 248–249
as a boundary tool, xiv, 5–6, 11, 22–24, 110
classification of, 38–43, 165
contentious, 40–42
neutral, 16, 74, 79–80, 93–97, 122
"public" and "private," 38–42, 83–91, 91–92, 93–97, 121, 143, 162–171, 242
variability of, 38–39
use of, in boundary work, 2
work, 135
See also home-work boundary, key

dimensions of, calendars; liminality
transitional shocks, 142
transitions (between home and work), 8, 11, 102, 105–148, 229–245, 280–290, 292
as behaviorally supported mental movement, 110–111, 123
as bridges, 108–110, 117, 148, 228
clothes and appearance-changing, 105
cognitive structure of, 106–110
commuting, 105–142, 224–226, 259–260
commuter clubs, 121–122
defined, 117
as liminality, 119–123
physical versus mental movement, 117–127
and privacy, 122–123, 199
routes, 105, 139–141 (*see also* transitions, routines, commuting)
defined, 8, 11–12, 27–28, 102–104, 105–106
difficulty with, 106–117, 116–117, 130, 142–145, 228, 231, 241, 243
dinner. *See* transitions, hellos and goodbyes, homecomings
eating and drinking, 105, 117, 127–132
alcohol, 115–116, 127–128
coffee and caffeine, 60, 115, 128–130, 258, 259
drugs, 117, 127–130
hot versus cold drinks, 130–131
snacks, 131–132
failed, 109–110, 118–119
fascination with, in people, 134–135
and fatigue, 231, 241, 243
frequency of, 109–110, 142–145
function of, 146–148
hellos and good-byes, 105, 123–127
homecomings, 124–126, 130, 231–232, 239–240, 242–243, 245, 258–259
and homeworkers, 106, 117–118
and liminality, 80, 119–123, 133–134
listening habits, 105–106, 141, 259
as mental gear-shifting, 106, 110–111, 113
need for, 102–104, 106–110, 124–127, 228
phone calls, 106, 142–145 (*see also* "work"-related constraints on home-work boundary, phone calls)
physical versus mental movement, 60–61, 117–127
predictability of, 109–110, 142–145
as ritual activity, 28, 145–148
rituals and, 28, 117
role of institutions in encouraging/discouraging individuals', 283–287
routines, 102, 105–106, 112–115, 117, 129–132, 137, 147, 276
bedtime, 112
commuting, 114–116, 139–140, 259–260
Monday versus Friday, 114–116, 139–140
morning versus evening, 112–116, 130–131, 139–140, 258–259
week versus weekend, 260–261
according to schedules, 117–118
showering, 133–134
sleep, 106, 112, 141–142
slides versus shocks, 142
stripping (-off clothes), 134–135
wristwatches, 105, 135–139

transitions (*continued*)
and writing, 111
See also Escher, M. C.; Jimmy; liminality; self, evocation/support of
transitions, other
between alcoholic and reformed alcoholic lifestyles, 284–285
between gender identities, 283
between life and death, 282–283
between scientific and nonscientific thoughtstyles, 283–284
between United States political administrations, 285–287
Tuan, Yi Fu, 110
Turner, Ralph, 57
Turner, Victor, 119–120

vacations, xi, 96–98
Van Gennep, Arnold, 79, 95, 110, 119–120, 123–124

Waugh, Linda, 21
"web of group affiliations," 57
Weber, Max, 13, 67, 155
Weiner, Lynn, 8
West, Candace, 54
worldview/weltanschauung, 13, 26
Whyte, William, 4
Williams, Christine, 52, 289
Williams, Raymond, 13
Williams, Richard, xvi, 289
Wood, Robert C., 23
work
as an experiential realm, 25–26, 28
as boundary constraining, physical space, 14–15, 22–25, 249
breaks from, daily, 91–96, 143 (*see also* lunch)
"craftsman" model of, 22, 91
creation of, 10
defined, 4, 18–24, 81
as a frame, 24–26
as a greedy institution, 25, 155, 196
versus leisure, 20
as a masculine realm, 19–20
organization of, 3
as paid labor, 19
personal versus historical images, 24–25
as a place and activity, 19
as public endeavor, 20–21, 81–83
and time awareness, 136–139, 248–249
union, 41–42, 153, 238–239
"utilitarian" model of, 22
See also home; home-work boundary
workplace
arrivals and departures, 125–126
signs, 126–127
bureaucratic, 153–155, 158, 161–162, 188
greedy, 153, 155–158, 162, 188
discretionary, 153, 157–162, 188
professional, 154–155
"work"-related constraints on home-work boundary, 6–7, 14, 100
accountability, 163
boundary reference groups, 153, 171–189
departments, 173, 182–185; "Happy" versus "Unhappy," 183–185
occupations, 173–182; training for and boundary expectations, 3, 174–182; (*see also* machinists; Personnel workers; scientists)
organizational strata/hierarchical position, 14, 173, 182, 187–188; and discretion, 162–163, 187–188, 253–254
work groups, 173, 185–187
break policies, 163–164
mail and mailboxes, 153, 165–167

phone calls, 153
privacy of, 165, 167–169
physical work environment, 154, 189–191
privacy, 162–171
time accounting procedures, 153, 163–165
trust, 162–171, 187–189
work accessibility, 154, 191–192, 251–253
work load, 192–193
work organization, 14, 152
work space, 153
privacy of, 38, 165, 169–171
See also home-work boundary, personal discretion and

Zelizer, Viviana, 203
Zerubavel, Eviatar, xi, xiv, xviii, 21, 24, 43, 53, 82, 91, 107, 110, 114, 121, 130, 146, 291
Zussman, Robert, xvii, 4, 58, 289